지은이 Jane Lee
펴낸이 정규도
펴낸곳 (주)다락원

초판 1쇄 발행 2017년 10월 30일
초판 3쇄 발행 2021년 8월 2일

책임편집 조상익, 곽빛나
디자인 김나경, 윤현주

다락원 경기도 파주시 문발로 211
내용문의: (02)736-2031 내선 553
구입문의: (02)736-2031 내선 250~252
Fax: (02)732-2037
출판등록 1977년 9월 16일 제406-2008-000007호

Copyright © 2017 Jane Lee

저자 및 출판사의 허락 없이 이 책의 일부 또는 전부를 무단 복제·전재·발췌할 수 없습니다. 구입 후 철회는 회사 내규에 부합하는 경우에 가능하므로 구입문의처에 문의하시기 바랍니다. 분실·파손 등에 따른 소비자 피해에 대해서는 공정거래위원회에서 고시한 소비자 분쟁 해결 기준에 따라 보상 가능합니다. 잘못된 책은 바꿔 드립니다.

값 16,800원

ISBN 978-89-277-0949-7 14740
       978-89-277-0947-3 14740 (set)

http://www.darakwon.co.kr

다락원 홈페이지를 방문하시면 상세한 출판정보와 함께 동영상강좌, MP3 자료 등 다양한 어학 정보를 얻으실 수 있습니다.

OPIc PUNCH
개정판!

Jane Lee 지음

오픽 펀치
IH & AL 공략

DARAKWON

머리말

Welcome, OPIc!

2008년 봄, OPIc 시험이 도입된 후 벌써 9년의 시간이 흘렀습니다. 삼성그룹이 그룹차원에서 영어면접의 평가도구로 OPIc을 도입하긴 했지만, OPIc은 이제 대기업과 공사 입사의 필수제출 조건으로 확고하게 자리매김하게 되었습니다. 지난 10년 남짓 영어회화 강사로 현장에서 수많은 학습자들을 가르쳐 온 저로서는 OPIc의 도입과 확대를 지켜보면서 OPIc이 '**제대로 된 영어회화 학습 방향을 제시해주는 시험**'이란 확신이 들었습니다. 개인적으로 OPIc 국내 1기 강사진으로 선발되어 OPIc 강의를 할 수 있게 된 점을 행운으로 여깁니다. 단순 회화나 시험만이 목적이 아닌, **의사소통능력의 증진과 그 활용을 위한 영어**를 지도할 수 있게 되었다고 믿었기 때문입니다.

Storytelling

OPIc도 다른 시험과 마찬가지로 나름의 룰이 있고, 득점 요령이 있습니다. 기본적으로 어느 정도는 암기가 필요한 것도 사실입니다. 그러나 본인만의 고유한 답안을 작성하지 않은 상태에서 다른 사람이 만들어 놓은 답안을 **단순 암기**하여 시험을 치르는 데에는 **한계**가 있습니다. 더구나 수많은 응시자들의 답안을 접하는 OPIc 평가 위원들은 여러분이 '타인의 답안'을 이야기하는지, '나만의 답안'을 이야기하는지 금새 알아차립니다. 하지만 각종 OPIc 기출 문제집이 출시되면서 많은 학생들 사이에 '**OPIc 준비=모범 답안 외우기**'라는 공식이 성립된 것 같아 매우 안타깝습니다. 이러한 방법으로 공부하는 분들은 결국 영어 학습의 장거리 경주에서 쉽게 뒤쳐지기 때문입니다.

Why OPIc Punch?

본 교재에도 기출 문제 및 모범 답안이 있습니다. 하지만 '답안' 자체보다 '**왜(why)**' 그러한 답안을 구성해야 하는지를 더 구체적으로 설명하고자 하였습니다. '**문제 의도를 정확히 파악**'하는 것이 좋은 답안을 이끌어 내는 핵심이기 때문입니다. 또한 학습자들이 기재된 모범 답안을 재구성하여 '**나만의 답안**'을 만들어 볼 수 있도록 노력했습니다. 한편 바쁜 시간을 쪼개어 영어 말하기 시험을 준비하는 학습자들의 입장을 고려하여 응시자들이 공감하기 쉬운 **Background Survey 4번~7번의 선택 항목 12가지**에 관한 기출변형문제 및 콤보 문제(combo questions), 롤플레이 문제(role-playing questions), 그리고 사회적 이슈(social issues)를 다루는 돌발 문제(random questions)를 정리하였습니다. 본 교재는 학습자들이 혼자서 최단기간으로 제시한 2주간의 집중 학습을 통해서 목표 등급에 도달하도록 도움을 드리기 위해 기획되었습니다. OPIc 응시생들이 의외로 그냥 지나치는 **OPIc의 3가지 핵심 포인트**를 짚어 드림으로써 학습 효과를 극대화하는 것을 목표로 하고 있습니다. 또한 학습자들의 공감대 형성과 현장 적응력을 키우기 위해 필자가 그동안 가르쳤던 응시생들이 **실전 시험에서 치뤘던 문제와 답안들**을 토대로 Model Answer을 실었습니다.

Special Thanks to...

2013년 OPIc Punch IM2 공략 출간을 시작으로 **OPIc Punch IH&AL 공략 개정판**을 내게 되었습니다. 2008년 봄 OPIc을 처음 강의하기 시작한 후 지금까지, 응시생들에게 실질적으로 도움을 주는 교재에 대한 고민의 결실입니다. 일방적인 주입식 강의는 OPIc의 성격과 본질적으로 맞지 않기 때문에 수년 동안 OPIc 시험의 동향과 한국 응시생들의 학습 성향을 분석하고 최대한 고려하여 교재를 구성하였습니다. 시중에 나온 수많은 교재의 장점을 흡수하면서도 차별화된 student-oriented book의 기획에 커다란 공감과 적극적인 지원을 해주신 다락원 편집부 일동에게 감사의 말씀 전합니다. 지난 OPIc Punch IM2 공략 개정판에 이어 OPIc Punch IH&AL 공략 개정판을 다시 한번 선택해주신 모든 수험생 여러분에게 행운을 빌어드립니다.

모두 승승장구 하십시오.

"You become what you believe."

2017년 10월 Jane Lee

CONTENTS

OPIc Punch IH&AL 공략 사용설명서 _8
NEW OPIc 소개 _10
Background Survery _12
OPIc 공략을 위한 효과적인 전략 _14
2주 완성 스케줄 _17
OPIc Town _18

Chapter 1 School Life 학교 생활

- Unit 01 Self-Introduction 자기소개_학생 _22
- Unit 02 School Courses 학교 수업 _26
- Unit 03 Classroom Device 수업 기기 _30
- Unit 04 School Campus 학교 캠퍼스 _34
- Unit 05 School Events 학교 행사 _38
- Unit 06 Language School 1 어학원 1 _42
- Unit 07 Language School 2 어학원 2 _46

Chapter 2 Work Life 직장 생활

- Unit 08 Self-Introduction 자기소개_직장인 _56
- Unit 09 Training Program 1 회사 연수 1 _60
- Unit 10 Training Program 2 회사 연수 2 _64
- Unit 11 Lunchtime 1 점심시간 1 _68
- Unit 12 Lunchtime 2 점심시간 2 _72
- Unit 13 Choosing a Career 1 취업 준비 1 _76
- Unit 14 Choosing a Career 2 취업 준비 2 _80

Chapter 3 Housing 주거 문화

- Unit 15 Korean Housing Culture 한국의 주거 문화 _90
- Unit 16 Korea's Housing Problem 한국 주거 문화의 문제 _94

Chapter 4 Free-Time Activities 여가 활동

- Unit 17 Watching Movies 1 영화보기 1 _102
- Unit 18 Watching Movies 2 영화보기 2 _106
- Unit 19 Night Clubbing 1 나이트클럽 가기 1 _110
- Unit 20 Night Clubbing 2 나이트클럽 가기 2 _114
- Unit 21 Text Message 1 문자 메시지 1 _118
- Unit 22 Text Message 2 문자 메시지 2 _122
- Unit 23 Shopping 1 쇼핑하기 1 _126
- Unit 24 Shopping 2 쇼핑하기 2 _130
- Unit 25 Home-Improvement Project 1 주거 개선 1 _134
- Unit 26 Home-Improvement Project 2 주거 개선 2 _138

Chapter 5 Hobbies 취미 활동

- Unit 27 Listening to Music 1 음악 감상하기 1 (기기) _148
- Unit 28 Listening to Music 2 음악 감상하기 2 (일반) _152
- Unit 29 Singing 1 혼자 노래 부르거나 합창하기 1 (롤플레이) _156
- Unit 30 Singing 2 혼자 노래 부르거나 합창하기 2 (롤플레이) _160
- Unit 31 Dancing 춤추기 _164
- Unit 32 Dancing Lessons 댄스 교습하기 _168
- Unit 33 Cooking 1 요리하기 1 _172
- Unit 34 Cooking 2 요리하기 2 _176
- Unit 35 Reading 1 독서하기 1 (E-reading) _180
- Unit 36 Reading 2 독서하기 2 (E-reading) _184

Chapter 6 Sports 운동

- Unit 37 Jogging (Walking) 1 조깅(걷기) 1 _194
- Unit 38 Jogging (Walking) 2 조깅(걷기) 2 _198
- Unit 39 Hiking/Trekking 하이킹/트레킹 _202
- Unit 40 Fitness 1 헬스클럽 1 _206
- Unit 41 Fitness 2 헬스클럽 2 _210

Chapter 7 Traveling 여행

- Unit 42 Domestic Business Trip 국내출장 _218
- Unit 43 Overseas Business Trip 해외출장 _222
- Unit 44 Vacation at Home 1 집에서 보내는 휴가 1 _226
- Unit 45 Vacation at Home 2 집에서 보내는 휴가 2 _230
- Unit 46 Domestic Travel 국내여행 _234
- Unit 47 Overseas Travel 해외여행 _238

Chapter 8 Social Issues 사회적 이슈

- Unit 48 Public Transportation 1 대중교통 1 _246
- Unit 49 Public Transportation 2 대중교통 2 _250
- Unit 50 Technology 1 테크놀로지 1 _254
- Unit 51 Technology 2 테크놀로지 2 _258
- Unit 52 Recycling 1 재활용 1 _262
- Unit 53 Recycling 2 재활용 2 _266
- Unit 54 Police Officer 1 경찰 1 _270
- Unit 55 Police Officer 2 경찰 2 _274
- Unit 56 Hospital 1 병원 1 _278
- Unit 57 Hospital 2 병원 2 _282
- Unit 58 Bank 1 은행 1 _286
- Unit 59 Bank 2 은행 2 _290
- Unit 60 Opening a Bank Account 은행 계좌 개설 _294

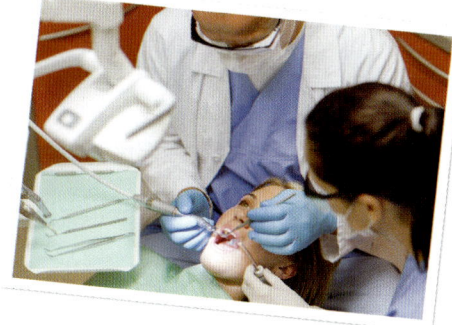

OPIc Punch IH&AL 공략 Actual Test _306

OPIc Punch IH&AL 공략 사용 설명서

OPIc Punch IH&AL 공략은…

자기주도적으로 2주 만에 IH~AL 등급을 목표로 하는 수험생들에게 권합니다. OPIc 말하기 시험은 많은 표현이나 어려운 어휘가 중요한 것이 아니라, 일상에서 자주 사용되는 실용적인 표현들을 상황에 맞도록 자연스럽게 사용해야 합니다. OPIc Punch는 이에 따라 수험생들의 자기주도적 교재(student-oriented book)로 목표 등급을 획득할 수 있도록 기획되었습니다.

OPIc Punch의 4가지 컨셉

- 라운드 One: 오픽 군살 제거! 꼭 필요한 주제와 표현만
- 라운드 Two: 자연스러운 대화하기에서 인터뷰 말하기로
- 라운드 Three: 입에 착착 붙는 오픽 스타일의 패턴 트레이닝
- 라운드 Four: 등급을 올리는 Secret 대공개

❶ Brainstorming Point
각 주제별 Chapter에서 나올 수 있는 예상 가능한 질문과 답변 소재를 6하 원칙으로 정리하여 답변 예측과 구성을 미리 '상상'해보도록 했습니다.

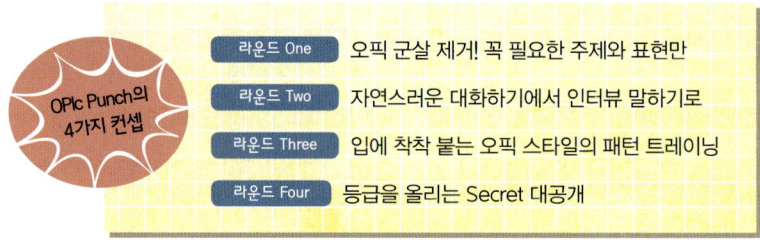

❷ Warm Up
- **Guess the Question & Answer:** 제시된 사진을 보고 질문과 답안을 떠올리기 위한 warm up 입니다.
- **Listen & Talk:** Model Answer의 전초전으로 자연스러운 대화하기를 거쳐 인터뷰 말하기로 유도합니다.

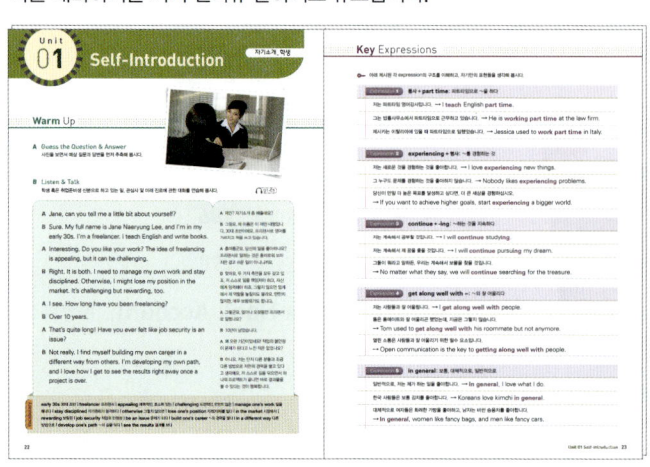

❸ Key Expressions
Listen & Talk와 Model Answer에 나오는 주요 표현을 '패턴화' 시켜서 연습하게 합니다. 쉬운 표현을 반복적으로 활용할 수 있도록 각 Unit별로 5개씩 뽑았습니다. 입에 착착 붙는 OPIc 스타일의 패턴 트레이닝을 경험할 수 있습니다.

④ Topic Question & Model Answer

- **Tip for the OPIc:** 답변 내용 구성과 요령을 위한 유용한 가이드 라인입니다.

- **Model Answer:** 다년 간의 기출문제와 예상문제에 따른 모범답안을 제시했습니다. Listen & Talk가 어떻게 이어지는지 확인할 수 있습니다. [Opening – Body – Closing]의 3단 구성을 통해 자연스러운 시작과 주요 내용 말하기 그리고 깔끔한 마무리를 어떻게 해야 하는지를 제시해줍니다.

- **More Questions:** 똑같은 질문이라도 수험생이 선택한 등급에 따라 질문의 길이와 난이도가 차이가 날 수 있습니다. 이에 대비해 Possible한 질문을 다양하게 제시해놓았습니다.

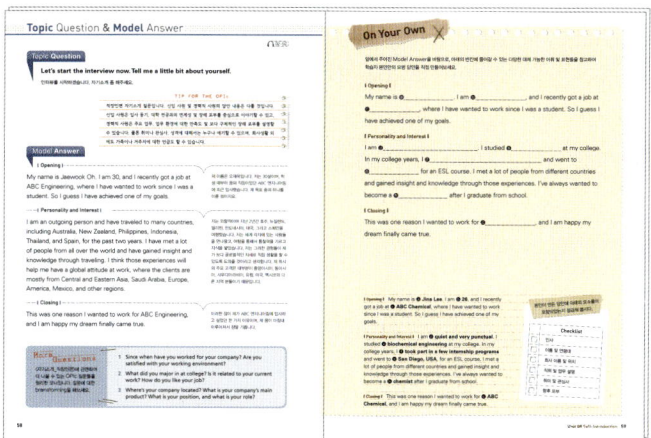

⑤ On Your Own

- **On Your Own:** Model Answer를 기초로 자신만의 답안을 빈칸에 쓰고 말해볼 수 있습니다. 모범답안의 재구성을 통해 On My Own이 됩니다.

- **Checklist:** 꺼진 불도 다시 보듯이 말할 거리를 빼놓지 않았는지 다시 확인해볼 수 있습니다.

⑥ The Music of Speech

발음 및 억양으로 최소한 1등급이 올라갑니다. 녹음된 원어민의 음성을 반복해서 듣고 따라 읽으면서 (shadowing) 어휘의 강세(accent) 구분, 문장 안에서의 올바른 끊어 읽기, 평서문의 문장 끝을 내려 읽는 연습을 해볼 수 있습니다.

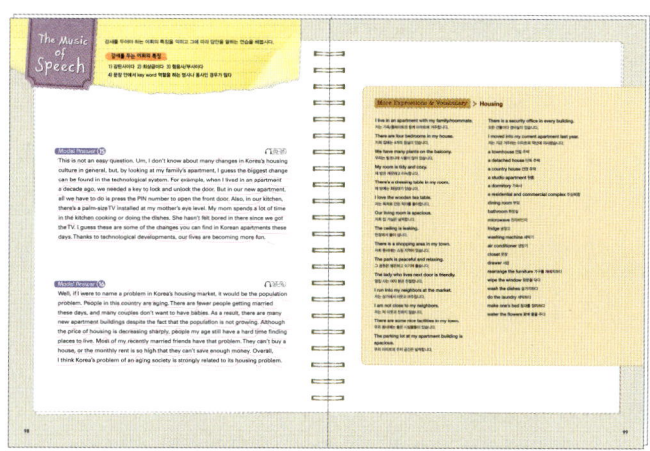

⑦ More Expressions & Vocabulary

해당 Chapter에서 나올 수 있는 표현과 어휘를 최대한 제시하여 답변에 활용할 수 있도록 했습니다.

⑧ OPIc Town

OPIc Town은 OPIc을 공부하기에 앞서 OPIc에서 나올 예상 질문과 연관된 소재와 상황을 자연스럽게 brainstorming하게 해주는 일종의 조감도입니다.

New OPIc 소개

OPIc 이란?

OPIc(Oral Proficiency Interview-computer)은 면대면 인터뷰인 OPI를 최대한 Interview와 가깝게 만든 컴퓨터를 통해 진행되는 iBT기반의 응시자 친화형 외국어 말하기 평가로, 외국어 전문 교육 연구 단체인 ACTFL(American Council on the Teaching of Foreign Languages)에서 개발한 공신력 있는 말하기 시험이다. 단순히 문법이나 어휘 등을 얼마나 많이 알고 있는가를 측정하는 시험이 아니라, 실제 생활에서 얼마나 효과적이고 적절하게 언어를 사용할 수 있는가를 측정하는 객관적인 언어 평가 도구로, 국내에서는 2007년 시작되어 현재 약 1,300여 개 기업 및 기관에서 OPIc을 채용과 인사고과 등에 활발하게 활용하고 있다.

OPIc 진행 Process

Orientation 20분
1. Background Survey
   평가문항을 위한 사전 설문
2. Self Assessment
   시험의 난이도 결정을 위한 자가평가
3. Overview of OPIc
   화면구성, 청취 및 답변방법 안내
4. Sample Question
   실제 답변 방법 연습

→

시험시간 40분
1. 1st Session
   - 개인 맞춤형 문항
   - 질문 청취 2회
   - 문항별 답변시간 제한 無
   - 약 7문항 출제
2. 난이도 재조정
   - Self Assessment (2차 난이도 선택)
   - 쉬운 질문/비슷한 질문/어려운 질문 中 선택
3. 2nd Session
   - 개인 맞춤형 문항
   - 질문청취 2회
   - 문항별 답변시간 제한 無
   - 약 7문항 출제

OPIc 등급

OPIc의 등급은 크게 세 가지, 작게는 일곱 가지로 세분화됩니다.

Novice
'초보자'라는 뜻으로 OPIc에서는 '초급' 단계의 등급입니다.
↓
Novice Low
Novice Mid
Novice High

Intermediate
'중간'이라는 뜻으로 OPIc에서는 '중급' 단계의 등급입니다.
↓
Intermediate Low
Intermediate Mid (1, 2, 3)
Intermediate High

Advanced
'고급의'라는 뜻으로 OPIc에서는 가장 높은 '고급' 단계의 등급입니다.
↓
Advanced Low

ACTFL Proficiency Guidelines

OPIc의 평가는 ACTFL Proficiency Guidelines-Speaking에 따라 절대 평가로 진행됩니다. 이는 말하기 능숙도(Oral Proficiency)에 대한 언어능력 기준입니다. ACTFL의 40년 노하우가 집적된 ACTFL Guidelines는 생활에서 얼마나 효과적이고 적절하게 언어를 사용할 수 있는가를 측정하는 가장 신뢰할 수 있는 평가 기준입니다.

Level		레벨별 요약설명
AL	Advanced LOW	사건을 서술할 때 일관적으로 동사 시제를 관리하고, 사람과 사물을 묘사할 때 다양한 형용사를 사용한다. 적절한 위치에서 접속사를 사용하기 때문에 문장간의 결속력도 높고 문단의 구조를 능숙하게 구성할 수 있다. 익숙하지 않은 복잡한 상황에서도 문제를 설명하고 해결할 수 있는 수준의 능숙도이다.
IH	Intermediate HIGH	개인에게 익숙하지 않거나 예측하지 못한 복잡한 상황을 만날 때, 대부분의 상황에서 사건을 설명하고 문제를 효과적으로 해결하곤 한다. 발화량이 많고, 다양한 어휘를 사용한다.
IM	Intermediate MID	일상적인 소재뿐 아니라 개인적으로 익숙한 상황에서는 문장을 나열하며 자연스럽게 말할 수 있다. 다양한 문장형식이나 어휘를 실험적으로 사용하려고 하며, 상대방이 조금만 배려해주면 오랜 시간 대화가 가능하다.
IL	Intermediate LOW	일상적인 소재에서는 문장으로 말할 수 있다. 대화에 참여하고 선호하는 소재에서는 자신감을 가지고 말할 수 있다.
NH	Novice HIGH	일상적인 대부분의 소재에 대해서 문장으로 말할 수 있다. 개인정보라면 질문을 하고 응답을 할 수 있다.
NM	Novice MID	이미 암기한 단어나 문장으로 말하기를 할 수 있다.
NL	Novice LOW	제한적인 수준이지만 영어 단어를 나열하며 말할 수 있다.

☐ Intermediate Mid의 경우 Fluency, Delivery, Production을 기준으로 Mid 3(상), Mid 2(중), Mid 1(하)로 세분화하여 제공됩니다.

☐ OPIc의 모체인 OPI에서는 Advanced도 Low, Mid, High로 구분되지만, 컴퓨터로 시험을 보는 OPIc에서는 Advanced Low라는 등급 하나만 부여됩니다.

Background Survey

이 Background Survey에 대한 응답을 기초로 개인 맞춤형 문항이 출제됩니다.

이 Background Survey에 대한 응답을 기초로 개인 맞춤형 문항이 출제됩니다. 질문을 자세히 읽고 답변해 주시기 바랍니다.

1 현재 귀하는 어느 분야에 종사하고 계십니까?
☐ 사업/회사   ☐ 재택근무/재택사업   ☐ 교사/교육자   ☐ 군 복무   ☐ 일 경험 없음

1.1 현재 귀하는 직업이 있으십니까?
☐ 네   ☐ 아니오
1.1.1 귀하의 근무 기간은 얼마나 되십니까?
☐ 첫 직장 – 2개월 미만   ☐ 첫 직장 – 2개월 이상   ☐ 첫 직장 아님 – 경험 많음
1.1.1.1 당신은 부하 직원을 관리하는 관리직을 맡고 있습니까?
☐ 네   ☐ 아니오

문항 1에서 [교사/교육자]로 답변했을 경우
1.1 당신은 어디에서 학생을 가르치십니까?
☐ 대학 이상   ☐ 초등/중/고등학교   ☐ 평생교육
1.1.1 귀하의 근무 기간은 얼마나 되십니까?
☐ 2개월 미만 – 첫 직장
☐ 2개월 미만 – 교직은 처음이지만 이전에 다른 직업을 가진 적이 있음
☐ 2개월 이상

2 현재 귀하는 학생이십니까?
☐ 네   ☐ 아니오

2.1 현재 어떤 강의를 듣고 있습니까?
☐ 학위 과정 수업   ☐ 전문 기술 향상을 위한 평생 학습   ☐ 어학 수업
2.2 최근 어떤 강의를 수강했습니까?
☐ 학위 과정 수업
☐ 전문 기술 향상을 위한 평생 학습
☐ 어학 수업
☐ 수업 등록 후 5년 이상 지남

3 현재 귀하는 어디에 살고 계십니까?
☐ 개인주택이나 아파트에 홀로 거주   ☐ 친구나 룸메이트와 함께 주택이나 아파트에 거주
☐ 가족(배우자/자녀/기타 가족 일원)과 함께 주택이나 아파트에 거주   ☐ 학교 기숙사   ☐ 군대 막사

아래의 4~7번 문항에서 12개 이상을 선택해 주시기 바랍니다.

4 귀하는 여가 활동으로 주로 무엇을 하십니까? (두 개 이상 선택)
☐ 영화보기 ☐ 클럽/나이트클럽 가기 ☐ 공연보기 ☐ 콘서트 보기
☐ 박물관 가기 ☐ 공원 가기 ☐ 캠핑하기 ☐ 해변 가기
☐ 스포츠 관람 ☐ 주거 개선 ☐ 술집/바에 가기 ☐ 카페/커피전문점 가기
☐ 게임하기(비디오, 카드, 보드, 휴대폰) ☐ 당구치기
☐ 체스하기 ☐ SNS에 글 올리기 ☐ 친구들과 문자대화하기
☐ 시험 대비 과정 수강하기 ☐ TV보기 ☐ 리얼리티쇼 시청하기
☐ 뉴스를 보거나 듣기 ☐ 요리 관련 프로그램 시청하기 ☐ 쇼핑하기
☐ 차로 드라이브하기 ☐ 스파/마사지샵 가기 ☐ 구직활동하기 ☐ 자원봉사하기

5 귀하의 취미나 관심사는 무엇입니까? (한 개 이상 선택)
☐ 아이에게 책 읽어 주기 ☐ 음악 감상하기 ☐ 악기 연주하기 ☐ 혼자 노래부르거나 합창하기
☐ 춤추기 ☐ 글쓰기(편지, 단문, 시 등) ☐ 그림 그리기 ☐ 요리하기 ☐ 애완동물 기르기
☐ 독서 ☐ 주식투자하기 ☐ 신문읽기 ☐ 여행관련 잡지나 블로그 읽기 ☐ 사진촬영하기

6 귀하는 주로 어떤 운동을 즐기십니까? (한 개 이상 선택)
☐ 농구 ☐ 야구/소프트 볼 ☐ 축구 ☐ 미식축구
☐ 하키 ☐ 크리켓 ☐ 골프 ☐ 배구 ☐ 테니스 ☐ 배드민턴
☐ 탁구 ☐ 수영 ☐ 자전거 ☐ 스키/스노보드 ☐ 아이스 스케이트
☐ 조깅 ☐ 걷기 ☐ 요가 ☐ 하이킹/트레킹 ☐ 낚시
☐ 헬스 ☐ 태권도 ☐ 운동 수업 수강하기 ☐ 운동을 전혀 하지 않음

7 당신은 어떤 휴가나 출장을 다녀온 경험이 있습니까? (한 개 이상 선택)
☐ 국내출장 ☐ 해외출장 ☐ 집에서 보내는 휴가
☐ 국내여행 ☐ 해외여행

OPIc 공략을 위한 효과적인 전략

OPIc의 3가지 핵심 포인트

- 핵심 포인트 1 : OPIc은 면접을 대체하는 시험이다!
- 핵심 포인트 2 : 발음 및 억양으로 1등급 이상 향상시켜라!
- 핵심 포인트 3 : 실용적인 표현을 반복적으로 자연스럽게 사용하라!

핵심 포인트 1

OPIc은 면접을 대체하는 시험이다!

국내 기업의 영어 면접 시험은 OPIc 도입 전과 후로 나눈다고 하여도 과언이 아닐 정도로 다수의 기업이 OPIc을 영어 면접 대체용 시험으로 활용하고 있습니다. 예전에는 기업에서 원어민 감독관을 임명하여 영어 면접을 진행했지만, 보다 공정하고 객관적인 평가를 위하여 미국의 인증된 면접 프로그램인 OPI(Oral Proficiency Interview)를 적용한 **computer-based test**를 도입한 것이지요. OPI는 현재 미국의 상당수 기업이 활용하고 있는 면접 제도이며, 국내에서는 삼성 그룹이 2008년 처음 OPIc를 도입한 이후 올해를 기준으로 국내 1천여 개 기업으로 확대되었습니다. 삼성 그룹의 전체 계열사는 채용 과정에서 뿐 아니라 입사 후 승진, 부서 이동 및 해외 발령 등을 가늠하는 인사고과 기준으로 OPIc 등급을 반영하고 있으며, 앞으로 더욱 많은 기업에서 유사 체제를 도입할 것으로 예상됩니다.

OPIc이 영어 면접을 대체하기 위해 도입된 시험인 것으로 미루어 볼 때, 그 평가 기준 역시 '실제 면접에서의 평가 기준'이 상당 부분 적용된다는 것을 짐작할 수 있습니다. 즉 실제 면접 시 심사위원들이 좋아하는 부분은 OPIc 평가 위원들도 좋아할 것이고, 반대로 실제 면접 시 피해야 할 부분은 OPIc에서도 피해야 할 것입니다. 그렇다면 면접 혹은 OPIc에서의 **Dos and Don'ts**는 무엇일까요? 간단히 정리해보면 아래와 같습니다.

'나만의 이야기'를 한다

면접에서 주목 받으려면 '나만의 스토리'가 있어야 합니다. OPIc에서도 마찬가지입니다. 그러나 막상 시험을 앞둔 분들 가운데 상당수가 '시간이 없어서' 혹은 '쉽게 공부하고 싶어서' 책 속의 모범 답안을 외우는 것에만 치우칩니다. 하지만 단순 암기만 하게 되면, 변형된 문제가 나오거나 문제의 방향이 달라지면 어떻게 해야 할지 막막해 합니다. 반면 충분한 brainstorming을 통해서 '나만의 답안'을 직접 써보고, 읽어보고, 외우신 분들은 문제의 유형 및 방향이 다소 달라지더라도 대처 능력이 훨씬 유연합니다. 또한 자신의 이야기를 하기 때문에 내용의 전달이 자연스럽습니다.

답은 1분 안팎으로 구성한다

다른 말하기 시험과 달리, OPIc은 문항 별로 답안에 대해 정해진 시간이 없는 게 특징입니다. 하지만 각 문제당 1분 안팎 정도가 가장 이상적인 답변 시간이라고 생각합니다. 시험 시간 40분 동안 12~15개 질문을 받게 되는 점을 고려할 때, 질문 내용을 청취하는 데에 소요되는 시간을 제외하면 한 문제당 평균 2분~2분 30초 정도 소요할 수 있는 셈입니다. 그러나 그마저도 다 사용할 필요는 없습니다. 학생들이 답안을 작성한 것을 외울 때, 보통 1분 안팎의 내용이면 100단어 내외를 사용하여 육하원칙이 포함된 기본 답안을 만들어 속도 등을 조절할 수 있습니다.

Replay Button 100% 활용하기!

OPIc의 '다시 듣기 시스템'을 적극 활용하라고 권장하고 싶습니다. 감점 없습니다! 실제 면접을 볼 때에도 면접관에게 질문한 내용을 다시 묻는다고 해서 불이익을 받지 않는 것과 마찬가지입니다. 질문의 내용을 정확히 이해해야만 출제 의도에 맞는 답안을 구성할 수 있겠죠? 또한 Replay Button을 누름으로써 질문을 듣고 답하기 전 최소 5초 이상의 시간을 얻게 되는 이점도 누릴 수 있습니다. 즉 질문을 받은 후 5초 안으로 Replay Button을 사용할 수 있는데, 각 질문의 길이가 보통 7초 이상임을 고려할 때 recording이 시작되기 전 답안을 머릿속으로 구상해 볼 수 있는 시간이 그만큼 늘어납니다.

구체적으로 답하라! (Storytelling)

OPIc 문제 유형을 보면, 허를 찌르는 질문들이 종종 출제됩니다. 그것은 바로, Why do you like to walk? 혹은 Describe your bike. 등과 같이, 15초면 답이 끝날 것 같은 내용의 질문을 말합니다. 아무리 영어를 원어민 수준으로 한다고 할지라도, 위와 같은 질문에 대해서는 몇 문장밖에 못하는 분들이 참으로 많습니다. 하지만 이와 같은 간단한 질문에 대해서도 골고루 살이 붙은 답안을 만들 수 있어야 AL에 가까워집니다.

Role-play 문제의 대답에는 맞장구를 치는 게 좋다!

Role-play question의 답안에서는 반드시 맞장구를 쳐야 합니다. 물론 "Leave a message."인 경우에는 그렇지 않겠지만, "Call and explain your situation." 혹은 "Ask three to four questions." 등의 문제에서는 상대방의 대답에 호응하는 표현이 들어가는 것은 필수입니다. 예를 들어, "Wow!", "Great!", "What?", "Thank you.", "That sounds cool!" 또는 대답하기 곤란한 질문의 경우, "That's a tough question." 의 반응을 해주는 것이 좋습니다.

자신감을 가져라!

자신감이 있다는 것은 목소리가 크고 밝다는 것만을 말하는 게 아닙니다. 목소리가 나직하더라도, 일관된 속도로 차분하게 대답하는 것이 바로 진정한 자신감을 의미합니다. 오버하는 톤은 오히려 감점 요인입니다. 목에 핏대를 세우고 무조건 큰 소리로 대답하는 것도 좋은 방법은 아닙

니다. 본인이 평소 교수님이나 친구들에게 이야기할 때 사용하는 톤으로 이야기하면 적절합니다.

목관리를 하라!

OPIc시험은 말 그대로 응시자가 컴퓨터에 녹음한 파일을 듣고 평가자가 점수를 주는 제도입니다. 따라서 목소리 컨디션을 관리하고 시험장에 들어가는 것이 상당히 중요합니다. 그러나 시험장에 가면 기침 및 재채기를 하는 사람이 꼭 있는데, 환절기나 겨울철에는 그 수가 더욱 많습니다. 최상의 컨디션으로 면접장에 가야 하듯이, OPIc 시험장에도 최상의 컨디션으로 가시기 바랍니다.

Don'ts

'문서를 낭독하는 듯한 답변' 혹은 '남의 말을 외운 듯한 답변'은 피한다

이것도 당연한 것이지만, 역시나 많은 응시자들이 다른 사람들이 만들어 놓은 모범 답안만 줄줄 암기하여 위의 두 가지 오류를 범하는 경우가 많습니다. 이런 경우, 응시자들이 말하기에 있어서 '전달 능력의 중요성' 및 '말하는 사람과 듣는 사람 간에 있는 상호 작용의 중요성'을 간과한 셈이지요.

말끝을 흐리거나 작은 목소리를 내지 않도록 유의한다.

많은 OPIc 응시자 분들이 범하는 오류는 바로 대답의 뒤로 갈수록 속도가 떨어지고 목소리가 기어들어간다는 것입니다. 이는 '이야깃거리가 바닥났다'는 증거인데요, 5초 이상의 pause가 지속될 경우, 말하지 못한 내용에 대한 미련을 버리고 당당하게 "That's all about my story." 혹은 "Thank you for listening."과 같은 말로 마무리하는 것이 백배 낫습니다. "너무 진부한 맺음말 아닌가요?"라고 묻는 분이 계시다면, "제발 진부한 표현이더라도 자신감 있게 사용하고 마무리 지으세요."라고 권합니다. 참고로 필자는 매번 시험 볼 때마다 Role-play questions을 제외한 모든 답안의 마지막에 "Thanks for listening."을 덧붙이고 마무리합니다. 이는 OPIc 평가자가 면접관이나 다름 없다고 여기기 때문입니다.

OPIc 공략을 위한 효과적인 전략

핵심 포인트 2

발음 및 억양으로 1등급 이상 향상시켜라!

OPIc에서 내가 녹음한 답안을 듣는 사람은 바로 평가 위원들입니다. 나의 답변이 잘 전달되려면 분명한 발음과 자연스러운 억양은 필수입니다. 저는 한국인들이 발음 교정을 얼마나 어렵게 생각하는지 잘 알고 있습니다. 그러나 좋은 발음은 외국인처럼 굴려야만 하는 것이 아닙니다. 여러분이 기본 발음 구분 (f/p) (v/b) (z/j) (r/l)만 하면 의미 전달이 훨씬 더 잘됩니다. R과 L발음 구분은 그 중 가장 어렵고 교정하는데 시간이 많이 걸리지만, 앞의 3가지 유사 발음 구분은 10분 안에 교정될 수 있습니다. 여러분의 입술과 혀, 그리고 치아를 어느 자리에 놓아야 하는지를 안다면, 발음 교정은 어렵지 않습니다.

발음보다도 더 강조하고 싶은 것이 바로 자연스러운 억양입니다. 원어민들이 가장 중요하게 여기는 영어 말하기의 key point는 바로 억양이라고 합니다. 각 어휘에 있는 강세(accent) 구분, 문장 안에서의 올바른 끊어 읽기, 평서문의 문장 끝을 내려 읽는 연습은 자연스러운 억양을 만들어 가는 과정입니다. 필자가 강의할 때 학생들에게 가장 많이 강조하는 부분도 이 3가지입니다. 아무리 좋은 내용이더라도 이 3가지 요소가 어긋날 경우 '볼품 없는' 답안으로 둔갑하게 됩니다. 사실 OPIc 답안을 작성하는 것을 보면 학생들 사이에 큰 차이가 없습니다. 문법의 차이가 있기는 하지만 내용의 차이는 도토리 키재기입니다. 즉, 학생들의 답안을 변별하는 중요 요소는 바로 차분한 톤과 속도, 정돈된 발음과 억양입니다.

핵심 포인트 3

쉬운 표현을 반복적으로 자연스럽게 사용하라!

IH이상(AL포함)을 공략하는 답안이 IM(1, 2, 3)을 공략하는 답안과 어떻게 다른지를 묻는 경우가 많습니다. 여러 가지 요소가 있겠지만, 중요한 것 중의 하나는 '질문에 대한 정확한 이해'라고 말해주고 싶습니다. Level 1, 2, 3의 질문과 Level 4, 5, 6의 질문은 당연히 다릅니다. 질문의 큰 틀은 비슷해도 그 내용은 다릅니다. 아마 큰 맘 먹고 Level 5, 6의 난이도를 선택해 본 분들이라면 질문 내용이 만만치 않음을 느꼈을 겁니다. Level이 높아질수록 질문의 배점도 향상되지만, 질문의 분량이 많은데다가 속도가 빨라지고 내용도 어려워져서 많은 응시자가 쩔쩔매는 경우가 허다합니다. 질문의 내용을 잘 이해하기 위해서는, 평소 청취를 반복적으로 연습하는 것이 중요합니다.

OPIc Punch 초, 중급 편 교재의 질문을 MP3로 반복해서 듣고, key word를 정리하고 따라다보면 질문에 대한 이해력이 빨라질 것입니다. 또한 질문의 key word를 답안을 구성할 때 활용하면 답안 내용이 보다 논리적이고 정갈하게 들립니다. 한편 매 시험마다 OPIc 시험의 질문내용이 조금씩 달라지긴 하지만, 소재별로 비슷한 질문들이 반복적으로 나옵니다. OPIc 질문의 경향을 잘 분석하고 그에 따른 brainstorming을 지속적으로 해두면 Level 5, 6의 질문들에 대한 두려움도 사라질 것입니다. IH이상 공략에서 중요한 또 다른 한 가지는 비교적 간단하지만 세련된 표현을 잘 활용하는 것입니다. 구어체적인 표현 가운데서도 표현이 늘어지지 않고 의사전달이 분명한 phrase(숙어)를 평소에 정리해두었다가 활용하면 좋습니다. OPIc Punch 교재의 Expressions 부분을 참고하거나 Model Answer에서 좋은 표현이라고 생각되는 것을 따로 표시해두었다가 활용하면 도움이 될 것입니다. 자, 그럼 지금부터, OPIc Punch와 함께 '실용적이면서도 세련된 표현'들을 함께 익혀봅시다!

취업 필수 OPIc! 2주 완성 스케줄

긴급하게 OPIc점수가 필요하거나 단기간에 OPIc시험을 준비하고 싶다면 Jane Lee선생님이 제안하는 2주 완성 스케줄을 이용해 IH 등급을 획득할 수 있습니다.

■ 학생 ■ 직장인 ■ 공통

1일	2일	3일	4일	5일	6일	7일
■ Unit 1, 2, 5 ■ Unit 8, 11, 12 자기소개하기 학교/회사에서 일어나는 일 얘기하기	■ Unit 3, 4 ■ Unit 9, 10, 13, 14 익숙한 공간 및 학생/직장인 신분에 연관된 활동 얘기하기	■ Unit 15, 16 한국의 주거 문화에 대해 설명하기	■ Unit 17, 18, 35, 36 이야기(영화, 책)에 관한 여가 및 취미활동에 관해 얘기하기	■ Unit 19, 20, 31, 32 춤(클럽, 댄스 교습)에 연관된 여가 및 취미 활동에 관해 얘기하기	■ Unit 21, 22, 23, 24 문자 메시지 및 쇼핑하기를 통한 여가 활동 묘사하기	■ Unit 25, 26, 33, 34, 44, 45 집과 연관된 여가 및 취미 활동그리고 휴가 생활에 대해 얘기하기
8일	**9일**	**10일**	**11일**	**12일**	**13일**	**14일**
■ Unit 27, 28, 29, 30 음악에 관한 취미활동 설명하기	■ Unit 37, 38, 39, 40, 41 거주지 근처에서 할 수 있는 운동에 대해 설명하기	■ Unit 42, 43, 46, 47 국내외 출장 및 여행에 관한 경험 얘기하기	■ Unit 48, 49, 50, 51 대중교통 및 테크놀로지에 관한 사회적 이슈 대비하기	■ Unit 52, 53, 54, 55 재활용 및 경찰에 관한 사회적 이슈 대비하기	■ Unit 56, 57, 58, 59, 60 병원 및 은행에 관한 사회적 이슈 대비하기	실전 모의고사

나만의 스타일! 나만의 스케줄

1일	2일	3일	4일	5일	6일	7일
8일	**9일**	**10일**	**11일**	**12일**	**13일**	**14일**
15일	**16일**	**17일**	**18일**	**19일**	**20일**	**21일**
22일	**23일**	**24일**	**25일**	**26일**	**27일**	**28일**

OPIc Town 소개

OPIc Town은, 학생들이 OPIc을 공부하기에 앞서 OPIc의 질문과 연관된 소재들을 자연스럽게 brainstorming하게 해주는 조감도입니다.

그림에서 보이는 산(mountain)과 등산객(hiker), 그 옆의 공원(park)과 공원 옆의 자전거 도로(trail) 및 자전거를 타는 사람(rider) 그리고 조깅하는 사람(jogger)은 Background Survey의 6번 항목(Sports)과 긴밀한 연관성이 있습니다.

한편 자전거 도로 옆에서 음악 듣는 사람(Listening to Music), 패스트푸드 식당(restaurant), 그 옆의 상가(Mart), 건너편의 경찰서(Police Station), 병원(Hospital), 영화관(Cinema) 그리고 맨 앞의 은행 (Bank)은 Background Survey의 4번, 5번 항목(Free-Time Activity, Hobbies & Interests) 및 돌발 문제(Random Questions)로 자주 출제되는 소재들입니다.

돌발 문제와 연관된 소재들은 또한, 우리 동네(Background Survey 3번 항목 관련)에서 쉽게 접할 수 있는 장소입니다. 또한 도로 위를 달리는 버스(bus)는 돌발 문제에 해당되는 교통(transportation)과 연관이 있습니다. 모든 것이 '우리의 일상'과 밀접하게 연관되었으므로, OPIc 시험을 위한 brainstorming이 훨씬 자연스럽게 다가올 것입니다.

오른쪽은 Background Survey의 2번 항목에 해당되는 학교(School Life)와 관련이 있음을 한눈에 알 수 있습니다. 학교 캠퍼스(School Campus), 캠퍼스에서 내가 좋아하는 장소라고 할 수 있는 벤치(bench), 학교 인물 묘사에 자주 나오는 교수님(professor) 및 일반 학생(student)의 모습을 보고, OPIc의 학생편 질문들을 떠올려보기 바랍니다.

사실 OPIc 시험은 상당한 '생활 밀착형' 소재들을 주로 다루고 있지만, 많은 학생들은 의외로 '일상의 소재'들에 대한 brainstorming이 평소 연습되지 않은 경우가 많습니다. OPIc Town 조감도를 바탕으로 OPIc에 나오는 단골 소재들을 자주 연상하며 많은 연습을 하시기 바랍니다.

CHAPTER 1 학교 생활
School Life

Unit 01	**Self-Introduction** 자기소개_학생
Unit 02	**School Courses** 학교 수업
Unit 03	**Classroom Device** 수업 기기
Unit 04	**School Campus** 학교 캠퍼스
Unit 05	**School Events** 학교 행사
Unit 06	**Language School 1** 어학원 1
Unit 07	**Language School 2** 어학원 2

Chapter 1은 학교 생활에 대해 다룹니다. 하지만 많은 학생들이 학교 수업과 별도로 어학원 수업을 듣고 있는 추세를 반영하여 어학원에 관한 질문도 자주 출제됩니다. IH 이상을 공략하는 Level 5~6에서는 학교 혹은 어학원의 과거 및 현재 모습, 구체적인 수업 내용, 그리고 교실 내부의 장비 및 기기 등에 대한 질문이 등장할 수 있습니다.

+ Brainstorming Point

When?
- when I made a presentation at school (학교에서 발표했던 경험)
- when I made a reservation for the lab (랩실을 예약한 경우)
- when I missed a class (수업에 결석한 경우)
- when I attended a language school (언제 어학원에 다녔는지)

Where?
- my classroom (교실)
- school campus (학교 캠퍼스)
- language school (어학원)

What?
- classroom devices (수업 장비)
- a school festival (학교 축제)
- course registration (수강 신청)
- work on school projects (학교 과제하기)
- what I like about the school campus (학교 캠퍼스의 좋은 점)
- what I learned at the language school (어학원에서 배운 것)
- language school facilities (어학원 시설)

Who?
- who I spent the school event with (학교 행사에 같이 참여했던 사람)
- who taught me how to use the device (기기 사용법을 가르쳐준 사람)
- my school team project members (그룹 과제를 함께 한 친구들)

Why?
- why the course is memorable (그 수업이 기억에 남는 이유)
- why I signed up for the course (그 수업을 수강했던 이유)
- why I chose my major (전공을 선택한 이유)

How?
- how I use the school library (학교 도서관 이용법)
- how I spend my day at school (학교에서 하루를 어떻게 보내는지)
- how I found the language school (어학원을 알게 된 경로)
- how I liked the language school programs (어학원 프로그램이 어떠했는지)

Unit 01 Self-Introduction

자기소개_학생

Warm Up

A Guess the Question & Answer
사진을 보면서 예상 질문과 답변을 먼저 추측해 봅시다.

B Listen & Talk
학생 혹은 취업준비생 신분으로 하고 있는 일, 관심사 및 미래 진로에 관한 대화를 연습해 봅시다.

🎧 01-01

A Jane, can you tell me a little bit about yourself?	**A** 제인? 자기소개 좀 해줄래요?
B Sure. My full name is Jane Naeryung Lee, and I'm in my early 30s. I'm a freelancer. I teach English and write books.	**B** 그럼요. 제 이름은 이 제인 내령입니다. 30대 초반이에요. 프리랜서로 영어를 가르치고 책을 쓰고 있습니다.
A Interesting. Do you like your work? The idea of freelancing is appealing, but it can be challenging.	**A** 흥미롭군요. 당신의 일을 좋아하나요? 프리랜서로 일하는 것은 흥미로워 보이지만 결코 쉬운 일이 아니까요.
B Right. It is both. I need to manage my own work and stay disciplined. Otherwise, I might lose my position in the market. It's challenging but rewarding, too.	**B** 맞아요. 두 가지 측면을 모두 갖고 있죠. 저 스스로 일을 책임져야 하고, 자신에게 엄격해야 하죠. 그렇지 않으면 업계에서 제 역할을 놓칠지도 몰라요. 만만치 않지만, 매우 보람되기도 합니다.
A I see. How long have you been freelancing?	**A** 그렇군요. 얼마나 오랫동안 프리랜서로 일했나요?
B Over 10 years.	**B** 10년이 넘었습니다.
A That's quite long! Have you ever felt like job security is an issue?	**A** 꽤 오랜 기간이었네요! 직업의 불안정이 문제가 된다고 느낀 적은 없었나요?
B Not really. I find myself building my own career in a different way from others. I'm developing my own path, and I love how I get to see the results right away once a project is over.	**B** 아니요. 저는 단지 다른 분들과 조금 다른 방법으로 저만의 경력을 쌓고 있다고 생각해요. 저 스스로 길을 닦으면서 하나의 프로젝트가 끝나면 바로 결과물을 볼 수 있다는 것이 행복합니다.

Vocabulary
early 30s 30대 초반 | **freelancer** 프리랜서 | **appealing** 매력적인, 호소력 있는 | **challenging** 도전적인, 만만치 않은 | **manage one's work** 일을 해내다 | **stay disciplined** 자기관리가 엄격하다 | **otherwise** 그렇지 않으면 | **lose one's position** 자리(지위)를 잃다 | **in the market** 시장에서 | **rewarding** 보람된 | **job security** 직업의 안정성 | **be an issue** 문제가 되다 | **build one's career** ~의 경력을 쌓다 | **in a different way** 다른 방법으로 | **develop one's path** ~의 길을 닦다 | **see the results** 결과를 보다

22

Key Expressions

🗝 아래 제시된 각 expression의 구조를 이해하고, 자기만의 표현들을 생각해 봅시다.

| Expression 1 | 동사 + part time: 파트타임으로 ~을 하다 |

저는 파트타임 영어강사입니다. → I **teach** English **part time**.

그는 법률사무소에서 파트타임으로 근무하고 있습니다. → He is **working part time** at the law firm.

제시카는 이탈리아에 있을 때 파트타임으로 일했었습니다. → Jessica used to **work part time** in Italy.

| Expression 2 | experiencing + 명사: ~를 경험하는 것 |

저는 새로운 것을 경험하는 것을 좋아합니다. → I love **experiencing** new things.

그 누구도 문제를 경험하는 것을 좋아하지 않습니다. → Nobody likes **experiencing** problems.

당신이 만일 더 높은 목표를 달성하고 싶다면, 더 큰 세상을 경험하십시오.
→ If you want to achieve higher goals, start **experiencing** a bigger world.

| Expression 3 | continue + -ing: ~하는 것을 지속하다 |

저는 계속해서 공부할 것입니다. → I will **continue** study**ing**.

저는 계속해서 제 꿈을 좇을 것입니다. → I will **continue** pursu**ing** my dream.

그들이 뭐라고 말하든, 우리는 계속해서 보물을 찾을 것입니다.
→ No matter what they say, we will **continue** search**ing** for the treasure.

| Expression 4 | get along well with ~: ~와 잘 어울리다 |

저는 사람들과 잘 어울립니다. → I **get along well with** people.

톰은 룸메이트와 잘 어울리곤 했었는데, 지금은 그렇지 않습니다.
→ Tom used to **get along well with** his roommate but not anymore.

열린 소통은 사람들과 잘 어울리기 위한 필수 요소입니다.
→ Open communication is the key to **getting along well with** people.

| Expression 5 | in general: 보통, 대체적으로, 일반적으로 |

일반적으로, 저는 제가 하는 일을 좋아합니다. → **In general**, I love what I do.

한국 사람들은 보통 김치를 좋아합니다. → Koreans love kimchi **in general**.

대체적으로 여자들은 화려한 가방을 좋아하고, 남자는 비싼 승용차를 좋아합니다.
→ **In general**, women like fancy bags, and men like fancy cars.

Topic Question & Model Answer

Topic Question

Let's start the interview. Tell me a little bit about yourself.

인터뷰를 시작하겠습니다. 당신에 대해 얘기해보세요.

> **TIP FOR THE OPIc**
> OPIc시험의 1번으로 출제되는 질문입니다. 자기소개는 보통 이름과 연령층, 그리고 종사하는 분야에 대해서 언급하는 것으로 시작하는 것이 좋습니다. 그 밖에 취미, 관심사, 혹은 하는 일에 대해서 보다 구체적으로 얘기할 수 있습니다. 가족 사항, 거주지, 장래 포부 등도 선택적으로 말할 수 있습니다. 여러 사항을 나열하기보다는, 1~2가지를 중점적으로 말하는 story-telling 형태가 바람직합니다.

Model Answer

Opening

Hi. My name is Jane Naeryung Lee, and I'm in my early 30s. I'm a freelancer and a student. I teach English part time and also study.

안녕하세요, 제 이름은 이 제인 내령이고요, 저는 30대 초반입니다. 저는 프리랜서이자 학생입니다. 저는 파트 타임으로 영어를 가르치며 공부를 하는 중입니다.

Interests and Personality

I love to study. People may think I'm crazy, but I love experiencing new things through books. So I've been studying various things and will continue studying this and that. I'm very much a people-person. I love to meet new people and communicate with them. I think I'm very sociable and love to hang out with different people. I'm also very positive and outgoing. I guess that's why I can always get along well with people.

저는 공부하는 것을 좋아합니다. 사람들은 제가 이상하다고 생각할지 모르지만, 저는 책을 통해서 새로운 것을 경험하는 것을 좋아합니다. 그래서 저는 지금껏 다양한 것을 공부해왔고 계속 이것저것 공부할 것입니다. 저는 사람들과 어울리는 것을 매우 좋아합니다. 새로운 사람을 만나고 그들과 얘기하는 것이 좋습니다. 저는 제가 매우 사교적이며 다른 사람들과 어울리는 것을 매우 좋아한다고 생각합니다. 저는 또한 매우 긍정적이며 활달합니다. 아마 그러한 성격 덕분에 늘 사람들과 잘 지내는 것 같습니다.

Closing: Where I live

On the other hand, I live in Bundang, which is about 30 minutes from downtown Seoul. I love this area. In general, I love my life.

다른 한편, 저는 분당에 거주하는데, 서울 중심가로부터 30분 정도 떨어진 곳입니다. 저는 이곳이 매우 좋습니다. 전반적으로 저는 제 인생을 소중하게 생각합니다.

More Questions

〈자기소개_학생편〉에 관련하여 더 나올 수 있는 OPIc 질문들을 정리한 코너입니다. 질문에 대한 brainstorming을 해보세요.

1. You said you are a student. What are you studying at school? How do you like your studies?
2. What do you like and dislike about your school life?
3. Tell me about your major. Is there any special reason you chose your major?

앞에서 주어진 Model Answer을 바탕으로, 아래의 빈칸에 들어갈 수 있는 다양한 대체 가능한 어휘 및 표현들을 참고하여 학습자 본인만의 모범 답안을 직접 만들어보세요.

I Opening I

Hi. My name is ⓐ_____, and I'm in my ⓑ_____. I'm a ⓒ_____ and a graduate student. ⓓ_____.

I Interests and Personality I

I love to ⓔ_____. I love experiencing new things through ⓕ_____. So, I've been ⓖ_____. I'm very ⓗ_____. I love to ⓘ_____. I think I'm very ⓙ_____ and love to ⓚ_____. I'm also very ⓛ_____ and ⓜ_____. I guess that's why I ⓝ_____.

I Closing: Where I live I

On the other hand, I live in ⓞ_____, which is about ⓟ_____ minutes/hours from downtown Seoul. I love this area. In general, I love my life.

I Opening I Hi. My name is ⓐ **Minseo Park**, and I'm in my ⓑ **mid-30s**. I'm a ⓒ **writer** and a graduate student. ⓓ **I write articles and also study**.

I Interests and Personality I I love to ⓔ **travel**. I love experiencing new things through ⓕ **traveling to different places**. So I've been ⓖ **traveling to many places around the world**. I'm very ⓗ **active**. I love to ⓘ **adventure**. I think I'm very ⓙ **dynamic** and love to ⓚ **meet new people**. I'm also very ⓛ **creative** and ⓜ **imaginative**. I guess that's why I ⓝ **can write inspiring articles on life and culture**.

I Closing: Where I live I On the other hand, I live in ⓞ **Seongbukdong**, which is about ⓟ **20** minutes from downtown Seoul. I love this area. In general, I love my life.

본인이 만든 답안에 아래의 요소들이 포함되었는지 점검해 봅시다.

	Checklist
☐	인사
☐	이름 및 연령대
☐	현재 하고 있는 일
☐	취미 및 관심사
☐	성격
☐	장래 포부
☐	거주지 등 일상에 관한 소개

Unit 02 School Courses

학교 수업

Warm Up

A Guess the Question & Answer
사진을 보면서 예상 질문과 답변을 먼저 추측해 봅시다.

B Listen & Talk
학교 수업 및 학점에 관한 대화입니다. 기억에 남는 수업과 그 이유에 대한 대화를 연습해 봅시다.

🎧 01-03

A How many courses are you taking this semester?

B I'm taking 6 courses. They are 20 credits in total.

A You must have a tight schedule.

B I do. But I'm trying to enjoy the classes as much as I can. I'm especially in love with my psychology class.

A Psychology? That's not even your major. Is it fun?

B It's very interesting. I've always wanted to have a solid understanding of the human mind and behavior. I'm sure it will be helpful for my future profession.

A That would be nice. What kinds of activities do you do in the class? I thought you would only read books for the entire semester.

B No way. We have class discussions where we can share ideas and learn how to think critically about various psychological issues.

A 이번 학기에 몇 과목 들어?

B 여섯 과목. 총 20학점이야.

A 엄청 빡빡하겠다.

B 맞아. 그렇지만 최대한 수업을 즐기려고 노력하고 있어. 특히 심리학 수업이 정말 재미있어.

A 심리학? 네 전공도 아니잖아. 재미있어?

B 정말 흥미로워. 난 늘 인간의 심리와 행동에 대한 깊은 이해를 하고 싶었거든. 미래의 직업을 갖는 데에도 도움이 될 거라고 확신해.

A 참 좋은 생각이네. 수업 시간에는 어떤 활동을 하게 되니? 난 한 학기 내내 책만 읽는 줄로 생각했어.

B 절대 안 그래. 토론 수업이 있을 때면 서로의 생각들을 공유하고, 다양한 심리학 문제에 대해 보다 비판적으로 생각하는 법을 배워.

Vocabulary
course 수업 | semester 학기 | credit 학점 | a tight schedule 빡빡한 스케줄 | in love with ~ ~가 정말 좋은 | psychology 심리, 심리학 | a solid understanding 견고한 이해 | human mind 사람 심리 | behavior 행동, 행위 | be helpful for ~ ~에 도움이 되다 | profession 직업 | critically 비판적으로

Key Expressions

아래 제시된 각 expression의 구조를 이해하고, 자기만의 표현들을 생각해 봅시다.

Expression 1   **out of curiosity:** 호기심에서

저는 호기심에서 그 수업을 신청했습니다. → I signed up for the class **out of curiosity**.

저는 호기심에서 길을 따라 걷기 시작했습니다. → I started to walk along the path **out of curiosity**.

그냥 호기심에서 물어보는 건데요, 하늘에는 몇 개의 별이 있나요?
→ I'm just asking **out of curiosity**, but how many stars are there in the sky?

Expression 2   **have nothing to do with ~:** ~와 아무 상관없다

그 수업은 제 전공과는 아무 상관도 없었습니다. → The class **had nothing to do with** my major.

이 문제는 당신과 아무 상관없는 일입니다. → This problem **has nothing to do with** you.

저는 혈액형은 성격과 아무 상관이 없다고 생각합니다.
→ I think blood types **have nothing to do with** personalities.

Expression 3   **observe:** 관찰하다, 목격하다

저는 다양한 페인팅과 점토 작품을 볼 수 있었습니다.
→ I was able to **observe** various paintings and clay art.

저는 오늘 아침 인터뷰 과정 전체를 보고 왔습니다.
→ I **observed** the entire interview process this morning.

사람들의 잠잘 때 버릇을 관찰하는 것은 재미있는 일이다.
→ It's funny to **observe** peoples' sleeping habits.

Expression 4   **have its own story:** 그만의 사연이 있다

각각의 작품마다 사연이 있는 듯 했습니다. → Each piece seemed to **have its own story**.

모든 노래에는 그만의 사연이 담겨 있다. → Every song **has its own story**.

모든 성공담에는 그만의 사연이 있기 마련이다. → Every success **has its own story**.

Expression 5   **reflect one's feeling:** ~의 감정을 반영하다

색채가 어떻게 사람의 감정을 반영하는지 볼 수 있는 특별한 경험이었습니다.
→ It was a special experience to see how colors **reflected people's feelings**.

그의 어조에는 그의 감정이 실려 있었습니다. → His tone **reflected his feelings**.

그 편지에는 그녀의 감정이 나타나 있었습니다. → The letter **reflected her feelings**.

Topic Question & Model Answer

Topic Question

Tell me about the most memorable class you have had. What's so special about it? Did anything unexpected happen?

당신이 들었던 가장 기억에 남는 수업에 대해 말해보세요. 그 수업에서 무엇이 그렇게 특별했나요? 당신이 예상치 못한 일이 일어났었나요?

TIP FOR THE OPIc

기억에 남는 수업에 관한 질문입니다. 수업은 학교생활의 상당 부분을 차지하는 활동입니다. 전공 관련 과목 혹은 과목과 관계없이, 인상적이었던 과목에 대해 얘기하면 됩니다. 교수님, 수업 내용, 힘들었던 과제, 발표 경험, 학과 친구들과 있었던 일 등에 대해 얘기할 수 있습니다. 현장 학습을 한 것, 새로운 경험, 예기치 못했던 사건 등에 대해서도 언급할 수 있습니다.

Model Answer

| Opening |

I would like to talk about the art therapy class I took when I was a freshman. It was an elective course, and I signed up for the class out of curiosity.

저는 대학교 1학년 때 들었던 미술 치료 수업에 대해 얘기해보겠습니다. 교양 수업이었는데, 호기심으로 수강 신청을 했었습니다.

| Introduction of the Class |

In fact, the class had nothing to do with my major. But, since I had been interested in the healing effects of art therapy, I thought it would be nice to learn about it by taking the class. I read in some books that art therapy is helpful to those who are emotionally scarred or physically disabled. However, I wasn't sure if it would really work by just drawing pictures and doing other creative activities. To find out more about art therapy, we visited hospitals, nursing homes, and special schools.

사실, 제 전공과는 아무런 관련이 없는 수업이었어요. 하지만 미술 치료의 효과에 대한 관심이 있어왔기 때문에, 수업을 들어서 배우는 게 좋을 것 같았어요. 몇 권의 책을 읽어보니 미술 치료가 정서적으로 상처를 입었거나 신체적으로 장애를 얻은 사람들에게 도움이 되더군요. 그렇지만 정말 그림을 그리거나 다른 창작 활동을 하는 것만으로 효과가 있는지는 확실히 알 수가 없었죠. 미술 치료에 대해 더 알아보기 위해, 우리는 병원과 양로원 및 특수학교를 방문했습니다.

| Lesson from the Class |

At those places, I was able to observe various paintings and clay art done by children and adults. Each piece seemed to have its own story, and I felt something warm deep in my heart. It was a special experience to see how colors and images reflected people's feelings.

그곳에서 저는 아이들과 어른들이 그린 다양한 그림 및 점토 미술 작품을 볼 수 있었습니다. 각 작품마다 사연이 있는 것 같았고, 저는 마음 깊은 곳에서 따스함을 느낄 수 있었습니다. 색채와 이미지가 사람들의 감정을 어떻게 담아내는지 볼 수 있는 특별한 경험이었습니다.

More Questions

〈학교 수업〉에 관련하여 더 나올 수 있는 OPIc 질문들을 정리한 코너입니다. 질문에 대한 brainstorming을 해보세요.

1. Are you close to any classmates or a professor? Why are you close to this person?
2. Have you ever faced an unexpected situation in class? What happened? Tell me everything that took place.

On Your Own

앞에서 주어진 Model Answer을 바탕으로, 아래의 빈칸에 들어갈 수 있는 다양한 대체 가능한 어휘 및 표현들을 참고하여 학습자 본인만의 모범 답안을 직접 만들어보세요.

I Opening I

I would like to talk about the ⓐ_____ class I took when I was a ⓑ_____. It was a/an ⓒ_____, and I signed up for the class ⓓ_____.

I Introduction of the Class I

In fact, the class was related to my major, International Relations. Since I had been interested in ⓔ_____, I thought it would be nice to learn about it by taking the class. I read in some books that ⓕ_____. However, I wasn't sure ⓖ_____. To find out more about ⓗ_____.

I Lesson from the Class I

At these events, I was able to ⓘ_____. It was a special experience to ⓙ_____.

I Opening I I would like to talk about the ⓐ **Human Rights in the Global Era** class I took when I was a ⓑ **junior**. It was a ⓒ **major elective course**, and I signed up for the class ⓓ **to gain an in-depth understanding of human rights in our society**.

I Introduction of the Class I In fact, the class was related to my major, International Relations. Since I had been interested in ⓔ **human rights for immigrants in Korea**, I thought it would be nice to learn about it by taking the class. I read in some articles that ⓕ **many immigrant workers in Korea are mistreated**. However, I wasn't sure ⓖ **what kinds of prejudice they were facing in our society**. To find out more about ⓗ **the present state of Korea's human rights, we attended the annual conference held by the National Human Rights Commission of Korea and also visited the Seoul Global Migrant Center**.

I Lesson from the Class I At these events, I was able to ⓘ **learn that protecting human rights starts by respecting individuals**. It was a special experience to ⓙ **get a close and personal look into the lives of multicultural families in Korea**.

본인이 만든 답안에 아래의 요소들이 포함되었는지 점검해 봅시다.

	Checklist
☐	기억에 남는 수업 이름
☐	전공 관련 여부
☐	수업 연계 활동
☐	인상 깊었던 일 (발표 경험, 교수님 등)
☐	수업을 통해 배운 점

Unit 03 Classroom Device

수업 기기

Warm Up

A Guess the Question & Answer
사진을 보면서 예상 질문과 답변을 먼저 추측해 봅시다.

B Listen & Talk
학교에서 자주 사용하게 되는 테크놀로지 및 기기에 대한 대화를 먼저 연습해 봅시다.

 01-05

A Korea is known to be one of the most digitalized nations. Is this true of your classrooms?

B I guess you want to know if the classrooms are also digitalized. They are. In my classroom, there are various devices such as an electronic board, an LCD TV, a beam projector, and more.

A I've never heard of an electronic board. How does it work?

B I have no idea how it works, but we don't use chalk or an eraser. Instead, the professor uses a stick to write on the board and then erases by clicking a button on the board.

A Sounds neat. What is your favorite device at school?

B I would say my laptop computer. I write papers, take notes during class, and even access the Internet on school campus. I can't imagine my school life without my laptop.

A Indeed. The computer is probably the most innovative product made by human beings.

A 한국은 세계적으로 가장 디지털화가 된 국가 중의 하나라고 하죠. 당신의 교실도 그런가요?

B 학교 교실도 디지털화가 되었는지 알고 싶으신 거군요. 맞습니다. 저희 교실에는 전자칠판, LCD TV, 빔 프로젝터 등과 같은 다양한 기기들이 있습니다.

A 전자 칠판이란 것은 들어본 적이 없어요. 어떻게 작동하나요?

B 저도 어떻게 작동하는지는 잘 모르지만, 분필이나 지우개를 사용하지 않아요. 대신 교수님께서 칠판에 어떤 막대기를 이용해서 쓴 후 전자 칠판에 있는 단추를 누르면 내용이 지워지더라고요.

A 재미있네요. 당신은 학교에서 사용하는 기기 중에 어떤 것을 가장 좋아하나요?

B 아마도 제 노트북 컴퓨터일 거예요. 과제도 쓸 수 있고 수업 내용을 필기할 뿐만 아니라 학교 캠퍼스에서 인터넷에도 접속할 수 있어요. 제 노트북 컴퓨터 없이는 학교생활을 상상할 수 없어요.

A 맞아요. 인간이 창조한 제품 가운데 아마 컴퓨터만큼 혁신적인 게 또 있을까 싶어요.

Vocabulary

be known to be ~ ~로 유명하다, 잘 알려지다 | **digitalized** 디지털화 된 | **device** 기기 | **electronic board** 전자칠판 | **beam projector** 빔 프로젝터 | **never heard of ~** ~에 대해 들어본 바가 없는 | **click a button** 단추를 클릭하다 | **write papers** 문서(리포트)를 작성하다 | **take notes** 필기를 하다 | **access the Internet** 인터넷에 접속하다 | **indeed** 정말, 참으로 | **innovative** 혁신적인

Key Expressions

아래 제시된 각 expression의 구조를 이해하고, 자기만의 표현들을 생각해 봅시다.

Expression 1   **install:** 설치하다

많은 교실에 컴퓨터가 설치되어 있습니다. → There are computers **installed** in many classrooms.

주차장에 CCTV 카메라가 몇 대 설치되어 있습니다.
→ There are several CCTV cameras **installed** in the parking lot.

우리 엄마는 그녀의 자동차에 네비게이터를 설치했습니다.
→ My mother **installed** a navigation system in her car.

Expression 2   **carry:** 들고 다니다, 가지고 다니다

저는 주로 학교에 제 노트북을 가져갑니다. → I usually **carry** my laptop to school.

우산 갖고 나가는 걸 잊지 마라. → Don't forget to **carry** your umbrella.

인찬은 조깅하러 갈 때마다 늘 그의 스마트폰을 들고 다닙니다.
→ Inchan always **carries** his smartphone when he jogs.

Expression 3   **take notes of ~:** ~의 내용을 필기하다, 받아 적다

저는 주로 강의 내용을 받아 적습니다. → I usually **take notes of** the lecture.

그 기자는 인터뷰 내용을 받아 적었습니다. → The journalist **took notes of** the interview.

저는 그 연설 내용을 기록하는 많은 사람들을 찾아볼 수 있었습니다.
→ I spotted many people **taking notes of** the speech.

Expression 4   **work on ~:** ~하는 데에 애쓰다, 노력하다, 공들이다

저는 제 노트북으로 학교 과제를 합니다. → I **work on** school projects with my laptop.

저는 요즘 제 책을 집필하는 데에 노력을 기울이고 있습니다. → I'm **working on** my book these days.

우리 팀은 하이브리드 자동차를 개발하는 데에 애를 쓰고 있습니다.
→ My team is **working on** the development of a hybrid car.

Expression 5   **access:** 들어가다, 접속하다, 연결되다; 접근(성)

제 노트북 컴퓨터로 인터넷에 접속하는 것은 쉽습니다.
→ It's easy to **access** the Internet with my laptop.

그 논문을 확인할 권리는 교수님에게만 있습니다.
→ Only the professor has the right to **access** the papers.

저는 바닷가 가까이에 있는 빌라에 살았더라면 하는 소망이 있습니다.
→ I wish I lived in a villa with easy **access** to the beach.

Topic Question & Model Answer

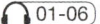

Topic Question

You said you are a student. What kinds of devices do you see in the classroom? What is your favorite device, and why?

당신은 학생이라고 대답했습니다. 교실에서 당신이 보는 기기의 종류는 무엇인가요? 당신이 가장 좋아하는 기기는 무엇이며 그 이유는 뭔가요?

TIP FOR THE OPIc
일상에서 자주 사용하는 기계 및 테크놀로지에 관한 질문입니다. 학교 교실이라고 장소를 한정하였지만, 사실 평소에 내가 좋아하는 기계를 중심으로 서술하면 됩니다. 물론, 교실 안에서만 볼 수 있는 기계가 따로 있을 것입니다. 수업 중 자주 활용되는 기계 1~2개에 관한 자세한 설명 및 본인이 좋아하는 기계의 사용 목적 등을 간략하게 언급할 수 있습니다.

Model Answer

| Opening |

In the classroom, there are various devices, such as an LCD TV, an electronic board, a beam projector, and computers.

저희 교실에는 LCD TV, 전자칠판, 빔 프로젝터 그리고 컴퓨터와 같은 다양한 기기들이 구비되어 있습니다.

| Purpose of Each Device |

When I attend my movie criticism class, we watch films and documentaries on the TV. Professors use the beam projector to show teaching materials, and many students use the projector for presentations. There are computers installed in many classrooms, but I prefer to use my own. I usually carry my laptop and my smartphone with me. My smartphone has a recording function that I use, but my favorite device is my laptop.

제가 영화 비평 수업을 들을 때는 TV로 영화 및 다큐멘터리를 시청합니다. 교수님들은 수업 자료를 보여주기 위해 빔 프로젝터를 사용하시고, 많은 학생들은 프레젠테이션을 하기 위해 빔 프로젝터를 사용합니다. 많은 교실에 컴퓨터가 설치되어 있지만, 저는 개인 컴퓨터를 사용하는 것을 선호합니다. 저는 주로 제 노트북 컴퓨터와 스마트폰을 가지고 다닙니다. 제 스마트폰에는 녹음 기능이 있는데, 그래도 제가 제일 좋아하는 것은 노트북 컴퓨터입니다.

| My Favorite Device |

I usually take notes of the lectures with my laptop and also work on school projects on it. Plus, it's very easy to access the Internet almost anywhere on campus! I can't think of a better device than this.

저는 제 노트북 컴퓨터로 강의 내용을 필기하고 학교 과제를 하기도 합니다. 게다가 학교 캠퍼스 어디에서든 인터넷에 접속할 수 있습니다! 이보다 좋은 기기가 있을지 모르겠습니다.

More Questions

〈수업 기기〉에 관련하여 더 나올 수 있는 OPIc 질문들을 정리한 코너입니다. 질문에 대한 brainstorming을 해보세요.

1. How did advanced technology change your school life? What are the merits and drawbacks of it?
2. What kinds of technology do you use in your class? Who taught you how to use that technology?
3. Do you often use technology at school? What do you use the most often? Why?

앞에서 주어진 Model Answer을 바탕으로, 아래의 빈칸에 들어갈 수 있는 다양한 대체 가능한 어휘 및 표현들을 참고하여 학습자 본인만의 모범 답안을 직접 만들어보세요.

I Opening I

In the classroom, there are various devices, such as ⓐ_____, ⓑ_____, ⓒ_____, and computers.

I Purpose of Each Device I

When I attend my ⓓ_____, we ⓔ_____.
Professors use the beam projector to show teaching materials, and many students use the projector for presentations. There are computers installed in many classrooms, but I prefer to use my own. I usually carry my laptop and my ⓕ_____ with me. ⓖ_____, but my favorite device is my laptop.

I My Favorite Device I

I usually take notes of the lectures with my laptop and also work on school projects on it. Plus, it's very easy to access the Internet almost anywhere on campus! I can't think of a better device than this.

I Opening I In the classroom, there are various devices, such as ⓐ **a microphone**, ⓑ **a projector screen**, ⓒ **a wall monitor**, and computers.

I Purpose of Each Device I When I attend my ⓓ **marketing research class**, we ⓔ **often use the screen to show graphs and charts for market analysis**. Professors use the beam projector to show teaching materials, and many students use the projector for presentations. There are computers installed in many classrooms, but I prefer to use my own. I usually carry my laptop and my ⓕ **electronic dictionary** with me. ⓖ **I search the electronic dictionary to look for financial jargon**, but my favorite device is my laptop. *jargon: 전문용어

I My Favorite Device I I usually take notes of the lectures with my laptop and also work on school projects on it. Plus, it's very easy to access the Internet almost anywhere on campus! I can't think of a better device than this.

본인이 만든 답안에 아래의 요소들이 포함되었는지 점검해 봅시다.

	Checklist
☐	교실 내부 기기
☐	기기의 용도와 사용 방법
☐	기기 사용법을 알려준 사람
☐	내가 좋아하는 기기
☐	좋아하는 기기의 사용 목적
☐	테크놀로지의 발달로 달라진 점

Unit 04 School Campus

학교 캠퍼스

Warm Up

A Guess the Question & Answer
사진을 보면서 예상 질문과 답변을 먼저 추측해 봅시다.

B Listen & Talk
학교 캠퍼스의 달라진 점에 관한 대화입니다. 캠퍼스의 시설물 및 환경이 달라진 점에 대한 대화를 연습해 봅시다.  01-07

A How do you like your new semester?	**A** 새 학기 되니까 어때?
B Good! Everything looks fresh and new.	**B** 아주 좋아! 모든 게 새롭고 신선해 보여.
A Really? Are there any changes on your school campus?	**A** 정말? 학교 캠퍼스에 달라진 거라도 있어?
B Yes, there are some changes. The buildings look the same, but, once you get into the library, you would be amazed.	**B** 응, 달라진 점이 몇 가지 있어. 건물은 다 똑같은데, 도서관에 들어가면 완전 놀랄 거야.
A Why? What's new about the library?	**A** 왜? 도서관이 어떻게 새로워졌는데?
B It is very digitalized. The seminar room in particular is equipped with state-of-the-art devices.	**B** 엄청 디지털화 되었어. 특히 세미나실이 최신식 장비들로 갖춰져 있더라고.
A I'm getting curious. Does it have automatic doors as well?	**A** 점점 궁금해진다. 자동문도 있는 거야?
B No, but it has a fingerprint-scanning system.	**B** 아니. 지문 감식 체계더라고.
A That's cool. What else?	**A** 멋지다. 다른 건 없어?
B There is a wall monitor, and a new whiteboard has also been installed.	**B** 응. 방에 벽걸이 모니터랑 새 화이트보드도 설치되어 있어.

Vocabulary
be amazed 놀라다, 감탄하다 ǀ **seminar room** 세미나 룸 ǀ **in particular** 특히 ǀ **be equipped with ~** ~의 장비를 갖추다 ǀ **state-of-the-art** 최신식의, 최첨단의 ǀ **get curious** 호기심이 일다 ǀ **automatic doors** 자동문 ǀ **fingerprint-scanning system** 지문 인식 시스템 ǀ **wall monitor** 벽걸이 모니터 ǀ **installed** 설치된

Key Expressions

> 아래 제시된 각 expression의 구조를 이해하고, 자기만의 표현들을 생각해 봅시다.

Expression 1 — **for sure:** 확실히, 분명히, 당연히

당연히 계절은 바뀌었습니다. → The season has changed **for sure**.

그는 확실히 성실한 사람이었습니다. → He was a sincere man **for sure**.

저는 반드시 올 여름에 당신을 방문할 것입니다. → I'll visit you this summer **for sure**.

Expression 2 — **enjoy the + 형용사 + weather:** ~한 날씨를 만끽하다

저는 날씨를 만끽하는 많은 사람들을 봅니다. → I see a lot of people **enjoying the weather**.

오늘, 아름다운 날씨를 만끽하세요! → **Enjoy the beautiful weather** today!

우리는 신혼여행 기간 동안에 그 섬의 따뜻한 날씨를 만끽했습니다.
→ We **enjoyed the lovely weather** of the island during our honeymoon.

Expression 3 — **after it was remodeled:** 리모델링 이후

리모델링 이후에 도서관에는 몇 가지 변화가 있었습니다.
→ There were some changes in the library **after it was remodeled**.

우리 사무실은 리모델링이 된 이후에 매우 정돈되어 보였습니다.
→ Our office looked very organized **after it was remodeled**.

제 방은 리모델링이 된 후에 현대적으로 바뀌었습니다.
→ My room became modern **after it was remodeled**.

Expression 4 — **digitalize:** 디지털화하다

많은 것들이 디지털화되었습니다. → Many things were **digitalized**.

한국은 매우 디지털화된 나라입니다. → South Korea is a highly **digitalized** country.

우리는 스마트폰 없이는 못 살게 되어버린 디지털 시대에 살고 있습니다.
→ We are living in a **digitalized** world where people can't live without smartphones.

Expression 5 — **with only ~:** ~만으로, ~만 있어도

학생증만 있으면, 책을 대여할 수 있습니다.
→ **With only** your student ID card, you can borrow books.

그녀는 커피 한 잔만 있으면 밤샐 수 있습니다. → **With only** a cup of coffee, she can stay up all night.

이 로션 한 방울만으로도 당신의 피부는 빛날 것입니다.
→ **With only** a drop of this lotion, your skin will be shiny.

Topic Question & Model Answer

Topic Question

Has your campus changed at all in the past semester? For example, are there any new buildings, dorms, or parks on campus? Please describe them in detail.

지난 학기와 비교했을 때 학교 캠퍼스에 달라진 점이 있나요? 예를 들어, 캠퍼스에 새로운 건물이나, 기숙사나 공원이라도 생겼나요? 그것들에 대해 자세히 얘기해 보세요.

TIP FOR THE OPIc

OPIc의 단골 질문인 '학교 캠퍼스 묘사하기'가 확장된 질문입니다. Level 5~6에서는 A와 B를 비교, 대조하는 질문이 자주 나옵니다. 캠퍼스의 이전과 현재 모습의 차이를 묘사할 때에는 건물의 외관이나 건물 내부의 시설물 변화, 계절의 변화, 새로 오신 교수님 혹은 학교 행정의 변화 등에 대해 얘기합니다. 비교적 많은 변화가 느껴지는 1~2가지에 대해 구체적으로 설명하고 느낌을 말하도록 하세요.

Model Answer

| Opening |

There have been a few changes on my school campus since last semester.

저희 학교 캠퍼스에는 지난 학기에 비해 달라진 점이 몇 가지 있습니다.

| Changes on the School Campus |

I got back to school a month ago, and the season has changed for sure. It's spring, so I see flowers blossoming in some places. The weather is good, too! I see a lot of people in lighter clothing who are enjoying the weather. On the other hand, there were some changes in the library after it was remodeled. Above all, many things were digitalized. For example, with only your student ID card, you can borrow books, enter the computer lab, and make reservations for the seminar room. It has become so much more convenient than it was in the past. Plus, the sofas and chairs in the lounge look more colorful and comfortable.

저는 한 달 전에 학교에 복학했는데, 우선 계절이 확실히 달라졌습니다. 봄이 되었기 때문에 여기저기 꽃이 핀 것을 볼 수 있습니다. 날씨도 정말 좋아요! 많은 사람들이 가벼운 옷차림으로 날씨를 만끽하는 것을 보게 됩니다. 다른 한편, 도서관이 리모델링된 이후에 변화가 생겼죠. 무엇보다도 많은 부분들이 디지털화되었습니다. 예를 들어, 학생증만 있으면, 책을 대여하고, 컴퓨터실에 출입하고 혹은 세미나룸을 예약할 수가 있습니다. 과거에 비해 훨씬 편리해졌지요. 더 나아가 휴게실에 있는 소파 및 의자의 색상이 화려해지고 더욱 편안해졌습니다.

| Closing |

These are some of the new things I've seen on my school campus.

이러한 점들이 제 학교 캠퍼스의 새로워진 몇 가지 사항들입니다.

More Questions

〈학교 캠퍼스〉에 관련하여 더 나올 수 있는 OPIc 질문들을 정리한 코너입니다. 질문에 대한 brainstorming을 해보세요.

1. What do you like about your school campus? Is there anything special about your school campus?
2. What kinds of facilities do you have on your school campus? Which one do you use the most often?

On Your Own

앞에서 주어진 Model Answer을 바탕으로, 아래의 빈칸에 들어갈 수 있는 다양한 대체 가능한 어휘 및 표현들을 참고하여 학습자 본인만의 모범 답안을 직접 만들어보세요.

| Opening |

There have been a few changes on my school campus since last semester.

| Changes on the School Campus |

I got back to school a month ago, and the season has changed for sure. It's ⓐ_____, so I see ⓑ_____ in some places. The weather is nice, too! I see a lot of people ⓒ_____ and enjoying the weather. In addition, there were some changes in the ⓓ_____ after it was remodeled. One of the best changes was the ⓔ_____. ⓕ_____. ⓖ_____. Plus, the sofas and chairs in the ⓗ_____ look more colorful and comfortable.

| Closing |

These are some of the new things I've seen on my school campus.

| Opening | There have been a few changes on my school campus since last semester.

| Changes on the School Campus | I got back to school a month ago, and the season had changed for sure. It's ⓐ **autumn**, so I see ⓑ **trees that have turned red and orange** in some places. The weather is nice, too! I see a lot of people ⓒ **sitting on the grass** and enjoying the weather. In addition, there were some changes in the ⓓ **cafeteria** after it was remodeled. One of the best changes was the ⓔ **new snack bar**. ⓕ **It used to sell only sandwiches and kimbap, but now it also sells hotdogs, panini, and bubble teas**. ⓖ **It's great to have more choices than in the past**. Plus, the sofas and chairs in the ⓗ **cafeteria** look more colorful and comfortable.

| Closing | These are some of the new things I've seen on my school campus.

본인이 만든 답안에 아래의 요소들이 포함되었는지 점검해 봅시다.

	Checklist
☐	새 학기를 맞이한 기분
☐	계절 변화로 인해 달라진 점
☐	학교 시설물 변화
☐	시설물 변화로 인한 영향
☐	캠퍼스의 새로운 모습에 대한 느낌

Unit 05 School Event

학교 행사

Warm Up

A Guess the Question & Answer
사진을 보면서 예상 질문과 답변을 먼저 추측해 봅시다.

B Listen & Talk
학교 축제에 관한 대화입니다. 축제 기간에 벌어지는 가수 초대, 일일주점, 벼룩시장 등에 관한 대화를 연습해 봅시다. 🎧 01-09

A Hey, how are you enjoying school life?

B It's so much fun. We are having the school festival next week, and people are excited about the events coming up.

A Right. It's the festival season in Korea. What kinds of events are you having at school?

B The practical music class students are inviting a well-known rock group and an indie band. I heard the tickets sold out in 20 minutes.

A I guess they must be very popular.

B I think they are. But they don't play music in my favorite genres, so I didn't get a ticket for myself.

A Are you taking part in any events?

B My classmates rented a bar near the campus, and we will throw our own party during the festival. We will sell food, play games, and even have a speed-dating event.

A Sounds fun! I hope you have a great time.

A 안녕, 학교생활 어때?

B 완전 재미있어. 다음 주면 학교 축제 기간인데, 다가올 행사들 때문에 사람들이 난리가 났어.

A 맞다. 한국에서는 지금이 축제 기간이지. 학교에서 어떤 축제 행사들을 하는데?

B 실용음악과 학생들은 유명한 록 그룹이랑 인디 밴드 하나를 초대한대. 듣기로는 20분 만에 표가 매진되었다고 하더라.

A 정말 인기가 많은 그룹들인가 보다.

B 그런 것 같아. 하지만 내가 좋아하는 음악 장르는 아니라서 난 티켓을 구하지 않았어.

A 네가 참여하는 행사는 없어?

B 우리 과 친구들은 학교 근처에 바 하나를 빌려서 축제 기간 내내 자체 파티를 열 거야. 음식도 팔고, 게임도 하고 스피드 데이팅도 할 거야.

A 재미있겠다! 좋은 시간 보내길 바래.

Vocabulary | **be excited about ~** ~에 대해 흥분하다 | **festival season** 축제의 계절 | **practical music class** 실용 음악 수업 | **sold out** 매진되다 | **take part in ~** ~에 참여하다 | **throw a party** 파티를 열다

Key Expressions

아래 제시된 각 expression의 구조를 이해하고, 자기만의 표현들을 생각해 봅시다.

Expression 1 **a great season for ~:** ~를 하기에 최적의 계절

축제를 벌이기에 최적의 계절입니다. → It's **a great season for** festivals.

봄은 소풍을 가기에 최적의 계절입니다. → Spring is **a great season for** picnics.

여름은 일광욕을 하기에 최적의 계절입니다. → Summer is **a great season for** sunbathing.

Expression 2 **favorite part of ~:** ~에서 가장 좋아하는 부분

그것이 제가 축제에서 가장 좋아하는 부분입니다. → It's my **favorite part of** the festival.

당신이 그 이야기에서 가장 좋아하는 부분은 무엇입니까? → What's your **favorite part of** the story?

그 장면은 그 영화에서 제가 가장 좋아하는 부분입니다. → That scene is my **favorite part of** the movie.

Expression 3 **on one side of ~:** ~의 한 쪽에

캠퍼스 한 쪽에는 벼룩시장이 있습니다. → There's a flea market **on one side of** the campus.

저는 들판 한 쪽에서 트럭 한 대를 보았습니다. → I saw a truck **on one side of** the field.

나는 탁자 한 쪽에서 쪽지 하나를 발견했습니다. → I found a note **on one side of** the table.

Expression 4 **at a bargain price:** 저렴한 가격에, 할인된 가격에

저는 그 스카프를 할인가에 구입했습니다. → I got the scarf **at a bargain price**.

세라는 그녀의 새 가방을 저렴한 가격에 샀습니다. → Serah got her new bag **at a bargain price**.

릭은 그 청바지를 할인가에 구입했습니다. → Rick purchased the jeans **at a bargain price**.

Expression 5 **be going to be crazy:** 열광적일 것이다, 매우 신날 것이다

파티는 정말 열광적일 것입니다. → The party **is going to be crazy**.

오늘 밤 싸이의 콘서트는 정말 열광적일 것입니다. → Psy's concert **is going to be crazy** tonight.

그것은 정말 큰 경기입니다. 사람들이 아주 열광적일 것이에요.
→ It's a big match. People **are going to be crazy**.

Topic Question & Model Answer

Topic Question

Do you have any special events at school? What kinds of activities do the students do when there's an event?

당신의 학교에서 특별한 행사들이 있나요? 행사가 있을 때 학생들은 어떤 활동을 하나요?

TIP FOR THE OPIc

학교 행사에 관한 질문입니다. 학교 행사에는 축제, 체육 대회, 동아리 관련 행사 및 전공 관련 세미나 등이 포함됩니다. 본인이 가장 흥미를 갖고 참여한 행사, 기억에 남는 일, 적극적으로 참여했던 이유 등에 대해 얘기해볼 수 있습니다. 답안을 통해 실제 학교 행사장의 생동감 있는 분위기를 연상할 수 있다면 아주 좋은 답안이 될 것입니다.

Model Answer

| Opening |

We have various events at school, such as seminars, sporting events, and a school festival. This festival, which is held in May every year, is the most popular event.

저희 학교에는 세미나, 체육 대회 및 교내 축제와 같은 다양한 행사들이 있습니다. 매년 5월에 열리는 축제가 가장 인기 있는 행사이죠.

| Details of the School Festival |

May is the most beautiful time of the year, so it's a great season for festivals. During the festival, we sometimes invite famous musicians to school and hold concerts. That's my favorite part of the festival. We also have a flea market on one side of the campus. Last year, I got a really nice flower-pattern scarf at a bargain price there. In addition, some students make food and sell them for low prices.

5월은 연중 가장 아름다운 시기이기 때문에 축제를 열기에 최적입니다. 축제 기간에 우리는 때로는 학교에 유명 가수들을 초대해서 콘서트를 열기도 합니다. 그것은 제가 가장 좋아하는 축제 순서이기도 합니다. 저희는 또한 축제 기간 중에 캠퍼스 한 쪽에서 벼룩시장을 열기도 합니다. 작년에 저는 그곳에서 꽃무늬 스카프를 할인가격에 구입했습니다. 뿐만 아니라 어떤 학생들은 음식을 만들어 저렴한 가격에 판매하기도 합니다.

| Plans and Closing |

This year, I'm planning to rent a venue near the school with my classmates to party. I'm sure it's going to be crazy.

올해 저는 과 친구들과 함께 학교 근처에 장소를 대여해서 파티를 열고자 합니다. 정말 재미있을 거예요.

More Questions

〈학교 행사〉에 관련하여 더 나올 수 있는 OPIc 질문들을 정리한 코너입니다. 질문에 대한 brainstorming을 해보세요.

1. When was the last time you took part in a school event? What did you do at the event?
2. What kinds of events do you have at school? Is there anything interesting about the events?
3. Tell me about the most popular event at your school. Why do you think it is popular?

On Your Own

앞에서 주어진 Model Answer을 바탕으로, 아래의 빈칸에 들어갈 수 있는 다양한 대체 가능한 어휘 및 표현들을 참고하여 학습자 본인만의 모범 답안을 직접 만들어보세요.

I Opening I

We have various events at school, such as ⓐ_____, ⓑ_____, and a ⓒ_____. The ⓒ_____ held in ⓓ_____ every year, is the most popular event.

I Details of the School Festival I

ⓔ_____, so it's a great season for ⓒ_____. During the ⓒ_____, we sometimes invite famous ⓕ_____. That's my favorite part of the ⓒ_____. We also get ⓖ_____ _____. Last year, I got some really ⓗ_____. In addition, some students ⓘ_____.

I Plans and Closing I

This year, I'm planning to ⓙ_____. I'm sure it's going to be ⓚ_____.

I Opening I We have various events at school, such as ⓐ **a speech contest**, ⓑ **a music performance**, and a ⓒ **job fair**. The ⓒ **job fair** held in ⓓ **September** every year, is the most popular event.

I Details of the School Festival I ⓔ **Fall is the most active recruiting season of the year**, so it's a great season for ⓒ **job fairs**. During the ⓒ **job fair**, we sometimes invite famous ⓕ **CEOs and leaders in various fields**. That's my favorite part of the ⓒ **job fair**. We also get ⓖ **free job consulting with HR managers from different companies during the fair**. Last year, I got some really ⓗ **helpful advice from an HR manager and was able to take part in an internship program**. In addition, some students ⓘ **get feedback on their résumés**.

I Plans and Closing I This year, I'm planning to ⓙ **apply for the mock interview session**. I'm sure it's going to be ⓚ **a great chance to build my interview skills**.

본인이 만든 답안에 아래의 요소들이 포함되었는지 점검해 봅시다.

Checklist

☐	다양한 학교 행사 종류
☐	학교 축제(내가 좋아하는 행사)에 관한 소개
☐	학교 축제 연계 행사
☐	기억에 남는 축제 에피소드
☐	내가 축제 때 하는 일
☐	축제에 대한 기대감

Unit 06 Language School 1

어학원 1

Warm Up

A Guess the Question & Answer
사진을 보면서 예상 질문과 답변을 먼저 추측해 봅시다.

B Listen & Talk
어학원에 관한 대화를 연습해 봅시다.

🎧 01-11

A Naejun, where did you learn English? You are so fluent.
B Thanks. I read English newspapers almost every day.
A What about your speaking? Have you ever lived overseas?
B No, but I have gone to several language schools since I was in elementary school.
A Wow. Then you must have met some nice teachers. You don't have an accent!
B Thanks. My parents were quite passionate about my education. I'm sure they did a lot of research before they sent me to the language schools.
A Did you like the classes at the language schools?
B Absolutely. It was always fun to be at the schools. We watched English videos and learned English songs at the institutes. I remember we also played games during class.
A It sounds like you really enjoyed attending the schools!
B Yes, but we also took spelling tests and grammar tests all the time.
A I wish I had studied English like you did.

A 내준아, 넌 영어를 어디서 배웠어? 영어가 무척 유창해서.
B 고마워. 난 거의 매일같이 영어 신문을 읽어.
A 말하기는 어떻게 배운 거야? 외국에서 산 적이 있니?
B 아니, 하지만 초등학교 때부터 어학원을 여러 군데 다녔어.
A 와. 그럼 넌 틀림없이 좋은 선생님들을 만났나봐. 발음이 마치 원어민 같아!
B 고마워. 부모님께서 교육에 대한 관심이 매우 크셨어. 나를 어학원에 보내시기 전에 아마 많이 알아보셨을 거야.
A 어학원 수업들은 재미있었어?
B 물론. 난 항상 학원에 가는 것이 재미있었어. 우리는 영어 비디오도 시청하고 영어 노래도 배웠지. 수업 시간에 게임을 한 기억도 있고.
A 듣자 하니 정말 학원 가는 것이 좋았나 보구나!
B 응. 하지만 우리는 늘 단어 시험이랑 문법 시험을 봤어.
A 나도 너처럼 영어를 공부했더라면 좋았을 텐데.

Vocabulary
fluent 유창한 | passionate 열정적인 | research 조사하다 | institute 연구 기관

Key Expressions

> 아래 제시된 각 expression의 구조를 이해하고, 자기만의 표현들을 생각해 봅시다.

Expression 1 — always believe + that절: 항상 ~라고 믿다

부모님께서는 항상 영어가 매우 중요하게 될 것이라고 믿으셨습니다.
→ My parents **always believed that** English would be very important.

저는 항상 제 꿈이 이루어질 것이라고 믿었습니다. → I **always believed that** my dream would come true.

우리는 언제나 정의를 위해 싸우는 것이 옳다고 믿었습니다.
→ We **always believed that** fighting for justice is the right thing to do.

Expression 2 — my siblings and I/me: 나와 내 형제 자매들

부모님께서는 저와 제 동생들을 영어 학원에 보내셨습니다.
→ My parents sent **my siblings and me** to an English institute.

저와 제 동생들은 종종 록 콘서트에 같이 갑니다. → **My siblings and I** often go to rock concerts together.

저와 제 형제들은 같은 학교에 다녔습니다. → **My siblings and I** went to the same school.

Expression 3 — be동사 + excited to: ~를 하게 되어 신나다

저희는 늘 그곳에 가는 것이 신났습니다. → We **were** always so **excited to** go there.

모두가 인질들이 풀려났다는 소식을 듣고 기뻐했습니다.
→ Everyone **was excited to** hear that the hostages had been released.

저는 오늘 밤 저희 프로그램에 대통령을 초대하여 인터뷰한다는 사실에 들떠 있습니다.
→ I **am** very **excited to** interview the president on our show tonight.

Expression 4 — coteach: (선생님 2명 이상이) 교대로 수업하다

한국인 선생님과 원어민 선생님이 교대로 수업하였습니다.
→ A Korean and a native teacher often **cotaught** the class.

저는 랜디와 교대로 오픽을 강의하곤 했습니다. → I used to **coteach** OPIc with Randy.

제가 대학생일 때, 교수님들이 교대로 강의하시는 수업이 인기 있었습니다.
→ **Coteaching** courses were popular when I was in college.

Expression 5 — can only remember: ~만을 기억하다

너무 오래 전 일이라 기억이 가물가물합니다.
→ It's been so many years that I **can only remember** a few things.

모든 일이 갑자기 일어나서 단지 거리 명만 기억납니다.
→ Everything happened so fast that I **can only remember** the street name.

Unit 06 Language School 1

Topic Question & Model Answer

Topic Question

Have you ever taken a class at a language school? If so, how did you like your class? What did you like the most about your language school?

당신은 어학원 수업을 수강한 적이 있습니까? 만일 수강한 적이 있다면 수업은 어떠했나요? 당신은 어학원의 어떤 점이 가장 좋았나요?

> **TIP FOR THE OPIc**
>
> 어학원에 관한 질문입니다. OPIc에서는 학교나 회사에서 이루어지는 일상적인 활동 및 경험에 대한 질문이 자주 출제됩니다. 그리고 그러한 질문 유형에는 그와 같은 활동에 대한 어릴 적 경험이나 기억에 남는 경험을 묻는 질문이 포함됩니다. 이러한 경우, 언제, 누구와 함께 있었던 일인지 상세하게 자신의 경험을 이야기하도록 합시다.

Model Answer

| Opening |

I have taken classes at several language schools since I was in elementary school. My parents always believed that English would be very important when we grew up. So they sent my siblings and me to an English institute in our neighborhood.

저는 초등학생이었을 때부터 여러 어학원에서 수업을 들었습니다. 부모님께서는 저희가 자라면 영어가 매우 중요하게 될 것이라고 늘 생각하셨습니다. 그래서 저와 제 동생들을 집 근처 영어 학원에 보내셨습니다.

| Memories of the Classes |

We were always so excited to go there. We watched English videos and learned English songs at the institute. I remember that we also played games during class. Sometimes, we had parties at the school. There were about 5 students and a teacher in the class. A Korean and a native teacher often cotaught the class.

학원에 가는 것은 언제나 즐거웠습니다. 저희는 학원에서 영어 비디오도 시청하고 영어 노래도 배웠습니다. 또한 수업 시간에 게임을 했던 기억도 납니다. 가끔은 학원에서 파티를 열기도 했습니다. 학급은 선생님 한 명에 다섯 명 정도의 학생들로 구성되어 있었습니다. 한국인 선생님 한 명과 원어민 선생님 한 명이 교대로 수업을 진행하였습니다.

| Closing |

It's been so many years that I can only remember a few things, but I still remember that I enjoyed the classes a lot. One day, I hope my husband and I can send our kids to similar classes. That would be awesome.

너무 오래 전 일이라 기억이 가물가물하지만 수업이 매우 재미있었던 기억이 납니다. 언젠가는 남편과 제가 저희 아이들도 비슷한 수업을 들을 수 있게 해주고 싶습니다. 정말 멋진 일이 될 것입니다.

〈어학원〉에 관련하여 더 나올 수 있는 OPIc 질문들을 정리한 코너입니다. 질문에 대한 brainstorming을 해보세요.

1. What languages did you study at the language school? Do you think the classes were helpful? Why?

2. Do you have a memorable experience at a language institute? When did it happen? Why is it so memorable? Please tell me about it from the beginning to the end.

3. Tell me about a specific class you took at a language school. What kinds of activities did you do in the class? How did you like them?

앞에서 주어진 Model Answer을 바탕으로, 아래의 빈칸에 들어갈 수 있는 다양한 대체 가능한 어휘 및 표현들을 참고하여 학습자 본인만의 모범 답안을 직접 만들어보세요.

I Opening I

I have taken classes at several language schools since I was ⓐ_____.
My parents always believed that English would be very important ⓑ_____.
So they sent ⓒ_____ to an English institute in our neighborhood.

I Memories of the Classes I

ⓓ_____ to go there. We watched English videos and learned English songs at the institute. I remember that we also played games during class. Sometimes, we had parties at the school. ⓔ_____.

ⓕ_____.

I Closing I

It's been so many years that I can only remember a few things, but I still remember that I enjoyed the classes a lot. One day, I hope ⓖ_____.
That would be awesome.

I Opening I I have taken classes at several language schools since I was ⓐ **five (나이)**. My parents always believed that English would be very important ⓑ **to learn for my future career**. So they sent ⓒ **me** to an English institute in our neighborhood.

I Memories of the Classes I ⓓ **It was fun** to go there. We watched English videos and learned English songs at the institute. I remember that we also played games during class. Sometimes, we had parties at the school. ⓔ **My favorite was the Christmas parties with carols and plays**. ⓕ **The gift exchanges were also a lot of fun**.

I Closing I It's been so many years that I can only remember a few things, but I still remember that I enjoyed the classes a lot. One day, I hope ⓖ **I will be able to work for a global company**. That would be awesome.

본인이 만든 답안에 아래의 요소들이 포함되었는지 점검해 봅시다.

	Checklist
☐	언제 어학원 수업을 수강했는지
☐	어학원을 찾게 된 경로
☐	수업에 관한 좋은 기억
☐	어학원 수업의 특징
☐	어학원에 다닌 소감

Unit 07 Language School 2

어학원 2

Warm Up

A Guess the Question & Answer
사진을 보면서 예상 질문과 답변을 먼저 추측해 봅시다.

B Listen & Talk
어학원 묘사에 관한 대화를 연습해 봅시다.

🎧 01-13

A How was the language school you went to last vacation?
B It was really nice. The program was helpful, and the teachers were very friendly.
A I'm glad to hear that! Which language school did you go to?
B I went to the Livingstone Language School. It's located in the school district.
A Nice. How many classrooms were there?
B I think there were about 10 classrooms. It wasn't a big school, but it had excellent curriculums.
A That's what really matters. So would you recommend that I go there?
B Of course. I'm sure you will like it as well.
A What did you enjoy the most during the classes?
B It was the internship program. Since it was a business English program, the school introduced a few qualified students to local companies for 6-week internships.
A Wow, that is awesome! I didn't know there was such a practical program at language schools.

A 지난 방학 때 다녔던 어학원 어땠니?
B 정말 좋았지. 프로그램이 도움이 됐고 선생님들께서도 아주 친절하셨어.
A 잘됐네! 어느 어학원에 다녔어?
B 리빙스톤 어학원이라는 곳에 다녔어. 학원들이 밀집한 지역에 위치해 있어.
A 좋다. 거기 교실은 몇 개나 있었는데?
B 10개 정도 있었던 것 같아. 큰 규모는 아니었지만 커리큘럼이 뛰어났어.
A 그게 진짜 중요한 거지. 그럼 넌 내가 그 어학원에 가는 것을 추천할 거니?
B 물론. 너도 좋아할 거라고 확신해.
A 수업에서 제일 좋았던 게 뭐야?
B 인턴쉽 프로그램이었어. 내가 들은 프로그램이 비즈니스 영어 과정이었는데, 어학원 측은 자격 요건을 갖춘 학생들을 인근 회사에 소개해줘서 6주간의 인턴쉽을 받을 수 있도록 해줬어.
A 와, 멋지다! 어학원에 그런 실무적인 과정이 있는 줄 몰랐네.

Vocabulary | district 지역, 관할구 | curriculum 교과 과정 | qualified 자격을 갖춘 | local 지역의, 인근의 | practical 실제적인, 실무적인

Key Expressions

아래 제시된 각 expression의 구조를 이해하고, 자기만의 표현들을 생각해 봅시다.

Expression 1   It's been such a long time since: ~로부터 상당한 시간이 흘렀다

어학원을 마지막으로 다닌 때는 정말 오래 전이었습니다
→ **It's been such a long time since** I last attended a language school.

그 빨간 원피스를 입은 지 참으로 오래되었습니다.
→ **It's been such a long time since** I wore that red dress.

그 낡은 오두막을 방문한 지 참으로 오래되었습니다.
→ **It's been such a long time since** we visited the old cabin.

Expression 2   vaguely remember: 기억이 애매모호하다

교실이 어떻게 생겼는지 기억이 가물가물합니다. → I **vaguely remember** what the classroom looked like.

그 집이 어디에 있었는지 잘 기억나지 않습니다. → I **vaguely remember** where the house is located.

저는 그가 좋아하던 노래 목록이 잘 기억나지 않습니다. → I **vaguely remember** his favorite music list.

Expression 3   practice + -ing: ~를 연습하다

그런 다음 저희는 청취 연습을 했습니다. → Then we **practiced** listen**ing**.

저는 밤새도록 컵케이크를 굽는 것을 연습했습니다. → I **practiced** bak**ing** cupcakes all night.

오늘 밤새도록 춤연습을 하는 것이 좋겠습니다. → We'd better **practice** danc**ing** all night.

Expression 4   memories of + 목적어 + be동사 + vivid: ~에 대한 기억이 선명하다

이 어학원에 대한 저의 기억이 훨씬 더 생생합니다.
→ My **memories of** this language school **are** so much more **vivid**.

숲 속에서 보낸 날들에 대한 그녀의 기억은 아직도 매우 선명합니다.
→ Her **memories of** her time in the forest **are** still very **vivid**.

개막식에 대한 그들의 기억은 놀라울 정도로 선명합니다.
→ Their **memories of** the opening ceremony **are** amazingly **vivid**.

Expression 5   during + 소유격 + childhood: ~의 어릴 적에

어릴 적 배운 수업들이 훨씬 더 재미있었습니다.
→ The classes were so much more fun **during my childhood**.

저는 어릴 적에 온갖 종류의 책을 읽었습니다. → I read all kinds of books **during my childhood**.

벨과 그녀의 오빠는 어릴 적에 하와이에서 살았습니다.
→ Belle and her brother lived in Hawaii **during their childhood**.

Topic Question & Model Answer

🎧 01-14

Topic Question

Tell me about a language school you attended. What did it look like? How many classrooms were there? Please describe the language school you attended in detail.

당신이 다녔던 어학원에 대해 이야기해 보세요. 어떻게 생겼나요? 몇 개의 교실이 있었나요? 당신이 다닌 어학원을 상세히 묘사해보세요.

TIP FOR THE OPIc

익숙한 장소의 내부(교실, 사무실, 침실, 병원, 은행 등)에 대해 묘사하라는 질문입니다. 그곳에 배치된 가구나 기기를 기준으로 장소를 묘사할 수도 있고 그곳에서 무엇을 하는지에 대해서도 이야기할 수 있습니다. 또한 관련 기기를 어떻게 사용하는지에 대해 설명한다면 보다 구체적인 답안이 만들어질 것입니다.

Model Answer

| Opening |

It's been such a long time since I last attended a language school. I vaguely remember what the classrooms looked like.

제가 어학원을 마지막으로 다닌 것은 정말 오래 전 일입니다. 교실이 어떻게 생겼는지 기억이 가물가물하네요.

| Classroom Facilities |

I think there were several classrooms in the institute. Every classroom had many chairs and a whiteboard. There was also a TV in the classroom, and we often watched videos. Sometimes, the teachers brought cassette/CD players to teach new songs or to use audio materials. Then, we practiced listening and dictation skills. These are the things I remember about the language school I attended when I was in elementary school.

학원에 교실은 여러 개 있었던 걸로 기억합니다. 각 교실에는 의자가 많이 있었고 화이트보드는 하나 있었습니다. 또한 교실에 TV도 한 대 있었는데 저희는 자주 비디오를 시청했습니다. 가끔은 선생님들께서 새로운 노래를 가르쳐주시거나 청취 자료를 들려주시기 위해 카세트나 CD 플레이어를 가져오셨습니다. 그러면 저희는 듣기 및 받아쓰기 연습을 했습니다. 이러한 것들이 바로 제가 초등학생 때 다녔던 어학원에 대한 기억입니다.

| Closing |

I attended a couple more language schools when I was in college. However, my memories of this language school are so much more vivid than the memories of those from my college years. I guess the reason is that the classes were so much more fun during my childhood.

저는 대학교에 다닐 때에도 어학원을 몇 군데 더 다녔습니다. 하지만 이 어학원에 대한 저의 기억들이 제가 대학생일 때 다닌 어학원에 대한 기억보다 더욱 생생합니다. 아마도 어릴 적에 배운 수업이 훨씬 더 재미있었기 때문일 것입니다.

More Questions

〈어학원〉에 관련하여 더 나올 수 있는 OPIc 질문들을 정리한 코너입니다. 질문에 대한 brainstorming을 해보세요.

1. Tell me about your language school. What does your language school look like? Please describe your language school in as much detail as possible.

2. Where is your language school located? How far is it from your house? What kinds of transportation do you use to get there?

3. Tell me about the first day at your language school. What was your first impression of the language school? Were the faculty members friendly?

On Your Own

앞에서 주어진 Model Answer을 바탕으로, 아래의 빈칸에 들어갈 수 있는 다양한 대체 가능한 어휘 및 표현들을 참고하여 학습자 본인만의 모범 답안을 직접 만들어보세요.

I Opening I

It's been ⓐ_____ since I last attended a language school. I vaguely remember what the classrooms looked like.

I Classroom Facilities I

I think there were several classrooms in the institute. Every classroom had ⓑ_____. There was also a ⓒ_____ in the classroom, ⓓ_____ we often watched videos. Sometimes, the teacher brought ⓔ_____. Then we practiced listening and dictation skills. These are the things I remember about the language school I attended when I was in ⓕ_____.

I Closing I

I attended a couple more language schools ⓖ_____. However, my memories of this language school are so much more vivid than the memories of those from the ⓗ_____ times. I guess the reason is that the classes were so much more fun during my childhood.

I Opening I It's been ⓐ **a while** since I last attended a language school. I vaguely remember what the classrooms looked like.

I Classroom Facilities I I think there were several classrooms in the institute. Every classroom had ⓑ **desks, chairs, and a podium**. There was also a ⓒ **projector** in the classroom, ⓓ **with which** we often watched videos. Sometimes, the teacher brought ⓔ **a globe and talked about different countries and their cultures**. Then we practiced listening and dictation skills. These are the things I remember about the language school I attended when I was in ⓕ **kindergarten**.

I Closing I I attended a couple more language schools ⓖ **while I was growing up**. However, my memories of this language school are so much more vivid than the memories of those from the ⓗ **other** times. I guess the reason is that the classes were so much more fun during my childhood.

본인이 만든 답안에 아래의 요소들이 포함되었는지 점검해 봅시다.

	Checklist
☐	어느 어학원이었는지
☐	어학원 시설의 특징
☐	교실 내부의 기기에 대한 묘사
☐	수업 분위기에 대한 기억
☐	어학원 수업을 수강한 효과

The Music of Speech

강세를 두어야 하는 어휘의 특징을 익히고 그에 따라 답안을 말하는 연습을 해봅시다.

강세를 두는 어휘의 특징
1) 감탄사이다 2) 최상급이다 3) 형용사/부사이다
4) 문장 안에서 key word 역할을 하는 명사나 동사인 경우가 많다

Model Answer 1　🎧 01-15

Hi. My name is Jane Naeryung Lee, and I'm in my early 30s. I'm a freelancer and a student. I teach English part time and also study. I love to study. People may think I'm crazy, but I love experiencing new things through books. So I've been studying various things and will continue studying this and that. I'm very much a people-person. I love to meet new people and communicate with them. I think I'm very sociable and love to hang out with different people. I'm also very positive and outgoing. I guess that's why I can always get along well with people. On the other hand, I live in Bundang, which is about 30 minutes from downtown Seoul. I love this area. In general, I love my life.

Model Answer 2　🎧 01-16

I would like to talk about the art therapy class I took when I was a freshman. It was an elective course, and I signed up for the class out of curiosity. In fact, the class had nothing to do with my major. But, since I had been interested in the healing effects of art therapy, I thought it would be nice to learn about it by taking the class. I read in some books that art therapy is helpful to those who are emotionally scarred or physically disabled. However, I wasn't sure if it would really work by just drawing pictures and doing other creative activities. To find out more about art therapy, we visited hospitals, nursing homes, and special schools. At those places, I was able to observe various paintings and clay art done by children and adults. Each piece seemed to have its own story, and I felt something warm deep in my heart. It was a special experience to see how colors and images reflected people's feelings.

Model Answer 3　🎧 01-17

In the classroom, there are various devices, such as an LCD TV, an electronic board, a beam projector, and computers. When I attend my movie criticism class, we watch films and documentaries on the TV. Professors use the beam projector to show teaching materials, and many students use the projector for presentations. There are computers installed in many classrooms, but I prefer to use my own. I usually carry my laptop and my smartphone with me. My smartphone has a recording function that

I use, but my favorite device is my laptop. I usually take notes of the lectures with my laptop and also work on school projects on it. Plus, it's very easy to access the Internet almost anywhere on campus! I can't think of a better device than this.

Model Answer 4   🎧 01-18

There have been a few changes on my school campus since last semester. I got back to school a month ago, and the season has changed for sure. It's spring, so I see flowers blossoming in some places. The weather is good, too! I see a lot of people in lighter clothing who are enjoying the weather. On the other hand, there were some changes in the library after it was remodeled. Above all, many things were digitalized. For example, with only your student ID card, you can borrow books, enter the computer lab, and make reservations for the seminar room. It has become so much more convenient than it was in the past. Plus, the sofas and chairs in the lounge look more colorful and comfortable. These are some of the new things I've seen on my school campus.

Model Answer 5   🎧 01-19

We have various events at school, such as seminars, sporting events, and a school festival. This festival, which is held in May every year, is the most popular event. May is the most beautiful time of the year, so it's a great season for festivals. During the festival, we sometimes invite famous musicians to school and hold concerts. That's my favorite part of the festival. We also have a flea market on one side of the campus. Last year, I got a really nice flower-pattern scarf at a bargain price there. In addition, some students make food and sell them for low prices. This year, I'm planning to rent a venue near the school with my classmates to party. I'm sure it's going to be crazy.

Model Answer 6 🎧 01-20

I have taken classes at several language schools since I was in elementary school. My parents always believed that English would be very important when we grew up. So they sent my siblings and me to an English institute in our neighborhood. We were always so excited to go there. We watched English videos and learned English songs at the institute. I remember that we also played games during class. Sometimes, we had parties at the school. There were about 5 students and a teacher in the class. A Korean and a native teacher often cotaught the class. It's been so many years that I can only remember a few things, but I still remember that I enjoyed the classes a lot. One day, I hope my husband and I can send our kids to similar classes. That would be awesome.

Model Answer 7 🎧 01-21

It's been such a long time since I last attended a language school. I vaguely remember what the classrooms looked like. I think there were several classrooms in the institute. Every classroom had many chairs and a whiteboard. There was also a TV in the classroom, and we often watched videos. Sometimes, the teachers brought cassette/CD players to teach new songs or to use audio materials. Then, we practiced listening and dictation skills. These are the things I remember about the language school I attended when I was in elementary school. I attended a couple more language schools when I was in college. However, my memories of this language school are so much more vivid than the memories of those from my college years. I guess the reason is that the classes were so much more fun during my childhood.

More Expressions & Vocabulary › School Life

I go to (학교 이름) University.
저는 ( ) 대학교를 다닙니다.

I graduated from (학교 이름) University.
저는 ( ) 대학교를 졸업했습니다.

I major in (전공 이름). 저는 ( )를 전공합니다.

My minor is (부전공 이름).
제 부전공은 ( )입니다.

I am a freshman/sophomore/junior/senior.
저는 1학년/2학년/3학년/4학년입니다.

I am taking (학점 수) credits.
저는 ( )학점을 수강하고 있습니다.

We sign up for classes online.
저희는 온라인으로 수강 신청을 합니다.

I dropped the class.
저는 그 수업을 중도 포기했습니다.

The class was full.
그 수업은 인원이 꽉 찼었습니다.

I made a presentation in the class.
저는 그 수업에서 발표를 했습니다.

I had to submit some papers to the professor.
저는 교수님께 과제를 제출해야 했습니다.

We take midterms/finals in May/July.
우리는 5월/7월에 중간/기말고사를 봅니다.

I am taking this semester off from school.
저는 금번 학기에 휴학 중입니다.

I am joining a dance club at school.
저는 학교에서 댄스 동아리에 들었습니다.

I had a hard time working on the paper.
저는 논문 작성으로 인해 힘든 시간을 보냈습니다.

graduate school 대학원
graduate student 대학원생
required course 필수 과목
elective course 교양 과목
course registration 수강 신청
semester 학기
student union 학생회
podium 교단

CHAPTER 2 직장 생활

Work Life

Unit 08	**Self-Introduction** 자기소개_직장인
Unit 09	**Training Program 1** 회사 연수 1
Unit 10	**Training Program 2** 회사 연수 2
Unit 11	**Lunchtime 1** 점심시간 1
Unit 12	**Lunchtime 2** 점심시간 2
Unit 13	**Choosing a Career 1** 취업 준비 1
Unit 14	**Choosing a Career 2** 취업 준비 2

Chapter 2는 취업 준비 및 회사 생활과 관련된 주제를 다룹니다. 자기소개와 관련된 질문은 물론, 담당 업무, 연수 과정, 사내 복지 제도, 점심 시간, 사무실 및 주변 환경에 대해 설명하라는 질문이 출제될 수 있습니다. 취업 준비생의 경우, 취업을 희망하는 기업 및 분야에 대해, 그리고 취업 준비 과정에 대한 질문이 출제될 수 있습니다.

+ Brainstorming Point

When?
- when I arrive at the office (언제 회사에 도착하는지)
- when I last went on a business trip (마지막으로 출장을 간 시기)
- when I usually get off from work (평소 퇴근하는 시간)
- when I got my last promotion (마지막 승진 시기)

Where?
- where my office is located (사무실 위치)
- where I went for a business trip (출장 간 곳)
- where I usually have lunch (평소에 점심을 먹는 곳)

What?
- main work in the office (사무실의 주요 업무)
- purpose of the business trip (출장 목적)
- results of the teamwork (부서 업무 결과)
- company projects (회사 프로젝트)
- what I like about my job (직업을 좋아하는 이유)
- training program classes (사내 연수 프로그램)
- popular companies/industries (인기 회사/산업)
- company benefits (회사 복지 및 혜택)

Who?
- who I often have lunch with (함께 점심 식사 하는 사람)
- co-workers (동료들)

Why?
- why I chose my current job (현재 직업을 선택한 이유)
- why I want to work in another area (다른 분야에서 일하고 싶은 이유)
- why I prefer either teamwork or individual work (개인 업무 혹은 팀 업무를 선호하는 이유)
- why I want to work for the company (그 회사에서 일하고 싶은 이유)

How?
- how I start my day at work (하루 일과를 어떻게 시작하는지)
- how long it takes to commute to work (통근 시간)
- how often I work overtime (얼마나 자주 야근을 하는지)
- how I am preparing for my future career (취업을 위해 어떤 준비를 하고 있는지)

Unit 08 Self-Introduction

자기소개_직장인

Warm Up

A Guess the Question & Answer
사진을 보면서 예상 질문과 답변을 먼저 추측해 봅시다.

B Listen & Talk
나를 소개하는 대화를 먼저 연습해 봅시다.

🎧 02-01

A Hello. Can you tell us about yourself?

B Sure. My full name is Kim Dongho. I'm 27. I just graduated from college.

A Okay. How many people are there in your family?

B There are 6 people in my family. They are my parents, older sister, two younger brothers, and me.

A That's a big family. Do you live with your family?

B No, we live in different cities. My sister is married, and her family lives in Vancouver, Canada. The others live in LA.

A I heard it's a nice city.

B It is. I miss the weather. Well, I'm not saying that the weather is bad in Korea.

A I know what you mean. Why do you want to work for our company?

B Most of all, I love traveling. Also, I'm very sociable and bright. I'm confident that I will be a good travel guide.

A 안녕하세요. 자기소개 좀 해주시겠어요?

B 네. 제 이름은 김동호입니다. 27살이고요, 대학교를 갓 졸업했습니다.

A 그렇군요. 가족은 몇 명인가요?

B 6명입니다. 부모님, 누나, 남동생 둘, 그리고 제가 있습니다.

A 정말 대가족이네요. 가족과 함께 살고 있나요?

B 아뇨, 각기 다른 곳에 거주하고 있어요. 누나는 결혼해서 가족과 함께 캐나다 밴쿠버에 살아요. 나머지 식구들은 LA에 삽니다.

A 좋은 곳이라고 들었어요.

B 맞아요. 날씨가 그리울 정도에요. 뭐, 한국 날씨가 안 좋다는 건 아니고요.

A 무슨 뜻인지 알아요. 저희 회사에 입사하고 싶은 이유는 뭐죠?

B 무엇보다도, 여행을 정말 좋아해요. 또한 저는 매우 사교적이고 밝은 성격입니다. 저는 제가 좋은 여행 가이드가 될 거라고 자신합니다.

Vocabulary
graduate from ~ ~를 졸업하다 | **a big family** 대가족 | **mean** 의미하다, 뜻하다 | **sociable** 사교적인 | **bright** 밝은, 명랑한 | **confident** 자신감 있는 | **travel guide** 여행 가이드

Key Expressions

○— 아래 제시된 각 expression의 구조를 이해하고, 자기만의 표현들을 생각해 봅시다.

Expression 1 **achieve a goal:** 목표를 이루다

저는 제 목표 중의 하나를 이루었습니다. → I have **achieved** one of my **goals**.

수는 푸드 스타일리스트가 되려는 그녀의 꿈을 결국 이루었습니다.
→ Sue eventually **achieved** her **goal** of becoming a food stylist.

당신의 목표를 이루기 위해서는 구체적이며 실천적이어야 합니다.
→ You need to be specific and take actions to **achieve** your **goals**.

Expression 2 **for the past + 숫자 + years:** 지난 몇 년 간

저는 지난 2년간 많은 국가를 여행했습니다.
→ I have traveled to many countries **for the past two years**.

요셉은 지난 13년간 감옥에 수감되어 있었습니다. → Joseph was imprisoned **for the past 13 years**.

저는 지난 10년간 패션 산업에 종사해왔습니다. → I've been in the fashion industry **for the past decade**.

Expression 3 **gain insight and knowledge:** 통찰력을 기르고 지식을 쌓다

저는 여행을 통해서 통찰력을 기르고 지식을 쌓았습니다.
→ I have **gained insight and knowledge** through traveling.

신문을 읽음으로써 통찰력을 기를 수 있습니다. → You can **gain insight** by reading the newspaper.

토론은 세상에 대한 지식을 쌓을 수 있는 좋은 방법입니다.
→ Discussion is a great way to **gain knowledge** of the world.

Expression 4 **global attitude:** 글로벌 태도, 자세

그와 같은 경험들은 제가 직장에서 글로벌 자세를 갖출 수 있도록 해줬습니다.
→ Those experiences helped me have a **global attitude** at work.

학생들이 긍정적인 글로벌 자세를 갖추는 것은 중요한 일입니다.
→ It's crucial for the students to have a positive **global attitude**.

북한 정부는 타국에 대한 글로벌 태도를 바꾸어야 할 것입니다.
→ The North Korean government should change its **global attitude** toward other nations.

Expression 5 **dream finally come true:** 꿈이 마침내 현실이 되다

저는 제 꿈이 마침내 현실이 되어서 기쁩니다. → I'm happy my **dream finally came true**.

그의 꿈은 오늘 마침내 이루어졌습니다. → His **dream finally came true** today.

승무원이 되고 싶었던 저의 꿈이 마침내 현실이 되었습니다.
→ My **dream** of becoming a flight attendant **finally came true**.

Topic Question & Model Answer

🎧 02-02

Topic Question

Let's start the interview now. Tell me a little bit about yourself.

인터뷰를 시작하겠습니다. 자기소개 좀 해주세요.

TIP FOR THE OPIc

직장인편 자기소개 질문입니다. 신입 사원 및 경력직 사원의 답안 내용은 다를 것입니다. 신입 사원은 입사 동기, 대학 전공과의 연계성 및 장래 포부를 중심으로 이야기할 수 있고, 경력직 사원은 주요 업무, 업무 환경에 대한 만족도 및 보다 구체적인 장래 포부를 설명할 수 있습니다. 물론 취미나 관심사, 성격에 대해서는 누구나 얘기할 수 있으며, 회사생활 외에도 가족이나 거주지에 대한 언급도 할 수 있습니다.

Model Answer

| Opening |

My name is Jaewook Oh. I am 30, and I recently got a job at ABC Engineering, where I have wanted to work since I was a student. So I guess I have achieved one of my goals.

제 이름은 오재욱입니다. 저는 30살이며, 학생 때부터 꿈의 직장이었던 ABC 엔지니어링에 최근 입사했습니다. 제 목표 중의 하나를 이룬 셈이지요.

| Personality and Interest |

I am an outgoing person and have traveled to many countries, including Australia, New Zealand, Philippines, Indonesia, Thailand, and Spain, for the past two years. I have met a lot of people from all over the world and have gained insight and knowledge through traveling. I think those experiences will help me have a global attitude at work, where the clients are mostly from Central and Eastern Asia, Saudi Arabia, Europe, America, Mexico, and other regions.

저는 외향적이며 지난 2년간 호주, 뉴질랜드, 필리핀, 인도네시아, 태국, 그리고 스페인을 여행했습니다. 저는 세계 각지에 있는 사람들을 만나왔고, 여행을 통해서 통찰력을 기르고 지식을 쌓았습니다. 저는 그러한 경험들이 제가 보다 글로벌적인 자세로 직장 생활을 할 수 있도록 도와줄 것이라고 생각합니다. 제 회사의 주요 고객은 대부분이 중앙아시아, 동아시아, 사우디아라비아, 유럽, 미국, 멕시코와 다른 지역 분들이기 때문입니다.

| Closing |

This was one reason I wanted to work for ABC Engineering, and I am happy my dream finally came true.

이러한 점이 제가 ABC 엔지니어링에 입사하고 싶었던 한 가지 이유이며, 제 꿈이 마침내 이루어져서 정말 기쁩니다.

More Questions

〈자기소개_직장인편〉에 관련하여 더 나올 수 있는 OPIc 질문들을 정리한 코너입니다. 질문에 대한 brainstorming을 해보세요.

1. Since when have you worked for your company? Are you satisfied with your working environment?
2. What did you major in at college? Is it related to your current work? How do you like your job?
3. Where's your company located? What is your company's main product? What is your position, and what is your role?

On Your Own

앞에서 주어진 Model Answer을 바탕으로, 아래의 빈칸에 들어갈 수 있는 다양한 대체 가능한 어휘 및 표현들을 참고하여 학습자 본인만의 모범 답안을 직접 만들어보세요.

| Opening |

My name is ⓐ_____. I am ⓑ_____, and I recently got a job at ⓒ_____, where I have wanted to work since I was a student. So I guess I have achieved one of my goals.

| Personality and Interest |

I am ⓓ_____. I studied ⓔ_____ at my college. In my college years, I ⓕ_____ and went to ⓖ_____ for an ESL course. I met a lot of people from different countries and gained insight and knowledge through those experiences. I've always wanted to become a ⓗ_____ after I graduate from school.

| Closing |

This was one reason I wanted to work for ⓒ_____, and I am happy my dream finally came true.

| Opening | My name is ⓐ **Jina Lee**. I am ⓑ **26**, and I recently got a job at ⓒ **ABC Chemical**, where I have wanted to work since I was a student. So I guess I have achieved one of my goals.

| Personality and Interest | I am ⓓ **quiet and very punctual**. I studied ⓔ **biochemical engineering** at my college. In my college years, I ⓕ **took part in a few internship programs** and went to ⓖ **San Diego, USA**, for an ESL course. I met a lot of people from different countries and gained insight and knowledge through those experiences. I've always wanted to become a ⓗ **chemist** after I graduate from school.

| Closing | This was one reason I wanted to work for ⓒ **ABC Chemical**, and I am happy my dream finally came true.

본인이 만든 답안에 아래의 요소들이 포함되었는지 점검해 봅시다.

	Checklist
☐	인사
☐	이름 및 연령대
☐	회사 이름 및 위치
☐	직위 및 업무 설명
☐	취미 및 관심사
☐	향후 포부

Unit 09 Training Program 1

회사 연수 1

Warm Up

A Guess the Question & Answer
사진을 보면서 예상 질문과 답변을 먼저 추측해 봅시다.

B Listen & Talk
사내 연수 과정에 관한 대화를 먼저 연습해 봅시다.

🎧 02-03

A Does your company have any training programs?

B Yes, we do. When I was a newcomer, I attended several training programs for 6 months. They're too much sometimes.

A I know what you mean. Training programs after a heavy workload can wear you out.

B Right. It seems like the work is endless.

A What kinds of training programs do you attend?

B Currently, I'm in an English conversation class as the teacher's assistant. I'm also attending a leadership course.

A Are they helpful?

B Well, I guess it depends, but I personally think both classes are very beneficial.

A 너희 회사에도 연수 프로그램이 있어?

B 응, 있어. 내가 신입사원 시절엔, 6개월동안 여러 개의 연수 프로그램에 참여했었어. 때로는 너무 많은 것 같아.

A 무슨 뜻인지 알겠다. 엄청난 업무량 외에 연수 과정까지 참여하려면 지치기 마련이지.

B 맞아. 일이 끝이 없는 것 같아.

A 너는 어떤 연수 프로그램에 참여하는데?

B 현재는 영어회화 수업 조교로 있어. 리더십 과정도 듣고 있고.

A 도움이 되는 것 같아?

B 음, 사람마다 다르겠지만, 개인적으로는 둘 다 배울 게 아주 많은 것 같아.

Vocabulary
training program 연수 프로그램(과정) | newcomer 새로운 사람, 신입사원 | (heavy) workload (과다한) 업무량 | endless 끝없는 | attend 참석하다 | currently 현재 | teacher's assistant 조교 | helpful 도움 되는 | depend ~에 달려있다 | personally 개인적으로 | beneficial 유익한

Key Expressions

🔑 아래 제시된 각 expression의 구조를 이해하고, 자기만의 표현들을 생각해 봅시다.

Expression 1   intense: 강도 높은, 극심한, 치열한

그것은 가장 강도 높은 프로그램입니다. → It is the most **intense** program.

그 방의 온도는 매우 높았습니다. → The heat in the room was very **intense**.

우리의 작업 환경은 상당히 강도가 높아요. → Our working environment is quite **intense**.

Expression 2   the highest satisfaction rate: 최고 만족도

그 수업은 언제나 가장 높은 만족도를 받습니다.
→ The class receives **the highest satisfaction rate** all the time.

실버 호텔은 설문조사에서 가장 높은 만족도를 기록했습니다.
→ The Silver Hotel received **the highest satisfaction rate** in the survey.

가장 높은 만족도를 받기 위해 우리가 바꿀 수 있는 부분은 무엇입니까?
→ What changes can we make to receive **the highest satisfaction rate**?

Expression 3   struggle with ~: ~로 고심하다, 어려운 시간을 보내다

그들은 영어 프레젠테이션 준비에 고심합니다. → They **struggle with** making English presentations.

죠는 파리에서 언어 장벽으로 고생했습니다. → Joe **struggled with** the language barrier in Paris.

저는 어릴 적에 수줍음으로 인해 많이 고심했습니다.
→ I used to **struggle with** being shy when I was young.

Expression 4   be beneficial for/to ~: ~에게 도움이 되다

저는 그 과정이 그들에게 매우 큰 도움이 된다고 확신합니다.
→ I'm sure the course **is** very **beneficial for** them.

영양적으로 균형잡힌 식단은 건강에 이롭습니다.
→ Nutritionally balanced foods **are beneficial for** people's health.

온라인 강의는 책을 싫어하는 아이들에게 도움이 될 수 있습니다.
→ Online learning can **be beneficial for** kids who don't like books.

Expression 5   core step: 필수 과정

그것은 그들의 승진에 있어서 필수 과정입니다. → It's a **core step** for their promotions.

성공적인 사업을 하기 위한 필수 과정에는 무엇이 있습니까?
→ What are the **core steps** to running a successful business?

OPIc 시험을 보는 것은 한국에서 경쟁력 있는 직업을 구하기 위한 필수 과정입니다.
→ Taking the OPIc test is a **core step** to getting a competitive job in Korea.

Topic Question & Model Answer

 02-04

Topic Question

What kinds of training programs do you have at your company? What do the employees say about the training programs? 당신의 회사에는 어떠한 연수 프로그램이 있나요? 직원들은 연수 프로그램에 대해 어떻게 얘기하나요?

TIP FOR THE OPIc

회사마다 업무 수행 능력의 향상을 위한 연수 과정이 있을 것입니다. 영어회화 과정 혹은 리더십 과정은 대표적인 회사 연수과정입니다. 그 밖에도 회사 고유 연수 프로그램이 있으면 소개해 보세요. 자신이 경험한 해당 연수 과정의 장점이나 효과에 대해 언급하도록 하세요.

Model Answer

| Opening |

There are several training programs at my company.

저희 회사에는 여러 개의 연수 프로그램이 있습니다.

| English Conversation Program |

The most intense and popular training program is the English conversation program. There are 30 employees that have taken part in the program, and it receives the highest satisfaction rates in the monthly evaluations. Since I speak English, I took part in the program as the teacher's assistant. The program is very lively and fun although many of the employees struggle with making presentations. Most of them are shy about speaking in front of a large group, but I know the practice is very beneficial for them.

그 중에서도 가장 강도가 높고 인기 있는 것은 바로 영어회화 과정입니다. 영어회화 과정에 참가하는 직원은 30명인데, 월말 평가에서 가장 높은 만족도를 나타내고 있습니다. 저는 영어를 구사할 수 있기 때문에, 해당 과정의 조교로 참여했습니다. 많은 직원들이 영어 프레젠테이션을 할 때 고충을 겪기 하지만, 이 프로그램은 활기차고 재미있습니다. 대부분은 많은 사람들 앞에서 말하는 것을 수줍어합니다. 하지만 저는 그러한 연습이 그들에게 매우 유익하다고 생각합니다.

| Computer Training Program |

On the other hand, my company also provides a computer training program for the engineers. It's a core step that can lead to a promotion. Finally, the most coveted training program among employees with over 3 years of experience is the leadership course.

한편, 저희 회사에는 엔지니어들을 위한 컴퓨터 연수 과정도 제공합니다. 그것은 엔지니어들의 승진에 있어 필수 과정입니다. 마지막으로, 입사한지 3년 이상 된 직원들에게 가장 사랑 받는 프로그램은 바로 리더십 과정입니다.

| Closing |

I guess these are some of the training programs you can find at my company.

이상으로 저희 회사에서 찾아볼 수 있는 몇 가지 프로그램에 대한 소개였습니다.

More Questions

〈회사 연수〉에 관련하여 더 나올 수 있는 OPIc 질문들을 정리한 코너입니다. 질문에 대한 brainstorming을 해보세요.

1. Does your company have any training programs for the newcomers? What is it? Do you think the program is helpful?
2. What was the most memorable training program you ever had at your company? Was it helpful for your work?

On Your Own

앞에서 주어진 Model Answer을 바탕으로, 아래의 빈칸에 들어갈 수 있는 다양한 대체 가능한 어휘 및 표현들을 참고하여 학습자 본인만의 모범 답안을 직접 만들어보세요.

I Opening I

There are several training programs at my company.

I Stress Management Program I

The most popular training program is ⓐ_____. There are ⓑ_____ employees that have taken part in the program, and it receives the highest satisfaction rates in the monthly evaluations. Since ⓒ_____, I took part in the program ⓓ_____. The program is very lively and fun. ⓔ_____.

I English Conversation Program I

In addition, my company also provides a/an ⓕ_____. It's a core course that can lead to a promotion. Finally, the most coveted training program is the leadership course.

I Closing I

I guess these are some of the training programs you can find at my company.

I Opening I There are several training programs at my company.

I Stress Management Program I The most popular training program is ⓐ **the stress management class**. There are ⓑ **50** employees that have taken part in the program, and it receives the highest satisfaction rates in the monthly evaluations. Since ⓒ **I easily get stressed from all of my paperwork and research**, I took part in the program ⓓ **to learn how to manage my stress more effectively**. The program is very lively and fun. ⓔ **The lecturer shares various case studies and tips on how to overcome stress in different situations**.

I English Conversation Program I In addition, my company also provides an ⓕ **English conversation program**. It's a core course that can lead to a promotion. Finally, the most coveted training program is the leadership course.

I Closing I I guess these are some of the training programs you can find at my company.

본인이 만든 답안에 아래의 요소들이 포함되었는지 점검해 봅시다.

Checklist
☐ 사내 연수 과정 소개
☐ 인기 사내 연수 과정
☐ 내가 참여하는 연수 과정
☐ 타사 연수 과정과의 차이
☐ 사내 연수 과정의 유익함

Unit 10 Training Program 2

회사 연수 2

Warm Up

A Guess the Question & Answer

사진을 보면서 예상 질문과 답변을 먼저 추측해 봅시다.

B Listen & Talk

개별 연수 과정 및 팀 연수 과정에 관한 대화를 먼저 연습해 봅시다.

🎧 02-05

A Among the training programs at your company, which do you prefer? The individual training program or team training program?	**A** 너희 회사 연수 과정 중에서 네가 선호하는 건 뭐야? 개인 연수 과정이야, 아니면 팀 연수 과정이야?
B The team training program for sure. I love to interact with people.	**B** 당연히 팀 연수 과정이지. 나 사람들이랑 어울리는 거 좋아하잖아.
A Right. You're such a people-person. Team training must be a lot more appealing to you.	**A** 맞다. 너 사람 정말 좋아하지. 너한테는 팀 연수 과정이 훨씬 매력적이겠다.
B Definitely. I think there's a lot to learn through the brainstorming process with people. It's a good way to expand my knowledge.	**B** 물론이지. 사람들과 브레인스토밍을 하면서 배울 점이 참 많은 것 같아. 지식의 범위도 확장되는 데 좋은 방법인 것 같아.
A Which class offers the most benefits for teamwork?	**A** 팀 업무에서 가장 배울 게 많은 수업은 뭐야?
B I would say it's the leadership class. We have a debate session once a month. It's a great way to learn how to be more persuasive and logical when you speak.	**B** 내 생각엔 리더십 수업 같아. 매달 한 번씩 토론 수업이 있거든. 말할 때 보다 설득적이고 논리적으로 하는 방법을 배우는 훌륭한 방식이거든.

Vocabulary

prefer 선호하다 | **individual** 개인의, 개별적인 | **interact with** ~와 상호작용을 하다, ~와 교감하다 | **people-person** 사교적인 사람 | **appealing** 호소력 있는, 매력 있는, 돋보이는 | **definitely** 당연히, 두 말할 것 없이 | **brainstorming process** 브레인스토밍 과정 | **expand one's knowledge** 지식을 확장하다 | **benefit** 혜택 | **debate session** 토론 세션 | **persuasive** 설득력 있는 | **logical** 논리적인

Key Expressions

○━ 아래 제시된 각 expression의 구조를 이해하고, 자기만의 표현들을 생각해 봅시다.

Expression 1   **interact with ~:** ~와 상호 작용하다, 교류하다, 소통하다

저는 동료들과 함께 교류할 수 있기 때문에 팀 업무를 선호합니다.
→ I prefer teamwork because I can **interact with** my co-workers.

민주는 그녀의 동료들과 소통을 잘합니다. → Minju **interacts** well **with** her colleagues.

학장은 학교 직원들과 소통을 잘합니다. → The dean **interacts** well **with** the school staff.

Expression 2   **appealing:** 매력 있는, 호소력 있는

우리는 보다 매력적인 프레젠테이션을 작성하는 법을 배웁니다.
→ We learn how to make presentations more **appealing**.

그 회사의 새 캠페인은 매우 호소력이 있습니다. → The company's new campaign is very **appealing**.

많은 방문객은 지은의 미술작품이 매우 매력적이라고 여깁니다.
→ Lots of visitors find Jieun's art piece very **appealing**.

Expression 3   **a window to + 명사:** ~의 창(창문)

그 수업은 우리에게 세상을 보는 창이 됩니다. → The class becomes **a window to** the world to us.

눈은 영혼의 창입니다. → The eyes are **a window to** the soul.

어떤 사람들은 TV가 세상의 창이 된다고 생각합니다.
→ Some people think TV is **a window to** the world.

Expression 4   **be persuasive:** 설득력이 있다

우리는 협상을 할 때 더 설득력있게 하는 법을 배웁니다.
→ We learn how to **be** more **persuasive** in negotiations.

당신은 거래를 성사시키기 위해서 더욱 설득력이 있어야 합니다.
→ You need to **be** more **persuasive** to make the deal.

시경은 그 얘기를 전할 때 매우 설득력이 있습니다.
→ Sikyung **is** very **persuasive** when he tells that story.

Expression 5   **gain credibility:** 신뢰도를 얻다

우리는 신뢰도를 얻기 위해 좋은 이미지를 가져야 합니다.
→ We need to possess a good image to **gain credibility**.

그는 신뢰도를 얻기 위해 정말 열심히 노력합니다. → He is trying very hard to **gain credibility**.

새 회장은 약자의 편에 섬으로써 신뢰를 얻었습니다.
→ The new president **gained credibility** by standing with the weak.

Topic Question & Model Answer

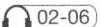

Topic Question

Between the individual training program and team training program, which do you prefer? Why? 당신은 개인 연수 과정과 팀 연수 과정 중에서 무엇을 더 선호하나요? 왜 그런가요?

TIP FOR THE OPIc

개인 중심 업무 및 팀 중심 업무 중 선호 여부를 묻는 질문입니다. 따라서 각각의 업무 특징을 2~3가지 언급해주면 됩니다. 개인 연수 과정, 과제 등을 할 때 본인의 생각대로 추진할 수 있는 것, 시간과 장소의 구애를 덜 받는 것 등을 이유로 들 수 있습니다. 팀 연수 과정이라면, 다양한 의견 도출을 통한 협력 과정 등을 장점으로 꼽을 수가 있을 것입니다.

Model Answer

| Opening |

I definitely prefer the team training program because it gives me an opportunity to interact with my co-workers. We can exchange different ideas and expand our knowledge through brainstorming. Most of all, I love to communicate with people. It's just more dynamic and fun.

저는 두말 할 나위 없이 팀 연수 과정을 좋아합니다. 왜냐하면 제 회사 동료들과 소통할 기회를 주기 때문입니다. 우리는 서로의 생각을 교류하고 함께 브레인스토밍을 하면서 지식을 확장할 수가 있습니다. 무엇보다도, 저는 사람들과 소통하는 것을 정말 좋아합니다. 훨씬 역동적이고 재미가 있어요.

| The Leadership Class |

In the leadership class that's held every Thursday, we learn how to make our presentations more appealing and engaging. There are always special lecturers from various fields, and the class becomes a window to the world. We also learn how to be more persuasive in our negotiations.

매주 목요일마다 열리는 리더십 수업에서는 보다 호소력 있고 매력적인 프레젠테이션을 하는 법을 배웁니다. 늘 다양한 분야에서 특별 강사를 모시는데, 수업은 세계를 향한 창이 됩니다. 우리는 또한 협상에서 좀 더 설득력 있도록 하는 방법도 배웁니다.

| Image Making Class |

My favorite part of the program is the class on maintaining your appearance. It may sound like this has nothing to do with leadership, but they teach you how to work on your own image to gain more credibility. I've learned a lot from the class. It's cool to see the make-overs of my co-workers as well.

제가 가장 좋아하는 프로그램은 바로 외모 관리 수업입니다. 리더십 과정과 아무런 관련이 없는 것 같지만, 그 수업을 통해 자신만의 이미지를 더욱 신뢰가 가도록 만드는 방법을 가르쳐 줍니다. 저는 수업을 통해 많은 것을 배웠습니다. 또한 동료들의 변신을 보는 것이 멋집니다.

| Closing |

Overall, I think the team training program has a lot more benefits than the individual training program.

아무쪼록 저는 개인 연수 과정보다 팀 연수 과정을 통해 얻는 점이 훨씬 많다고 생각합니다.

More Questions

〈회사 연수〉에 관련하여 더 나올 수 있는 OPIc 질문들을 정리한 코너입니다. 질문에 대한 brainstorming을 해보세요.

1. If you could request a new training program for your company, which program would you suggest? Why?
2. Are you comfortable doing teamwork? If so, what do you like about teamwork? If not, what is difficult about teamwork?

On Your Own

앞에서 주어진 Model Answer을 바탕으로, 아래의 빈칸에 들어갈 수 있는 다양한 대체 가능한 어휘 및 표현들을 참고하여 학습자 본인만의 모범 답안을 직접 만들어보세요.

I Opening I

I definitely prefer the team training program because it gives me an opportunity to interact with my co-workers. We can exchange different ideas and expand our knowledge through brainstorming. Most of all, I love to communicate with people.

I The Business English I

In the ⓐ_____ that's held ⓑ_____, we learn how to ⓒ_____. There are always special lecturers from various fields, and the class becomes a window to the world. We also learn how to be more persuasive in our negotiations.

I The Speech Class I

My favorite part of the program is the ⓓ_____. It teaches you how to ⓔ_____. I've learned a lot in the class.

I Closing I

Overall, I think team training program has a lot more benefits than the individual training program.

I Opening I I definitely prefer the team training program because it gives me an opportunity to interact with my co-workers. We can exchange different ideas and expand our knowledge through brainstorming. Most of all, I love to communicate with people.

I The Business English I In the ⓐ **business English class** that's held ⓑ **every Tuesday**, we learn how to ⓒ **write, present, and debate in English**. There are always special lecturers from various fields, and the class becomes a window to the world. We also learn how to be more persuasive in our negotiations.

I The Speech Class I My favorite part of the program is the ⓓ **speech class**. It teaches you how to ⓔ **make concise and logical speeches**. I've learned a lot in the class.

I Closing I Overall, I think the team training program has a lot more benefits than the individual training program.

본인이 만든 답안에 아래의 요소들이 포함되었는지 점검해 봅시다.

	Checklist
☐	사내 연수 과정 종류
☐	개인(팀) 연수 과정의 장점
☐	현재 참여하는 연수 과정
☐	연수 과정을 통해 배우는 점
☐	기억에 남는 에피소드
☐	연수 담당 강사 소개

Unit 11 Lunchtime 1

점심시간 1

Warm Up

A Guess the Question & Answer
사진을 보면서 예상 질문과 답변을 먼저 추측해 봅시다.

B Listen & Talk
회사 점심시간에 관한 대화를 먼저 연습해 봅시다.

🎧 02-07

A The meeting is finally over, and it's lunchtime.

B Is it already?

A It's 12 o'clock. See?

B Time flies. Where shall we go today?

A What about JS Bakery? It has special discounts every Thursday.

B Sure, let's go. I love the salami sandwiches and broccoli soup there.

A My favorite is the chocolate fondue. I'm going to make it for my boyfriend on Valentine's Day.

B So romantic! Thinking about them is making my mouth water. I can't wait to eat them.

A Let's hurry.

A 드디어 회의 끝이고 점심시간이다!

B 벌써 그렇게 됐어?

A 12시잖아. 보여?

B 시간 정말 빠르다. 오늘 우리 어디 가서 먹을까?

A JS 제과점 어때? 매주 목요일마다 특별 할인해주잖아.

B 그래, 어서 가자. 그 집 살라미 샌드위치랑 브로콜리 스프랑 정말 좋아해.

A 난 초콜릿 퐁듀가 제일 좋더라. 발렌타인 데이에 남자 친구를 위해 만들어 줄 거야.

B 정말 낭만적이구나! 생각만해도 군침 돈다. 먹고 싶어 못 참겠다.

A 어서 가자.

Vocabulary Times flies. 시간이 화살같다. | special discount 특별 할인 | salami 살라미 소시지 | broccoli 브로콜리 | fondue 퐁듀 (와인을 넣어 녹인 치즈에 빵을 찍어 먹는 요리 / 뜨거운 오일에 고기, 야채 등을 찍어 먹는 요리) | romantic 낭만적인 | make one's mouth water 군침이 돌게 하다 | can't wait to + 동사 ~를 하고 싶어 못 참겠다, 정말로 ~하고 싶다

Key Expressions

🔑 아래 제시된 각 expression의 구조를 이해하고, 자기만의 표현들을 생각해 봅시다.

| Expression 1 | **offer:** 제공하다, 제안하다 |

저희 회사 구내식당은 다양한 메뉴를 제공합니다. → Our company cafeteria **offers** various meals.

그녀는 친절히 그에게 음료를 제공했습니다. → She kindly **offered** him a drink.

많은 오디션 프로그램은 시청자에게 스타가 될 수 있는 기회를 제공합니다.
→ Many audition programs **offer** the chance for viewers to become stars.

| Expression 2 | **hang out with ~:** ~와 어울리다 |

저는 그녀와 어울리는 것을 좋아합니다. → I love to **hang out with** her.

제 아이들은 이웃과 어울리는 것을 좋아합니다. → My kids like to **hang out with** our neighbors.

창현은 야구팀 멤버들과 어울리는 것을 좋아합니다.
→ Changhyun likes to **hang out with** the members of the baseball team.

| Expression 3 | **have similar tastes (in):** (~의) 취향이 비슷하다, 선호도가 비슷하다 |

우리는 음식에 대한 취향이 비슷합니다. → We **have similar tastes in** food.

우리는 영화에 관한 한 취향이 비슷합니다. → We **have similar tastes** when it comes to movies.

그 커플은 가구를 선택하는 데 있어서 안목이 비슷합니다.
→ The couple **has similar tastes** when choosing furniture.

| Expression 4 | **last long:** 오래 지속되다 |

저희 점심시간은 그리 오래 가지 않습니다. → Our lunchtime doesn't **last long**.

침묵은 오래가지 않았습니다. → The silence didn't **last long**.

현재의 고난의 시기는 오래가지 않을 것입니다. → This period of hardship won't **last long**.

| Expression 5 | **as always:** 언제나처럼 |

언제나처럼 기분 좋은 식사였습니다. → It was an enjoyable meal **as always**.

음식은 언제나처럼 훌륭했습니다. → The food was great **as always**.

찰스는 언제나처럼 다정했습니다. → Charles was sweet and gentle **as always**.

Topic Question & Model Answer

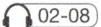

Topic Question

Having lunch with your co-workers is always a lot of fun. When was the last time you had lunch with your co-workers? Who did you go with, and what did you eat? 직장 동료들과 함께 점심을 먹는 것은 언제나 즐거운 일입니다. 당신이 동료들과 함께 마지막으로 점심을 먹은 것은 언제였나요? 누구와 함께 갔으며, 무엇을 먹었나요?

TIP FOR THE OPIc

하루 일과 중 점심시간은 누구에게나 주어지는 시간이고 익숙한 상황이지만, 막상 질문이 나오면 당황할 수도 있습니다. 평소에 자주 가는 식당, 즐겨 먹는 메뉴, 함께 식사하는 동료 등에 대해 얘기하면 됩니다. 더불어 식당의 분위기, 동료와의 대화 내용을 언급합니다.

Model Answer

| Opening |

The last time I had lunch with my co-workers was this afternoon. I usually have lunch with my co-workers, and we often go to the company cafeteria in the basement. Our company cafeteria offers various meals and is a very nice facility.

제가 마지막으로 직장 동료들과 함께 점심을 먹은 것은 오늘 점심이었습니다. 저는 주로 제 동료들과 점심 식사를 하는데, 우리는 주로 회사 지하에 있는 구내 식당에 갑니다. 저희 회사 구내식당은 다양한 종류의 메뉴를 제공하고 있으며 시설도 아주 우수합니다.

| My Last Lunchtime |

This afternoon, I went to a nearby restaurant with my co-worker Minyoung, who works in another department. I love to hang out with her since we have many things in common, including similar tastes in food. Since our lunchtime doesn't last long, we don't go that far. One of our favorite places is *Krajo Burger*, which is a Korean burger house. The food is good, and the prices are reasonable. Above all, it's never that crowded!

오늘 오후에, 저는 다른 부서에서 일하는 제 동료 민영과 함께 인근 식당에 갔습니다. 저는 그녀와 어울리는 것을 좋아하는데, 공통점이 많을 뿐 아니라 입맛도 비슷하기 때문입니다. 회사 점심시간이 그리 길지 않기 때문에 우리는 그다지 멀리 가지는 못합니다. 우리가 좋아하는 식당 중의 하나는 한국표 햄버거 집인 '크라조 버거'입니다. 거기 음식은 맛이 있고 가격이 합리적이기 때문입니다. 무엇보다도, 식당이 붐비는 일이 결코 없습니다!

| Closing |

We had a great meal and had a good talk. It was an enjoyable meal as always.

우리는 맛있는 점심 식사를 했고 얘기도 많이 나누었습니다. 언제나처럼 기분 좋은 식사였습니다.

More Questions

〈회사 점심시간〉에 관련하여 더 나올 수 있는 OPIc 질문들을 정리한 코너입니다. 질문에 대한 brainstorming을 해보세요.

1. Tell me about your typical day at work. What do you do from the moment you arrive at your office to when you leave the office?
2. What kinds of facilities and buildings do you have around your workplace? Give me a good description of them.
3. Tell me about your favorite dining place near your workplace. Why do you like the restaurant? Who do you go there with?

On Your Own

앞에서 주어진 Model Answer을 바탕으로, 아래의 빈칸에 들어갈 수 있는 다양한 대체 가능한 어휘 및 표현들을 참고하여 학습자 본인만의 모범 답안을 직접 만들어보세요.

| Opening |

The last time I had lunch with my co-workers was ⓐ_____. I usually have lunch with my co-workers, and we often ⓑ_____.

ⓒ_____.

| My Last Lunchtime |

ⓐ_____, I went to a nearby restaurant with my co-worker ⓓ_____. I love to hang out with him since we have many things in common, including similar tastes in food. Since our lunchtime doesn't last long, we don't go that far. One of our favorite places is ⓔ_____, which is ⓕ_____. The food is good, and the prices are reasonable. Above all, it's never that crowded!

| Closing |

We had a great meal and had a good talk. It was an enjoyable meal as always.

| Opening | The last time I had lunch with my co-workers was ⓐ **last Friday**. I usually have lunch with my co-workers, and we often ⓑ **bring our own lunches and share our meals**. ⓒ **I think homemade meals are the best. They are nutritious, and we can save money and time during lunch**.

| My Last Lunchtime | ⓐ **Last Friday**, I went to a nearby restaurant with my co-worker ⓓ **Minjae, who works in another department**. I love to hang out with him since we have many things in common, including similar tastes in food. Since our lunchtime doesn't last long, we don't go that far. One of our favorite places is ⓔ **Bang-ga**, which is ⓕ **famous for Indian cuisine**. The food is good, and the prices are reasonable. Above all, it's never that crowded!

| Closing | We had a great meal and had a good talk. It was an enjoyable meal as always.

본인이 만든 답안에 아래의 요소들이 포함되었는지 점검해 봅시다.

Checklist

☐	마지막 점심을 한 지가 언제인지
☐	누구와 함께 식사했는지
☐	평소 좋아하는 점심 식사 장소
☐	주로 점심에 어떤 메뉴를 먹는지
☐	식사하면서 나눈 대화 내용

Unit 12 Lunchtime 2

점심시간 2

Warm Up

A Guess the Question & Answer
사진을 보면서 예상 질문과 답변을 먼저 추측해 봅시다.

B Listen & Talk
기억에 남는 점심에 관한 대화를 연습해 봅시다.

 02-09

A Do you have any special memories of lunch?	**A** 넌 뭐 특별히 기억에 남는 점심시간 있어?
B I have a few. The lunch hour can be routine, but I'm quite adventurous.	**B** 응, 몇 번 있지. 점심시간이야 일상적인 일이지만, 난 꽤나 모험적이잖아.
A Adventurous at lunch?	**A** 점심시간에 모험을 한다고?
B Why not? I love to hunt down different places and try new dishes. There are a number of places to venture near my workplace.	**B** 안 될 게 뭐야? 난 여기 저기 다니면서 새로운 메뉴를 맛보는 걸 좋아해. 우리 회사 주변 곳곳에 모험할 만한 숨은 맛집이 있거든.
A Tell me about it. You work in the best town for dining.	**A** 당연하겠지. 맛집으로 최고인 동네에서 일하잖아.
B I know! I feel really fortunate to work in the Samcheong-dong area. It's also one of the most romantic places in Seoul.	**B** 그러니깐! 삼청동 주변에서 일하는 걸 정말 감사하게 생각해. 서울에서 가장 로맨틱한 곳이기도 하지.
A It sure is. Let's go for lunch now. I'm dying of hunger.	**A** 맞아. 우리 이제 밥 먹으러 가자. 배고파 죽겠다.

Vocabulary routine 일상적인, 반복되는 | adventurous 모험적인 | hunt down 찾아 다니다, 추적하다 | venture 모험하다 | Tell me about it. 내 말이 바로 그거야. (상대방의 말에 동의할 때 사용하는 표현) | feel fortunate to ~ ~하게 되어 다행이다, ~를 감사하게 여기다 | die of hunger 배고파 죽다

Key Expressions

🔑 아래 제시된 각 expression의 구조를 이해하고, 자기만의 표현들을 생각해 봅시다.

Expression 1   be planning to + 동사: ~할 예정이다, 계획이다

저는 근무 후에 파티를 가질 예정이었습니다. → I **was planning to** have a party after work.

저는 새로운 도시로 이사를 갈 예정입니다. → I **am planning to** move to a new city.

상진은 다른 분야에서 일을 찾을 계획입니다. → Sangjin **is planning to** find a job in another field.

Expression 2   totally a surprise: 완전히 놀랄만한, 전혀 예상치 못한, 뜻밖에

그것은 완전 깜짝 놀랄 일이었습니다. → It was **totally a surprise**.

그의 프러포즈는 깜짝 놀랄만한 일이었습니다. → His proposal was **totally a surprise**.

베컴의 한국 방문은 전혀 예상치 못한 일이었습니다. → Beckham's visit to Korea was **totally a surprise**.

Expression 3   feel so blessed to + 동사: ~하게 되어 대단히 감사하게 여기다, 축복으로 여기다

저는 그처럼 훌륭한 사람들이 제 주변에 있다는 사실을 대단히 감사하게 여깁니다.
→ I **felt so blessed to** have such great people around me.

우리는 그녀와 같은 선생님을 만난 것을 큰 축복이라고 여깁니다.
→ We **felt so blessed to** have a teacher like her.

저는 자연으로 둘러싸인 곳에서 산다는 게 대단히 축복이라고 여깁니다.
→ I **feel so blessed to** live in a place surrounded by nature.

Expression 4   the same way: 같은 방식의, 같은 모습의

같은 방식이어야 함을 얘기하는 것은 아닙니다. → I don't mean it in **the same way**.

우리는 같은 방식으로 생각하지는 않습니다. → We don't think **the same way**.

그 걸그룹 멤버들은 똑같은 의상을 입었습니다. → The girl group members dressed **the same way**.

Expression 5   look forward to + -ing: ~하게 되길 고대하다, 기대하다

저는 언젠가 또 다시 그런 멋진 저녁 만찬을 하게 되길 기대합니다.
→ I **look forward to** hav**ing** a nice dinner sometime again.

저는 시드니를 여행하게 되길 고대합니다. → I'm **looking forward to** travel**ing** to Sydney.

줄리엣은 왕궁으로부터 초대장을 받기를 기대하고 있습니다.
→ Juliet is **looking forward to** receiv**ing** the invitation from the royal family.

Topic Question & Model Answer

🎧 02-10

Topic Question

What is the most memorable lunch you've ever had with your co-workers? Why was it so memorable? What happened, and what did you like about it?

직장 동료와의 점심 식사 가운데 가장 기억에 남는 점심은 언제였나요? 기억에 남는 이유가 뭔가요? 무슨 일이 있었으며 무엇이 마음에 들었나요?

TIP FOR THE OPIc

점심을 먹는 것은 일상적인 행위이지만 특별한 기억으로 남을 점심시간도 있을 것입니다. 친한 친구의 깜짝 방문, 팀 동료들과의 회식, 연인과의 점심 데이트, 회사 행사 때의 점심시간 등에 대해 얘기할 수 있을 것입니다. 만일 점심시간의 기억이 없다면, 평소 바랐던 점심시간의 모습, 예를 들어 시간이 더 길었으면 좋겠다든지를 말해도 무방합니다.

Model Answer

| Opening |

The most memorable lunch I ever had was probably last summer on my birthday.

제게 가장 기억에 남는 점심은 아마도 작년 제 생일날일 것입니다.

| The Most Memorable Lunchtime |

Since I had to go to work, I was planning to have a party after work. But guess what? On that day, my boyfriend came to my office with a bunch of flowers and a big smile during lunch hour. It was totally a surprise. He took me to a fancy restaurant nearby and also invited some of my co-workers. We all had a very nice time together. I felt so blessed to have such great people around me.

그날도 저는 출근을 해야 해서, 퇴근 후에 파티를 갖고자 했습니다. 그런데 무슨 일이 있었는지 아세요? 그날, 제 남자친구가 점심시간에 꽃을 한 다발 들고 활짝 웃으며 사무실을 찾아온 것이었습니다. 정말 놀라지 않을 수 없었습니다. 그는 저를 인근의 고급 식당에 데려갔고, 제 동료들도 몇 명 초대했습니다. 우리는 모두 좋은 시간을 함께 했습니다. 저는 주변에 그런 좋은 사람들이 있다는 것에 대해 매우 축복 받은 느낌이었습니다.

| Closing |

I hope to have another great lunch sometime. I don't mean in the same way, but I look forward to having a nice lunch sometime again.

언젠가 근사한 점심 식사를 또 하게 될 소망합니다. 작년 생일날 같지는 않아도 되지만, 머지않아 기분 좋은 점심 식사를 하게 될 것을 기대합니다.

More Questions

〈회사 점심시간〉에 관련하여 더 나올 수 있는 OPIc 질문들을 정리한 코너입니다. 질문에 대한 brainstorming을 해보세요.

1. Do you think your lunch hour is long enough? Why or why not?
2. Do you prefer to have Korean food or Western food for lunch? Why? What kind of dishes do you have for lunch in general?
3. Here is a situation I want you to act out. Your boss asked you to make a lunch reservation at a decent place near your office. Call the restaurant and ask 3 to 4 questions before making the reservation.

On Your Own

앞에서 주어진 Model Answer을 바탕으로, 아래의 빈칸에 들어갈 수 있는 다양한 대체 가능한 어휘 및 표현들을 참고하여 학습자 본인만의 모범 답안을 직접 만들어보세요.

| Opening |

The most memorable lunch I ever had was ⓐ_____.

| The Most Memorable Lunchtime |

Since I had to go to work, I was planning to have a party after work. But guess what? On that day, my ⓑ_____.
It was totally a surprise. ⓒ_____.
ⓓ_____. We all had a very nice time together. I felt so blessed to have such a great lunch time.

| Closing |

I hope to have another great lunch sometime. I don't mean in the same way, but I look forward to having a nice lunch sometime again.

| Opening | The most memorable lunch I ever had was ⓐ **on Christmas Eve last year**.

| The Most Memorable Lunchtime | Since I had to go to work, I was planning to have a party after work. But guess what? On that day, my ⓑ **boss announced that we were going to get a half-day off when we arrived at the office**. It was totally a surprise. ⓒ **My boss is very strict with our working hours, and nobody thought we would get a half-day off.** ⓓ **Our team went to a fancy restaurant nearby and had a special meal for Christmas**. We all had a very nice time together. I felt so blessed to have such a great lunch.

| Closing | I hope to have another great lunch sometime. I don't mean in the same way, but I look forward to having a nice lunch sometime again.

본인이 만든 답안에 아래의 요소들이 포함되었는지 점검해 봅시다.

	Checklist
☐	기억에 남는 점심이 언제인지
☐	누구와 함께 한 점심이었는지
☐	특별한 날이었는지 (생일, 승진, 회식 등)
☐	어떤 사건이 일어났는지
☐	어디에서 식사를 했는지

Unit 13 Choosing a Career 1

취업 준비 1

Warm Up

A Guess the Question & Answer
사진을 보면서 예상 질문과 답변을 먼저 추측해 봅시다.

B Listen & Talk
취업을 희망하는 회사에 관한 대화를 연습해 봅시다.

🎧 02-11

A Do you think that there are certain companies people want to work for?

B People that I know generally talk about the fields they are interested in but not companies in particular.

A Then what do people around you consider when they choose a job?

B I think my friends usually consider their major and the vision of the company when they choose a job.

A That's quite ideal! Actually, we should all focus more on our interests and strong points rather than simply chasing after a company's name.

B I agree. But I think most people find it difficult to discover what their true interests are.

A Well, the key is to build as much experience as you can. Then, it will be so much easier for them to understand both their interests and strong points.

B That's right. I feel bad when people just chase higher salaries or company benefits. Such people seem not to know what is truly important in life.

A 사람들이 일하고 싶어하는 특정 회사가 있다고 생각해?

B 내가 아는 사람들은 주로 자기가 어떤 분야에서 일하고 싶은지에 대해서만 얘기하고 특정 회사에 대해서는 얘기하지 않아.

A 그럼 네 주변에 있는 사람들은 직장을 고를 때 어떤 점을 고려해?

B 내 친구들은 직장을 고를 때 주로 전공과 회사의 비전을 고려하는 것 같아.

A 그것 참 이상적이군! 사실 우리 모두가 회사 이름만 쫓기보다는 자신의 관심 및 장점을 고려해야 하는데 말이야.

B 나도 동의해. 하지만 대부분의 사람들은 자신의 진정한 관심이 무엇인지 알아내는데 어려움을 겪는 듯 보여.

A 음, 그에 대한 관건은 최대한 많은 경험을 쌓는 거야. 그러면 관심이 가는 일이 무엇인지, 또 자신의 장점이 무엇인지 이해하는 것이 훨씬 쉬워질 거야.

B 맞아. 사람들이 고액 연봉이나 회사의 복지 제도만 쫓는 걸 보면 안타까운 마음이 들어. 그런 사람들은 인생에서 정말로 중요한 것이 무엇인지 잘 모르는 것 같아.

Vocabulary
certain 특정한, 확실한 | particular 특정한 | consider 고려하다 | chase 쫓다 | build experience 경험을 쌓다

Key Expressions

아래 제시된 각 expression의 구조를 이해하고, 자기만의 표현들을 생각해 봅시다.

Expression 1　　**comes from ~ background:** 과거 ~ 분야에 몸을 담았다

제 남편은 과거에 컴퓨터 프로그램 개발자였습니다.
→ My husband **comes from** a computer programming **background**.

저스틴은 물류 분야에 몸을 담았었습니다. → Justin **comes from** a logistics **background**.

사라는 범죄 수사 분야에 몸을 담았었습니다. → Sarah **comes from** a criminal investigation **background**.

Expression 2　　**start a new journey as a + 명사:** ~로서의 새 삶을 시작하다

그는 사진작가로서 새 삶을 시작했습니다! → He **started a new journey as** a photographer!

성종은 바리스타로서 새 삶을 시작했습니다. → Sungjong **started a new journey as** a barista.

제인은 작가로서 새 길을 걷기 시작했습니다. → Jane **started a new journey as** a writer.

Expression 3　　**take another path:** 다른 길을 택하다

그는 예전 직장을 관두고 새 길에 접어들었습니다. → He left his previous job and **took another path**.

그 정치인은 다른 길을 걷기로 결심했습니다. → The governor decided to **take another path**.

크리스티나는 사법고시에 두 번 실패한 후 다른 길을 가기로 마음먹었습니다.
→ Christina decided to **take another path** after failing the bar exam twice.

Expression 4　　**career change:** 직종 전환

저는 그가 성공적으로 직종을 전환했다고 생각합니다. → I think he made a successful **career change**.

40대에 직종을 전환을 하는 것은 상당한 용기가 필요한 일입니다.
→ Making a **career change** in one's 40s takes a lot of courage.

직종을 변경하기 위한 상세한 계획이 있나요? → Do you have any action plan for a **career change**?

Expression 5　　**pursue + 소유격 + vision:** ~의 비전을 추구하다

저는 진정한 보람은 비전을 추구하는 것으로부터 나온다고 믿습니다.
→ I believe that a true reward comes from **pursuing one's vision**.

존스는 평생 동안 자신의 비전을 추구했습니다.
→ Jones has been **pursuing his vision** all throughout his life.

저는 저의 비전을 쫓으면서 많은 난관에 부딪혔습니다.
→ I faced lots of challenges as I **pursued my vision**.

Topic Question & Model Answer

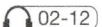

Topic Question

Do you think that there are certain companies people want to work for? Which companies do the people around you want to work at? Why do you think people want to work at those companies? 당신은 사람들이 특별히 일하고 싶어하는 회사가 있다고 생각하나요? 당신 주변 사람들은 어떤 회사에서 일하고 싶어 하나요? 왜 사람들이 해당 회사들에서 일하고 싶어한다고 생각하나요?

> **TIP FOR THE OPIc**
> 취업에 관한 질문입니다. 내가 일하고 싶은 분야 및 그 분야에서 일하고 싶은 이유와 그러한 목표를 달성하기 위해 어떤 준비를 하고 있는지에 대해 물어볼 수 있습니다. 평소 본인의 진로 및 관심사에 대해 체계적으로 생각하고 말하는 훈련을 기르는 것이 중요합니다.

Model Answer

| Opening |

I haven't met a lot of people who want to work for a certain company. Most people I know choose a job according to their interests and background.

저는 특정 회사에서 일하고 싶은 사람들을 만난 적이 별로 없습니다. 제가 아는 대부분의 사람들은 자신의 관심 및 배경에 따라 직장을 선택합니다.

| Inspiring Career Story |

For example, my husband comes from a computer programming background. He used to develop computer software programs for national security. He was successful, but he resigned to explore more of the world. He started a new journey as a photographer! I think it is awesome that he left his previous job and took another path to pursue his true vision. He is now sharing the wonder of God's creation with others through his photographs. His work is displayed in galleries in different cities and places. He also has a website. It's www.jperryimages.com.

예를 들어 제 남편은 예전에 컴퓨터 프로그램 개발 분야에 몸을 담았었습니다. 그는 국가 보안을 담당하는 컴퓨터 소프트웨어 프로그램 개발자였습니다. 그는 성공했지만 보다 넓은 세상을 경험하기 위하여 직장을 그만두었습니다. 그리고 사진작가로서의 새 삶을 시작했습니다! 저는 남편이 진정한 비전을 추구하기 위해 예전 직장을 그만두고 새로운 길에 접어든 것이 멋지다고 생각합니다. 그는 이제 사진 작업을 통해 하느님의 신비한 창조 섭리를 세상에 보여줍니다. 그의 사진 작품은 여러 도시의 미술관에 전시되어 있습니다. 홈페이지도 있는데 주소는 www.jperryimages.com입니다.

| Closing |

I think he made a successful career change. Getting a job is not just about earning a better salary or getting more benefits through a company. I believe that a true reward comes from pursuing one's vision.

저는 그가 성공적으로 직종을 전환했다고 생각합니다. 일을 하는 것은 단지 회사에서 높은 연봉과 수당을 받기 위한 것은 아니라고 봅니다. 저는 진정한 보람은 자신의 비전을 추구하는 것으로부터 나온다고 믿습니다.

More Questions

〈취업 준비〉에 관련하여 더 나올 수 있는 OPIc 질문들을 정리한 코너입니다. 질문에 대한 brainstorming을 해보세요.

1. You indicated in the survey that you are a student. How are you preparing for your future career? Is your major relevant to your future goal?

2. You said you are a student. Is there a specific area you want to work in the future? How did you get interested in that area?

On Your Own

앞에서 주어진 Model Answer을 바탕으로, 아래의 빈칸에 들어갈 수 있는 다양한 대체 가능한 어휘 및 표현들을 참고하여 학습자 본인만의 모범 답안을 직접 만들어보세요.

I Opening I

ⓐ_____ work for a certain company. Most people I know choose their jobs according to their ⓑ_____.

I Inspiring Career Story I

For example, my ⓒ_____. He used to ⓓ_____ computer ⓔ_____. He ⓕ_____, but he resigned to explore more of the world. He ⓖ_____! I think it is awesome that he left his previous job and took another path to pursue his true ⓗ_____. He is now ⓘ_____.

I Closing I

I think he made a successful career change. Getting a job is not just about earning a better salary or getting more benefits through a company welfare system. I believe that a true reward comes from pursuing one's vision.

I Opening I ⓐ **I have few friends who want to** work for a certain company. Most people I know choose their jobs according to their ⓑ **college major and experience**.

I Inspiring Career Story I For example, my ⓒ **brother majored in computer engineering**. He used to ⓓ **be in charge of** computer ⓔ **network systems at his old company**. He ⓕ **had a stable job**, but he resigned to explore more of the world. He ⓖ **went to graduate school to study a different field**! I think it is awesome that he left his previous job and took another path to pursue his true ⓗ **interests**. He is now ⓘ **working as an intern for a very promising company**.

I Closing I I think he made a successful career change. Getting a job is not just about earning a better salary or getting more benefits through a company welfare system. I believe that a true reward comes from pursuing one's vision.

본인이 만든 답안에 아래의 요소들이 포함되었는지 점검해 봅시다.

	Checklist
☐	사람들이 선호하는 회사(들)
☐	사람들이 선호하는 회사(들)의 특징
☐	그 회사(들)을 선호하는 이유
☐	주변 사람들의 관련 사례
☐	내가 생각하는 바람직한 취업관

Unit 13 Choosing a Career 1

Unit 14 Choosing a Career 2

취업 준비 2

Warm Up

A Guess the Question & Answer
사진을 보면서 예상 질문과 답변을 먼저 추측해 봅시다.

B Listen & Talk
인기 직종에 관한 대화를 연습해 봅시다.

🎧 02-13

A Do you know what kinds of jobs are popular these days?

B I only know that a recent survey stated that over 50% of high school students in Korea want to be TV celebrities.

A What about college students? Which industries are popular with them?

B I am not sure which industries are popular, but many of my students are applying for jobs in the IT industry. In addition, the mobile application industry seems to have a lot of job openings lately.

A What about the beauty and fashion industries? Korean cosmetics are selling really well overseas these days.

B I know. I heard that Korean cosmetic businesses are expanding overseas and through e-commerce. In fact, they are popular all over Asia and even in the United States.

A I think the Korean Wave has made a huge contribution.

B Absolutely. I hear people talking about K-pop culture wherever I go.

A Wow. That's really cool.

A 요즘 어떤 직업이 인기 있는 줄 아니?

B 최근 한 설문조사에 의하면 50% 이상의 한국 고등학생들이 연예인이 되고 싶어한다는 정도는 알아.

A 대학생들은 어때? 대학생들한테는 어떤 분야가 인기가 있지?

B 어떤 분야가 인기 있는지는 잘 모르겠지만 내 학생들 중 다수가 IT 업종에 지원하더라고. 그 밖에도 최근에는 휴대폰 앱 개발 분야도 일자리가 많은 것 같아.

A 뷰티와 패션 산업은 어때? 한국 화장품이 요즘 해외에서 정말 잘 팔리잖아.

B 알아. 한국 화장품 산업이 해외에서뿐 아니라 이커머스 상에서도 확대되고 있다고 들었어. 실제로 아시아 전역에서 인기가 있는 데다가 미국에서도 인기가 많데.

A 내 생각엔 한류 신드롬이 한몫 한 거 같아.

B 그렇고 말고. 가는 곳마다 사람들이 K-pop에 대해 이야기하는 것이 들려.

A 와. 정말 멋진 일이다.

Vocabulary

industry 산업, 사업 | **mobile application** 휴대폰 어플리케이션 | **rising** 떠오르는, 부상하는 | **expand** 확장하다 | **make a contribution** 공헌하다

Key Expressions

아래 제시된 각 expression의 구조를 이해하고, 자기만의 표현들을 생각해 봅시다.

Expression 1 grow constantly: 지속적인 성장을 하다

이 산업들은 꾸준하게 성장하고 있습니다. → These industries have been **growing constantly**.

래빈이의 화장품 사업은 지속적인 성장을 해왔습니다.
→ Raebin's cosmetic business has been **growing constantly**.

내준이의 지혜는 날로 성장했습니다. → Naejun's wisdom **grew constantly**.

Expression 2 computer geek: 컴퓨터에 많은 시간을 할애하는 괴짜

우리는 컴퓨터 괴짜들이나 컴퓨터와 연관된 일을 한다고 생각했었습니다.
→ We thought that only **computer geeks** worked with computers.

잭 스미스는 평생 컴퓨터 괴짜로 살았습니다. → Jack Smith was a **computer geek** all his life.

닉은 틈만 나면 컴퓨터로 시간을 보내는 컴퓨터 괴짜입니다.
→ Nick is a **computer geek** who spends all his free time on the computer.

Expression 3 see potential in/of: ~에서 잠재력을 발견하다

그녀는 온라인 시장의 잠재성을 보았습니다. → She **saw potential in** the online market.

그 대표는 그에게서 잠재력을 보았습니다. → The CEO **saw potential in** him.

저희는 그 나라의 잠재력을 보았습니다. → We **saw the potential of** the country.

Expression 4 at the center of + 명사 + exist + 명사: ~의 중심에는 ~가 있다

테크놀로지의 중심에는 컴퓨터와 인터넷이 있습니다.
→ **At the center of** technology **exist** the computer and the Internet.

회오리 바람과 같은 사건의 중심에는 그 회사의 전 대표가 연루되어 있습니다.
→ **At the center of** the whirlwind **exists** the former CEO of the company.

분쟁의 중심에는 권력을 잡기 위한 양측의 술책이 존재하고 있습니다.
→ **At the center of** the dispute **exists** a power game between the two.

Expression 5 relevant industry: 관련 산업

연관 산업들은 계속 성장할 것입니다. → **Relevant industries** will keep growing.

우리는 항상 관련 산업의 추이를 눈여겨보아야 합니다.
→ We always have to keep our eyes on the changes in the **relevant industries**.

관련 산업으로부터 고립된다면 큰 실수가 될 것입니다.
→ It is a huge mistake to be isolated from the **relevant industries**.

Topic Question & Model Answer

Topic Question

Each generation has different preferences in choosing jobs. Which industry is popular with people nowadays? Why do you think so?

각 연령층은 직업에 대한 선호도가 다릅니다. 요즘 젊은 사람들에게는 어떤 산업이 인기가 있나요? 왜 그렇다고 생각하나요?

> **TIP FOR THE OPIc**
> AL을 목표로 하는 난이도 5 이상의 질문은 개인적인 질문에서 더 나아가 사회적 경향을 분석하라는 요청을 하기도 합니다. 예를 들어, 개인적인 취업관을 넘어서, 요즘 인기 있는 산업 분야가 무엇이며 그 분야가 있기 있는 이유가 무엇인지 설명해보라고 할 수도 있습니다.

Model Answer

| Opening |

Honestly, the people I usually meet don't talk about jobs that much. We talk about our families and lives more often.

솔직히 저는 사람들과 만나서 직업에 대한 이야기는 잘 하지 않습니다. 저희는 주로 가족과 인생에 대한 이야기를 합니다.

| Popular Industries |

But I have met several people who wanted to work in the IT industry, the computer game industry, and the mobile app industry. These industries have been growing constantly. In the past, we thought that only computer geeks worked with computers. Nowadays, people with all kinds of backgrounds use computers for their work and hobbies. For example, my sister majored in textile design, but she saw potential in the online market and received her graphic designer's certificate. Now she is the owner of an online company. Of course, she uses her computer every day!

하지만 저는 IT 산업, 컴퓨터 게임 산업, 그리고 핸드폰 앱 산업에 종사하길 원하는 사람들을 여러 번 만난 적이 있습니다. 해당 산업들은 꾸준한 성장을 해왔습니다. 과거에 사람들은 컴퓨터 괴짜이나 컴퓨터와 연관된 일을 한다고 생각했습니다. 요즘은 다양한 배경을 가진 사람들이 일 혹은 취미 생활을 위해 컴퓨터를 사용합니다. 예를 들어 제 여동생은 섬유 디자인을 전공했는데, 온라인 사업의 잠재성을 보고 그래픽디자이너 자격증을 땄습니다. 지금 그녀는 온라인 회사 대표입니다. 물론 동생은 매일 컴퓨터를 사용합니다!

| Closing |

Technology is continually evolving. At the center of technology exist the computer and the Internet. Therefore, relevant industries will keep growing. I think that is why I find many people want to work in the IT, computer, and mobile-app industries.

테크놀로지는 계속해서 발전하고 있습니다. 테크놀로지의 중심에는 컴퓨터와 인터넷이 있습니다. 따라서 연관 산업들은 계속 성장할 것입니다. 그것이 바로 제 주변에 IT, 컴퓨터 그리고 핸드폰 앱 산업에 종사하려는 사람이 많은 이유라고 생각합니다.

More Questions

〈취업 준비〉에 관련하여 더 나올 수 있는 OPIc 질문들을 정리한 코너입니다. 질문에 대한 brainstorming을 해보세요.

1. I want to know about the job market in your country. What are the most important qualifications to get a job? Why are they so important?

2. Imagine you are having a face-to-face interview at a company next week. What will you do to prepare for the interview?

앞에서 주어진 Model Answer을 바탕으로, 아래의 빈칸에 들어갈 수 있는 다양한 대체 가능한 어휘 및 표현들을 참고하여 학습자 본인만의 모범 답안을 직접 만들어보세요.

| Opening |

Honestly, ⓐ_____. ⓑ_____, so we talk about our families and lives more often.

| Popular Industries |

But I have met several people who wanted to work in the IT industry, ⓒ_____. These industries have been growing constantly. In the past, we thought that only ⓓ_____. Nowadays, people with all kinds of backgrounds ⓔ_____. For example, ⓕ_____ majored in ⓖ_____! Now ⓗ_____.

| Closing |

Technology is continually evolving. At the center of technology exist ⓘ_____. Therefore, relevant industries will keep growing. I think that is why I find many people want to work in the IT and ⓙ_____ industries.

| Opening | Honestly, ⓐ **I don't know much about other peoples' career interests.** ⓑ **The people around me already have jobs**, so we talk about our families and lives more often.

| Popular Industries | But I have met several people who wanted to work in the IT industry, ⓒ **the automobile industry, and the biotechnology industry**. These industries have been growing constantly. In the past, we thought that only ⓓ **special people worked in these industries**. Nowadays, people with all kinds of backgrounds ⓔ **can be useful in the IT industry and the biotechnology industry**. For example, ⓕ **I** majored in ⓖ **business communication and got a job at a leading IT company**! Now ⓗ **I am the manager of the Sales Department and have to deal with IT products every day**.

| Closing | Technology is continually evolving. At the center of technology exist ⓘ **information and technology and bioscience**. Therefore, relevant industries will keep growing. I think that is why I find many people want to work in the IT and ⓙ **biotechnology** industries.

본인이 만든 답안에 아래의 요소들이 포함되었는지 점검해 봅시다.

Checklist
☐ 젊은 사람들에게 인기 있는 산업
☐ 그 산업이 인기 있는 이유
☐ 인기 산업의 사회적 의미
☐ 인기 산업 종사자의 사례
☐ 인기 산업에 대한 내 관점

The Music of Speech

강세를 두어야 하는 어휘의 특징을 익히고 그에 따라 답안을 말하는 연습을 해봅시다.

강세를 두는 어휘의 특징
1) 감탄사이다 2) 최상급이다 3) 형용사/부사이다
4) 문장 안에서 key word 역할을 하는 명사나 동사인 경우가 많다

Model Answer 8   🎧 02-15

My name is Jaewook Oh. I am 30, and I recently got a job at ABC Engineering, where I have wanted to work since I was a student. So I guess I have achieved one of my goals. I am an outgoing person and have traveled to many countries, including Australia, New Zealand, Philippines, Indonesia, Thailand, and Spain, for the past two years. I have met a lot of people from all over the world and have gained insight and knowledge through traveling. I think those experiences will help me have a global attitude at work, where the clients are mostly from Central and Eastern Asia, Saudi Arabia, Europe, America, Mexico, and other regions. This was one reason I wanted to work for ABC Engineering, and I am happy my dream finally came true.

Model Answer 9   🎧 02-16

There are several training programs at my company. The most intense and popular training program is the English conversation program. There are 30 employees that have taken part in the program, and it receives the highest satisfaction rates in the monthly evaluations. Since I speak English, I took part in the program as the teacher's assistant. The program is very lively and fun although many of the employees struggle with making presentations. Most of them are shy about speaking in front of a large group, but I know the practice is very beneficial for them. On the other hand, my company also provides a computer training program for the engineers. It's a core step that can lead to a promotion. Finally, the most coveted training program among employees with over 3 years of experience is the leadership course. I guess these are some of the training programs you can find at my company.

Model Answer 10   🎧 02-17

I definitely prefer the team training program because it gives me an opportunity to interact with my co-workers. We can exchange different ideas and expand our knowledge through brainstorming. Most of all, I love to communicate with people. It's just more dynamic and fun. In the leadership class that's held every Thursday, we learn how to make our presentations more appealing and engaging. There are always special lecturers from various fields, and the class becomes a window to the world. We also learn how to be more persuasive in our negotiations. My favorite part of the program is the class on maintaining your appearance. It may sound like this has nothing to do with leadership, but they teach you how to work on your own image to gain more credibility. I've learned a lot from the class. It's cool to see the make-overs of my co-workers as well. Overall, I think the team training program has a lot more benefits than the individual training program.

Model Answer 11   02-18

The last time I had lunch with my co-workers was this afternoon. I usually have lunch with my co-workers, and we often go to the company cafeteria in the basement. Our company cafeteria offers various meals and is a very nice facility. This afternoon, I went to a nearby restaurant with my co-worker Minyoung, who works in another department. I love to hang out with her since we have many things in common, including similar tastes in food. Since our lunchtime doesn't last long, we don't go that far. One of our favorite places is *Krajo Burger*, which is a Korean burger house. The food is good, and the prices are reasonable. Above all, it's never that crowded! We had a great meal and had a good talk. It was an enjoyable meal as always.

Model Answer 12   02-19

The most memorable lunch I ever had was probably last summer on my birthday. Since I had to go to work, I was planning to have a party after work. But guess what? On that day, my boyfriend came to my office with a bunch of flowers and a big smile during lunch hour. It was totally a surprise. He took me to a fancy restaurant nearby and also invited some of my co-workers. We all had a very nice time together. I felt so blessed to have such great people around me. I hope to have another great lunch sometime. I don't mean in the same way, but I look forward to having a nice lunch sometime again.

Model Answer 13 🎧 02-20

I haven't met a lot of people who want to work for a certain company. Most people I know choose a job according to their interests and background. For example, my husband comes from a computer programming background. He used to develop computer software programs for national security. He was successful, but he resigned to explore more of the world. He started a new journey as a photographer! I think it is awesome that he left his previous job and took another path to pursue his true vision. He is now sharing the wonder of God's creation with others through his photographs. His work is displayed in galleries in different cities and places. He also has a website. It's www.jperryimages.com. I think he made a successful career change. Getting a job is not just about earning a better salary or getting more benefits through a company. I believe that a true reward comes from pursuing one's vision.

Model Answer 14 🎧 02-21

Honestly, the people I usually meet don't talk about jobs that much. We talk about our families and lives more often. But I have met several people who wanted to work in the IT industry, the computer game industry, and the mobile app industry. These industries have been growing constantly. In the past, we thought that only computer geeks worked with computers. Nowadays, people with all kinds of backgrounds use computers for their work and hobbies. For example, my sister majored in textile design, but she saw potential in the online market and received her graphic designer's certificate. Now she is the owner of an online company. Of course, she uses her computer every day! Technology is continually evolving. At the center of technology exist the computer and the Internet. Therefore, relevant industries will keep growing. I think that is why I find many people want to work in the IT, computer, and mobile-app industries.

More Expressions & Vocabulary ≫ Work Life

Office Life

I work for a major company. 저는 대기업에 다닙니다.
I work for/at (회사 이름). 저는 ~에서 근무합니다.
I run my own business. 저는 개인 사업을 합니다.
I have been working for (연차) years.
저는 ~년 동안 일해 왔습니다.
I am in the (부서명) Department. 저는 ~ 부서에서 일합니다.
I work from nine to six.
저는 오전 9시부터 저녁 6시까지 일합니다.
I have lunch in the company cafeteria.
저는 회사 구내식당에서 점심 식사를 합니다.
My boss is very professional. 제 상사는 전문가답습니다.
I usually wear a suit to work.
저는 주로 정장을 입고 회사에 갑니다.
I dress casually for work.
저는 캐주얼한 차림으로 회사에 갑니다.
I check my email when I arrive at the office.
저는 사무실에 도착하면 이메일을 확인합니다.

I attend meetings in the morning.
저는 아침에 회의에 참석합니다.
I often work late. 저는 자주 야근을 합니다.
It's difficult to deal with customers.
고객을 응대하는 것은 어렵습니다.
The secretary arranges my schedule.
제 스케줄은 비서가 정리해줍니다.

Choosing a Career

cover letter 커버레터 (지원동기 및 약력을 간략히 1페이지 이내로 정리하는 자기소개서로, 보통 이력서와 함께 전송한다)
have an interview 인터뷰를 하다
do an internship 인턴쉽에 참여하다
go to a job fair 취업박람회에 가다
background check (미국에서 하는) 입사 전 신원조회
reference 추천서
probation (정규직으로 채용되기 전에 주어지는) 견습 기간

CHAPTER 3 주거 문화

Housing

| Unit 15 | **Korean Housing Culture** 한국의 주거 문화 |
| Unit 16 | **Korea's Housing Problem** 한국 주거 문화의 문제 |

Chapter 3은 주거 문화에 대해 다룹니다. 초급단계에서 다룬 이웃(neighborhood) 또는 이웃 사람들(neighbors)과의 관계나 활동을 포함한, 보다 수준이 있는 질문 유형이 등장합니다. 예를 들어 가족 혹은 룸메이트 또는 혼자 살고 있는 거주지 및 주변 환경에 관한 질문이 나올 수 있습니다. Level 4 이상에서는 한국 주거 문화의 특징, 아파트 문화와 주택 문화의 차이, 유년기 거주지와 현재 거주지의 변화, 거주지 내부 묘사, 동네 시설물 묘사, 문화와 기술 변화로 인한 가족 구성원과의 관계도 질문할 수 있습니다.

+ Brainstorming Point

When?	since when I have been living in my current house (집에 언제부터 거주했는지) when I last spent time with my neighbors (이웃과 함께 한 마지막 시간)
Where?	where my house is located (우리집 위치) where I used to live in my childhood (어릴 적 거주지) where in my town I like to visit (자주 가는 동네 장소)
What?	the differences between my past house and current house (과거와 현재 거주지 차이) what I like about my town (동네의 장점) what kinds of furniture we have at home (집에 있는 가구) the buildings and facilities in my neighborhood (동네에 있는 건물 및 시설물) a memorable episode with my neighbors (이웃과 있었던 기억에 남는 일)
Who?	my next-door neighbor (옆집 이웃) who I live with (함께 거주하는 사람) who in my family I spend the most time with (가장 함께 하는 시간이 많은 가족 구성원)
Why?	why Korea is facing certain housing problems (한국만의 특정한 주거 문제) why I like my current place (현재 거주지가 좋은 이유) why I'm close/not close to my neighbors (이웃과 친한/안 친한 이유) why I like certain places in my town (동네 특정 장소를 좋아하는 이유)
How?	how I feel about Korea's housing culture (한국 주거 문화에 대한 견해) how Korean houses have changed in the past few years (지난 수년 동안 한국 주택이 변화된 점)

Unit 15 Korean Housing Culture

한국의 주거 문화

Warm Up

A Guess the Question & Answer
사진을 보면서 예상 질문과 답변을 먼저 추측해 봅시다.

B Listen & Talk
새로운 거주지에 관한 대화를 먼저 연습해 봅시다.

🎧 03-01

A How do you like your new apartment?

B It's complicated to get to. I can't find my own house.

A It's only been a week. You will get used to it. It took 3 months for me to recognize all the buildings around my house.

B Okay. That makes me feel better.

A Come on. There must be something you like about your new place. Have you met your neighbors?

B Yeah, the ones who live across from us. They seem nice except that the man smokes in the stairwell every day.

A Sorry to hear that. What kinds of facilities does the town have?

B There are a laundry, DVD rental store, supermarket, restaurants, and a coffee shop, and the park has a beautiful view.

A Good. I'm sure you'll become familiar with your new place.

A 새로 이사 간 아파트는 어때?

B 찾기 정말 복잡해. 내 집을 못 찾아가겠어.

A 아직 일주일 밖에 안 됐잖아. 익숙해질 거야. 난 집 주변 건물들만 익히는 데에도 3개월이 걸렸어.

B 그래. 네 얘기 들으니까 좀 낫다.

A 이봐, 새 집에 대해 좋은 점도 있을 것 아냐. 이웃 사람들은 좀 만나봤어?

B 응, 앞집 사람들만. 좋은 사람들 같긴 한데, 남자가 맨날 계단에서 담배를 피는 남자만 빼곤.

A 저런. 동네 시설물은 뭐가 있는데?

B 세탁소, DVD 대여점, 슈퍼마켓, 식당, 커피숍, 그리고 경치가 아름다운 공원이 있어.

A 잘 됐네. 좀 있으면 새 집이랑 많이 친숙해질 거야.

Vocabulary
complicated 복잡한 | recognize 인식하다, 알아차리다 | neighbor 이웃 | stairwell (아파트) 복도 계단 | facility 시설물 | rental store 대여점 | be familiar with ~ ~와 친밀하다, 익숙하다

Key Expressions

아래 제시된 각 expression의 구조를 이해하고, 자기만의 표현들을 생각해 봅시다.

Expression 1 **not an easy** + 명사: 쉬운 ~가 아닌

이것은 쉬운 질문이 아닙니다. → This is **not an easy** question.

오늘은 정말 힘든 하루였습니다. → It was **not an easy** day.

우리는 쉬운 문제를 다루고 있는 것이 아닙니다. → We are **not** dealing with **an easy** matter.

Expression 2 **be found in** ~: ~에서 발견되다

가장 큰 변화는 기술적인 체제에서 발견될 수 있습니다. → The biggest change can **be found in** the technological system.

정답은 책에서 발견할 수 있습니다. → The answer can **be found in** the book.

가장 혁신적인 업적은 창의성을 맘껏 발휘하는 사람들에게서 나타납니다.
→ The most innovative work is to **be found in** those who let their creativity run free.

Expression 3 **a decade ago:** 10년 전에

저는 10년 전에 삼신 아파트에 살았습니다. → I lived in Samsin Apartment **a decade ago**.

그는 10년 전에 캐나다에 머물렀습니다. → He stayed in Canada **a decade ago**.

유미는 10년 전에 미인 대회에서 1등을 했습니다. → Yumi won a beauty pageant **a decade ago**.

Expression 4 **all we [you] have to do is** + 동사원형/to부정사: 우리가[당신이] 할 일은 ~뿐입니다

저희가 할 것은 개인 비밀번호를 입력하는 것뿐입니다. → **All we have to do is** press the PIN number.

당신이 할 일은 샐러드에 드레싱 소스를 얹는 것뿐입니다.
→ **All you have to do is** add the dressing to the salad.

당신이 빨간 버튼만 누르면 장치는 곧바로 작동하기 시작할 것입니다.
→ **All you have to do is** touch the red button, and the device will work right away.

Expression 5 **a palm-size(d)** + 명사: 손바닥만한 크기의 물건

저희 엄마 눈높이에 맞는 손바닥만한 TV가 설치되어 있습니다. → Installed is **a palm-size** TV that is the same as my mom's eye level.

내령은 손바닥만한 크기의 강아지를 키웁니다. → Naeryung is raising **a palm-sized** puppy.

제이크루사는 손바닥만한 미디어플레이어를 공개 행사때 전시했습니다.
→ J-crew displayed **a palm-sized** media player at the showcase.

Topic Question & Model Answer

🎧 03-02

Topic Question

Tell me about the housing culture in your country. How has it changed in the past few years? Have there been any changes in terms of design or architecture? Have homes become very modern? Tell me about some changes in the housing culture of your country. 당신 국가의 주거문화에 대해 말해보세요. 지난 몇 년간 어떻게 달라졌나요? 주거 환경의 디자인이나 건축 방식에 대한 변화가 있었나요? 집이 훨씬 현대적으로 바뀌었나요? 당신 국가의 주거 문화의 변화에 대해 얘기해보세요.

TIP FOR THE OPIc

한국의 주거 문화의 특징과 그 변화에 관한 질문입니다. 어려운 질문일수록 최대한 단순화시켜서 1~2가지 요점만 짚어주는 것이 좋습니다. 한국 주거지의 디자인 및 건축의 변화에 대해 답하라고 한정지었으므로 내가 살고 있는 집이 과거에 비해 어떻게 달라졌는지 말할 수 있습니다. 현관문을 여는 방식 혹은 냉방장치의 설치 혹은 1인 가구의 증가로 인한 오피스텔의 급증, 아파트 단지 내에 스포츠센터 등 편의시설의 확대에 대해 말할 수 있습니다.

Model Answer

| Opening |

This is not an easy question. Um, I don't know about many changes in Korea's housing culture in general, but, by looking at my family's apartment, I guess the biggest change can be found in the technological system.

이건 정말 만만치 않은 질문이네요. 음, 저는 일반적인 한국 주거 문화의 변화에 대해서는 잘 모르지만, 저희 가족이 거주하는 아파트를 본다면, 아마도 테크놀로지의 진보가 큰 변화를 가져온 것 같습니다.

| Changes in Korea's Housing Culture |

For example, when I lived in an apartment a decade ago, we needed a key to lock and unlock the door. But in our new apartment, all we have to do is press the PIN number to open the front door. Also, in our kitchen, there's a palm-size TV installed at my mother's eye level. My mom spends a lot of time in the kitchen cooking or doing the dishes. She hasn't felt bored in there since we got the TV.

예를 들어, 제가 10년 전에 아파트에 살았을 때는, 현관문을 잠그고 열기 위해서는 열쇠가 필요했습니다. 하지만 지금의 새 아파트에서는, 현관문을 열기 위해 비밀번호만 입력하면 됩니다. 또한, 주방에는 어머니 눈높이에 맞는 손바닥만한 크기의 TV가 설치되어 있습니다. 저희 어머니는 주방에서 음식을 만들거나 설거지를 하는 데에 많은 시간을 보내십니다. 하지만 TV를 설치한 후로 어머니는 주방 일을 지루해하시지 않습니다.

| Closing |

I guess these are some of the changes you can find in Korean apartments these days. Thanks to technological developments, our lives are becoming more fun.

제가 생각할 때 바로 이러한 점들이 요즘 한국의 아파트에서 볼 수 있는 몇 가지 변화인 것 같습니다. 테크놀로지의 발전 덕분에, 우리의 삶이 더 재미있어지고 있어요.

More Questions

〈한국의 주거 문화〉에 관련하여 더 나올 수 있는 OPIc 질문들을 정리한 코너입니다. 질문에 대한 brainstorming을 해보세요.

1. You indicated in the survey that you live with your family. Where's your house located? How big is your family?
2. Suppose that you moved to a new apartment. Your neighbors who live upstairs play their music too loud every night. Talk to your neighbor and make suggestions to solve the problem.

On Your Own

앞에서 주어진 Model Answer을 바탕으로, 아래의 빈칸에 들어갈 수 있는 다양한 대체 가능한 어휘 및 표현들을 참고하여 학습자 본인만의 모범 답안을 직접 만들어보세요.

| Opening |

This is not an easy question. I don't know about many changes in Korea's housing culture in general, but, by looking at my family's apartment, I guess the biggest change can be found in the ⓐ_____.

| Changes in Korea's Housing Culture |

For example, when I lived in an apartment a decade ago,
ⓑ_____. But in our new apartment,
ⓒ_____. Each resident has to carry his or her own ID card to enter the gate. Also, in our ⓓ_____, there's a palm-sized ⓔ_____.
ⓕ_____.

| Closing |

I guess these are some of the changes you can find in Korean apartments these days. Thanks to ⓖ_____, our lives are becoming ⓗ_____.

본인이 만든 답안에 아래의 요소들이 포함되었는지 점검해 봅시다.

| Opening | This is not an easy question. I don't know about many changes in Korea's housing culture in general, but, by looking at my family's apartment, I guess the biggest change can be found in the ⓐ **security system**.

| Changes in Korea's Housing Culture | For example, when I lived in an apartment a decade ago, ⓑ **the janitor was the only person who could prevent strangers coming into the apartment building**. But in our new apartment, ⓒ **there's a scanning system installed that recognizes the residents who are at the apartment gate**. Each resident has to carry his or her own ID card to enter the gate. Also, in our ⓓ **living room**, there's a palm-sized ⓔ **screen installed to show visitors who are standing outside the front door**. ⓕ **As we can clearly see the visitors without opening the front door, we can prevent strangers from coming into our house**.

| Closing | I guess these are some of the changes you can find in Korean apartments these days. Thanks to ⓖ **advanced security systems**, our lives are becoming ⓗ **safer and more convenient**.

	Checklist
☐	어릴 적 집의 특징
☐	현재 거주지의 특징
☐	집안 구조의 변화
☐	집안 시설물의 변화
☐	아파트(주택) 외관의 변화
☐	동네 시설물의 변화

Unit 16 Korea's Housing Problem

한국 주거 문화의 문제

Warm Up

A Guess the Question & Answer

사진을 보면서 예상 질문과 답변을 먼저 추측해 봅시다.

B Listen & Talk

한국의 주택 문제에 관한 대화를 먼저 연습해 봅시다.

🎧 03-03

A How do you find your life in Korea?

B I love the people and food.

A What about your living environment?

B Well, that's what I'm really not used to. I used to live in a house with a yard and a pool. Although my Korean apartment feels too small for me, the rent for this house seems to be high.

A I understand. But you have one of the finest views in town.

B True. The night view of the Han River is amazing.

A What about your neighbors? Are they nice?

B They are friendly, but they don't speak English. Also, there are few people around my age. Most of my neighbors are old couples.

A Right. It's expected since our current society has a large aging population.

A 한국에서 살아보니까 어때?

B 사람들이랑 음식은 정말 좋아.

A 거주 환경은 어떤데?

B 음. 그 점이 바로 정말 익숙하지 않은 부분이지. 난 뜰이랑 수영장이 있는 집에서 살았는데 말이야. 지금 사는 한국 아파트는 너무 작게 느껴지는데도, 월세가 비싼 것 같아.

A 이해해. 하지만 넌 동네에서 제일 멋진 경관이 내려다보이는 곳에 살잖아.

B 맞아. 한강의 야경은 끝내주지.

A 네 이웃은 어때? 친절해?

B 응. 친절한데 영어는 못해. 내 또래 사람들도 드물어. 대부분이 노년 부부더라고.

A 응. 그럴 수밖에 없는 것이 이젠 한국도 고령 사회거든.

Vocabulary | **living environment** 주거환경 | **rent** 집 대여료 (월세, 전세) | **night view** 야경 | **current society** 현대 사회 | **aging population** 고령화 인구 | **large population** 큰 규모의 인구

Key Expressions

아래 제시된 각 expression의 구조를 이해하고, 자기만의 표현들을 생각해 봅시다.

Expression 1　population problem: 인구 문제

인구 문제는 한국의 주택 시장의 중요한 사안입니다.
→ There is a huge **population problem** in Korea's housing market.

인도는 과잉 인구 문제로 잘 알려져 있습니다.
→ India is well-known for its over**population problem**.

많은 나라들은 인구의 고령화 문제에 직면하고 있습니다.
→ Many countries are facing an aging **population problem**.

Expression 2　decrease sharply: 폭락하다

주택 가격이 급격히 하락하고 있습니다. → The price of housing is **decreasing sharply**.

우리의 시장 점유율이 올해 심하게 줄어들었다.
→ Our share of the market has **decreased sharply** this year.

정부의 강경책 덕분에 교통사고가 현저히 줄었습니다.
→ Traffic accidents have **decreased sharply** thanks to the government's strict policies.

Expression 3　have a hard time + -ing: ~하는 데 어려운 시간을 보내다, ~하느라 고생하다

제 또래의 사람들은 살 곳을 찾는 데에 쉽지 않은 시간을 보냅니다.
→ People my age still **have a hard time finding** places to live.

소년들은 캠핑 장소를 찾느라 고생했습니다. → The boys **had a hard time finding** the camping site.

수지는 요리를 배우는 데에 힘든 시간을 보냈습니다. → Suji **had a hard time learning** how to cook.

Expression 4　save money [income]: 돈[수입]을 저축하다

결혼한 지 얼마 안 된 제 친구들 대부분은 저축을 잘 못합니다.
→ Most of my recently married friends can't **save** enough **money**.

저는 매달 월급의 70%를 저축하고 있습니다. → I'm **saving** 70% of my monthly **income**.

준호는 회사의 파산으로 인해 돈을 충분히 저축하지 못했습니다.
→ Junho wasn't able to **save** enough **money** due to the company's bankruptcy.

Expression 5　be related to ~: ~와 연관되다

한국의 주택문제는 인구의 고령화와 관련이 있습니다.
→ Korea's housing problem **is related to** its aging population.

맑은 공기는 녹색 환경과 관련이 있습니다. → Fresh air **is related to** a green environment.

한 일간지에 의하면, 눈 건강은 뇌 건강과 연관되어 있습니다.
→ According to a daily newspaper, eye health **is related to** brain health.

Unit 16 Korea's Housing Problem

Topic Question & Model Answer

🎧 03-04

Topic Question

What are some housing problems your country is facing? Like problems with cost, safety, and so on. Tell me about the problems in your country's housing market.

당신 나라가 직면하고 있는 주거 문제는 무엇인가요? 예를 들어 주택비용, 안전 등의 문제 말입니다. 당신 나라의 주택 시장에 대한 문제점들에 대해 얘기해보세요.

TIP FOR THE OPIc

Level 5 이상에서 나올 수 있는 질문입니다. 개인이 거주하는 주거 환경의 문제점과 더불어 나아가 한국 사회의 주거 문화 및 문제점을 질문할 수 있습니다. 평소 주택 시장의 문제 등에 대해 생각해봤을지라도 영어로 답안을 구사하기 쉽지 않습니다. 이럴 때는 주제어 1~2가지만 정확히 짚어내도 답안 내용이 훨씬 짜임새있게 들립니다. 또한 사회 전체적인 현상은 간략하게 언급하고, 주변의 사례를 들어 설명하는 것이 설득력 있고 답안을 구성하기에도 좋습니다.

Model Answer

| Opening |

Well, if I were to name a problem in Korea's housing market, it would be the population problem.

음, 한국의 주택 시장에 관한 문제점을 꼽으라고 한다면, 아마도 인구 문제일 것입니다.

| Aging Society and Its Problems |

People in this country are aging. There are fewer people getting married these days, and many couples don't want to have babies. As a result, there are many new apartment buildings despite the fact that the population is not growing. Although the price of housing is decreasing sharply, people my age still have a hard time finding places to live. Most of my recently married friends have that problem. They can't buy a house, or the monthly rent is so high that they can't save enough money.

한국의 인구는 점점 고령화되고 있습니다. 요즘에는 결혼하는 사람들이 줄어들고 있으며, 많은 부부들은 아이를 원치 않습니다. 그 결과, 인구는 증가하고 있지 않는 사실에도 불구하고 신축 아파트는 많이 있습니다. 비록 주택 가격은 급격히 하락하고 있음에도 제 연령대의 사람들은 살 곳을 찾는 데에 여전히 어려움을 느낍니다. 최근에 결혼한 제 친구들 대부분이 역시 이러한 문제를 겪고 있습니다. 그들은 집을 구입할 수가 없고, 혹은 월세가 너무 높은 관계로 저축을 제대로 할 수 없습니다.

| Closing |

Overall, I think Korea's problem of an aging society is strongly related to its housing problem.

전반적으로 볼 때, 저는 한국의 고령화 문제가 주택 시장의 문제와 밀접한 연관이 있다고 봅니다.

More Questions

〈한국 주거 문화의 문제〉에 관련하여 더 나올 수 있는 OPIc 질문들을 정리한 코너입니다. 질문에 대한 brainstorming을 해보세요.

1. Is there anything you want to change about your neighborhood? What is it? Why do you want to change it?

2. What kinds of facilities are there in your neighborhood? Do you think they are useful? Which one do you use the most often?

3. Do you often talk to your neighbors? What do you talk about when you meet your neighbors? Give me some details.

On Your Own

앞에서 주어진 Model Answer을 바탕으로, 아래의 빈칸에 들어갈 수 있는 다양한 대체 가능한 어휘 및 표현들을 참고하여 학습자 본인만의 모범 답안을 직접 만들어보세요.

I Opening I

Well, if I were to name a problem in Korea's housing market, it would be the

ⓐ_____.

I Aging Society and Its Problems I

ⓑ_____. As a result, there are

ⓒ_____.

ⓓ_____. Therefore, people my age have a hard time

finding places to live. ⓔ_____. They can't buy a house,

or the monthly rent is so high that they can't save enough money.

I Closing I

Overall, I think Korea's problem of ⓕ_____ are strongly

related to its housing problem.

I Opening I Well, if I were to name a problem in Korea's housing market, it would be the ⓐ **growth of single households**.

I Aging Society and Its Problems I ⓑ **The divorce rate is growing while fewer people are getting married**. As a result, there are ⓒ **more people living by themselves while there are a limited number of houses constructed for one person**. ⓓ **Rent is increasing as well**. Therefore, people my age have a hard time finding places to live. ⓔ **The problem is an issue for recently married couples as well**. They can't buy a house, or the monthly rent is so high that they can't save enough money.

I Closing I Overall, I think Korea's problems of ⓕ **a high divorce rate and low marriage rate** are strongly related to its housing problem.

본인이 만든 답안에 아래의 요소들이 포함되었는지 점검해 봅시다.

Checklist
☐ 보편적인 주거 문화의 문제
☐ 집값의 부담
☐ 1인 가구 증가에 비한 공급 부족
☐ 내가 거주하면서 느낀 문제
☐ 이웃과의 사이에서 생긴 문제
☐ 동네에서 생긴 문제 (도둑고양이, 주차문제, 분리수거 등)

Unit 16 Korea's Housing Problem

The Music of Speech

강세를 두어야 하는 어휘의 특징을 익히고 그에 따라 답안을 말하는 연습을 해봅시다.

강세를 두는 어휘의 특징

1) 감탄사이다 2) 최상급이다 3) 형용사/부사이다
4) 문장 안에서 key word 역할을 하는 명사나 동사인 경우가 많다

Model Answer 15 🎧 03-05

This is not an easy question. Um, I don't know about many changes in Korea's housing culture in general, but, by looking at my family's apartment, I guess the biggest change can be found in the technological system. For example, when I lived in an apartment a decade ago, we needed a key to lock and unlock the door. But in our new apartment, all we have to do is press the PIN number to open the front door. Also, in our kitchen, there's a palm-size TV installed at my mother's eye level. My mom spends a lot of time in the kitchen cooking or doing the dishes. She hasn't felt bored in there since we got the TV. I guess these are some of the changes you can find in Korean apartments these days. Thanks to technological developments, our lives are becoming more fun.

Model Answer 16 🎧 03-06

Well, if I were to name a problem in Korea's housing market, it would be the population problem. People in this country are aging. There are fewer people getting married these days, and many couples don't want to have babies. As a result, there are many new apartment buildings despite the fact that the population is not growing. Although the price of housing is decreasing sharply, people my age still have a hard time finding places to live. Most of my recently married friends have that problem. They can't buy a house, or the monthly rent is so high that they can't save enough money. Overall, I think Korea's problem of an aging society is strongly related to its housing problem.

More Expressions & Vocabulary ≫ Housing

I live in an apartment with my family/roommate.
저는 가족/룸메이트와 함께 아파트에 거주합니다.

There are four bedrooms in my house.
저희 집에는 4개의 침실이 있습니다.

We have many plants on the balcony.
우리는 발코니에 식물이 많이 있습니다.

My room is tidy and cozy.
제 방은 깨끗하고 아늑합니다.

There's a dressing table in my room.
제 방에는 화장대가 있습니다.

I love the wooden tea table.
저는 목재로 만든 탁자를 좋아합니다.

Our living room is spacious.
저희 집 거실은 널찍합니다.

The ceiling is leaking.
천장에서 물이 샙니다.

There is a shopping area in my town.
저희 동네에는 쇼핑 지역이 있습니다.

The park is peaceful and relaxing.
그 공원은 평온하고 쉬기에 좋습니다.

The lady who lives next door is friendly.
옆집 사는 여자 분은 친절합니다.

I run into my neighbors at the market.
저는 상가에서 이웃과 마주칩니다.

I am not close to my neighbors.
저는 제 이웃과 친하지 않습니다.

There are some nice facilities in my town.
우리 동네에는 좋은 시설물들이 있습니다.

The parking lot at my apartment building is spacious.
우리 아파트의 주차 공간은 널찍합니다.

There is a security office in every building.
모든 건물마다 경비실이 있습니다.

I moved into my current apartment last year.
저는 지금 거주하는 아파트에 작년에 이사왔습니다.

a townhouse 연립 주택
a detached house 단독 주택
a country house 전원 주택
a studio apartment 원룸
a dormitory 기숙사
a residential and commercial complex 주상복합
dining room 부엌
bathroom 화장실
microwave 전자레인지
fridge 냉장고
washing machine 세탁기
air conditioner 냉방기
closet 옷장
drawer 서랍
rearrange the furniture 가구를 재배치하다
wipe the window 창문을 닦다
wash the dishes 설거지하다
do the laundry 세탁하다
make one's bed 침대를 정리하다
water the flowers 꽃에 물을 주다

CHAPTER 4 여가 활동

Free-Time Activities

Unit 17	**Watching Movies 1** 영화보기 1
Unit 18	**Watching Movies 2** 영화보기 2
Unit 19	**Night Clubbing 1** 나이트클럽 가기 1
Unit 20	**Night Clubbing 2** 나이트클럽 가기 2
Unit 21	**Text Message 1** 문자 메시지 1
Unit 22	**Text Message 2** 문자 메시지 2
Unit 23	**Shopping 1** 쇼핑하기 1
Unit 24	**Shopping 2** 쇼핑하기 2
Unit 25	**Home-Improvement Project 1** 주거 개선 1
Unit 26	**Home-Improvement Project 2** 주거 개선 2

Chapter 4는 여가 활동에 관한 질문을 다룹니다. 주로 영화 보기, 쇼핑하기, 문자로 대화하기, 나이트 클럽 가기, 주거 개선하기에 대해 다룹니다. 일상적으로 자주 접하는 활동에 관한 질문이 출제되기도 하지만 난이도가 높은 예상 밖의 질문이 나오는 경우도 많습니다. 좋아하는 영화 장르, 배우, 클럽, 쇼핑 방식과 관련된 기본적인 주제에서부터 집안일을 하다 생긴 사고, 클럽에서 우연히 만난 사람, 한국과 다른 나라의 쇼핑 문화의 차이, 문자로 대화하는 것의 장단점에 이르기까지 다양한 심화 주제들이 언급될 수 있습니다.

✚ Brainstorming Point

When?
- the first/last time I watched a movie/went to a concert/cleaned my house/went clubbing (처음/마지막으로 영화를 본/콘서트에 간/청소를 한/클럽에 간 때)
- the first time I watched a movie/went clubbing/purchased a cell phone (처음 영화를 본/클럽에 간/휴대폰을 구입한 때)
- the last time I went shopping/got a refund on an item/cleaned my house (마지막으로 쇼핑한/환불한/청소를 한 때)

Where?
- my favorite movie theater/club/concert hall/room (가장 좋아하는 영화관/클럽/콘서트 장/방)
- my favorite movie theater/club/shopping mall/room (가장 좋아하는 영화관/클럽/쇼핑 장소/방)

What?
- my all-time-favorite movie (생애 최고의 영화)
- an embarrassing moment at a club (클럽에서 당황했던 순간)
- an accident that occurred while cleaning the house (청소하다 벌어진 사건)
- refunded items (환불한 제품들)
- advantages/disadvantages of text messaging (문자로 대화하기의 장단점)

Who?
- my favorite movie actor/actress/director (좋아하는 영화 배우/감독)
- who I met at the club (클럽에서 만난 사람)
- who I like to watch movies with (함께 영화를 보고 싶은 사람)

Why?
- why I like clubbing/doing household chores (클럽 가기/집안일 하기를 좋아하는 이유)
- why I like the theater/concert hall/club (왜 그 영화관/콘서트 장/클럽을 좋아하는지)
- why I had to do the household chores (집안일을 해야만 했던 이유)
- why I like the actor/actress/director (그 배우/감독을 좋아하는 이유)
- why I like the theater/club/shopping mall/text messaging (왜 그 영화관/클럽/쇼핑 장소/문자로 대화하기를 좋아하는지)

How?
- how I got interested in clubbing (클럽 가는 것을 좋아하게 된 계기)
- how often I watch movies/go clubbing/go shopping/do the household chores (얼마나 자주 영화를 보는지/클럽에 가는지/쇼핑이나 집안일을 하는지)

Unit 17 Watching Movies 1

영화보기 1

Warm Up

A Guess the Question & Answer
사진을 보면서 예상 질문과 답변을 먼저 추측해 봅시다.

B Listen & Talk
내가 처음 본 영화에 관한 대화를 먼저 연습해 봅시다.

🎧 04-01

A What's the first movie you ever watched?

B I think it was *Who Framed Roger Rabbit*.

A *Who Framed Roger Rabbit*? The film which combined live action and animation?

B That's right. Many people remember the movie as the one with a sexy lady in a red dress and hair, but it also starred the toughest rabbit on Earth.

A True. But I didn't think you'd be familiar with that movie. You don't look like you come from that generation.

B I'll take that as a compliment. Thanks.

A Really. You look younger than that. Anyway, how did you like the movie?

B It was very funny and interesting. I can't quite remember the storyline, but some images from the movie still remain.

A It was a sensational movie. I wish they would remake the movie into a 21st-century version. That would be really cool.

A 네가 처음 본 영화가 뭐였어?

B '누가 로져 래빗을 모함했나'이었던 것 같아.

A '누가 로져 래빗을 모함했나'? 실사와 애니메이션을 조합한 영화 말이야?

B 맞아. 많은 사람들이 그 영화를 떠올리면 빨간 머리에 빨간 드레스를 입은 섹시한 여주인공을 기억하는데, 사실 세상에서 가장 터프한 토끼도 등장하지.

A 그렇지. 그런데 난 네가 그 영화가 친숙한 줄은 생각 못했지. 그 세대 사람이 아닌 것 같은데.

B 그 말 칭찬으로 받아들일게. 고마워.

A 진짜야. 그 영화를 기억하기엔 정말 어려 보여. 아무튼, 그 영화 재미있게 봤어?

B 응 정말 웃기고 재미있었지. 줄거리는 잘 생각이 안 나는데 영화 속 몇몇 장면은 기억에 남아.

A 엄청 화제가 된 영화였잖아. 21세기 버전으로 그 영화를 다시 만들면 좋겠어. 정말 굉장할 것 같은데 말이야.

Vocabulary | **combine** 합치다, 섞다 | **live action** (영화의) 실사 | **animation** 애니메이션 | **star** ~를 주인공으로 하다 | **on earth** 지구상에서, 세상에서 | **come from a generation** ~시대의 사람이다 | **take something as a compliment** 칭찬으로 받아들이다 | **remain** 남아있다 | **sensational** 센세이션을 일으킨, 상당한 화젯거리의 | **remake** 다시 만들다

Key Expressions

아래 제시된 각 expression의 구조를 이해하고, 자기만의 표현들을 생각해 봅시다.

Expression 1   **the first + 명사 + I ever + 과거동사 + be동사 ~:** 제가 가장 처음 ~한 것은 ~였다

제가 가장 처음 본 영화는 바로 '쥬라기 공원'이었습니다.
→ **The first** movie **I ever watched was** *Jurassic Park*.

제가 가장 처음 만들었던 케익은 바로 녹차 쉬폰 케익이었습니다.
→ **The first** cake **I ever made was** a green tea chiffon cake.

제가 처음으로 꽃을 선물로 받은 것은 제 16살 생일이었습니다.
→ **The first** flower **I ever received was** on my 16th birthday.

Expression 2   **star:** ~를 주인공으로 하다

그 영화는 맷 데이먼이 주인공입니다. → The movie is **starring** Matt Damon.

우디 앨런의 최신 영화는 페넬로페 크루즈를 주인공으로 내세우고 있습니다.
→ Woody Allen's latest movie is **starring** Penelope Cruz.

미나는 레이첼 맥아담스를 주인공으로 하는 모든 DVD영화를 갖고 있습니다.
→ Mina has all the movies **starring** Rachel McAdams on DVD.

Expression 3   **be pretty cool to ~:** ~하게 되어 좋다, ~해서 멋지다고 생각하다

커다란 스크린을 보니 멋지다는 생각이 들었습니다. → It **was pretty cool to** see the huge screen.

타워 맨 꼭대기에 올라와보니 꽤 멋있다. → It **is pretty cool to** be on the top of the tower.

새처럼 하늘을 날 수 있다면 정말 멋질 것입니다. → It must **be pretty cool to** fly in the air like birds.

Expression 4   **stay in ~:** ~에 머물다, ~에 가만히 있다

2시간 동안 제 자리에 가만히 있는 것은 쉽지 않았습니다.
→ It wasn't easy to **stay in** my seat for 2 hours.

저는 아이들에게 경찰관이 도착할 때까지 다락방에 있으라고 말했습니다.
→ I told the kids to **stay in** the attic until the cops arrived.

그 호랑이는 여정 기간 내내 캐비닛 안에 있었습니다.
→ The tiger **stayed in** the cabinet during the entire journey.

Expression 5   **after + -ing:** ~하고 난 후

콜라와 팝콘을 너무 많이 먹었더니 정말 배불렀습니다.
→ I felt really full **after** hav**ing** so much coke and popcorn.

그들은 그 소식을 듣더니 거의 기절할 뻔 했습니다. → They almost fainted **after** hear**ing** the news.

카지노에서 돈을 너무 많이 쓰고 났더니, 빈털터리가 됐습니다.
→ **After** spend**ing** so much money at the casino, I was broke.

Topic Question & Model Answer

Topic Question

Tell me about the first movie you ever watched. When was it? How did you like the movie? Do you still like the same kinds of movies now as you did in the past? 당신이 처음 본 영화에 대해 얘기해보세요. 언제 처음 영화를 봤나요? 영화는 재미있게 봤나요? 그 때나 지금이나 좋아하는 영화 장르는 같은가요?

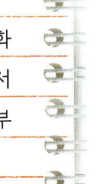

TIP FOR THE OPIc

자신이 가장 처음 본 영화를 묻는 질문입니다. 어릴 적 본 영화 가운데 기억에 남는 영화 한 편에 대해 묘사하면 됩니다. 가족과 함께 본 영화일 수도 있고, 친구들과 처음 극장에서 본 영화일 수도 있습니다. 간단한 상황 묘사를 한 뒤에는 영화 장르, 줄거리, 감동적인 부분 등을 언급하면 됩니다.

Model Answer

| Opening |

The first movie I ever watched at a theater was *Home Alone* starring Macaulay Culkin. I had watched many other movies on TV before, but that was probably the first movie I ever watched in a theater.

제가 처음으로 영화관에서 봤던 영화는 바로 맥컬리 컬킨 주연의 '나 홀로 집에'입니다. 저는 이전에도 TV에서 많은 영화를 봤지만, 아마 제가 영화관에서 처음 본 영화는 그 영화일 것입니다.

| Memories about the First Movie I Watched |

I think I went there with my parents and my little sister and brother. It may sound funny, but if I have to talk about my first impression of the theater, I would say, "It was dark." Also, it was pretty cool to see the huge screen in the front and to sit with so many people. However, it was not easy to stay in my seat for nearly 2 hours after having so much coke and popcorn during the movie. The movie was great. It was a funny, touching movie — a nice family movie.

저는 당시 부모님과 제 여동생 그리고 남동생과 함께 영화를 보러 갔던 것으로 기억합니다. 우습게 들릴 지 모르지만, 제가 영화관에 대해 가졌던 첫인상은 바로, '깜깜했다' 입니다. 또한, 앞에 있는 커다란 스크린과 주변의 많은 관객들이 있다는 사실이 멋지게 느껴졌습니다. 하지만 영화를 보는 2시간 가까이 콜라와 팝콘을 잔뜩 먹은 채로 가만히 자리에 앉아 있는 것이 쉽지 않았습니다. 영화는 최고였습니다. 재미있고 감동도 있는 유쾌한 가족 영화였습니다.

| Types of Movies I Like |

I still like to watch movies such as comedies and dramas. I don't like bloody action movies. I guess I've always liked gentle and light-hearted movies with humor, and they are still my favorites.

저는 여전히 코미디나 드라마 장르를 좋아합니다. 피투성이 액션 영화는 싫습니다. 저는 늘 잔잔하고 웃음과 감동을 주는 영화를 좋아했고, 여전히 그런 영화 장르를 좋아합니다.

More Questions

〈영화 관람〉에 관련하여 더 나올 수 있는 OPIc 질문들을 정리한 코너입니다. 질문에 대한 brainstorming을 해보세요.

1. What kinds of movie genres did you like in your childhood? How is that different from now?
2. Do you watch movies at a movie theater or do you rent DVDs? Which do you prefer? Why?
3. Is there any movie that inspired you? What was the movie about? How did it change your life?

On Your Own

앞에서 주어진 Model Answer을 바탕으로, 아래의 빈칸에 들어갈 수 있는 다양한 대체 가능한 어휘 및 표현들을 참고하여 학습자 본인만의 모범 답안을 직접 만들어보세요.

I Opening I

The first movie I ever watched at a theater was ❶_____ starring ❷_____.

I Memories about the First Movie I Watched I

I think ❸_____. It may sound funny, but if I have to talk about my first impression of the theater, I would say, "It was dark." Also, it was pretty cool to see the huge screen in the front and to sit with so many people. The movie was great. It was funny ❹_____.

I Types of Movies I Like I

I still like to watch movies such as ❺_____. I don't like ❻_____. I guess I've always liked ❼_____, and they are still my favorites.

I Opening I The first movie I ever watched at a theater was ❶ **Men in Black** starring ❷ **Will Smith**.

I Memories about the First Movie I Watched I I think ❸ **watched the movie with my friends**. It may sound funny, but if I have to talk about my first impression of the theater, I would say, "It was dark." Also, it was pretty cool to see the huge screen in the front and to sit with so many people. The movie was great. It was funny ❹ **with spectacular CG and sound effects**.

I Types of Movies I Like I I still like to watch movies such as ❺ **science fiction and action**. I don't like ❻ **bloody horror movies**. I guess I've always liked ❼ **movies with a simple plot and a huge scale**, and they are still my favorites.

본인이 만든 답안에 아래의 요소들이 포함되었는지 점검해 봅시다.

	Checklist
☐	내가 처음 본 영화 제목
☐	어디에서 봤는지 (영화관, TV)
☐	누구와 함께 봤는지
☐	출연한 영화배우
☐	영화 줄거리 (기억에 남는 점)
☐	나의 영화 성향

Unit 17 Watching Movies 1

Unit 18 Watching Movies 2

영화보기 2

Warm Up

A Guess the Question & Answer
사진을 보면서 예상 질문과 답변을 먼저 추측해 봅시다.

B Listen & Talk
가장 좋아하는 영화배우에 관한 대화를 먼저 연습해 봅시다.

🎧 04-03

A Which star have you had a crush on?

B Me? Do I have to choose just one?

A No, no. You can name anyone.

B Well, my number one is Brad Pitt, the hottest man in Hollywood.

A To you, I guess.

B What do you mean? There's no one that beats him!

A Okay, cool down. But I think Daniel Craig is very attractive.

B Oh, the 007 hero?

A Right. I love his British accent. Sounds so s–e–x–y!

B Calm down! It sounds like you're in love with him.

A 한 눈에 반한 영화배우 있었어?

B 나 말이야? 한 명만 골라야 되는 거야?

A 아냐, 아냐. 얼마든지 얘기해.

B 음, 1번은 당연히 브래드 피트지. 할리우드에서 가장 멋진 남자.

A 너한테 그런 거겠지.

B 무슨 말이야? 그보다 멋진 남자가 어디 있다고.

A 알았어, 열 받지 마. 그런데 난 대니얼 크레이그가 정말 매력적인 것 같더라.

B 아, 그 007 주인공?

A 맞아. 그 사람 영국식 발음이 좋아. 정말 섹시한 것 같아!

B 좀 침착해! 완전 푹 빠진 것 같네.

Vocabulary have a crush on ~ ~에게 반하다 | name someone ~의 이름을 대다 | beat someone ~를 이기다 (때리다) | cool down 열을 식히다 | calm down 진정하다 | be in love with someone ~와 사랑에 빠지다

Key Expressions

> 아래 제시된 각 expression의 구조를 이해하고, 자기만의 표현들을 생각해 봅시다.

Expression 1   in person: 실제로, 직접

그를 실제로 만난다면 정말 놀라울 것입니다. → It would be amazing to meet him **in person**.

그는 그 모델과 직접 얘기하고 싶어서 무대 뒤에서 기다렸습니다.
→ He waited backstage to talk to the model **in person**.

소포를 가져가려면 직접 사무실을 방문해야 합니다.
→ You need to visit the office **in person** to pick up your parcel.

Expression 2   be married to ~: ~와 결혼하다

그는 저명 인사와 결혼했습니다. → He **is married to** a celebrity.

내 사촌은 발레리나와 결혼했습니다. → My cousin **is married to** a ballerina.

세진이는 고등학교 때 남자친구와 결혼했습니다. → Sejin **is married to** her high school boyfriend.

Expression 3   manage: 다루다, 해내다, 감당하다

그녀는 어떻게 그의 직업과 가정을 모두 감당할 수 있을까요?
→ How does she **manage** both her career and her family?

제가 그 일을 해낼 수 있을지 약속 드리기는 어렵습니다. → I can't promise that I can **manage** the work.

당신은 효주가 그것을 혼자서 감당할 수 있을 것이라고 생각하나요?
→ Do you think Hyoju can **manage** it by herself?

Expression 4   maintain one's + 명사: ~의 ~을 유지하다

오래도록 명성을 유지하는 배우는 드뭅니다. → Few movie stars **maintain their fame** for so long.

명성을 유지하기 위해 패리스 밀튼은 언론에 매우 친절한 편입니다.
→ To **maintain her fame**, Paris Milton is very media friendly.

스미스 가문은 그들의 부를 유지하기 위해 열심히 일했습니다.
→ The Smith family worked hard to **maintain their wealth**.

Expression 5   very challenging: 아주 어려운, 만만치 않은, 난제의

좋은 아빠 노릇을 하기란 만만치 않을 것입니다. → Being a good father must be **very challenging**.

그 일을 성취하는 것은 매우 어려운 일이었습니다. → Accomplishing the task was **very challenging**.

환자의 상태에 따라 수술이 매우 어려워질 수도 있습니다.
→ The surgery may become **very challenging** depending on the patient's condition.

Topic Question & Model Answer

🎧 04-04

Topic Question

You said you like to watch movies. If you had a chance to meet a movie star in person, who would you like to meet? Why? What do you want to ask him or her?

당신은 영화 보는 것이 좋다고 했습니다. 만일 영화배우를 직접 만날 기회가 있다면, 당신은 누구를 만나고 싶나요? 왜 그런가요? 당신은 그/그녀에게 무엇을 물어보고 싶나요?

> **TIP FOR THE OPIc**
> 흔히 일어나기 힘든 일에 대해 얘기하라는 질문을 받으면 다소 당황스러울 수 있습니다. 하지만 평소 좋아하던 배우에 대한 설명을 하는 것이라고 생각하세요. 좋아하는 배우의 이름, 출연한 영화 제목 1~2개, 배우를 좋아하는 이유 등을 언급한 후, 배우를 실제 만났을 때 물어보고 싶은 일상적인 질문 2~3개를 하는 답안을 구성할 수 있습니다.

Model Answer

| Opening |

It would be amazing to meet my favorite movie star in person. If I had to choose, I would definitely say Brad Pitt. I'm sure you know who he is.

제가 좋아하는 영화배우를 실제로 만난다면 정말 굉장할 것 같네요. 만일 한 명을 선택해야 한다면, 저는 분명히 브래드 피트라고 얘기할 거에요. 아마 당신도 그가 누군지 알 것입니다.

| My Favorite Movie Actor |

He is a famous Hollywood star and is married to another hot celebrity, Angelina Jolie. They are an awesome couple. If I got to meet Brad Pitt, I would ask how he is able to manage both his career and his family successfully. I mean, he has had such a long career, and he still has a very nice image. Not many movie stars are able to maintain their fame for so long. Also, he has a bunch of kids — both adopted and biological — with Angelina Jolie. Being a good father must be very challenging as well as being a good actor. I'd want to know if he has his own philosophy on how to be a good father. Plus, I'm very curious to know if he wants to be in any Korean movies in the future. I wonder if he knows any Korean actresses.

그는 유명한 할리우드 배우이며 또 다른 인기 배우 안젤리나 졸리와 결혼했습니다. 그들은 대단한 부부입니다. 만일 브래드 피트를 만나게 된다면, 저는 그가 어떻게 그의 직업과 가정을 모두 성공적으로 감당할 수 있는지 묻고 싶습니다. 그는 영화계에 몸을 담은 지가 정말 오래됐는데 여전히 아주 좋은 이미지를 갖고 있기 때문입니다. 그토록 오랫동안 명성을 유지할 수 있는 영화배우는 많지 않습니다. 또한 그는 안젤리나 졸리와의 슬하에 입양한 자녀 및 직접 낳은 아이들을 여러 명 두고 있습니다. 좋은 아빠의 역할이란 좋은 배우로 일하는 것만큼이나 어려운 일일 것입니다. 브래드 피트만의 좋은 자녀 교육 철학이 있는지 궁금합니다. 또한 저는 그가 향후 한국 영화에 출연하고 싶은지도 알고 싶습니다. 그가 알고 있는 한국 여배우도 있는지 궁금합니다.

| Closing |

Well, I guess these are a few things I would ask if I got to meet Brad Pitt!

음, 아마 브래드 피트를 만나면 위와 같은 질문들을 할 것 같아요!

More Questions

〈영화 관람〉에 관련하여 더 나올 수 있는 OPIc 질문들을 정리한 코너입니다. 질문에 대한 brainstorming을 해보세요.

1. Tell me about one of the actors/actresses in your country. Which movie was he/she in? What do you like about him/her?
2. Who is your favorite actor or director? Why do you like him/her?

앞에서 주어진 Model Answer을 바탕으로, 아래의 빈칸에 들어갈 수 있는 다양한 대체 가능한 어휘 및 표현들을 참고하여 학습자 본인만의 모범 답안을 직접 만들어보세요.

I Opening I

It would be amazing to meet my favorite movie star in person. If I had to choose, I would definitely say ⓐ_____. I'm sure you know who he is.

I My Favorite Movie Actor I

He is a famous Hollywood star and is married ⓑ_____. If I got to meet ⓐ_____, I would ask how he is able to manage both his career and his family successfully. I mean, he has had such a long career, and he still has a very nice image. Not many movie stars are able to maintain their fame for so long. Also, being a good father must be very challenging as well as being a good actor. I'd want to know if he has his own philosophy on how to be a good father. Plus, I'm very curious to know if he wants to be in any Korean movies in the future. I wonder if he knows any Korean actresses.

I Closing I

Well, I guess these are a few things I would ask if I got to meet ⓐ_____!

I Opening I It would be amazing to meet my favorite movie star in person. If I had to choose, I would definitely say ⓐ **Hugh Jackman**. I'm sure you know who he is.

I My Favorite Movie Actor I He is a famous Hollywood star and is married ⓑ **with two kids**. If I got to meet ⓐ **Hugh Jackman**, I would ask how he is able to manage both his career and his family successfully. I mean, he has had such a long career, and he still has a very nice image. Not many movie stars are able to maintain their fame for so long. Also, being a good father must be very challenging as well as being a good actor. I'd want to know if he has his own philosophy on how to be a good father. Plus, I'm very curious to know if he wants to be in any Korean movies in the future. I wonder if he knows any Korean actresses.

I Closing I Well, I guess these are a few things I would ask if I got to meet ⓐ **Hugh Jackman**!

본인이 만든 답안에 아래의 요소들이 포함되었는지 점검해 봅시다.

	Checklist
☐	좋아하는 영화배우 이름
☐	영화배우가 출연한 대표작
☐	영화배우가 좋은 이유 (매력)
☐	배우에 관해 궁금한 점

Unit 19 Night Clubbing 1

나이트 클럽 가기 1

Warm Up

A Guess the Question & Answer
사진을 보면서 예상 질문과 답변을 먼저 추측해 봅시다.

B Listen & Talk
친구와 클럽에 가는 것에 관한 대화를 먼저 연습해 봅시다.

🎧 04-05

A Hey, Taehui! You look gorgeous today! Are you going to a party?	**A** 이봐, 태희야! 오늘 정말 멋진데! 파티라도 가는 거야?
B Thanks. I'm going clubbing in Hongdae.	**B** 고마워. 오늘 홍대에 있는 클럽에 가.
A Wow. You all dressed up for clubbing. I thought you were going to a wedding banquet.	**A** 와. 클럽 가기에는 꽤나 차려 입었네. 결혼 피로연이라도 가는 줄 알았어.
B You're very kind to say that. I just don't know how to dress up properly for clubs.	**B** 그렇게 얘기해줘서 고마워. 난 클럽 갈 때 옷차림이 어때야 하는지도 잘 몰라.
A Which club are you going to tonight?	**A** 오늘 밤 어느 클럽 가는데?
B There's a new nightclub called Foxy. My friends and I are thinking of checking it out.	**B** '폭시'라는 새로 연 나이트클럽이 있어. 나랑 친구들이랑 가서 한 번 둘러보려고.
A That's a catchy name! So are you one of those foxy girls?	**A** 귀에 쏙 들어오는 이름이네! 그럼 너도 그 여우같은 여자들 중에 한 명인 거야?
B No way. I think they named it that way to attract more male customers.	**B** 아냐. 남자 고객들을 유치하려고 그런 이름을 지은 것 같아.
A Sure. Have fun tonight! But be careful of the guys. Remember that all men are wolves.	**A** 그래. 오늘 재미있게 놀아! 하지만 남자들은 조심하고. 남자는 다 늑대라는 거 명심해.

Vocabulary
gorgeous 아주 멋진, 아름다운 | **dress up for ~** ~를 위해 차려입다 | **banquet** 연회, 만찬 | **dress up properly** 알맞게 차려입다 | **check out** 확인하다, 알아보다 | **catchy** 귀에 쏙 들어오는 | **attract** 끌어들이다

Key Expressions

○━ 아래 제시된 각 expression의 구조를 이해하고, 자기만의 표현들을 생각해 봅시다.

Expression 1 **not ~ anymore:** 더 이상~하지 않다

저는 더 이상 클럽에 가지를 않습니다. → I **don't** go clubbing **anymore**.

내 아버지는 더 이상 담배를 피우지 않습니다. → My father **doesn't** smoke **anymore**.

그녀의 언니는 더 이상 캐나다에 살지 않습니다. → Her sister **doesn't** live in Canada **anymore**.

Expression 2 **be busy with ~:** ~로 인해 바쁘다

저는 일로 인해 바쁩니다. → **I'm busy with** work.

저희 팀은 월례 보고서 작성으로 인해 매우 바쁩니다.
→ Our team **is** very **busy with** the monthly report.

그 회사는 새로 출시된 상품으로 인해 바쁩니다.
→ The company **is busy with** the newly launched product.

Expression 3 **tune into ~:** ~로 채널을 맞추다, 열심히 듣다

저는 제가 좋아하는 음악은 어떤 것이든 듣습니다. → I **tune into** any kind of music I like.

제 남동생은 음악 프로그램을 보는 것을 좋아합니다. → My brother loves to **tune into** music programs.

전 세계 수백만 명의 시청자들은 매일 아침 그녀의 토크쇼를 시청합니다.
→ Millions of viewers around the world **tune into** her talk show every morning.

Expression 4 **dress up:** 옷을 차려 입다

나는 옷을 차려 입을 필요가 없다. → I don't need to **dress up**.

세진이는 결혼식이 있을 때마다 옷을 차려 입는 것을 좋아합니다.
→ Sejin loves to **dress up** whenever there's a wedding.

우리는 모두 사진 촬영을 하기 위해 남색 정장으로 차려 입었습니다.
→ We all **dressed up** in navy-blue suits for the photo shoot.

Expression 5 **on one's own:** 스스로, 혼자서, 독립적으로

저는 혼자서 기타치는 법을 배웠습니다. → I just learned how to play guitar **on my own**.

윤호는 독립해서 살고 있습니다. → Yunho is living **on his own**.

다른 사람에게 의존하기보다는 스스로 하는 것이 언제나 더 좋습니다.
→ It's always better to be **on your own** than to rely on another person.

Topic Question & Model Answer

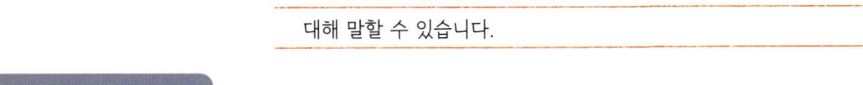

Topic Question

You indicated in the survey that you like dancing. Where do you go to dance? Do you go clubbing or take private lessons? Tell me where you like to dance.

당신은 설문조사에서 춤추기를 좋아한다고 했습니다. 당신은 주로 어디에 가서 춤을 추나요? 클럽에 가나요, 아니면 개인 교습을 받나요? 당신이 어디에 가서 춤추는 것을 좋아하는지 말해보세요.

TIP FOR THE OPIc

'클럽/나이트 가기' 및 '춤추기' 항목과 연계된 질문입니다. 내가 좋아하는 클럽, 춤을 배운 적이 있는지를 물어보고 있지만, 자주 가는 클럽의 위치 및 분위기를 언급하면서 왜 춤추는 것을 좋아하는지에 대해 얘기해도 됩니다. 댄스 수업을 받은 경험이 있다면 그것에 관한 사례를 언급할 수 있지만, 그렇지 않을 경우에는 어떻게 춤을 좋아하게 되었는지에 대해 말할 수 있습니다.

Model Answer

| Opening |

I used to go clubbing in the past, but I don't go anymore. I love dancing, but now I dance in my room.

저는 예전에는 주로 클럽에 가는 것을 좋아했는데, 더 이상은 가지 않습니다. 저는 춤추는 것을 좋아하지만, 이제는 제 방에서 춤을 춥니다.

| Dancing in the Room |

Since I'm busy with work, I don't have time to go clubbing. When I'm in my room, I tune into any kind of music I like and dance to the songs. I feel so free when I dance in my room. I don't need to dress up, and I have enough space for myself!

저는 일로 바쁘기 때문에, 클럽에 갈 시간이 없습니다. 제 방에 있을 때는, 좋아하는 음악을 틀고 노래에 맞춰 춤을 춥니다. 제 방에서 춤을 추면 정말 자유로운 기분입니다. 옷을 차려 입지 않아도 되고, 춤출 공간도 넉넉하니까요!

| How I Learned to Dance |

When I was younger, I took dance classes at a private institute for 6 months. It was fun, but I don't think it actually taught me how to dance. I just learned how to dance on my own.

제가 더 어릴 적에는 사설 학원에서 6개월 동안 댄스 수업을 받았습니다. 재미는 있었지만 그 수업을 듣고 춤을 배웠다고 생각하지는 않습니다. 그냥 혼자서 춤추는 법을 터득했습니다.

More Questions

〈클럽/나이트가기〉에 관련하여 더 나올 수 있는 OPIc 질문들을 정리한 코너입니다. 질문에 대한 brainstorming을 해보세요.

1. How do you dress up when you go clubbing? Is there any special dress code for clubbing in your country?
2. Tell me about your favorite club. Where's it located? What kinds of music does it play? How's it different from other clubs?
3. Is there any memorable person you've met at a club? Why was the person memorable?

On Your Own

앞에서 주어진 Model Answer을 바탕으로, 아래의 빈칸에 들어갈 수 있는 다양한 대체 가능한 어휘 및 표현들을 참고하여 학습자 본인만의 모범 답안을 직접 만들어보세요.

I Opening I

ⓐ_____. I love dancing, and

ⓑ_____.

I Dancing in the Club I

ⓒ_____.

ⓓ_____. I feel so free when I dance at the club. ⓔ_____!

I How I Learned to Dance I

When I was younger, I took dance classes at a private institute for 6 months. It was fun, but I don't think it actually taught me how to dance. I just learned how to dance on my own.

I Opening I ⓐ **I go clubbing every season**. I love dancing, and ⓑ **I like to go to a club where my close friend is a DJ**.

I Dancing in the Club I ⓒ **This club is called the Iron Club, and the people there are always in a party mood**. ⓓ **The DJ usually plays house music and electronic music**. I feel so free when I dance at the club. ⓔ **There is a nonsmoking area, so the air is not bad, and the room is quite spacious**!

I How I Learned to Dance I When I was younger, I took dance classes at a private institute for 6 months. It was fun, but I don't think it actually taught me how to dance. I just learned how to dance on my own.

본인이 만든 답안에 아래의 요소들이 포함되었는지 점검해 봅시다.

	Checklist
☐	어디서 춤추는 걸 좋아하는지
☐	자주 가는 클럽 이름
☐	왜 그곳에서 춤추는지
☐	누구와 춤추는 걸 좋아하는지
☐	어떻게 춤을 배웠는지
☐	춤출 때 듣는 음악

Unit 20 Night Clubbing 2

나이트 클럽 가기 2

Warm Up

A Guess the Question & Answer
사진을 보면서 예상 질문과 답변을 먼저 추측해 봅시다.

B Listen & Talk
춤추기를 좋아하는 친구에 관한 대화를 먼저 연습해 봅시다.

🎧 04-07

A Wow, look at your moves! Did you get trained in dancing?

B Nah, I just dance along to the songs I like.

A But that was really good! I had no idea you were that good at dancing. Since when did you start dancing?

B I think I was about 6. There was a family gathering, and everyone was sitting around the TV. I remember that I started dancing like the singer on the show.

A That must have been very cute of you. Where do you dance these days?

B I am on an amateur B-boy team at my school. We perform on stage once a month. That helps me a lot to keep up with my dance skills.

A Sounds cool! When is your next performance?

B Next Saturday at 2 p.m. in the Daehangno area. Are you going to come?

A I would love to.

A 와, 네 춤 동작 좀 봐! 춤 배운 적 있어?

B 아니, 그냥 좋아하는 노래 나오면 춤추는 정도야.

A 그런데 방금 정말 춤 잘 추더라! 네가 그렇게 춤을 잘 추는 줄은 몰랐어. 언제부터 춤추기 시작했어?

B 6살 때부터였던 것 같아. 가족 모임이 있었는데, 모두가 TV주변에 둘러앉았거든. 내 기억으로는 내가 쇼에 나오는 가수를 따라서 춤을 추기 시작했던 것 같아.

A 너 진짜 귀여웠겠다. 요새는 어디에서 춤 춰?

B 학교에 있는 아마추어 비보이 팀에 있어. 한 달에 한 번 무대에서 공연을 해. 그렇게 해서 춤을 더 연마하게 되는 것 같아.

A 멋진데! 다음 공연은 언제야?

B 다음 주 토요일 오후 2시, 대학로 근처에서 해. 너도 오려고?

A 응, 가고 싶어.

Vocabulary

get trained in ~ ~에 대한 훈련을 받다 | dance along to ~ ~에 맞춰 춤추다 | have no idea ~에 대해 전혀 알지 못하다 | family gathering 가족 모임 | perform on stage 무대 위에서 공연하다 | keep up with ~ ~를 유지하다, 지속하다

Key Expressions

아래 제시된 각 expression의 구조를 이해하고, 자기만의 표현들을 생각해 봅시다.

Expression 1   **months ago:** 몇 달 전에

저는 두 달 전에 클럽에 갔습니다. → I went clubbing 2 **months ago**.

그 책은 한 달 전에 출판되었습니다. → The book was published a **month ago**.

나는 그 가방이 상가에 진열되어 있는 것을 몇 달 전에 보았습니다.
→ I saw the bag displayed at the store several **months ago**.

Expression 2   **celebrate:** 기념하다, 축하하다

제 친구는 그녀의 생일 파티를 클럽에서 기념하고 싶어 했습니다.
→ My friend wanted to **celebrate** her birthday at the club.

그 커플은 10주년 결혼기념일을 그 섬에서 보냈습니다.
→ The couple **celebrated** their 10th wedding anniversary on the island.

한국에서는 12월 31일을 어떻게 기념하나요? → How do you **celebrate** New Year's Eve in Korea?

Expression 3   **all night:** 밤새도록

과제를 작성하느라 밤을 샜어. → I was up **all night** working on a paper.

저는 그 시험 준비를 위해 밤새도록 공부했습니다. → I studied for the exam **all night**.

그 소년들은 밤새도록 거리를 헤맸습니다. → The boys wandered through the streets **all night**.

Expression 4   **win ~ competition:** ~ 대회에서 우승을 하다

그녀는 그날 밤 춤 경연 대회에서 우승을 했습니다. → She **won** the dance **competition** that night.

그는 쇼트트랙 대회에서 우승했습니다. → He **won** the short-track **competition**.

우리는 최경주가 골프 대회에서 우승했다는 소식을 듣고 매우 기뻤습니다.
→ We were excited to hear that K. J. Choi **won** the golf **competition**.

Expression 5   **unforgettable:** 잊을 수 없는, 기억에 남는

그것은 정말 잊을 수 없는 경험이었습니다. → It was truly an **unforgettable** experience.

알래스카에서의 기억은 잊을 수가 없습니다. → My memories from Alaska are **unforgettable**.

그 재즈 콘서트는 제게 있어 잊을 수 없는 경험입니다.
→ The jazz concert was an **unforgettable** experience for me.

Topic Question & Model Answer

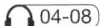 04-08

Topic Question

Tell me about your latest clubbing experience. What did you do at the club? Was there anything fun or interesting? Tell me everything that you did at the club that day.

당신이 최근에 갔던 클럽 경험에 대해 말해보세요. 클럽에서 무엇을 했나요? 재밌고 흥미로웠던 일은 없었나요? 그날 클럽에서 있었던 모든 일을 얘기해보세요.

TIP FOR THE OPIc

앞서 나온 '클럽/나이트 가기' 및 '춤추기' 항목과 연계된 콤보 질문입니다. 클럽이나 나이트에 갔을 때 기억에 남을 만한 특별한 상황이 있었는지에 대해 얘기할 수 있습니다. 만일 없다면, 마지막으로 언제, 누구와 함께 어느 곳에 갔는지를 말할 수 있습니다. 또한 어떤 점이 재미있었고, 옷차림은 어땠는지, 분위기는 어땠는지에 대해서 언급해도 좋습니다.

Model Answer

| Opening |

The last time I went clubbing was a couple of months ago.

제가 마지막으로 클럽에 간 것은 몇 달 전이었습니다.

| My Latest Clubbing Experience |

I don't really go clubbing anymore, but one of my friends wanted to celebrate her birthday at the club, so we went to one of the hottest clubs in town. It's called The Glam. It was a fun girls' night out. We dressed up and partied all night.

저는 더 이상 클럽에 가지는 않지만, 친구 한 명이 클럽에서 자신의 생일파티를 축하하고 싶어 했기 때문에 가장 뜬다는 클럽 중의 한 곳을 갔어요. 그곳은 '글램'이라는 곳이에요. 여자들끼리 신나게 밤새워 놀았습니다. 한껏 차려 입고 밤새도록 파티를 즐겼어요.

| A Fun Experience at the Club |

The most memorable thing that happened was that the birthday-girl won the dance competition that night. She won a free travel package to New York, and we all got jealous. It was truly an unforgettable experience.

그날 가장 기억에 남았던 일은 바로 생일을 맞았던 친구가 그날 밤 있었던 댄스 경연에서 우승을 한 것입니다. 그녀는 공짜 뉴욕 여행 패키지를 따냈고, 우리는 모두 부러워 어쩔 줄 몰랐습니다. 정말로 잊지 못할 경험이었습니다.

More Questions

〈클럽/나이트가기〉에 관련하여 더 나올 수 있는 OPIc 질문들을 정리한 코너입니다. 질문에 대한 brainstorming을 해보세요.

1. Suppose you meet a drunken person at a club. The person insists on dancing with you, but you don't want to. What would you do? Have you ever experienced something similar to this?
2. Is clubbing popular in your country? If yes, why do you think so?
3. When was the first time you went clubbing? Was it a special occasion? Who did you go with?

On Your Own

앞에서 주어진 Model Answer을 바탕으로, 아래의 빈칸에 들어갈 수 있는 다양한 대체 가능한 어휘 및 표현들을 참고하여 학습자 본인만의 모범 답안을 직접 만들어보세요.

I Opening I

The last time I went clubbing was ⓐ_____.

I My Latest Clubbing Experience I

I don't really go clubbing anymore, but one of my friends

ⓑ_____. It's called

ⓒ_____. It was a fun night. We dressed up and partied all night.

I A Fun Experience at the Club I

The most memorable thing that happened was that

ⓓ_____.

ⓔ_____. It was truly an

unforgettable experience.

I Opening I Well, the last time I went clubbing was ⓐ **last Friday**.

I My Latest Clubbing Experience I I don't really go clubbing anymore, but one of my friends ⓑ **was leaving the town, so we threw a farewell party at our favorite club**. It's called ⓒ **The Mystery**. It was a fun night. We dressed up and partied all night.

I A Fun Experience at the Club I The most memorable thing that happened was that ⓓ **we met some of our college friends there**. ⓔ **We all laughed and went to a nearby bar for some drinks**. It was truly an unforgettable experience.

본인이 만든 답안에 아래의 요소들이 포함되었는지 점검해 봅시다.

	Checklist
☐	언제 마지막으로 클럽에 갔는지
☐	누구와 함께 갔었는지
☐	그날 왜 클럽에 갔는지
☐	어느 클럽에 갔었는지
☐	클럽에서 생긴 특별한 사건

Unit 21 Text Messages 1

문자 메시지 1

Warm Up

A Guess the Question & Answer
사진을 보면서 예상 질문과 답변을 먼저 추측해 봅시다.

B Listen & Talk
문자로 소통하다가 발생한 오해에 관한 대화를 연습해 봅시다.

🎧 04-09

A Did you get my text message last night?	**A** 내가 어젯밤에 보낸 문자 받았어?
B Do you mean the one in which you asked if I'd like to go to the movies?	**B** 영화 보러 가자고 한 문자 말이야?
A Yes. I was wondering if you wanted to go or not.	**A** 응. 네가 같이 갈 건지 가지 않을 건지 궁금해서.
B I was waiting for the movie website link I asked you for. I didn't hear from you after the last message I sent you.	**B** 난 네가 영화 홈페이지 링크 보내주기만을 기다렸지. 마지막으로 문자 보내고 아직 답을 못 받았어.
A No way! I sent you the link right after I got your message!	**A** 그럴 리가! 네 문자 보고 바로 답장을 보냈는데?
B You did? Wait a minute. Oh, I am sorry. I didn't see that message in the box.	**B** 그랬어? 잠깐만. 어머나, 미안. 문자 온 걸 못 봤네.
A I should have called you instead of continuing to text you.	**A** 문자를 보내는 대신 전화를 할 걸 그랬어.
B Please call me if I don't get back to you soon enough the next time. I receive so many messages, including spam messages, and I sometimes miss the important ones.	**B** 다음에도 내가 한참 동안 답이 없으면 꼭 전화를 줘. 문자를 아주 많이 받는데 스팸 문자까지 오니까 가끔은 중요한 것들을 놓치게 돼.
A You are not the only one. That's why I don't trust communicating through text messages very much. It's a bit frustrating when some people mainly want to talk through Mamao Talk instead of making phone calls.	**A** 너만 겪는 일이 아니야. 그래서 난 문자로 이야기하는 것을 별로 신뢰하지 않아. 어떤 사람들은 전화하는 대신에 마마오톡으로만 이야기를 해서 답답해.
B I know. Short messages are fine for texting, but I will call a person if I want to have a conversation with him or her.	**B** 알아. 문자로는 간단한 얘기를 주고받는 건 좋은데 만일 상대방과 대화하고 싶으면 난 전화를 해.

Vocabulary

soon enough 얼마 지나지 않아 | **include** 포함하다 | **frustrating** 답답한, 절망적인

Key Expressions

아래 제시된 각 expression의 구조를 이해하고, 자기만의 표현들을 생각해 봅시다.

Expression 1 get a data connection: 데이터 연결을 하다

데이터 연결을 할 수 있으면 어디서나 문자 발송이 가능합니다.
→ As long as you can **get a data connection**, you can send texts from any location.

로비에서 무료로 데이터를 사용할 수 있나요? → Can I **get a** free **data connection** in the lobby?

우리는 배에서 데이터 연결을 하기 위해 특수 장치를 설치했습니다.
→ We installed a special device to **get a data connection** on the boat.

Expression 2 communication tool: 통신 수단

SMS는 중요한 커뮤니케이션 수단이 되었습니다. → SMS became an important **communication tool**.

SMS는 인기 있는 통신 수단입니다. → SMS is a popular **communication tool**.

온스타그램은 막강한 영향력을 가진 통신 수단입니다. → Onstagram is a powerful **communication tool**.

Expression 3 make arrangement: 일정을 잡다

그들은 짤막한 문자 메시지로 일정을 신속히 조정합니다.
→ They **make** quick **arrangements** by sending short messages.

일정을 잡기 전에 미리 알려 주십시오. → Please give us notice before you **make arrangements**.

그녀는 비서를 통해서만 일정을 잡습니다. → She **makes arrangements** only through her secretary.

Expression 4 face-to-face: 얼굴을 맞대고 하는

요즘 사람들은 얼굴을 맞대고 이야기하기보다 문자로 더 자주 대화합니다.
→ Nowadays, people text each other more often than to talk **face-to-face**.

저는 사람과 직접 만나서 얘기하는 것을 좋아하기 때문에 메신저를 사용하지 않습니다. → I don't use instant messenger programs because I like to have **face-to-face** communications.

저는 사람들이 직접 만나서 대화하는 것이 상호간의 오해를 줄이는 방법이라고 믿습니다.
→ I believe that **face-to-face** communications reduce misunderstandings between people.

Expression 5 balance (between) A and B: A와 B사이의 균형

문자로 대화하는 것과 직접 만나서 하는 커뮤니케이션 간의 균형을 맞추어야 합니다. → We need some **balance between** texting **and** having person-to-person communications.

저의 가장 큰 난관은 일과 가정 사이의 균형을 맞추는 것입니다.
→ My biggest challenge is **balancing** my work **and** family.

경제 성장과 환경 보호 사이의 균형을 이루는 것은 상당한 난제입니다.
→ How to **balance** economic growth **and** environmental sustainability is a huge dilemma.

Topic Question & Model Answer

 04-10

Topic Question

Lots of people send text messages these days. Text messaging has become a new communication method, replacing many old communication tools. What kinds of problems can text messages generate? 요즘 많은 사람들이 문자를 사용합니다. 문자는 새로운 커뮤니케이션 수단이 되었으며 전통적인 커뮤니케이션 방식을 대체하고 있습니다. 문자 사용으로 발생할 수 있는 문제점은 무엇인가요?

> **TIP FOR THE OPIc**
> OPIc에서는 특정 사안의 장단점 및 과거와 현재(전통적인 것과 새로운 것)의 차이점에 대해 서술하라는 질문이 종종 출제됩니다. 평소 경험한 것을 사례로 활용하여 답안을 구성하는 것이 좋습니다.

Model Answer

| Opening |

I see both pros and cons in text messaging. Text messaging is fast and easy to use. As long as you can get a data connection, you can send texts from any location. Naturally, texting has become one of the most common communication tools in the 21st century.

저는 문자 사용에 장단점이 모두 있다고 생각합니다. 문자 메시지는 빠르고 사용하기가 쉽습니다. 데이터 연결만 가능하면 어디서나 문자 발송이 가능합니다. 따라서 21세기에 들어서 문자는 가장 흔한 커뮤니케이션 수단이 되었습니다.

| Advantages and Disadvantages |

Texting is not only widely used between friends but is also used in the business world. SMS has become an important communication tool in lots of workplaces. Text messages are valued in the business world as people make quick arrangements by sending short messages. However, we should not overlook the negative aspects of sending text messages. Nowadays, people text each other more often than to talk face-to-face.

문자는 비단 친구들 사이에서만 사용되는 것이 아니라 직장에서도 사용됩니다. SMS는 많은 직장에서 중요한 커뮤니케이션 수단이 되었습니다. 문자 전송은 직장에서 중요하게 여겨지는데, 그 이유는 짤막한 문자를 통해 일정 조정을 빠르게 할 수 있기 때문입니다. 하지만 우리는 문자 사용의 이면을 간과해서는 안 됩니다. 요즘 사람들은 얼굴을 맞대고 이야기하기 보다 문자로 더 자주 대화합니다.

| Closing |

As a consequence, surveys show that people feel less connected to others and feel lonelier in the modern age. Though we see the benefits of text messaging, we need some balance between that and person-to-person communications.

그 결과, 설문조사에 의하면, 현대 사람들은 고립감과 외로움을 더 많이 느낀다고 합니다. 문자 사용의 혜택이 많지만, 사람들과 얼굴을 마주하고 대화하는 것과의 균형을 맞추면서 살아야겠습니다.

〈문자 메시지〉에 관련하여 더 나올 수 있는 OPIc 질문들을 정리한 코너입니다. 질문에 대한 brainstorming을 해보세요.

1. Lots of people communicate by sending text messages these days. What kinds problems can they generate? How can they be solved?

2. Why do you think text messaging has become an important communication tool? What are the benefits of sending text messages?

On Your Own

앞에서 주어진 Model Answer을 바탕으로, 아래의 빈칸에 들어갈 수 있는 다양한 대체 가능한 어휘 및 표현들을 참고하여 학습자 본인만의 모범 답안을 직접 만들어보세요.

| Opening |

I see both pros and cons in text messaging. Text messaging is fast and easy to use. As long as you can get a data connection, you can send texts from any location. Naturally, texting has become one of the most ⓐ_____ communication tools.

| Advantages and Disadvantages |

Texting is not only widely used between friends but is also used in the business world. SMS has been adapted as an important communication tool in ⓑ_____. Text messages are valued in the business world as people make quick arrangements by sending short messages. However, we should ⓒ_____ the negative aspects of sending text messages. Texting culture has been ⓓ_____.

| Closing |

As a consequence, surveys show that ⓔ_____. Though we see the benefits of text messaging, we need some balance between that and person-to-person communications.

| Opening | I see both pros and cons in text messaging. Text messaging is fast and easy to use. As long as you can get a data connection, you can send texts from any location. Naturally, texting has become one of the most ⓐ **popular** communication tools.

| Advantages and Disadvantages | Texting is not only widely used between friends but is also used in the business world. SMS has been adapted as an important communication tool in ⓑ **all kinds of industries.** Text messages are valued in the business world as people make quick arrangements by sending short messages. However, we should ⓒ **be aware of** the negative aspects of sending text messages. Texting culture has been ⓓ **keeping people from having in-depth conversations.**

| Closing | As a consequence, surveys show that ⓔ **text messages generate more miscommunications than face-to-face communications.** Though we see the benefits of text messaging, we need some balance between that and person-to-person communications.

본인이 만든 답안에 아래의 요소들이 포함되었는지 점검해 봅시다.

Checklist

☐	커뮤니케이션 수단의 과거와 현재
☐	문자 보내기의 특징
☐	문자 보내기의 영향력 증대
☐	문자 보내기의 장단점
☐	바람직한 커뮤니케이션에 대한 의견

Unit 22 Text Messages 2

문자 메시지 2

Warm Up

A Guess the Question & Answer
사진을 보면서 예상 질문과 답변을 먼저 추측해 봅시다.

B Listen & Talk
문자 소통의 한계에 관한 대화를 연습해 봅시다. 🎧 04-11

A Do you see your family often?	A 가족들을 자주 만나?
B I try to. I've been to Busan for every vacation so far. But I don't know if I can make it this time. I have to study English really hard.	B 그렇게 하려고 노력해. 이제까지는 방학 때마다 부산에 갔지. 하지만 이번에도 갈 수 있을지는 모르겠어. 영어 공부를 정말 열심히 해야 하거든.
A Oh, you can still go and see your family for a few days!	A 에이, 그래도 며칠 동안은 가족을 보러 다녀올 수 있잖아!
B I'm crossing my fingers. Do you talk to your parents often?	B 그러길 바라고 있어. 넌 부모님과 자주 대화하니?
A I think so. My mom sends me text messages every day. I miss her so much.	A 그런 편이야. 엄마가 매일 문자를 보내서. 엄마가 무척 그리워.
B I miss my mother, too. How often do you call your parents?	B 나도 그래. 넌 얼마나 자주 부모님께 전화를 드리니?
A Every other week. It's not easy because there are so many things going on.	A 격주로 드려. 일이 많아서 자주 전화 드리지는 못해.
B You should still try to talk to your parents more often. They must miss you a lot, too.	B 그래도 더 자주 부모님께 전화 드리도록 해. 네가 매우 보고싶으실 거야.
A I know. I wish I could spend quality time with my parents more often. I really miss talking to them face to face.	A 알아. 나도 부모님과 더 자주 알찬 시간을 보내고 싶어. 부모님 얼굴을 뵙고 얘기하던 때가 정말 그리워.
B Same here. My parents and I text each other very often, but texting is never as good as talking face to face.	B 나도 마찬가지야. 부모님과 나도 자주 문자를 주고받지만 그것이 결코 얼굴 보고 이야기하는 것만큼 좋지는 않지.
A Exactly. I just want to be next to my parents more often.	A 그러게 말이야. 부모님을 더 자주 뵐 수 있으면 좋겠어.

Vocabulary | **so far** 이제까지 | **cross one's fingers** 행운을 빌다 | **every other** 한 번 건너 한 번 | **quality time** 매우 알찬 시간 | **face to face** 얼굴을 마주보면서

Key Expressions

> 아래 제시된 각 expression의 구조를 이해하고, 자기만의 표현들을 생각해 봅시다.

Expression 1   **social life:** (대인 관계 등의) 사회 생활

딸은 학교 생활이나 대인 관계나 모두 좋다고 말했습니다.
→ The daughter said her school life and her **social life** were both good.

저는 사만다를 회사에서만 봅니다. 그녀의 사회 생활에 대해서는 모릅니다.
→ I only see Samantha at work. I don't know about her **social life**.

일을 마친 후 사교의 기회가 더 많으면 좋겠습니다. → I wish we had more of a **social life** after work.

Expression 2   **communicate through SMS:** 문자로 소통하다

SMS를 통해 대화하는 것으로는 충분하지 않습니다. → **Communicating through SMS** is not enough.

가끔은 문자로 이야기하는 것이 더 쉬울 수도 있습니다.
→ Sometimes, **communicating through SMS** can be easier.

문자로 비즈니스에 대해 소통하는 것은 종종 불확실한 결과를 낳습니다.
→ **Communicating through SMS** for business often results in uncertainty.

Expression 3   **nonverbal communication:** (눈맞춤, 제스쳐 등의) 비언어적 소통 방식

비언어적 의사소통을 이용하면 감정을 더 쉽게 속일 수가 있습니다.
→ It is easier to hide our true feelings by using **nonverbal communications**.

눈맞춤은 비언어적 의사소통의 핵심 형태입니다.
→ Eye contact is a key form of **nonverbal communications**.

비언어적 의사소통은 우리의 일상에서 매우 중요합니다.
→ **Nonverbal communication** is very important in our day to day lives.

Expression 4   **fake + 소유격 + feelings:** ~의 감정을 연출하다

우리는 언제든지 거짓으로 감정을 연출할 수 있습니다. → We can **fake our feelings** anytime.

자신의 감정을 꾸미는 사람들이 있다는 것은 불편한 일입니다.
→ It is uncomfortable that some people **fake their feelings**.

저는 그녀의 기분이 상하지 않도록 감정을 연출해야만 했습니다.
→ I had to **fake my feelings** to avoid making her feel worse.

Expression 5   **traditional method of:** 전통적인 방식의

그것이 바로 전통적인 의사소통 방식이 여전히 가치 있는 이유입니다.
→ That is why **traditional methods of** communication are still very important.

몇몇 사람들은 전통적인 요리법을 가치 있게 여깁니다.
→ Some people value **traditional methods of** cooking.

Topic Question & Model Answer

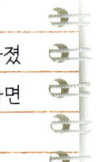

Topic Question

How is texting different from traditional ways of communication? Do you think texting can be as effective as talking on the phone? Why? 문자는 전통적인 커뮤니케이션 방식과 어떻게 다른가요? 당신은 문자가 전화 통화만큼의 효과적이라고 생각하나요? 왜 그렇게 생각하나요?

TIP FOR THE OPIc
위 질문은 휴대폰의 문자 기능을 통해 과거와 현재의 통신 문화가 어떻게 달라졌는지를 말해보라는 질문입니다. 문자로 소통하는 것의 한계를 느낀 적이 있다면 그러한 경험을 사례로 드는 것도 좋습니다.

Model Answer

| Opening |

I do not agree that texting can be as effective as talking on the phone. Texting can actually hinder people from having real conversations.

저는 문자로 대화하는 것이 전화 통화만큼 효과적이라고 생각하지 않습니다. 문자 사용은 도리어 진정한 대화에 방해가 된다고 생각합니다.

| Texting Messages is Imperfect |

Once, I read an article about a mother and her college daughter, who texted back and forth for hours. The daughter said her school life and her social life were both good. However, the mother discovered it later that her daughter had been bullied for a long time. This story shows that communicating through SMS is not enough. It is easier to hide our true feelings by using nonverbal communications. By texting and adding emoticons, we can fake our feelings anytime. This results in a miscommunication.

저는 언젠가 대학생 딸과 그 엄마가 몇 시간 동안 문자로 대화를 했다는 기사를 읽은 적이 있습니다. 그 딸은 문자로 학교 생활이나 대인 관계나 모두 좋다고 말했습니다. 하지만 나중에 그 엄마는 자신의 딸이 오랫동안 학우들로부터 괴롭힘을 당했다는 사실을 알게되었습니다. 이 이야기는 SMS를 통해 대화하는 것으로는 충분한 소통이 되지 않다는 점을 보여줍니다. 비언어적 의사소통을 사용함으로써 우리의 감정을 더 쉽게 속일 수 있습니다. 문자 메시지나 이모티콘을 사용함으로써 우리는 언제든지 가짜 감정을 연출할 수 있습니다. 그 결과 이는 잘못된 의사소통으로 이어집니다.

| Closing |

Communication is not only about letters and words. People also communicate by using gestures and facial expressions and by changing the tones of their voices. This is why traditional methods of communication are still so important in this digital age.

의사소통은 단순히 글자나 단어로만 이루어지는 것이 아닙니다. 사람들은 제스처나 얼굴 표정 그리고 목소리의 톤을 통해서도 의사소통을 합니다. 그것이 바로 현 디지털 시대에서도 전통적인 의사소통 방식이 여전히 가치 있는 이유입니다.

More Questions

〈문자 메시지〉에 관련하여 더 나올 수 있는 OPIc 질문들을 정리한 코너입니다. 질문에 대한 brainstorming을 해보세요.

1. You said you like to send text messages. What do you like about that? How often do you send text messages?
2. Texting messages became a popular communication method these days. What is your favorite method of communication?
3. Do you have an embarrassing experience related to text messaging? What happened? Give me all the details.

On Your Own

앞에서 주어진 Model Answer을 바탕으로, 아래의 빈칸에 들어갈 수 있는 다양한 대체 가능한 어휘 및 표현들을 참고하여 학습자 본인만의 모범 답안을 직접 만들어보세요.

| Opening |

I do not agree that texting can be as effective as talking on the phone. Texting can actually hinder people from having real conversations.

| Texting Messages is Imperfect |

ⓐ_____. ⓑ_____.

ⓒ_____. ⓓ_____.

ⓔ_____.

| Closing |

ⓕ_____ communication is not only about letters and words. People also communicate by using gestures and facial expressions and by changing the tones of their voices. That is why traditional methods of communication are still so important in this digital age.

| Opening | I do not agree that texting can be as effective as talking on the phone. Texting can actually hinder people from having real conversations.

| Texting Messages is Imperfect | ⓐ **When we have face-to-face conversations, we can focus on people while we are talking.** ⓑ **However, when you communicate by sending and receiving text messages, it is easier to get distracted.** ⓒ **For example, you can receive multiple messages from different people at the same time.** ⓓ **This may confuse you and may lead to miscommunications.** ⓔ **The worst-case scenario is that you may even send a text message to the wrong person.**

| Closing | ⓕ **But most of all, I believe that** communication is not only about letters and words. People also communicate by using gestures and facial expressions and by changing the tones of their voices. That is why traditional methods of communication are still so important in this digital age.

본인이 만든 답안에 아래의 요소들이 포함되었는지 점검해 봅시다.

	Checklist
☐	전통적인 커뮤니케이션 방식
☐	현대 사회의 커뮤니케이션 방식
☐	전화와 문자의 차이
☐	문자 보내기의 한계에 관한 사례
☐	문자 보내기에 대한 내 의견

Unit 23 Shopping 1

쇼핑하기 1

Warm Up

A Guess the Question & Answer
사진을 보면서 예상 질문과 답변을 먼저 추측해 봅시다.

B Listen & Talk
물건을 환불하는 상황에 관한 대화를 연습해 봅시다.

🎧 04-13

A Hi. How can I help you?

B Hi. I would like to return these pants.

A Do you have the receipt?

B Yes, here it is.

A Thank you. Can I ask why you want to return the pants?

B Well, I figured out that the fabric is of very poor quality.

A Oh, did you wash them in hot water by chance? It's written on the tag that these should only be washed in cold water.

B I used cold water. But after they were out in the sun for a few hours to dry, the color totally changed. They were blue, but now they look gray.

A Really? Oh, they look gray to me, too. I'm terribly sorry. I'll talk to my manager and take care of it.

B Do you have to talk to your manager? I don't have much time. I have to leave soon.

A She has to see the product. She will be here in a minute. I'm sorry about the inconvenience.

A 안녕하세요. 어떻게 도와 드릴까요?

B 안녕하세요. 이 바지를 환불하고 싶어요.

A 영수증 있으세요?

B 네, 여기 있어요.

A 감사합니다. 바지를 왜 환불하고 싶으신지 여쭤봐도 될까요?

B 음, 바지 재질이 아주 안 좋더라고요.

A 아, 혹시 뜨거운 물로 세탁하셨나요? 태그에 찬물로만 세탁해야 한다고 적혀 있거든요.

B 찬물로 세탁했어요. 하지만 몇 시간 동안 햇볕에 말린 다음에는 색깔이 완전히 변했어요. 파란색이었는데 이제는 회색처럼 보여요.

A 정말요? 어머, 제가 봐도 회색 같네요. 정말 죄송합니다. 매니저님께 말씀을 드려서 해결해 드릴게요.

B 매니저와 꼭 이야기를 나누셔야 하나요? 제가 시간이 없어서요. 곧 가봐야 해요.

A 제품을 직접 보셔야 하거든요. 금방 오실 거예요. 불편을 드려서 죄송합니다.

Vocabulary

figure out 발견하다, 해결하다 | **of poor quality** 품질이 나쁜 | **terribly** 매우, 끔찍하게 | **inconvenience** 불편

Key Expressions

아래 제시된 각 expression의 구조를 이해하고, 자기만의 표현들을 생각해 봅시다.

Expression 1   among the items: 물품들 중에

그 중에는 수면 양말 여섯 켤레도 포함되어 있었습니다.
→ **Among the items**, there were 6 pairs of bed socks.

물품 가운데 베개 커버도 있었습니다. → There were pillow covers **among the items**.

그 중에는 시댁 식구를 위한 초콜릿 상자도 포함되어 있었습니다.
→ **Among the items**, there were boxes of chocolate for my in-laws.

Expression 2   plenty of + 명사: 충분한 양의 ~

엄마께서 제 수면 양말을 여러 켤레 주문하셨습니다. → My mom ordered **plenty of** bed socks for me.

음식이 충분하니 마음껏 더 드세요. → We have **plenty of** food, so feel free to have some more.

방에 있는 모든 사람들에게 필요한 만큼의 베개가 있습니다.
→ There are **plenty of** pillows for everyone in the room.

Expression 3   at half price / half the price: 절반 가격의

더구나 엄마는 제가 지불한 가격의 절반밖에 되지 않는 가격으로 구입을 했습니다.
→ She even got them for only **half the price** that I had paid.

그 매장은 곧 문 닫을 예정이라 모든 제품을 절반 가격에 판매하고 있습니다.
→ The store is closing, so it is selling everything **at half price**.

붉은 선반에 있는 모든 제품은 내일까지 절반 가격으로 판매됩니다.
→ All of the items on the red shelf are available **at half price** till tomorrow.

Expression 4   be not a big deal: 대수로운 일이 아니다

대수로운 일은 아니었지만 저는 한 가지 교훈을 배웠습니다. → It **was not a big deal**, but I learned a lesson.

매일 아침 물탱크를 채우는 것은 대수로운 일이 아닙니다.
→ It **is not a big deal** to fill up the water tank every morning.

그녀에게 있어 매일 새벽 5시에 일어나는 것은 대수롭지 않은 일이었습니다.
→ Waking up at 5 a.m. every day **was not a big deal** for her.

Expression 5   think twice before: ~ 하기 전에 두 번 생각하다

상표를 떼어내기 전에 심사숙고 할 필요가 있습니다. → I shall **think twice before** I take off the tags.

제가 드리는 조언은 직장을 그만두기 전에 두 번 생각하라는 것입니다.
→ My advice is to **think twice before** you quit your job.

떠나기 전에 두 번 생각하십시오. → **Think twice before** leaving.

Topic Question & Model Answer

🎧 04-14

Topic Question

You indicated in the survey that you like to go shopping. When was the last time you got a refund for an item you purchased? What didn't you like about it? Did you face any problems when you were returning the item?

당신은 설문조사에서 쇼핑하기를 좋아한다고 했습니다. 당신이 마지막으로 제품을 구매하고 환불한 것이 언제였나요? 당신은 왜 그 제품이 마음에 들지 않았나요? 제품을 환불하면서 겪은 어려움은 없었나요?

TIP FOR THE OPIc

환불 경험에 관한 질문입니다. 오프라인 쇼핑뿐만 아니라 온라인 쇼핑, 홈쇼핑 등을 통해 구매했던 물건을 환불한 사례에 대해 얘기해줍니다. 어떠한 물건을 왜 (충동 구매, 기대와 다른 상품 도착, 품질이 좋지 못해서 등의 이유로) 환불하게 되었고 그 절차는 어떠했는지 등에 대해 설명합니다.

Model Answer

| Opening |

A couple of weeks ago, I visited K-Mart to get a few winter items. Among the items, I got 6 pairs of bed socks. They were cute, fluffy, and comfortable.

몇 주 전, 저는 겨울철에 필요한 것을 몇 가지 사기 위해서 K마트에 갔습니다. 그 가운데는 수면 양말 여섯 켤레도 포함되어 있었습니다. 양말은 귀엽고 푹신하고 착용감이 편했습니다.

| Refund Experience |

However, when I got home, my mom told me that she had ordered plenty of bed socks for me. She knew that I had needed extra pairs of bed socks. She even got them for only half the price that I had paid. Since they were gifts from my mom, I decided to get a refund on the ones that I bought. Then, I remembered that I had taken off the tags on all of my socks. I had my receipt, but there was no way to get a refund. I still went back to the store and asked a staff member for a refund. The answer was, "Sorry, but no."

그런데 집에 도착하니까 엄마께서 제 수면 양말을 여러 켤레 주문해놓으셨다고 말씀하셨습니다. 엄마는 제게 수면 양말이 더 필요하다는 걸 알고 있었습니다. 더구나 제가 지불한 가격의 절반밖에 되지 않는 가격으로 양말을 구입하셨습니다. 그 양말들은 엄마의 선물이었기 때문에 저는 제가 산 양말을 환불하기로 결심했습니다. 그때, 제가 양말에 붙어있던 상표를 모두 떼어냈다는 점이 기억났습니다. 저는 영수증을 가지고 있었지만 환불할 방법이 없었습니다. 그래도 저는 다시 매장에 가서 직원에게 환불할 수 있는지 물어봤습니다. 돌아온 대답은 "죄송하지만 안 됩니다."였습니다.

| Closing |

Well, it was not a big deal, but I learned a lesson: I shall think twice before I take the tags off items I purchase.

뭐 그리 대수로운 일은 아니었지만 저는 한 가지 교훈을 얻었습니다: 제품 구매 후 상표를 떼어내기 전에는 심사숙고할 필요가 있다는 것입니다.

More Questions

〈쇼핑하기〉에 관련하여 더 나올 수 있는 OPIc 질문들을 정리한 코너입니다. 질문에 대한 brainstorming을 해보세요.

1. When was the last time you went shopping? Where did you go to? Who did you go with? What did you buy?
2. Do you have an unforgettable shopping experience? When was it? Why is it so memorable?
3. You said you like shopping. Where do you usually go shopping? Why do you like that place?

On Your Own

앞에서 주어진 Model Answer을 바탕으로, 아래의 빈칸에 들어갈 수 있는 다양한 대체 가능한 어휘 및 표현들을 참고하여 학습자 본인만의 모범 답안을 직접 만들어보세요.

I Opening I

A couple of weeks ago, I visited ⓐ_____ to get a few ⓑ_____. Among the items, I got ⓒ_____. They were ⓓ_____.

I Refund Experience I

However, when I got home, my ⓔ_____ told me that ⓕ_____ had ordered plenty of ⓖ_____ for ⓗ_____. ⓘ_____ knew that I ⓙ_____ extra ⓚ_____. ⓛ_____ even got them for only half the price that I had paid. Since they were gifts from my ⓔ_____, I decided to get a refund on the ones that I bought. Then, I remembered that I had taken the off the tags on all of the ⓒ_____. I had my receipt, but there was no way to get a refund. I still went back to the store and asked a staff member for a refund. The answer was, "Sorry, but no."

I Closing I

Well, it was not a big deal, but I learned a lesson: I shall think twice before I take the tags off items I purchase.

I Opening I A couple of weeks ago, I visited ⓐ **Furniture World** to get a few ⓑ **items for my new bedroom**. Among the items, I got ⓒ **pillow covers**. They were ⓓ **silky and comfortable**.

I Refund Experience I However, when I got home, my ⓔ **wife** told me that ⓕ **she** had ordered plenty of ⓖ **pillow covers** for ⓗ **us**. ⓘ **She** knew that I ⓙ **had wanted** extra ⓚ **pillow covers**. ⓛ **She** even got them for only half the price that I had paid. Since they were gifts from my ⓔ **wife**, I decided to get a refund on the ones that I bought. Then, I remembered that I had taken the off the tags on all of the ⓒ **pillow covers**. I had my receipt, but there was no way to get a refund. I still went back to the store and asked a staff member for a refund. The answer was, "Sorry, but no."

I Closing I Well, it was not a big deal, but I learned a lesson: I shall think twice before I take the tags off items I purchase.

본인이 만든 답안에 아래의 요소들이 포함되었는지 점검해 봅시다.

Checklist
☐ 언제 마지막으로 환불했는지
☐ 어디에서 구입했던 제품인지
☐ 어떤 제품을 환불했는지
☐ 왜 환불했는지
☐ 환불 과정에 대한 설명

Unit 24 Shopping 2

쇼핑하기 2

Warm Up

A Guess the Question & Answer
사진을 보면서 예상 질문과 답변을 먼저 추측해 봅시다.

B Listen & Talk
쇼핑 문화의 다양성에 관한 대화를 연습해 봅시다.

🎧 04-15

A The lines are so long!
B Why don't we use the self-checkout counter?
A What is the self-checkout counter?
B It is a machine that helps you with the purchasing process. You can scan the products that you are purchasing and also pay for them by yourself.
A Wow. I've never done that before. Yeah, the lines are so long. We can try the self-checkout machine.
B Isn't the self-checkout service common in Korea?
A No, not as far as I know. Some stores might offer it, but I've never seen it before.
B I see. In fact, I have noticed that shopping in Korea and the States is a bit different.
A I agree. I don't see many free samples being given out in American stores.
B No, it is not common here. I miss the free samples you can get in Korean stores. I never had to feel guilty for eating free samples again and again.

A 줄이 엄청 길어!
B 셀프 계산대를 사용하는 것이 어때?
A 셀프 계산대가 뭐야?
B 계산 과정을 도와주는 기계야. 사려고 하는 제품을 직접 스캔해서 혼자서 결제를 할 수 있지.
A 와. 난 한 번도 해본 적이 없어. 그러게, 줄이 너무 길다. 셀프 계산대를 이용하면 되겠다.
B 한국에서는 셀프 계산 서비스가 흔치 않니?
A 응, 내가 아는 한 그렇지 않아. 셀프 계산대가 설치된 곳이 있을지도 모르지만 난 한 번도 보지 못했어.
B 그렇구나. 사실은 나도 한국과 미국의 쇼핑이 약간 다르다는 걸 깨닫고 있어.
A 나도 그래. 미국 매장에서는 시식 코너를 잘 못 찾겠더라고.
B 맞아, 여기서는 잘 없어. 한국 매장의 시식 문화가 그리워. 아무리 많이 시식해도 미안한 마음이 들지 않았지.

Vocabulary self-checkout machine 셀프 계산대 (고객이 직원의 도움 없이 직접 물건을 계산할 수 있도록 만든 기계) | scan 스캔하다 | purchasing process 구매 과정 | guilty 죄책감

Key Expressions

아래 제시된 각 expression의 구조를 이해하고, 자기만의 표현들을 생각해 봅시다.

Expression 1   a slight difference between: ~ 사이의 근소한 차이

한국과 미국의 장보기에는 약간의 차이가 있습니다.
→ There is **a slight difference between** grocery shopping in Korea and in the U.S.

저는 이 두 개의 무늬에서 작은 차이점을 발견했습니다.
→ I found **a slight difference between** these two patterns.

저는 진짜 보석과 가짜 보석에서 약간의 차이점을 발견했습니다.
→ I spotted **a slight difference between** the real jewel and the fake one.

Expression 2   usually happen in: 주로 ~에서 발생하다

이러한 일은 주로 정육 코너에서 발생합니다. → This **usually happens in** the meat department.

그러한 사고는 주로 직장에서 일어납니다. → Those kind of accident **usually happens in** workplace.

그 질병은 주로 어린 아이들에게 발생합니다. → The disease **usually happens in** young children.

Expression 3   go to a pharmacy: 약국에 가다

한국에서는 약국에 가야 합니다. → In Korea, you have to **go to a pharmacy**.

저는 이 처방전 때문에 약국에 가야만 합니다. → I need to **go to a pharmacy** for this prescription.

병원에 가지 말고 약국에 가십시오. → **Go to a pharmacy** instead of seeing a doctor.

Expression 4   self-checkout service: 셀프 계산 서비스

뿐만 아니라 미국의 식료품 매장에서는 셀프 계산 서비스가 보편화되었습니다.
→ In addition, **self-checkout service** is common in American grocery stores.

구매하는 제품이 몇 개 안 될 경우에는 셀프 계산 서비스가 편리합니다.
→ **Self-checkout service** is convenient when you only have a few items.

셀프 계산 서비스는 주유소 및 공항에서도 이용되고 있습니다.
→ **Self-checkout service** is also used at gas stations and airports.

Expression 5   scan barcode(s): 바코드를 스캔하다

셀프 서비스 코너는 상품의 바코드를 직접 스캔할 수 있는 코너입니다.
→ The self-service section is where you can **scan the barcodes** of the products by yourself.

요즘은 스마트폰으로 바코드를 스캔할 수 있습니다.
→ These days, you can **scan barcodes** with your smartphone.

저는 오늘 아침 방문객 명찰에 있는 바코드를 70개 정도 스캔했습니다.
→ I **scanned** around 70 **barcodes** on visitors' name tags this morning.

Topic Question & Model Answer

Topic Question

I'd like to know about grocery shopping in your country. How is shopping for groceries in your country different than shopping for groceries in other countries? Compare them in detail.

당신이 사는 나라의 장보기에 대해 알고 싶습니다. 당신 나라의 식료품 쇼핑은 다른 나라의 식료품 쇼핑과 어떻게 다른가요? 자세히 비교해보세요.

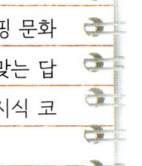

TIP FOR THE OPIc

한국의 쇼핑 문화를 다른 나라와 비교하라는 질문입니다. 다른 나라의 쇼핑 문화를 잘 모르더라도 한국 쇼핑 문화의 특징을 잘 정리해주면 질문 의도에 맞는 답안이 완성될 수 있습니다. 떨이 제품, 명동/동대문의 할인 행사, 다양한 시식 코너 등이 한국의 흥미로운 쇼핑 문화에 포함될 것입니다.

Model Answer

| Opening |

I only know about grocery shopping in Korea and the United States. There is a slight difference between shopping for groceries in Korea and shopping for groceries in the U.S.

저는 한국과 미국의 장보기에 대해서만 알고 있습니다. 한국의 식료품 쇼핑은 미국의 식료품 쇼핑과 약간의 차이가 있습니다.

| Different Shopping Culture |

First of all, in Korea, there are many people yelling at customers to buy their products. This usually happens in the meat department or if there is a special sale on a certain item. Another difference is that in the U.S., you can buy medicine like aspirin and stomach medicine at grocery stores. In Korea, you have to go to a pharmacy. In addition, self-service is common at U.S. grocery stores while it is not very popular in Korea. The self-service section is where you can scan the barcodes of the products yourself and pay for them instead of going to a cashier.

먼저 한국에서는 식료품 매장에 가면 장을 보러 온 사람들에게 큰 소리로 물건을 사라고 하는 사람들이 많습니다. 이는 주로 정육점 코너나 반짝 세일이 진행될 경우에 그렇습니다. 또 다른 점은 미국에서는 아스피린이나 배탈 났을 때 먹는 약 등을 식료품 가게에서 구입할 수 있습니다. 한국에서는 약국에 가야만 약을 살 수가 있습니다. 뿐만 아니라 미국에서는 셀프 서비스가 보편화되었는데 한국에서는 별로 사용되지 않고 있습니다. 셀프 서비스 코너는 점원의 도움 없이 고객이 직접 바코드를 스캔하여 결제를 하는 곳입니다.

| Closing |

These are a few of the differences between grocery shopping in Korea and in the U.S.

이러한 점이 한국과 미국의 장보기의 몇 가지 차이점입니다.

More Questions

〈쇼핑하기〉에 관련하여 더 나올 수 있는 OPIc 질문들을 정리한 코너입니다. 질문에 대한 brainstorming을 해보세요.

1. Tell me about your shopping habits. Are you an impulsive shopper or not? Why do you think so?
2. Online shopping mall is increasing and is very popular. What are the pros and cons of online shopping malls?
3. Do you like to go shopping with your friends or by yourself? Why do you prefer shopping like that?

On Your Own

앞에서 주어진 Model Answer을 바탕으로, 아래의 빈칸에 들어갈 수 있는 다양한 대체 가능한 어휘 및 표현들을 참고하여 학습자 본인만의 모범 답안을 직접 만들어보세요.

I Opening I

I only know about grocery shopping in Korea and the United States. There ⓐ_____ between shopping for groceries in Korea and shopping for groceries in the U.S.

I Different Shopping Culture I

First of all, in Korea, there are many people yelling at customers to buy their products. This usually happens ⓑ_____. Another difference is that in the U.S., ⓒ_____. ⓓ_____. In Korea, ⓔ_____. In addition, self-service is common in U.S. grocery stores while it is not very popular in Korea. The self-service section is where you can scan the barcodes of the products yourself and pay for them instead of going to the cashier.

I Closing I

These are a few of the differences between grocery shopping in Korea and in the U.S.

I Opening I I only know about grocery shopping in Korea and the United States. There ⓐ **are some differences** between shopping for groceries in Korea and shopping for groceries in the U.S.

I Different Shopping Culture I First of all, in Korea, there are many people yelling at customers to buy their products. This usually happens ⓑ **when there is a big sale in the store**. Another difference is that in the U.S., ⓒ **the price you see on the tag is not the price that you pay**. ⓓ **Sales tax is charged on each product**. In Korea, ⓔ **the tax is already included in the price that is printed on the tag**. In addition, self-service is common in U.S. grocery stores while it is not very popular in Korea. The self-service section is where you can scan the barcodes of the products yourself and pay for them instead of going to the cashier.

I Closing I These are a few of the differences between grocery shopping in Korea and in the U.S.

본인이 만든 답안에 아래의 요소들이 포함되었는지 점검해 봅시다.

Checklist
☐ 한국의 장보기 문화의 특징
☐ 나의 경험 및 주변 사례
☐ 외국의 장보기 문화의 특징
☐ 나의 경험 혹은 TV 및 기사에서 본 사례
☐ 장보기 문화의 차이점에 대한 생각

Unit 25 Home-Improvement Project 1
주거 개선 1

Warm Up

A Guess the Question & Answer
사진을 보면서 예상 질문과 답변을 먼저 추측해 봅시다.

B Listen & Talk
집의 창문이 깨지는 사고에 관한 대화를 먼저 연습해 봅시다.

🎧 04-17

A Oh, no! Watch out!	**A** 어머, 안 돼! 조심해요!
B What's going on?	**B** 무슨 일이야?
A I think somebody hit the window with a ball.	**A** 누가 공으로 창문을 친 것 같아요.
B Look at this mess! What should we do?	**B** 이 난장판을 봐! 우리 어떡하지?
A Call the police. We've got to catch whoever did this.	**A** 경찰을 불러요. 누가 이렇게 한 건지 붙잡아야만 해요.
B Honey, I see a boy with a blue cap running down the road!	**B** 여보, 길을 뛰어 내려가는 저 파란색 모자 쓴 아이가 보여요!
A Go after him! You can catch him.	**A** 그 아이를 쫓아가요! 당신이 붙잡을 수 있잖아요.
B He's just a little kid. He probably didn't know what he was doing.	**B** 그냥 어린 아이일 뿐이야. 자기가 무슨 일을 하는 건지 모르고 그랬을 거야.
A Darn. What should we do? There are pieces of broken glass everywhere.	**A** 이런. 어떻게 하죠? 여기 저기 깨진 유리 파편이 가득해요.
B Calm down, sweetheart. Let's call the repair shop. They will fix it right away.	**B** 진정해, 여보. 수리점에 전화합시다. 바로 고쳐줄 거야.

Vocabulary
mess 엉망인 상황, 난장판 | **run down the road** 길을 따라 뛰어 내려가다 | **go after someone** ~를 쫓아가다 | **darn** 영어로 '빌어먹을'을 순화한 표현 | **repair shop** 수리 센터

Key Expressions

아래 제시된 각 expression의 구조를 이해하고, 자기만의 표현들을 생각해 봅시다.

Expression 1 — call + 사람 + to ask ~: ~를 물어보기 위해 전화하다

당신이 와서 창문을 수리할 수 있는지 물어보려고 전화했습니다.
→ I'm **calling to ask** if you can come and fix the window.

유진이는 그 여행에 관해 물어보기 위해 저에게 전화했습니다. → Yujin **called me to ask** about the trip.

인국은 의사에게 전화해서 그의 눈에 아무 이상이 없는지를 물었습니다.
→ Ingook **called the doctor to ask** if there were any problem with his eyes.

Expression 2 — be shattered: 산산조각 나다, 산산이 부서지다

제 방에 있는 창문이 오늘 아침 산산조각이 났습니다.
→ The window in my room **was shattered** this morning.

그에 대한 환상이 다 깨져 버렸다. → All my illusion about him **were shattered**.

자정이 지나자 새 삶에 대한 신데렐라의 꿈은 산산이 부서졌습니다.
→ Cinderella's hopes for a new life **were shattered** after midnight.

Expression 3 — need + 목적어 + 과거분사: ~이 필요하다, ~이 되어야 한다

저는 그 창문의 수리가 필요합니다. → I **need** the window **repaired**.

셔츠의 사이즈는 정확히 측정되어야 합니다. → The size of the shirt **needs to be measured** correctly.

제 고객은 내일까지 그 업무의 완료가 필요합니다.
→ My client **needs** the work **to be done** by tomorrow.

Expression 4 — in an hour: 한 시간 안에

당신은 한 시간 안에 올 수 있나요? → Would you be able to come **in an hour**?

대표단은 한 시간 안에 도착합니다. → The delegation is arriving **in an hour**.

우리는 한 시간 안에 공항에 도착할 것입니다. → We will reach the airport **in an hour**.

Expression 5 — be replaced: 대체되다, 교체되다

창문 전체가 교체되어야 합니다. → The entire window needs to **be replaced**.

죄송하지만 저희 생각에는 코치가 교체되어야 할 것 같습니다.
→ I'm sorry, but we think the coach needs to **be replaced**.

요즘에는 신문이 인터넷의 기사로 대체되고 있습니다.
→ Newspapers are **being replaced** by stories on the Internet.

Topic Question & Model Answer

 04-18

Topic Question

Here is a situation you have to act out. Your window is broken. Call the repair shop and ask 3 to 4 questions to the staff for help.

여기 상황극이 있습니다. 당신의 창문이 깨졌습니다. 수리점에 전화해서 직원에게 3~4가지 질문을 하여 도움을 요청하세요.

TIP FOR THE OPIc

'주거 개선' 항목과 연계된 롤플레이 질문입니다. 집안의 그릇이나 창문이 깨지는 일은 흔합니다. 창문이 깨지면 수리점에 전화하여 어떻게 일어난 상황인지, 어느 정도로 심각한 상황인지를 설명하고 방문수리를 요청해 보세요. 긴급하고 당황한 목소리로 말하면 더욱 전달력이 높아지고 등급에도 긍정적인 영향을 끼칠 수 있습니다.

Model Answer

| Opening |

Hello. Is this the ABC Repair Shop? Hi. My name is Jiyoung, and I live at Hangook apartment in Suwon.

안녕하세요, ABC 수리점인가요? 네, 제 이름은 지영이고요, 수원에 있는 한국 아파트에 살아요.

| Broken Window at Home |

I'm calling to ask if you can come to fix the window in my apartment. The window in my room was shattered this morning. Somebody's ball hit the window and shattered the entire glass. I wiped the floor and vacuumed, so the floor is clean, so I just need the window repaired.

제 집 창문 좀 방문 수리해달라고 전화 드렸어요. 오늘 아침 제 방 창문이 산산조각 났어요. 누군가의 공이 창문을 쳤는데 유리 전체가 완전히 부서졌어요. 제가 바닥도 닦고 청소기로 정리했기 때문에 바닥은 깨끗하니까, 창문만 수리해주시면 돼요.

| Request to the Repair Shop |

Would you be able to come in an hour? Good. It looks like the entire window needs to be replaced. The width is 2 meters, and the height is 1 meter. How many staffers can I expect? Two? Okay. What's the price for the repairs? 30,000 won? I got it. Great. I'll see you in about an hour! Oh, my number is 010-1122-4555.

1시간 안으로 방문 가능하신가요? 좋아요. 창문 전체를 새것으로 교체해야겠어요. 가로는 2m, 세로는 1m에요. 몇 분이나 오시죠? 2명이요? 알겠어요. 수리비용은 얼마인가요? 30,000원이요? 그래요. 좋아요, 그럼 1시간 안에 뵙겠습니다! 아, 제 전화번호는 010-1122-4555에요.

| Closing |

Thank you. See you soon. Bye.

감사합니다. 곧 뵐게요. 안녕히 계세요.

More Questions

〈주거 개선〉에 관련하여 더 나올 수 있는 OPIc 질문들을 정리한 코너입니다. 질문에 대한 brainstorming을 해보세요.

1. You indicated in the survey that you do household chores. What kinds of household chores do you do?

2. Do you often do the household chores? When was the last time you did the household chores? What did you like about doing them?

On Your Own

앞에서 주어진 Model Answer을 바탕으로, 아래의 빈칸에 들어갈 수 있는 다양한 대체 가능한 어휘 및 표현들을 참고하여 학습자 본인만의 모범 답안을 직접 만들어보세요.

| Opening |

Hello. Is this the ABC Repair Shop? Hi. My name is ⓐ_____, and I live at ⓑ_____ in ⓒ_____.

| Broken Window at Home |

I'm calling to ask if you can come to fix the window in my apartment. The window in my room was shattered this morning. ⓓ_____.

| Request to the Repair Shop |

Would you be able to come in an hour? Good. It looks like the entire window needs to be replaced. The width is 2 meters, and the height is 1 meter. How many staffers can I expect? Two? Okay. What's the price for the repairs? 30,000 won? I got it. Great. I'll see you in about an hour! Oh, my number is 010-1122-4555.

| Closing |

Thank you. See you soon. Bye.

| Opening | Hello. Is this the ABC Repair Shop? Hi. My name is ⓐ **Misook**, and I live at ⓑ **Shilla Apartment** in ⓒ **Sadangdong**.

| Broken Window at Home | I'm calling to ask if you can come to fix a window in my apartment. The window in my room was shattered this morning. ⓓ **There was a small crack in the window, and the storm last night was too strong for the window to stand**.

| Request to the Repair Shop | Would you be able to come in an hour? Good. It looks like the entire window needs to be replaced. The width is 2 meters, and the height is 1 meter. How many staffers can I expect? Two? Okay. What's the price for the repairs? 30,000 won? I got it. Great. I'll see you in about an hour! Oh, my number is 010-1122-4555.

| Closing | Thank you. See you soon. Bye.

본인이 만든 답안에 아래의 요소들이 포함되었는지 점검해 봅시다.

Checklist
☐ 전화 걸 때 인사말
☐ 상대방 확인 및 신분 밝히기
☐ 전화 건 목적 (수리 요청)
☐ 무엇을, 왜 수리할지 설명
☐ 관련 사항 문의
☐ 방문 시간 및 장소 확인
☐ 마무리 인사

Unit 26 Home-Improvement Project 2

주거 개선 2

Warm Up

A Guess the Question & Answer
사진을 보면서 예상 질문과 답변을 먼저 추측해 봅시다.

B Listen & Talk
창문 수리에 관한 대화를 연습해 봅시다.

🎧 04-19

A ABC Repair Shop?

B Yes, ma'am.

A Hi. I'm Mrs. Han. I live on 14th Street. I spoke to one of your staff members, manager Park, an hour ago. He said he would come to fix my window, but now he says he can't!

B Mrs. Han, we are very sorry. But manager Park has an urgent family matter. Please understand.

A What about us? My living room window is completely shattered. There's a storm coming tonight! Didn't you hear the weather forecast?

B Hold on, ma'am. I'll find someone else to visit you. Oh, we are able to send you a team by 4 p.m. Is that okay?

A Fine. Thanks for your help. Bye.

A ABC 수리 센터인가요?

B 네, 그렇습니다.

A 안녕하세요, 저는 14번가에 사는 한씨 부인이에요. 한 시간 전에 박팀장이라는 직원 분과 통화를 했었어요. 그 분이 저희 집에 와서 창문을 고쳐주기로 했는데, 이제 와서 못하겠다고 하네요!

B 부인, 정말 죄송합니다. 하지만 박팀장은 좀 다급한 가족 문제가 생겼어요. 양해 부탁 드립니다.

A 그럼 저희는 어떡하라고요? 저희 집 거실 창문이 산산조각이 났단 말이에요. 오늘 밤 태풍이 상륙한다고요! 일기 예보 못 들으셨어요?

B 잠시만요, 부인. 다른 분을 보낼 수 있는지 알아봐 드릴게요. 아, 오후 4시까지 사람들을 보내드릴 수 있겠네요. 괜찮으시겠어요?

A 그래요. 감사합니다. 안녕히 계세요.

Vocabulary | **urgent** 다급한, 시급한 | **family matter** 가족 문제 | **shattered** 산산조각 난 | **weather forecast** 기상 예보

Key Expressions

아래 제시된 각 expression의 구조를 이해하고, 자기만의 표현들을 생각해 봅시다.

Expression 1   inform + 사람 + that/about ~: 누구에게 ~을 알려주다

제가 오늘 아침 저희 집 창문이 산산조각 났다고 알려드렸었는데요.
→ I **informed you that** my window was shattered this morning.

그 남자는 우리에게 잠재적인 사이버 공격에 대해 귀띔해줬습니다.
→ The man **informed us about** the potential cyberattack.

그들의 재정적 상황에 대해서 좀 알려주시겠습니까?
→ Could you please **inform me about** their financial status?

Expression 2   completely: 완전히

제 창문은 완전히 부서졌습니다. → My window was **completely** shattered.

제 생각에는 당신이 제 요지를 완전히 잘못 이해하고 있는 것 같습니다.
→ I think you are **completely** misunderstanding my point.

위원회는 모든 정치적인 행위를 완전히 금지하였습니다.
→ The committee **completely** banned any political actions.

Expression 3   every part of ~: ~의 모든 부분

유리 전체가 완전히 깨졌습니다. → **Every part of** the glass is gone.

우리 가족은 그녀 삶의 모든 부분을 축복했습니다. → My family blessed **every part of** her life.

우리는 펜트하우스의 모든 부분이 맘에 들었습니다. → We liked **every part of** the penthouse.

Expression 4   nowhere else: 다른 어디에도 없는

나는 갈 곳이 아무 데도 없다. → I have **nowhere else** to go.

보물들을 숨길 곳이 다른 어디에도 없습니다. → There is **nowhere else** to hide the jewels.

그 가족이 하룻밤을 보낼 곳은 다른 어디에도 없었습니다.
→ The family had **nowhere else** to spend the night.

Expression 5   a good deal: 상호 만족하는 거래

그럼 그렇게 하시죠. → It's **a good deal** then.

제 생각에 그 승용차가 2만 달러면 좋은 가격 같습니다. → I think $20,000 for the sedan is **a good deal**.

내 상사는 출장 기간 동안에 좋은 거래를 성사시켰습니다.
→ My boss made **a good deal** during her business trip.

Topic Question & Model Answer

🎧 04-20

Topic Question

A problem occurred. The window repairman cannot come over to your place until next week. Call the repair shop and tell the staff member why he or she has to fix your window as soon as possible. 문제가 발생했습니다. 창문 수리점 직원이 다음 주까지 당신의 집을 방문할 수가 없습니다. 수리점에 전화해서 직원에게 왜 그/그녀가 최대한 빨리 당신 집 창문을 수리해야 하는지 설명해 보세요.

TIP FOR THE OPIc

앞서 나온 질문의 심화 롤플레이 질문입니다. 수리점 직원의 방문 요청이 절박하다면, 그에 맞는 이유를 제시해야 합니다. 창문의 보수가 절박할 때는, 궂은 날씨, 외부의 침입으로부터의 안전, 집안의 중요한 행사 등을 이유로 들 수가 있습니다. 답안의 내용도 중요하지만, 실제 말하기를 할 때 목소리에 '절박함'이 묻어나면 좋은 등급을 받을 것입니다.

Model Answer

| Opening |

Hello? This is the ABC Repair Shop, right? Hi. This is Jiyoung in Suwon.

안녕하세요? ABC 수리점 맞죠? 네, 수원에 사는 지영이에요.

| Problem |

I just got a text message from one of your staff members. He said that he cannot come to fix my window until next week. What seems to be the problem? Is it possible for you to send someone else then?

조금 전 직원 분 중 한 분으로부터 문자를 받았는데요. 다음 주까지 저희 집 창문 수리가 어렵다고 하셔서요. 무슨 문제인가요? 다른 직원 분을 보내주시면 안 되나요?

| A Request for an Urgent Visit |

I believe that I informed you that my window was completely shattered this morning. Every part of the glass is gone! I need it to be fixed by tonight before I can go to bed. Please try to understand. I live in a tiny little house. I have nowhere else to go. Please.

아까 제가 저희 집 창문이 오늘 아침 완전히 부서졌다고 말씀 드렸던 것 같은데요. 유리가 한 조각도 남김없이 다 부서졌어요! 오늘밤 잠들기 전에 고쳐야 해요. 제발 제 입장 좀 헤아리고 노력해주세요. 저는 아주 조그만 집에 살고 있단 말이에요. 다른 데 갈 곳이 없단 말이에요. 제발요.

| Suggestions and Closing |

Can you just carry the window by yourself and come? What if I pay you 50,000 won instead of 30,000 won? Sound good? It's a deal then. I'll see you in an hour. Thank you. Bye.

그냥 혼자 들고 오실 수는 없나요? 만일 제가 3만원이 아니라 5만원을 드리면 어때요? 좋아요? 그럼 그렇게 하죠. 1시간 안에 뵐게요. 감사합니다. 안녕히 계세요.

More Questions

〈주거 개선〉에 관련하여 더 나올 수 있는 OPIc 질문들을 정리한 코너입니다. 질문에 대한 brainstorming을 해보세요.

1. Tell me about the steps you take to do household chores.
2. Which part of the house do you clean up the most often? Why? What do you do to clean up?
3. Tell me about some changes you've made at your home recently. Were you happy with the results?

On Your Own

앞에서 주어진 Model Answer을 바탕으로, 아래의 빈칸에 들어갈 수 있는 다양한 대체 가능한 어휘 및 표현들을 참고하여 학습자 본인만의 모범 답안을 직접 만들어보세요.

| Opening |

Hello? This is the ABC Repair Shop, right? Hi. This is ⓐ_____ in
ⓑ_____.

| Problem |

I just got a text message from one of your staff members. He said that he cannot come to fix my window until next week. What seems to be the problem? Is it possible for you to send someone else then?

| A Request for an Urgent Visit |

I believe that I informed you that my window was completely shattered this morning. Every part of the glass is gone! I need it to be fixed by ⓒ_____. Please try to understand. ⓓ_____.
Please.

| Suggestions and Closing |

Can you just carry the window by yourself and come? What if I pay you 50,000 won instead of 30,000 won? Sound good? It's a deal then. I'll see you in an hour. Thank you.

| Opening | Hello? This is the ABC Repair Shop, right? Hi. This is
ⓐ **Miyoung** in ⓑ **Mapo**.

| Problem | I just got a text message from one of your staff members. He said that he cannot come to fix my window until next week. What seems to be the problem? Is it possible for you to send someone else then?

| A Request for an Urgent Visit | I believe that I informed you that my window was completely shattered this morning. Every part of the glass is gone! I need it to be fixed by ⓒ **5 in the evening**. Please try to understand. ⓓ **I have a housewarming party at 7 p.m. I need to prepare food and decorate the house for my visitors. I can't cancel the party**.
Please.

| Suggestions and Closing | Can you just carry the window by yourself and come? What if I pay you 50,000 won instead of 30,000 won? Sound good? It's a deal then. I'll see you in an hour. Thank you.

본인이 만든 답안에 아래의 요소들이 포함되었는지 점검해 봅시다.

Checklist
☐ 전화 걸 때 인사말
☐ 상대방 확인 및 신분 밝히기
☐ 방문 수리가 안 되는 이유 확인
☐ 다급히 수리해야 하는 상황 설명
☐ 방문 수리를 위한 대안 제시
☐ 문제 해결 및 마무리

The Music of Speech

강세를 두어야 하는 어휘의 특징을 익히고 그에 따라 답안을 말하는 연습을 해봅시다.

강세를 두는 어휘의 특징
1) 감탄사이다 2) 최상급이다 3) 형용사/부사이다
4) 문장 안에서 key word 역할을 하는 명사나 동사인 경우가 많다

Model Answer 17 🎧 04-21

The first movie I ever watched at a theater was *Home Alone* starring Macaulay Culkin. I had watched many other movies on TV before, but that was probably the first movie I ever watched in a theater. I think I went there with my parents and my little sister and brother. It may sound funny, but if I have to talk about my first impression of the theater, I would say, "It was dark." Also, it was pretty cool to see the huge screen in the front and to sit with so many people. However, it was not easy to stay in my seat for nearly 2 hours after having so much coke and popcorn during the movie. The movie was great. It was a funny, touching movie—a nice family movie. I still like to watch movies such as comedies and dramas. I don't like bloody action movies. I guess I've always liked gentle and light-hearted movies with humor, and they are still my favorites.

Model Answer 18 🎧 04-22

It would be amazing to meet my favorite movie star in person. If I had to choose, I would definitely say Brad Pitt. I'm sure you know who he is. He is a famous Hollywood star and is married to another hot celebrity, Angelina Jolie. They are an awesome couple. If I got to meet Brad Pitt, I would ask how he is able to manage both his career and his family successfully. I mean, he has had such a long career, and he still has a very nice image. Not many movie stars are able to maintain their fame for so long. Also, he has a bunch of kids—both adopted and biological—with Angelina Jolie. Being a good father must be very challenging as well as being a good actor. I'd want to know if he has his own philosophy on how to be a good father. Plus, I'm very curious to know if he wants to be in any Korean movies in the future. I wonder if he knows any Korean actresses. Well, I guess these are a few things I would ask if I got to meet Brad Pitt!

Model Answer 19 🎧 04-23

I used to go clubbing in the past, but I don't go anymore. I love dancing, but now I dance in my room. Since I'm busy with work, I don't have time to go clubbing. When I'm in my room, I tune into any kind of music I like and dance to the songs. I feel so free when I dance in my room. I don't need to dress up, and I have enough space for myself! When I was younger, I took dance classes at a private institute for 6 months.

It was fun, but I don't think it actually taught me how to dance. I just learned how to dance on my own.

Model Answer 20 🎧 04-24

The last time I went clubbing was a couple of months ago. I don't really go clubbing anymore, but one of my friends wanted to celebrate her birthday at the club, so we went to one of the hottest clubs in town. It's called `The Glam`. It was a fun girls' night out. We dressed up and partied all night. The most memorable thing that happened was that the birthday-girl won the dance competition that night. She won a free travel package to New York, and we all got jealous. It was truly an unforgettable experience.

Model Answer 21 🎧 04-25

I see both pros and cons in text messaging. Text messaging is fast and easy to use. As long as you can get a data connection, you can send texts from any location. Naturally, texting has become one of the most common communication tools in the 21st century. Texting is not only widely used between friends but is also used in the business world. SMS has become an important communication tool in lots of workplaces. Text messages are valued in the business world as people make quick arrangements by sending short messages. However, we should not overlook the negative aspects of sending text messages. Nowadays, people text each other more often than to talk face-to-face. As a consequence, surveys show that people feel less connected to others and feel lonelier in the modern age. Though we see the benefits of text messaging, we need some balance between that and person-to-person communications.

Model Answer 22 🎧 04-26

I do not agree that texting can be as effective as talking on the phone. Texting can actually hinder people from having real conversations. Once, I read an article about a mother and her college daughter, who texted back and forth for hours. The daughter said her school life and her social life were both good. However, the mother discovered it later that her daughter had been bullied for a long time. This story shows that communicating through SMS is not enough. It is easier to hide our true feelings by using nonverbal communications. By texting and adding emoticons, we can fake our feelings anytime. This results in a miscommunication. Communication is not only about letters and words. People also communicate by using gestures and facial expressions and by changing the tones of their voices. This is why traditional methods of communication are still so important in this digital age.

Model Answer 23 04-27

A couple of weeks ago, I visited K-Mart to get a few winter items. Among the items, I got 6 pairs of bed socks. They were cute, fluffy, and comfortable. However, when I got home, my mom told me that she had ordered plenty of bed socks for me. She knew that I had needed extra pairs of bed socks. She even got them for only half the price that I had paid. Since they were gifts from my mom, I decided to get a refund on the ones that I bought. Then, I remembered that I had taken off the tags on all of my socks. I had my receipt, but there was no way to get a refund. I still went back to the store and asked a staff member for a refund. The answer was, "Sorry, but no." Well, it was not a big deal, but I learned a lesson: I shall think twice before I take the tags off items I purchase.

Model Answer 24 04-28

I only know about grocery shopping in Korea and the United States. There is a slight difference between shopping for groceries in Korea and shopping for groceries in the U.S. First of all, in Korea, there are many people yelling at customers to buy their products. This usually happens in the meat department or if there is a special sale on a certain item. Another difference is that in the U.S., you can buy medicine like aspirin and stomach medicine at grocery stores. In Korea, you have to go to a pharmacy. In addition, self-service is common at U.S. grocery stores while it is not very popular in Korea. The self-service section is where you can scan the barcodes of the products yourself and pay for them instead of going to a cashier. These are a few of the differences between grocery shopping in Korea and in the U.S.

Model Answer 25 04-29

Hello. Is this the ABC Repair Shop? Hi. My name is Jiyoung, and I live at Hangook apartment in Suwon. I'm calling to ask if you can come to fix the window in my apartment. The window in my room was shattered this morning. Somebody's ball hit the window and shattered the entire glass. I wiped the floor and vacuumed, so the floor is clean, so I just need the window repaired. Would you be able to come in an hour? Good. It looks like the entire window needs to be replaced. The width is 2 meters, and the height is 1 meter. How many staffers can I expect? Two? Okay. What's the price for the repairs? 30,000 won? I got it. Great. I'll see you in about an hour! Oh, my number is 010-1122-4555. Thank you. See you soon. Bye.

Model Answer 26 🎧 04-30

Hello? This is the ABC Repair Shop, right? Hi. This is Jiyoung in Suwon. I just got a text message from one of your staff members. He said that he cannot come to fix my window until next week. What seems to be the problem? Is it possible for you to send someone else then? I believe that I informed you that my window was completely shattered this morning. Every part of the glass is gone! I need it to be fixed by tonight before I can go to bed. Please try to understand. I live in a tiny little house. I have nowhere else to go. Please. Can you just carry the window by yourself and come? What if I pay you 50,000 won instead of 30,000 won? Sound good? It's a deal then. I'll see you in an hour. Thank you. Bye.

More Expressions & Vocabulary ≫ Free-Time Activities

Movies

favorite director 좋아하는 감독
favorite actor/actress 좋아하는 남자 배우/여자 배우
movie release 영화 개봉
blockbuster 흥행 작품
special effects 특수 효과
sound effects 음향 효과
all-time-favorite 생애 최고의
spectacular movie scene 화려한 영화 장면
romantic comedy 로맨틱 코미디
horror 공포
science fiction 공상 과학
drama 드라마
action 액션
animation 만화
movie genre 영화 장르
OST (original soundtrack) 영화 음악
The movie trailer was great. 영화 예고편은 훌륭했습니다.

I read the movie reviews. 저는 그 영화 평론을 읽었습니다.
I made a reservation for the movie. 저는 그 영화의 표를 예매했습니다.
I got some popcorn and a soda. 저는 팝콘과 탄산음료를 샀습니다.
I like the snack bar at the theater. 저는 그 영화관의 매점이 좋습니다.

Park

There is a nice trail in the park. 그 공원에는 좋은 산책로가 있습니다.
The night view at the park is awesome. 그 공원의 야경은 끝내줍니다.
There is a fountain in the park. 그 공원에는 분수대가 있습니다.
We often go on picnics at the park. 우리는 종종 공원으로 소풍을 갑니다.
I like to sit on the bench and enjoy the view. 저는 벤치에 앉아서 경치를 감상하는 것을 좋아합니다.

Clubbing

We go clubbing every Friday. 우리는 금요일마다 클럽에 갑니다.
We partied at the club all night. 우리는 클럽에서 밤새 파티를 했습니다.

Shopping

a good deal 만족스러운 거래
impulsive shopping 충동구매
clearance 할인 품목
GMO product(s) 유전자변형 식품
organic product(s) 유기농 제품
overpriced 품질에 비해 가격이 비싼
planned shopping 계획구매
rewards card (할인, 포인트누적 등의 혜택을 주는) 멤버쉽 카드
non-GMO product(s) 유전자변형을 하지 않은 식품

CHAPTER 5 취미 활동

Hobbies

Unit 27	**Listening to Music 1** 음악 감상하기 1 (기기)
Unit 28	**Listening to Music 2** 음악 감상하기 2 (일반)
Unit 29	**Singing 1** 혼자 노래 부르거나 합창하기 1 (롤플레이)
Unit 30	**Singing 2** 혼자 노래 부르거나 합창하기 2 (롤플레이)
Unit 31	**Dancing** 춤추기
Unit 32	**Dancing Lessons** 댄스 교습하기
Unit 33	**Cooking 1** 요리하기 1
Unit 34	**Cooking 2** 요리하기 2
Unit 35	**Reading 1** 독서하기 1 (E-reading)
Unit 36	**Reading 2** 독서하기 2 (E-reading)

Chapter 5는 음악 감상, 노래 부르기, 춤추기, 댄스, 요리 및 독서에 대해 다룹니다. 취미 활동에 관한 주제라도 사회 현상과 연계된 주제를 물으면 난이도가 높은 질문이 될 수도 있습니다. 예를 들어 사람들이 음악을 듣거나 독서하는 방식이 시대별로 어떻게 달라졌는지 등을 물을 수도 있습니다. 또한 롤플레이 형식의 문제도 등장할 수 있는데, 예를 들면 춤추기에 관해서는 댄스 학원에 등록하는 상황을 가정하여 이야기를 해보라는 문제가 나올 수 있고, 요리에 관해서는 집들이를 갈 때 어떤 음식을 준비해갈 것인지를 묻는 문제가 출제될 수 있습니다. 한편 노래 부르기에 관해서는 본인이 겪었던 창피한 경험에 대해 물어볼 수도 있습니다. 이러한 질문에 답하기 위해서는 취미 활동과 연계된 다양한 상황에 대해 브레인스토밍하는 연습이 요구됩니다.

+ Brainstorming Point

When?
- when I like to listen to music/sing/dance/cook (언제 음악 감상/노래/춤추기/요리하는 것을 좋아하는지)
- the last time I went clubbing/cooked (마지막으로 클럽 간/요리한 때)

Where?
- where I like to dance (어디서 춤을 추는지)
- where the singing/dancing institute is located (노래/댄스 교습 장소)
- my favorite dining place (좋아하는 식당)

What?
- the music device I use (사용하는 음악 기기)
- my favorite music genre (가장 좋아하는 음악 장르)
- what I like to cook (어떤 요리를 하는 것을 좋아하는지)
- what I think about e-books (전자책에 대한 내 생각)

Who?
- my favorite musician (가장 좋아하는 뮤지션)
- who I go clubbing with (함께 클럽에 가는 사람)
- who taught me how to sing/dance (노래 부르는/춤추는 법을 가르쳐준 사람)

Why?
- why I like to listen to music/sing/dance/cook (음악 감상/노래/춤추기/요리를 좋아하는 이유)
- why I like the musician (그 뮤지션을 좋아하는 이유)
- why an experience is so memorable (경험이 기억에 남는 이유)
- why I prefer paper/electronic books (종이책/전자책을 선호하는 이유)

How?
- how I got interested in singing/dancing/cooking (노래하기/춤추기/요리에 관심을 갖게 된 계기)
- how often I go clubbing (얼마나 자주 클럽에 가는지)
- how good I am at singing/dancing/cooking (노래/춤/요리를 얼마나 잘하는지)
- how I purchase books (어떻게 책을 구입하는지)

Unit 27 Listening to Music 1

음악 감상하기 1 (기기)

Warm Up

A Guess the Question & Answer
사진을 보면서 예상 질문과 답변을 먼저 추측해 봅시다.

B Listen & Talk
음악 감상할 때 사용하는 기기에 관한 대화를 먼저 연습해 봅시다.   🎧 05-01

A Look! I got a new MP4 player this morning.	**A** 이것 봐! 오늘 아침에 새로 MP4 플레이어를 샀어.
B That's cute. How's it different from an MP3 player?	**B** 정말 귀엽다! MP3 플레이어랑 어떻게 달라?
A It's like a smartphone. It plays both music and videos.	**A** 응, 스마트폰이랑 비슷해. 음악도 나오고 영상도 틀 수 있어.
B Then why didn't you just stick with your smartphone?	**B** 그렇다면 그냥 네 스마트폰 사용하지 그랬어?
A Oh, I don't want to be bothered by all those calls and messages while I'm jogging. I bought this for when I jog.	**A** 아, 조깅할 땐 전화 오고 문자 오는 게 귀찮아서. 조깅할 때 사용하려고 샀어.
B Okay! I love the big screen on your MP4 player. How many songs do you have on it?	**B** 그렇구나! 네 MP4 플레이어 화면 커서 좋네. 음악은 몇 개나 저장했어?
A 300 so far.	**A** 지금까지 300곡.
B Woah. You're a total music addict.	**B** 우와. 넌 정말 음악에 푹 빠졌구나.

Vocabulary be different from ~ ~와 다르다 | both A and B A와 B 모두 | be bothered by ~ ~에 의해 방해받다 | stick with ~ ~을 고집하다 | so far 이제까지 | music addict 음악에 중독되다시피 한 사람

Key Expressions

아래 제시된 각 expression의 구조를 이해하고, 자기만의 표현들을 생각해 봅시다.

Expression 1   **I remember ~:** 제 기억에는 ~ 했습니다

제 기억으로 1990년대에 CD 플레이어는 인기 많은 기기였습니다.
→ **I remember** that the CD player was a popular device in the 90s.

제 기억으로 그가 대학생일 때는 통통했었습니다.
→ **I remember** he used to be chubby when he was in college.

제 기억으로 제가 어릴 적에는 막대 아이스크림이 100원도 안 되었습니다.
→ **I remember** an ice cream bar used to be less than 100 won in my youth.

Expression 2   **people of all ages:** 모든 연령대의 사람들

'워크맨'은 모든 연령대의 사람들로부터 사랑 받았습니다.
→ The Walkman was loved by **people of all ages**.

그 책은 모든 연령대의 사람들로부터 읽힙니다. → The book is read by **people of all ages**.

그의 노래는 전 연령대의 사람들로부터 사랑받고 있습니다. → His song is adored by **people of all ages**.

Expression 3   **functional:** 기능적인

기기들은 더욱 더 기능적으로 변했습니다. → Gadgets have become much more **functional**.

이 공기청정기는 매우 기능적입니다. 가습기 기능까지 있습니다.
→ This air purifier is very **functional**. It even has a humidity function.

제 새 스마트폰은 기능이 참 많습니다. 영상채팅도 할 수 있어요.
→ My new smartphone is very **functional**. I can video-chat with it.

Expression 4   **chat on ~:** ~로 얘기하다, 채팅하다

카카오톡으로 무료 채팅을 할 수 있습니다. → You can **chat** for free **on** Kakao-Talk.

인터넷으로 채팅을 한다는 것은 멋진 일입니다. → It's awesome to **chat on** the Internet.

어머니는 지금 전화로 말씀 중이십니다. → My mom is **chatting on** the phone at this moment.

Expression 5   **simplify:** 단순화시키다

진보된 기술은 그 과정을 단순화시켰습니다. → Advanced technology has **simplified** the process.

당신의 생산성을 증대시키기 위해서는 삶을 단순화시켜야 합니다.
→ **Simplify** your life to increase your productivity.

아이디어를 실천에 옮기려면 그것을 단순화시키는 것이 항상 좋습니다.
→ It's always better to **simplify** your ideas to put them into practice.

Topic Question & Model Answer

 05-02

Topic Question

What kinds of gadgets and technologies do people use for music these days? How have they changed the way people play or listen to music? 요즘은 사람들이 음악을 듣기 위해 어떠한 기기 혹은 기술을 사용하나요? 그로 인해 사람들이 음악을 연주하거나 감상하는 방식이 어떻게 달라졌나요?

TIP FOR THE OPIc

테크놀로지의 발달로 인한 음악 감상 패턴이나 연주법, 작곡 기법의 변화를 묻는 질문입니다. '음악 감상' 항목과 연계된 질문이지만, 돌발 문제처럼 보일 정도로 난이도가 있는 질문입니다. 가장 무난한 대답은 음악 기기의 변화를 설명하는 것입니다. 또한 악기연주나 작곡을 할 때 달라진 점 등도 얘기할 수 있습니다.

Model Answer

| Opening |

There have been a lot of changes in the ways we use gadgets to listen to music.

사람들이 음악을 듣기 위해 사용하는 도구에는 많은 변화가 있었습니다.

| Gadgets in the Past |

I remember that the CD player was a very popular device to listen to music in the 90s. Also, a small cassette player called the Walkman was loved by people of all ages.

제 기억으로 1990년대에는 CD 플레이어가 음악을 듣는 도구로써 한창 인기 있었습니다. 또한, '워크맨'이라고 불리는 작은 카세트 플레이어가 남녀노소 모두에게 사랑받았습니다.

| Music Devices in the Present |

These days, gadgets have become much smaller and much more functional. Many people carry their smartphones to listen to music. Most of the smartphones are only the size of your palm, so they are very light. With a smartphone, you can also access the Internet, watch movies, chat for free on Kakao-Talk, and do much more. Advanced technology has even simplified the composing process. A close friend of mine is a composer, and he uses his iPad to make music. He says that it has become a lot easier to write music because the device has all kinds of different instrumental sounds.

요즘에는, 음악을 듣는 도구가 훨씬 작아지고 또한 더욱 기능적으로 바뀌었습니다. 많은 사람들은 음악을 듣기 위해 스마트폰을 휴대하고 다닙니다. 대부분의 스마트폰은 손바닥만 한 크기 정도라서 아주 가볍습니다. 또한 스마트폰으로 인터넷에 접속할 수도 있고, 영화를 보고, 카카오톡으로 무료 채팅을 하는 등 많은 것을 할 수 있습니다. 기술의 진보는 작곡의 과정까지도 단순화시켰습니다. 제 친한 친구 한 명은 작곡가인데, 그는 아이패드를 사용해서 작곡을 합니다. 그의 말로는, 아이패드에는 다양한 종류의 악기 소리가 저장되어 있어서, 작곡을 하기가 훨씬 쉬워졌다고 합니다.

| Closing |

Overall, I think current technology has brought many changes in the way people play and listen to music.

아무쪼록 저는 현대의 테크놀로지가 사람들이 음악을 연주하거나 감상하는데 있어서 많은 변화를 가져왔다고 생각합니다.

More Questions

〈음악 감상하기〉에 관련하여 더 나올 수 있는 OPIc 질문들을 정리한 코너입니다. 질문에 대한 brainstorming을 해보세요.

1 When do you like to listen to music? In the morning? Before you go to bed? Why?

2 How does music affect you? What are some good things about listening to music?

앞에서 주어진 Model Answer을 바탕으로, 아래의 빈칸에 들어갈 수 있는 다양한 대체 가능한 어휘 및 표현들을 참고하여 학습자 본인만의 모범 답안을 직접 만들어보세요.

I Opening I
There have been a lot of changes in the ways we use gadgets to listen to music.

I Gadgets in the Past I
I remember that the CD player was a very popular device to listen to music in the 90s. Also, a small cassette player called the Walkman was loved by people of all ages.

I Music Devices in the Present I
These days, gadgets have become much smaller and much more functional. Many people carry ⓐ_____ to listen to music. Most ⓐ_____ are only the size of your palm, so they are very light. With ⓐ_____, you can ⓑ_____. In addition, ⓒ_____. Advanced technology has even simplified the composing process. A close friend of mine is a composer, and he uses his iPad to make music because the device has all kinds of different instrumental sounds.

I Closing I
Overall, I think current technology has resulted in many changes in the way people play and listen to music.

I Opening I There have been a lot of changes in the ways we use gadgets to listen to music.

I Gadgets in the Past I I remember that the CD player was a very popular device to listen to music in the 90s. Also, a small cassette player called the Walkman was loved by people of all ages.

I Music Devices in the Present I These days, gadgets have become much smaller and much more functional. Many people carry ⓐ **MP3 players** to listen to music. Most ⓐ **MP3 players** are only the size of your palm, so they are very light. With ⓐ **MP3 players**, you can ⓑ **save hundreds of songs**. In addition, ⓒ **it's easy to download new songs**. Advanced technology has even simplified the composing process. A close friend of mine is a composer, and he uses his iPad to make music because the device has all kinds of different instrumental sounds.

I Closing I Overall, I think current technology has resulted in many changes in the way people play and listen to music.

본인이 만든 답안에 아래의 요소들이 포함되었는지 점검해 봅시다.

	Checklist
☐	과거 음악 감상 방식
☐	CD 플레이어 및 워크맨 언급
☐	현재 음악 감상 방식
☐	인터넷
☐	MP3 플레이어 및 스마트폰
☐	과거 현재 모두 듣는 라디오

Unit 28 Listening to Music 2

음악 감상하기 2 (일반)

Warm Up

A Guess the Question & Answer
사진을 보면서 예상 질문과 답변을 먼저 추측해 봅시다.

B Listen & Talk
음악적 취향의 변화에 관한 대화를 연습해 봅시다.

🎧 05-03

A What kinds of music do you like?
B I like all kinds of music but heavy metal. I think heavy metal is just too loud.
A Then do you prefer quiet music?
B It depends. Sometimes I like quiet music, but I also like dance music.
A What about rock?
B I love rock. I never listened to rock before I met my husband. But since he listens to rock all the time, I naturally listen to it often, and now I enjoy it.
A Did your taste in music change after you met your husband?
B My taste in music has gradually changed. I used to like hip-hop the most, but I don't listen to it anymore. I prefer listening to classical music and CCM these days.
A That's a huge change!
B I know. I think it happened when I went to graduate school. I played quieter songs to concentrate better when I was working on my papers.

A 어떤 음악 좋아하니?
B 헤비메탈 빼고 다 좋아해. 헤비메탈은 그냥 너무 시끄러운 것 같아.
A 그럼 조용한 음악 좋아해?
B 기분에 따라 달라. 때로는 조용한 음악이 좋지만 댄스 음악도 좋아해.
A 록은 어때?
B 많이 좋아해. 남편을 만나기 전에는 록을 들어본 적이 없었어. 하지만 남편이 늘 듣다 보니 나도 자연스럽게 자주 듣게 되어서 이제는 즐겨 듣고 있지.
A 남편을 만난 후에 음악적 취향이 달라졌니?
B 내 음악적 취향은 점차적으로 바뀌었어. 예전에는 힙합을 제일 좋아했는데 요즘에는 더 이상 듣지 않지. 지금은 클래식 음악이나 크리스챤 음악을 좋아해.
A 상당히 달라졌구나!
B 맞아. 대학원에 다니면서였던 것 같아. 집중하기 위해서 조용한 음악을 틀어놓고 보고서를 썼어.

Vocabulary

naturally 자연스럽게 | **taste in music** 음악적 취향, 음악적 기호 | **gradually** 점진적으로 | **work on papers** 보고서/학교 과제 등을 작성하다

Key Expressions

🔑 아래 제시된 각 expression의 구조를 이해하고, 자기만의 표현들을 생각해 봅시다.

Expression 1   a variety of genres from A to B: A부터 B에 이르는 다양한 장르

저는 재즈부터 록까지 다양한 장르를 듣습니다. → I listen to **a variety of genres from** jazz **to** rock.

저는 논픽션부터 시에 이르기까지 다양한 장르를 읽습니다.
→ I read **a variety of genres from** nonfiction **to** poems.

그녀는 드라마부터 액션 영화에 이르기까지 다양한 장르에 출연했습니다.
→ She was in **a variety of genres from** dramas **to** action films.

Expression 2   fall in love with + 명사: ~와 사랑에 빠지다

20대 중반에 저는 클래식 음악에 빠졌습니다.
→ When I was in my mid-20s, I **fell in love with** classical music.

저희는 한국에 있을 때 등산에 푹 빠졌습니다. → We **fell in love with** hiking when we were in Korea.

제 주변에는 한국 대중 가요의 매력에 빠진 외국인 친구들이 많이 있습니다.
→ I have many foreign friends who **fell in love with** K-pop.

Expression 3   with + 음악 + on: ~ 음악을 틀어놓은 상태에서

클래식 곡을 들으면서 학교 과제를 하면 집중력이 향상되었습니다.
→ It was easier to concentrate on my school assignments **with classical music on**.

운전할 때 시끄러운 음악을 틀어놓으면 졸음 운전을 피할 수 있습니다.
→ It is easier to stay awake **with loud music on** when I am driving.

흥겨운 노래가 나오는 파티는 지루할 수가 없습니다. → Parties cannot be boring **with fun music on**.

Expression 4   the lyrics are therapeutic: 그 가사는 마음을 치유해준다

CCM이 좋은 이유는 가사가 마음을 치유해주기 때문입니다.
→ I like CCM songs because **the lyrics are therapeutic**.

저는 마음을 치유하는 가사를 듣고 눈물을 흘렸습니다.
→ I burst into tears because **the lyrics are therapeutic**.

그녀의 노래들은 마음을 치유하는 가사로 인해 많이 사랑받고 있습니다.
→ Her songs are widely loved because **the lyrics are therapeutic**.

Expression 5   play + 명사 + on my cell phone: 내 핸드폰으로 ~를 틀다/보다

저는 제 핸드폰에 저장된 곡이나 라디오를 통해서 음악을 듣습니다.
→ I either **play** my favorite list **on my cell phone** or tune into the radio.

저희는 종종 제 핸드폰으로 영화를 봅니다. → I often **play** movies **on my cell phone**.

저는 핸드폰으로 동영상을 보는 것을 좋아합니다. → I like to **play** videos **on my cell phone**.

Topic Question & Model Answer

🎧 05-04

Topic Question

You indicated in the survey that you like music. What kind of music do you like? When do you usually listen to it? I want to know everything about it. 당신은 설문조사에서 음악 감상을 좋아한다고 했습니다. 어떤 종류의 음악을 좋아하나요? 언제 주로 듣나요? 당신의 음악 감상 활동에 대해 모두 이야기해보세요.

TIP FOR THE OPIc

음악 감상(취미 활동)에 관한 질문입니다. 본인이 좋아하는 음악 장르가 무엇인지, 어떤 상황에서 듣는 것을 좋아하는지, 좋아하는 가수(밴드)나 작곡가는 누구이며 나의 현재 음악적 취향은 과거와 어떻게 다른지 등에 대해 물어볼 수 있습니다.

Model Answer

| Opening |

I like to listen to all kinds of music. My taste in music changes depending on what I do and how I am feeling. Generally, I listen to a variety of genres from jazz to rock music.

저는 모든 종류의 음악을 좋아합니다. 음악에 대한 기호는 제가 무엇을 하고 있고 어떤 기분인지에 따라 달라집니다. 일반적으로 저는 재즈부터 록 음악까지 다양한 장르를 즐겨 듣습니다.

| Why I Liked Classic |

Back in my early 20s, my favorite music genre was hip-hop. However, when I was in my mid-20s, I fell in love with classical music. I often listened to classical music when I was working on papers in my room. It was easier to concentrate on my school assignments with classical music on because it doesn't have lyrics.

제가 20대 초반이었을 때에는 힙합을 가장 좋아했습니다. 하지만 20대 중반에 이르러 클래식 음악에 빠져들었습니다. 저는 주로 방에서 문서 작성을 할 때 클래식 음악을 들었습니다. 클래식 곡에는 가사가 없기 때문에 학교 과제 등을 할 때 클래식 음악을 들으면 집중력이 향상되었습니다.

| CCM Heals My Heart |

These days, I listen to CCM songs the most. I like CCM songs because the melodies are touching, and the lyrics are therapeutic. I usually play CCM songs when I do the dishes or cook. When I listen to music, I either play my favorite list on my cell phone or tune into the radio. That way, I can enjoy music almost anytime.

요즘 제가 가장 즐겨 듣는 음악은 CCM입니다. CCM이 좋은 이유는 멜로디가 감동적이고 가사가 마음을 치유해주기 때문입니다. 저는 주로 설거지를 하거나 요리를 할 때 CCM을 듣습니다. 주로 제 핸드폰에 저장된 곡을 듣거나 라디오를 통해 듣습니다. 그렇게 하면 거의 언제든지 음악을 들을 수 있습니다.

| Closing |

Music is something that is precious to me. It is something we should be grateful to have in our lives.

음악은 제게 있어서 소중한 것입니다. 우리의 삶 가운데 음악이 있다는 것은 감사히 여길 만한 일입니다.

More Questions

〈음악 감상하기〉에 관련하여 더 나올 수 있는 OPIc 질문들을 정리한 코너입니다. 질문에 대한 brainstorming을 해보세요.

1. Do you listen to different music depending on the situation? What kinds of music do you listen to in the morning? Why?

2. You said you like to listen to music. What's your favorite musical instrument? Why is it your favorite? Do you know how to play that instrument?

On Your Own

앞에서 주어진 Model Answer을 바탕으로, 아래의 빈칸에 들어갈 수 있는 다양한 대체 가능한 어휘 및 표현들을 참고하여 학습자 본인만의 모범 답안을 직접 만들어보세요.

I Opening I
I like to listen to all kinds of music. My taste in music changes depending on what I do and how I am feeling. ⓐ_____.

I Why I Liked Rock I
Back in my ⓑ_____ years, my favorite ⓒ_____. However, when I was in my ⓓ_____, I fell in love with ⓔ_____. I often listened to ⓕ_____ when I ⓖ_____. It was easier to ⓗ_____.

I Jazz Relaxes Me I
These days, I listen to ⓘ_____ the most. I like ⓙ_____ because the melodies are touching and ⓙ_____. I usually play ⓙ_____ when I ⓚ_____. When I listen to music, I either play my favorite list on my cell phone or tune into the radio. That way, I can enjoy music almost anytime.

I Closing I
Music is something that is precious to me. It is something we should be grateful to have in our lives.

I Opening I I like to listen to all kinds of music. My taste in music changes depending on what I do and how I am feeling. ⓐ **However, I listen to rock music the most often.**

I Why I Liked Rock I Back in my ⓑ **junior high school** years, my favorite ⓒ **rock band was Led Zeppelin**. However, when I was in my ⓓ **20s**, I fell in love with ⓔ **Queen**. I often listened to ⓕ **their music** when I ⓖ **was driving my car**. It was easier to ⓗ **stay awake with their music on**.

I Jazz Relaxes Me I These days, I listen to ⓘ **jazz** the most. I like ⓙ **jazz** because the melodies are touching and ⓙ **powerful**. I usually play ⓙ **jazz** when I ⓚ **want to relax**. When I listen to music, I either play my favorite list on my cell phone or tune into the radio. That way, I can enjoy music almost anytime.

I Closing I Music is something that is precious to me. It is something we should be grateful to have in our lives.

본인이 만든 답안에 아래의 요소들이 포함되었는지 점검해 봅시다.

	Checklist
☐	내가 좋아하는 음악
☐	내가 좋아하는 뮤지션
☐	음악적 기호에 영향을 준 요인
☐	언제 음악을 듣는 것을 좋아하는지
☐	음악 감상이 유익한 이유

Unit 29 Singing 1

혼자 노래 부르거나 합창하기 1 (롤플레이)

Warm Up

A Guess the Question & Answer
사진을 보면서 예상 질문과 답변을 먼저 추측해 봅시다.

B Listen & Talk
혼자 노래하기에 관한 대화를 먼저 연습해 봅시다.

🎧 05-05

A Was it you who was just singing?	A 방금 노래한 거 너였어?
B Oops. I thought nobody was there. Sorry.	B 어머. 밖에 아무도 없는 줄 알았는데. 미안.
A It was impressive. Actually, I thought it was from the radio.	A 아주 인상적이었어. 사실 난 라디오에서 나오는 노래인 줄 알았어.
B That's flattering.	B 과찬이야.
A I'm serious. I think you should audition.	A 정말이야. 오디션에 한 번 나가봐.
B Thanks, but I don't sing in front of people.	B 고마워. 하지만 난 사람들 앞에서는 노래 못해.
A What a shame. Your voice is extraordinary! Have you ever taken singing lessons?	A 안타깝다. 네 목소리 보통이 아니야! 노래 강습 받은 적 있어?
B No. I just follow the songs that I like. I'm happy you liked it.	B 아니. 그냥 좋아하는 노래를 따라 불러. 네가 좋게 봐주니까 기분 좋다.

Vocabulary | **impressive** 인상적인 | **That's flattering.** 과찬입니다. (과찬을 받고 어쩔 줄 모를 때 쓰는 말) | **audition** 오디션을 보다 | **What a shame.** 안타깝다. | **extraordinary** 보통이 아닌, 비범한 | **take a lesson** 강습을 받다

Key Expressions

🔑 아래 제시된 각 expression의 구조를 이해하고, 자기만의 표현들을 생각해 봅시다.

Expression 1 **be interested in ~:** ~에 관심 있다

저는 보컬 트레이닝 수업에 관심이 있습니다. → **I'm interested in** your vocal training class.

태연이는 연기에 상당한 관심이 있습니다. → Taeyun **is** very **interested in** acting.

동호는 사회적 문제에 매우 큰 관심이 있습니다.
→ Dongho **is** very much **interested in** social problems.

Expression 2 **difference in ~:** ~의 차이

저는 가격의 차이를 알고 싶습니다. → I'd like to know the **difference in** the cost.

그가 사석과 공석에서 행동하는 방식에는 큰 차이가 있었습니다.
→ There was a huge **difference in** the way he behaved in public and in private.

만일 당신의 삶에 변화를 만들고 싶다면, 역동적인 활동을 계획하기 시작해보세요.
→ If you want to make a **difference in** your life, start planning more activities.

Expression 3 **one-to-one:** 일대일

일대일 강의의 비용은 어떻게 되나요? → What's the cost of the **one-to-one** class?

영국대사관은 일대일 영어 수업을 열고 있습니다.
→ The British Embassy offers **one-to-one** English classes.

민서는 요즘 일대일 요가 수업에 참여하고 있습니다.
→ Minseo is taking **one-to-one** yoga classes these days.

Expression 4 **can't [can] afford ~:** ~할 여유가 없다[있다]

저는 일대일 수업료를 지불할 만한 여유가 없습니다. → I **can't afford** the one-to-one lesson.

사고 싶은 마음은 굴뚝같지만, 저는 이 시계를 살 만한 여유가 없습니다.
→ It's really tempting, but I **can't afford** to buy this watch.

결혼 초기부터 집을 장만할 여유가 되는 사람은 극히 드뭅니다.
→ Few people **can afford** a house at the beginning of their married lives.

Expression 5 **within** + 시간/거리 : ~안에, ~이내에

일주일 안에 방문하겠습니다. → I'll visit you **within** a week.

한 시간 안에 꽃이 배달될 것입니다. → The flowers will be delivered **within** the hour.

공항은 제 이모 댁으로부터 5km 이내에 있습니다.
→ The airport is **within** 5 kilometers of my aunt's place.

Topic Question & Model Answer

 05-06

Topic Question

Here's a situation I want you to act out. Suppose you were going to take singing lessons at a private institute. Call the person in charge and ask 3 to 4 things you should know before you start the lessons.

여기 상황극이 하나 있습니다. 당신이 사설 학원의 노래교실에 등록하려고 합니다. 담당자에게 전화해서 수업을 시작하기 전에 알아두어야 할 3~4가지를 질문해 보세요.

> **TIP FOR THE OPIc**
> 노래 교습을 받으러 학원에 등록하기 전에 관련 정보를 확인하라는 질문입니다. 수업을 듣기 위한 과정인 만큼 강의료, 수업 시간, 강사 등에 관한 사항을 기본적으로 물어볼 수 있습니다. 또한 학원의 위치, 타 학원과의 차별화된 제도 등에 대한 질문도 가능합니다. 수업에 참여하기 위해 필요한 도구 및 준비 사항도 질문에 포함될 수 있을 것입니다.

Model Answer

| Opening |

Hello? Is this the Doremi Music School? Hi. My name is Suji, and I'm interested in your vocal training class.

여보세요? 도레미 음악 교실인가요? 네, 제 이름은 수지이구요, 당신 학원의 보컬 트레이닝 반을 수강하고 싶어서요.

| Questions about Singing Lessons |

I guess I am a beginner. I've never had vocal training before. I'd like to know the difference in the cost of the one-to-one class and the group class. It's nearly five times more expensive! In that case, I will take the group lesson. I don't think I can afford the one-to-one lesson. Do you have an afternoon class? Cool. Is there anything I should prepare for the class? Just eat well and drink enough water? That's easy. Do you offer any kind of discount if I invite a friend to take the class as well? 10% off? Nice! My last question: Who's going to be my teacher? It's Yuri from J.O.P. Entertainment? Great!

저는 초보자에 해당되는 것 같아요. 한 번도 보컬 트레이닝을 받아 본 적이 없거든요. 일대일 수업과 그룹 강의 비용이 얼마나 다른지 궁금해요. 거의 5배나 비싸군요! 그럴 경우, 그룹 수업에 등록하겠습니다. 일대일 수업은 좀 부담되네요. 오후 수업도 있나요? 잘됐네요. 수업 전에 준비할 사항은 없나요? 그냥 잘 먹고 충분한 양의 물을 마시고 오라고요? 쉽네요. 혹시 제가 친구를 초대하면 할인이 되나요? 10% 할인이라고요? 좋아요! 마지막 질문인데요, 제 선생님은 누가 되나요? J.O.P. 엔터테인먼트 출신의 유리 선생님이라고요? 최고에요!

| Closing |

I'll visit your institute within a week. Thank you. Bye.

이번 주 안으로 학원에 가겠습니다. 감사합니다. 안녕히 계세요.

More Questions

<노래하기>에 관련하여 더 나올 수 있는 OPIc 질문들을 정리한 코너입니다. 질문에 대한 brainstorming을 해보세요.

1. Have you ever taken any singing lessons? When were they? Were they helpful to you?
2. What's your favorite song that you like to sing? Why do you like the song?
3. Where do you like to sing? Some people sing in the shower. Do you have a special place where you like to sing by yourself?

앞에서 주어진 Model Answer을 바탕으로, 아래의 빈칸에 들어갈 수 있는 다양한 대체 가능한 어휘 및 표현들을 참고하여 학습자 본인만의 모범 답안을 직접 만들어보세요.

| Opening |

Hello? Is this the Doremi Music School? Hi. My name is Suji, and I'm interested in your vocal training class.

| Questions about Singing Lessons |

I guess I am a beginner. I've never had vocal training before.

ⓐ_____.

ⓑ_____? I'd like to know the difference in the cost of the one-to-one class and the group class. It's nearly five times more expensive! In that case, I will take the group lesson. I don't think I can afford the one-to-one lesson. Do you have ⓒ_____? Cool. Is there anything I should prepare for the class? Just eat well and drink enough water? That's easy. Do you offer any kind of discount if I invite a friend to take the class as well? 10% off? Nice! My last question: Who's going to be my teacher? It's Yuri from J.O.P. Entertainment? Great!

| Closing |

I'll visit your institute within a week. Thank you. Bye.

| Opening | Hello? Is this the Doremi Music School? Hi. My name is Suji, and I'm interested in your vocal training class.

| Questions about Singing Lessons | I guess I am a beginner. I've never had vocal training before. ⓐ **But people say I'm quite good, and I want to audition sometime soon.** ⓑ **Which class should I take?** I'd like to know the difference in the cost of the one-to-one class and the group class. It's nearly five times more expensive! In that case, I will take the group lesson. I don't think I can afford the one-to-one lesson. Do you have ⓒ **a class for audition participants only**? Cool. Is there anything I should prepare for the class? Just eat well and drink enough water? That's easy. Do you offer any kind of discount if I invite a friend to take the class as well? 10% off? Nice! My last question: Who's going to be my teacher? It's Yuri from J.O.P. Entertainment? Great!

| Closing | I'll visit your institute within a week. Thank you. Bye.

본인이 만든 답안에 아래의 요소들이 포함되었는지 점검해 봅시다.

Checklist
☐ 전화 걸 때 인사말
☐ 신분 밝히기
☐ 전화 건 목적(노래 교실 수강) 설명
☐ 문의 사항 (강습료, 할인 혜택, 강사, 준비사항)
☐ 마무리 인사

Unit 30 Singing 2

혼자 노래 부르거나 합창하기 2 (롤플레이)

Warm Up

A Guess the Question & Answer
사진을 보면서 예상 질문과 답변을 먼저 추측해 봅시다.

B Listen & Talk
노래 교실 등록에 관한 대화를 먼저 연습해 봅시다.

 05-07

A Would you be interested in taking singing lessons with me?

B Singing lessons? Why do you need singing lessons?

A Oh, I just want a change in my life.

B Sure. Music is a good way to recharge. I will join you if the price is reasonable.

A The place offers a discount if we sign up for a class as a group of 3.

B And how much will that be per person?

A 30,000 won an hour per person. It's just once a week, and the teacher is fabulous.

B Who's teaching?

A Hold your breath. It's Martin Kwon from J3 Entertainment!

B Really? Let's go and sign up right away!

A 너 나랑 같이 노래 강습 받을래?

B 노래 강습? 네가 왜 노래 강습이 필요해?

A 아, 삶에 변화를 좀 주고 싶어서.

B 그래. 음악은 재충전을 하는 데에 좋은 방법이지. 가격이 괜찮으면 같이 배워볼게.

A 음, 한 반에 3명을 채우면 할인해준대.

B 그렇게 되면 한 명당 얼마씩인데?

A 한 사람당 한 시간에 30,000원이야. 1주일에 1번이고 선생님이 굉장해.

B 누가 가르치는데?

A 심장 멎을지 몰라. J3 엔터테인먼트 출신의 마틴 권이야!

B 정말? 지금 당장 가서 등록하자!

Vocabulary be interested in ~ ~에 흥미 있다, ~에 관심 있다 | want a change 변화를 갖고 싶다 | recharge 재충전하다 | reasonable 합리적인 | offer a discount 할인해주다 | sign up for ~ ~에 등록하다 | per person 한 사람 당 | fabulous 엄청난, 굉장한

Key Expressions

아래 제시된 각 expression의 구조를 이해하고, 자기만의 표현들을 생각해 봅시다.

Expression 1　sign up for ~: ~에 등록하다

저는 오늘 아침 당신 수업에 등록했습니다. → I **signed up for** your class this morning.

소연은 바리스타 과정에 등록했습니다. → Soyeon **signed up for** a barista course.

서둘러 등록하세요. 그렇지 않으면 기회를 놓칠지도 모릅니다.
→ Hurry and **sign up**. Otherwise, you might miss your chance.

Expression 2　come up: 발생하다, 일어나다

저는 막바지에 문제가 좀 생겼습니다. → I had some issues **come up** at the last minute.

그러한 문제들은 가끔씩 일어납니다. → Those problems **come up** from time to time.

질문이 생기면 저희에게 연락을 주십시오. → Please contact us if any question **comes up**.

Expression 3　make arrangements: 준비를 하다

제 상사는 저에게 회의에 관한 준비를 하라고 주문하였습니다.
→ My boss asked me to **make arrangements** for the meeting.

우리 팀은 선적을 위한 모든 것을 준비했습니다. → Our team **made** all the **arrangements** for shipping.

제가 관광 투어를 위한 준비를 할 것입니다. → I will **make arrangements** for the sightseeing tour.

Expression 4　be out of + 장소: 부재중이다, 자리를 비우다

저는 다음 주 일주일 내내 자리를 비우게 됩니다. → I'll **be out of** town the entire week.

부장님은 내일 사무실에 안 계실 것입니다. → My manager will **be out of** the office tomorrow.

우리가 집을 비울 동안에는 이웃 사람들이 우리 강아지를 돌봐줍니다.
→ Our neighbors take care of our dog when we **are out of** town.

Expression 5　delay: 연기하다, 미루다

제 친구가 첫 수업을 미루는 것이 가능한가요?
→ Is it possible for my friend to **delay** the start of her class?

우리의 항공편은 폭풍으로 인해 연기되었습니다. → Our flight was **delayed** due to the storm.

그 회의는 다음 달로 연기될 것입니다. → The conference will be **delayed** until next month.

Topic Question & Model Answer

🎧 05-08

Topic Question

A problem occurred. You have a problem and have to miss the next two classes. Call the instructor and give 3 to 4 alternatives concerning missing the classes.

문제가 발생했습니다. 당신에게 문제가 발생한 관계로 다음 2회의 수업을 결석하게 되었습니다. 강사에게 전화해서 결강에 대한 3~4가지 대안을 제시해달라고 얘기해보세요.

TIP FOR THE OPIc

개인 사정상 수업에 결석하게 되는 상황을 제시하였습니다. 이럴 때 현실적으로 어떠한 대안을 요청할 수 있는지 빠르게 생각해봐야 합니다. 수업을 연기하거나, 보강을 요청하거나, 다른 시간대에 참여하거나 하는 방법 여부를 물어볼 수 있습니다. 대안을 요청하기 전에는 우선 어떠한 사정 때문에 결석을 하는지 간단히 설명하고, 결석을 하는 것에 대한 양해를 구하는 것이 좋겠죠?

Model Answer

| Opening |

Hello. Is this Yuri? Hi. This is Suji. I signed up for your vocal training class this Monday.

안녕하세요, 유리 선생님인가요? 아, 저는 수지라고 해요. 이번 주 월요일에 선생님의 보컬 트레이닝 수업에 등록했어요.

| Missing Classes |

I'm terribly sorry, Yuri, but I had some issues come up at the last minute. I have to go out of town for an urgent business trip next week. My boss just called me this morning to make the arrangements. I'll be out of town the entire week next week, so I will miss the next two classes.

선생님, 정말 죄송하지만 문제가 발생했어요. 다음 주에 갑자기 중요한 출장이 생겼어요. 오늘 아침 사장님께서 전화하시더니 일정을 잡으셨네요. 다음 주 일주일 내내 자리를 비우게 돼서 다음 수업을 2번 연속으로 빠지게 되네요.

| Make-up Class Request |

I wonder if I might make up the classes I miss another time. That's great. I didn't know you had such a system in place. When is the makeup class scheduled? You have it every Saturday? Sure, I can be there. Also, is it possible for my friend to delay the start of her class, too? She's very shy and doesn't want to attend class without me. Thank you. That's so nice of you.

혹시 제가 보강을 할 수 있는지 궁금합니다. 정말 잘됐네요. 그런 제도가 있는 줄은 몰랐어요. 그럼 보강 수업은 언제 잡혀있나요? 매주 토요일에 있다고요? 그럼요, 참여할 수 있죠. 아, 그리고 혹시 제 친구도 수업을 연장할 수 있나요? 친구가 수줍음이 많아서 저 없이는 수업을 못 듣겠대요. 감사합니다. 정말 친절하시네요.

| Closing |

Thank you again. I'll get back to you when I return from my trip. Bye.

다시 한번 감사하고요, 출장 갔다 오면 다시 연락 드리겠습니다. 안녕히 계세요.

More Questions

〈노래하기〉에 관련하여 더 나올 수 있는 OPIc 질문들을 정리한 코너입니다. 질문에 대한 brainstorming을 해보세요.

1. Did you ever sing in front of others? When did you do that? What song did you sing?
2. I also like to sing. Ask me several questions about my favorite musician and song. In addition, ask me some of my singing habits.

On Your Own

앞에서 주어진 Model Answer을 바탕으로, 아래의 빈칸에 들어갈 수 있는 다양한 대체 가능한 어휘 및 표현들을 참고하여 학습자 본인만의 모범 답안을 직접 만들어보세요.

I Opening I

Hello. Is this Yuri? Hi. This is Suji. I signed up for your vocal training class this Monday.

I Missing Classes I

I'm terribly sorry, Yuri, but I had some issues come up at the last minute. I have to **ⓐ**_____ next week. **ⓑ**_____. I'll be **ⓒ**_____ the entire week next week, so I will miss the next two classes.

I Make-up Class Request I

I wonder if I might make up the classes I miss another time. That's great. I didn't know you had such a system in place. When is the makeup class scheduled? You have it every Saturday? Sure, I can be there. In addition, is it possible for my friend to delay the start of her class, too? She's very shy and doesn't want to attend class without me. Thank you. That's so nice of you.

I Closing I

Thank you again. I'll get back to you when **ⓓ**_____. Bye.

I Opening I Hello. Is this Yuri? Hi. This is Suji. I signed up for your vocal training class this Monday.

I Missing Classes I I'm terribly sorry, Yuri, but I had some issues come up at the last minute. I have to **ⓐ prepare for an upcoming school event** next week. **ⓑ I work in the PR office and have to design and print a brochure to promote the event.** I'll be **ⓒ tied up with work** the entire week next week, so I will miss the next two classes.

I Make-up Class Request I I wonder if I might make up the classes I miss another time. That's great! I didn't know you had such a system in place. When is the makeup class scheduled? You have it every Saturday? Sure, I can be there. In addition, is it possible for my friend to delay the start of her class, too? She's very shy and doesn't want to attend class without me. Thank you. That's so nice of you.

I Closing I Thank you again. I'll get back to you when **ⓓ the school event is over**. Bye.

본인이 만든 답안에 아래의 요소들이 포함되었는지 점검해 봅시다.

	Checklist
☐	전화 걸 때 인사말
☐	신분 밝히기
☐	전화 건 목적(수업 결석) 말하기
☐	보강 가능 여부 문의
☐	수업 연기 여부 문의
☐	마무리 인사

Unit 30 Singing 2

Unit 31 Dancing

춤추기

Warm Up

A Guess the Question & Answer
사진을 보면서 예상 질문과 답변을 먼저 추측해 봅시다.

B Listen & Talk
댄스 동아리에 관한 대화를 먼저 연습해 봅시다.

🎧 05-09

A Look at your moves. Where did you learn them?

B I just follow the moves of the singers I see on TV.

A I didn't know you could dance so well. Do you practice on your own?

B I mostly do that. But I belong to an amateur B-boy group and practice with them once a week.

A An amateur B-boy group? That sounds very interesting. How did you join them?

B I found them through an online community. I've been with them for two years.

A Do you perform on stage anytime?

B We do that every summer and winter. Are you interested in coming?

A Sure. I love to see dance performances. Also, hip-hop is one of my favorite genres.

B That's awesome. I'll invite you to our summer performance.

A 네 춤 동작 좀 봐. 어디서 배웠어?

B TV에서 가수들이 춤추는 걸 보고 따라 하는 거야.

A 네가 그렇게 춤을 잘 추는지 몰랐어. 혼자서 연습하는 거야?

B 대게 그래. 그렇지만 난 아마츄어 비보이 그룹에 속해 있어서 1주일에 한 번은 함께 연습해.

A 아마추어 비보이 그룹이라고? 굉장히 흥미롭다. 어떻게 같이 하게 됐어?

B 온라인 커뮤니티 통해서 알게 됐어. 2년째 함께 활동하고 있어.

A 무대에서 공연하기도 하니?

B 매 여름이랑 겨울에 해. 너 공연에 관심 있어?

A 그럼. 난 춤 공연 보는 거 정말 좋아해. 더구나 힙합은 내가 제일 좋아하는 장르 중에 하나야.

B 잘됐네! 이번 여름 공연 때 내가 초대할게.

Vocabulary
follow the moves 동작을 따라하다 | on one's own 혼자 (스스로) | belong to something ~에 소속되다 | amateur 아마추어 | online community 온라인 커뮤니티 | perform on stage 무대 위에서 공연하다 | genre 장르 | performance 공연

Key Expressions

아래 제시된 각 expression의 구조를 이해하고, 자기만의 표현들을 생각해 봅시다.

Expression 1 **ever since:** 그 후로 계속

저는 그 때부터 계속해서 춤추는 걸 좋아합니다! → I have enjoyed dancing **ever since**!

그를 만난 후로 제 인생은 정말 밝아졌습니다. → My life has turned so bright **ever since** I met him.

영국으로 이사 온 후, 저는 매일같이 차를 마셨습니다.
→ **Ever since** I moved to England, I have drunk tea every day.

Expression 2 **in front of ~:** ~앞에서

저는 사람들 앞에서 춤췄습니다. → I danced **in front of** people.

우리는 절벽 앞에 있는 빈 집을 찾았습니다. → We found an empty house **in front of** a cliff.

저는 제가 사람들 앞에서 보다 자신감이 있었으면 좋겠습니다.
→ I wish I could be more confident **in front of** people.

Expression 3 **a natural talent:** 천부적인 재능, 타고난 재능

저는 춤에 대한 타고난 재능이 있습니다. → I have **a natural talent** for dancing.

제이미 올리버는 요리에 타고난 재능이 있습니다. → Jamie Oliver has **a natural talent** for cooking.

악동뮤지션은 작곡에 천부적인 재능이 있습니다.
→ Akdong Musician has **a natural talent** for composing songs.

Expression 4 **no matter ~:** ~와 상관없이

저는 시간과 장소에 상관없이 노래에 따라 춤을 춥니다.
→ I dance along to songs **no matter** when it is or where I am.

네가 얼마나 화가 났던 간에, 말을 내뱉기 전에 두 번 생각하도록 하여라.
→ **No matter** how angry you are, think twice before you speak.

그는 사람들이 불평하든 말든 상관없이 밤에 음악을 크게 틀었습니다.
→ He played loud music at night **no matter** how much people complained.

Expression 5 **express oneself:** 스스로를 표현하다

저는 그것이 스스로를 표현하는 가장 좋은 방법 중의 하나라고 생각합니다.
→ I think it's one of the best ways to **express myself**.

많은 아이들은 감정을 표현하기 위해 그림을 그립니다.
→ Lots of children draw pictures to **express themselves**.

이소룡은 생전에 무술이 스스로를 표현할 수 있는 훌륭한 방법 중의 하나라고 했습니다.
→ Bruce Lee said that martial arts are a great way to **express oneself**.

Topic Question & Model Answer

 05-10

> **Topic Question**
>
> **Since when did you become interested in dancing? Did you learn how to dance from anyone? What makes you so interested in dancing?**
>
> 당신은 언제부터 춤추기에 관심이 있었나요? 누군가로부터 춤추는 법을 배웠나요? 당신은 춤추는 것이 왜 그렇게 좋나요?

TIP FOR THE OPIc

댄스 교습이라고 하면 흔히 학원에서 교습받는 것을 떠올리는데, 학원에 다니지 않는 경우라 하더라도 '어떻게 춤을 배웠는가'에 대해 말하면 됩니다. 예를 들면 친구로부터 춤을 배웠을 수도 있고, TV를 보면서 가수 안무를 따라하다가 배웠을 수도 있습니다. 혹은 댄스 동아리에서 춤을 연습할 수도 있고 인터넷 영상을 보며 춤을 익힐 수도 있습니다. 그냥 '몸이 가는 대로' 막춤을 출지도 모릅니다. 본인이 '춤을 추게 된 계기'에 대해 구체적으로 얘기하면 해당 질문에 대한 답안 구성이 자연스럽게 될 것입니다.

Model Answer

| Opening |

I think I've been interested in dancing since I was young.

저는 어렸을 적부터 춤추는 것에 흥미를 가졌던 것 같습니다.

| How I Got Interested in Dancing |

I remember the first time I danced in front of people. I was 6. There was a family gathering, and good music was on TV. I naturally started dancing and have enjoyed it ever since. I guess I have a natural talent for dancing. As long as there's good music, I just dance along to the song no matter when it is or where I am.

저는 제가 사람들 앞에서 처음 춤을 췄던 때가 기억이 납니다. 제가 6살 때였습니다. 그날 가족 모임이 있었는데, TV에서 좋은 음악이 나오고 있었습니다. 저는 자연스럽게 춤을 추기 시작했고, 그 후로 계속 춤추는 것을 즐깁니다. 저는 춤추는 데에 타고난 재능이 있는 것 같습니다. 좋은 음악만 있으면 저는 언제, 어디든지 상관없이 노래에 따라 춤을 춥니다.

| Why I Like to Dance |

I feel free when I'm dancing, and I think it's one of the best ways to express myself. It's also a good way to relieve my stress.

저는 춤을 출 때 자유로움을 느끼며, 춤추는 것이 제 자신을 표현하는 가장 좋은 방법 중 하나라고 생각합니다. 또한 제 스트레스를 해소하는 건전한 방법이기도 합니다.

More Questions

〈춤추기〉에 관련하여 더 나올 수 있는 OPIc 질문들을 정리한 코너입니다. 질문에 대한 brainstorming을 해보세요.

1. You indicated in the survey that you like to dance. What is good about dancing? How do you feel when you dance?
2. How did you get interested in dancing? Do you practice dancing often?
3. Tell me what you do before and after you go to the dance institute.

On Your Own

앞에서 주어진 Model Answer을 바탕으로, 아래의 빈칸에 들어갈 수 있는 다양한 대체 가능한 어휘 및 표현들을 참고하여 학습자 본인만의 모범 답안을 직접 만들어보세요.

| Opening |

I think I've been interested in dancing since I was young.

| How I Got Interested in Dancing |

I remember the first time I danced in front of people. I was ⓐ_____.

ⓑ_____.

I naturally started dancing and have enjoyed it ever since. I guess I have a natural talent for dancing. As long as there's good music, I just dance along to the song no matter when it is or where I am.

| Why I Like to Dance |

I feel free when I'm dancing, and I think it's ⓒ_____.

It's also a good way to relieve my stress.

| Opening | I think I've been interested in dancing since I was young.

| How I Got Interested in Dancing | I remember the first time I danced in front of people. I was ⓐ **16**. ⓑ **We went on a school picnic, and there was a dance time. We played several hit songs from the time**. I naturally started dancing and have enjoyed it ever since. I guess I have a natural talent for dancing. As long as there's good music, I just dance along to the song no matter when it is or where I am.

| Why I Like to Dance | I feel free when I'm dancing, and I think it's ⓒ **just exciting to dance to the music**. It's also a good way to relieve my stress.

Checklist

- ☐ 춤에 흥미를 가지게 된 동기
- ☐ 처음 춤을 췄던 기억
- ☐ 언제 주로 춤추는지
- ☐ 어디서 주로 춤추는지
- ☐ 왜 춤추는 게 좋은지
- ☐ 어떤 음악에 맞춰 춤추는지

본인이 만든 답안에 아래의 요소들이 포함되었는지 점검해 봅시다.

Unit 32 Dancing Lessons

댄스 교습하기

Warm Up

A Guess the Question & Answer
사진을 보면서 예상 질문과 답변을 먼저 추측해 봅시다.

B Listen & Talk
댄스 학원 등록에 관한 대화를 먼저 연습해 봅시다.

🎧 05-11

A Hi. I registered for the moonwalk class last week and was just about to join your class. But I couldn't find my name on the list. What's wrong?

B Hi. Can I have your first name, please?

A My name is Catherine.

B And your last name, please?

A Hwang. H-w-a-n-g.

B Catherine Hwang. Hmm. We don't have that name on the list. Sorry, but do you have the receipt?

A No, but I remember that I wired you online on April 23. Can you check your bank account?

B Sure. Oh, I think we do have your name printed on our bank account. It seems to be misspelled though. We have Cathy Hong on the list.

A That happens sometimes. Well, now can I join the class?

B Please go ahead.

A 안녕하세요. 지난주에 문워크 수업에 등록해서 조금 전 수업에 참여하려고 했어요. 그런데 제 이름이 명단에 없네요. 무슨 일이죠?

B 성함이 어떻게 되시죠?

A 제 이름은 캐서린입니다.

B 성이 어떻게 되시죠?

A 황씨에요. H-w-a-n-g라고 쓰죠.

B 캐서린 황. 음. 명단에 성함을 찾을 수가 없네요. 실례지만 영수증은 있으신가요?

A 아뇨, 하지만 4월 23일에 온라인 입금을 했던 것으로 기억해요. 은행 계좌 좀 확인해 주시겠어요?

B 네. 아, 저희 계좌에서 고객님 성함을 찾은 것 같네요. 그런데 잘못 표기가 된 것 같네요. 캐시 홍이라고 적혀있어요.

A 가끔 일어나는 일이죠. 그럼 이제 수업에 참여해도 되나요?

B 네, 어서 시작하세요.

Vocabulary | register for ~ ~에 등록하다 | moonwalk class 문워크 춤 강습반 | be about to ~ 막~하려고 하다 | receipt 영수증 | bank account 계좌 | wire 송금하다 | misspell 철자가 잘못 되다 | on the list 명단에 적힌 | go ahead 먼저 말하다, 계속하다, 들어가다

Key Expressions

> 아래 제시된 각 expression의 구조를 이해하고, 자기만의 표현들을 생각해 봅시다.

Expression 1 take a class: 수업을 듣다

저는 재즈 수업을 듣고 싶었습니다. → I want to **take** the jazz dance **class**.

저는 이번 학기에 3 과목을 수강하고 있습니다. → I am **taking** 3 **classes** this semester.

한번에 그렇게 많은 과목을 수강하는 것은 어렵다. → It's hard to **take** so many **classes** all at once.

Expression 2 put one's name on the list: 명단에 이름을 올리다

그는 제 이름을 명단에 올려놨습니다. → He **put my name on the list**.

연회 참석자 명단에 부디 제 이름을 올려놔주세요. → Please **put my name on the list** for the banquet.

나는 오늘 아침 후보자 명단에서 네 이름을 봤다.
→ I saw **your name on the list** of candidates this morning.

Expression 3 open class: 오픈 수업, 참관 수업

저는 오픈 수업에 참여하고 싶었습니다. → I wanted to join the **open class**.

학교는 모든 학부모님을 오픈 수업에 초대했습니다.
→ The school invited all the parents to its **open class**.

선생님들은 다가오는 오픈 수업으로 인해 매우 긴장하고 있습니다.
→ The teachers are nervous about the upcoming **open class**.

Expression 4 go wrong: 잘못되다, 잘못된 방향으로 가다

뭐가 잘못된 건지 확인해주시겠어요? → Would you please check what **went wrong**?

이제 와서 보니 그 프로젝트에 있어 정말 많은 것이 잘못되어 왔음을 알 수 있습니다.
→ I can now see that many things are **going wrong** with the project.

우리는 컴퓨터 시스템에 어떤 문제가 있는지 찾아낼 필요가 있다.
→ We need to figure out what's **going wrong** with the computer system.

Expression 5 misspell: 철자를 잘못 표기하다

그가 제 이름의 철자를 잘못 기입했습니다. → He **misspelled** my name.

그 지역에는 잘못 표기된 도로명이 많습니다. → Lots of street names are **misspelled** in that area.

저는 문서에 단어 몇 개의 철자를 잘못 표기한 것 같습니다.
→ I'm afraid I **misspelled** some words in the document.

Topic Question & Model Answer

🎧 05-12

Topic Question

Suppose you registered for a dance class and went to the studio but encountered a problem. Your name is not on the list. What do you do? Ask the secretary for help and also see if there are any alternative choices.

당신이 댄스 수업을 등록한 후 학원에 갔는데 문제가 생겼다고 가정해보세요. 당신의 이름이 명단에서 누락되었습니다. 어떻게 할 건가요? 비서에게 도움을 요청하고 다른 대안이 있는지 확인해보세요.

TIP FOR THE OPIc

앞서 나온 댄스 교습 학원 등록 과정에서 문제가 발생했다는 가정 하에 해당 상황을 해결해보라는 질문입니다. 특정 기관의 등록 과정에서 이름이 잘못 쓰여졌다든지, 지불 사항에 대한 기록이 누락되는 등의 사건이 일어날 수 있습니다. 이럴 때는 상대방에게 차분하게 먼저 언제, 누구를 통해 등록을 했는지를 설명한 후 도움을 요청하면 됩니다. 본인이 특별히 어떻게 도움 받고 싶은지를 자세히 요구하는 것도 좋습니다.

Model Answer

| Opening |

Hi. Are you the secretary of this dance school? Okay. Hi, Mijoo. My name is Jiyoung and I want to take the jazz dance class.

안녕하세요. 당신이 이 댄스 학원의 비서인가요? 네. 안녕하세요, 미주씨. 제 이름은 지영이고요, 재즈 댄스 수업을 듣고 싶어요.

| Name Is Missing from the List |

I talked to one of your staff members the other day and asked the person to put my name on the list for the open class. I just came to join the class, but I can't find my name on the list! I'm not sure what happened. Would you please check what went wrong? Can I still take the open class? Yes, I brought my ID card. Here you go. Well, thank you for your help. I guess the other staff member made a mistake.

며칠 전에 학원 직원 한 분과 통화하면서 공개 수업 참가자 명단에 이름을 적어달라고 했었어요. 방금 공개 수업을 들으러 왔는데, 명단에서 제 이름을 못 찾겠어요! 무슨 일인지 모르겠네요. 뭐가 잘못됐는지 확인해주시겠어요? 공개 수업에 참여할 수 있는 건가요? 네, 제 신분증을 가져왔어요. 여기 있어요. 도와주셔서 감사합니다. 다른 직원이 실수를 한 것 같네요.

| Problem Solving and Closing |

Oh, so he misspelled my name. Jaehyung? No, no. My name is J-I-Y-O-U-N-G. Not Jaehyung. It's all right. Thank you for your help. Bye.

아, 제 이름을 잘못 적었군요. 재형이라고 적혀 있다고요? 아니, 아니에요. 제 이름은 지영, J-I-Y-O-U-N-G라고 써요. 재형이 아니에요. 괜찮아요. 도와주셔서 감사합니다. 안녕히 계세요.

More Questions

〈댄스 교습하기〉에 관련하여 더 나올 수 있는 OPIc 질문들을 정리한 코너입니다. 질문에 대한 brainstorming을 해보세요.

1. What kind of dance do you like? Salsa? Tango? Hip-hop? Jazz dance? Tell me about your favorite type of dance in detail.

2. Are you taking any dance classes these days? Or have you ever taken a dance class before? Tell me about the dance institute you attended.

앞에서 주어진 Model Answer을 바탕으로, 아래의 빈칸에 들어갈 수 있는 다양한 대체 가능한 어휘 및 표현들을 참고하여 학습자 본인만의 모범 답안을 직접 만들어보세요.

l Opening l

Hi. Are you the secretary of this dance school? Okay. Hi, Mijoo. My name is Jiyoung and I want to take the ⓐ_____.

l Name Is Missing from the List l

I talked to one of your staff members the other day and asked the person to put my name on the list for the open class. I just came to join the class, but I can't find my name on the list! I'm not sure what happened. Would you please check what went wrong? Can I still take the open class? Yes, I brought my ID card. Here you go. Well, thank you for your help. I guess the other staff member made a mistake.

l Problem Solving and Closing l

Oh, so ⓑ_____? It's all right. Thank you for your help. Bye.

---

l Opening l Hi. Are you the secretary of this dance school? Okay. Hi, Mijoo. My name is Jiyoung, and I want to take the ⓐ **salsa dance class**.

l Name Is Missing from the List l I talked to one of your staff members the other day and asked the person to put my name on the list for the open class. I just came to join the class, but I can't find my name on the list! I'm not sure what happened. Would you please check what went wrong? Can I still take the open class? Yes, I brought my ID card. Here you go. Well, thank you for your help. I guess the other staff member made a mistake.

l Problem Solving and Closing l Oh, so ⓑ **my name was on the wrong list**? It's all right. Thank you for your help. Bye.

본인이 만든 답안에 아래의 요소들이 포함되었는지 점검해 봅시다.

Checklist
☐ 도움 받을 사람 찾기
☐ 신분 밝히기
☐ 문제 상황(이름 누락) 설명하기
☐ 해결 방안 문의하기
☐ 문제 해결하기 (이름 확인)
☐ 감사 표현. 마무리

Unit 32 Dancing Lessons

Unit 33 Cooking 1

요리하기 1

Warm Up

A Guess the Question & Answer
사진을 보면서 예상 질문과 답변을 먼저 추측해 봅시다.

B Listen & Talk
친구 집에 방문할 때 음식을 준비해가는 것에 대한 대화를 먼저 연습해 봅시다.

🎧 05-13

A Suji is throwing a potluck party tonight. Are you going?

B Oh, I thought it was a sleep-over party for the girls.

A The sleep-over is after the potluck party. Make sure to take your pajamas.

B What food are you bringing?

A Some appetizers from a Vietnamese restaurant. I ordered some spring rolls, dim-sum, and a rice noodle salad.

B Sounds yummy. I'm going to get some lasagna and meatball pasta.

A Wow. I'll be able to eat like a horse when the party starts.

B Me too. I can't wait!

A 오늘 수지가 포틀럭 파티를 연대. 너도 갈 거야?

B 아, 나는 여자들끼리 밤새 놀다 자고 오는 건 줄 알았는데.

A 포틀럭 파티 끝나면 그렇게 할거야. 잠옷 챙겨오는 거 잊지 마.

B 넌 어떤 음식 가지고 올 거야?

A 베트남 음식점에서 전채 요리 좀 가져오려고. 이미 스프링 롤이랑 딤섬이랑 쌀국수 샐러드 주문해놨어.

B 맛있겠다. 난 라자냐랑 미트볼 파스타를 조금씩 싸오려고.

A 와. 난 파티 시작하면 완전 돼지처럼 먹을 거야.

B 나도. 못 참겠어!

Vocabulary | **throw a party** 파티를 열다 | **sleep-over party** 하룻밤 자고 가는 파티 | **potluck party** 각자 먹을 것을 가져와서 나눠 먹는 파티 | **make sure to ~** ~하는 것을 확실히 하다 | **appetizer** 전채요리, 식전 요리 | **dim-sum** 만두류 요리 | **lasagna** 라쟈냐 | **meatball pasta** 작은 공 모양으로 고기를 만들어 넣은 파스타 | **eat like a horse** 돼지 같이 먹다, 많이 먹다

Key Expressions

> 아래 제시된 각 expression의 구조를 이해하고, 자기만의 표현들을 생각해 봅시다.

Expression 1 potluck party: 포틀럭 파티 (각자 음식을 조금씩 가져 와서 나눠 먹는 식사)

당신은 포틀럭 파티를 여시죠, 맞죠? → You are having a **potluck party**, right?

내령은 오늘밤 포틀럭 파티를 엽니다. 와서 함께 하세요.
→ Naeryung is throwing a **potluck party** tonight. Come and join us.

노아의 가족은 매년 크리스마스 때마다 포틀럭 파티를 주최합니다.
→ Noah's family throws a **potluck party** during the Christmas season each year.

Expression 2 a little bit of everything: 조금씩 모두 다

아, 당신은 모든 걸 조심씩 다 원하는군요? → Oh, you want **a little bit of everything**?

우리는 부페 음식을 조금씩 모두 다 먹어봤습니다. → We tried **a little bit of everything** at the buffet.

이 진열창에 있는 것을 모두 다 조금씩 포장해주시겠어요?
→ Can you please gift-wrap **a little bit of everything** in this display window?

Expression 3 거리/시간 + away: ~만큼의 거리/시간이 걸리는

그곳은 역으로부터 두 블록만 더 가면 있습니다. → It's only **two blocks away** from the station.

그 사진관은 대문으로부터 열 발자국 정도 떨어진 곳에 있습니다.
→ The studio is about **10 steps away** from the gate.

저희 할머니는 베벌리힐스에서 20마일 떨어진 곳에 살고 계십니다.
→ My grandmother lives only **20 miles away** from Beverly Hills.

Expression 4 stop by (at) ~: ~에 들르다

근처 아이스크림 가게에 잠시 들를 수 있습니다. → I can **stop by at** a nearby ice cream shop.

주유소에 잠시 들르는 게 좋겠습니다. → We'd better **stop by** the gas station.

모든 승객은 수하물 찾는 구역에 들렀습니다.
→ All the passengers **stopped by** the baggage claim area.

Expression 5 can't wait for/to 부정사: ~이 매우 기다려지다

저는 파티가 굉장히 기다려집니다. → I **can't wait for** the party.

우리는 그의 특별 앨범 발매가 매우 기다려집니다. → We **can't wait for** his special album release.

저는 제 절친의 변신을 얼른 보고 싶습니다. → I **can't wait to** see my best friend's make-over.

Topic Question & Model Answer

Topic Question

Your friend is having a party, and you have to bring some food. Call your friend and ask her or him 3 to 4 questions.

당신의 친구가 파티를 여는데 당신은 음식을 가져가야 합니다. 친구에게 전화해서 3~4가지 질문을 해보세요.

> **TIP FOR THE OPIc**
> '집에서 휴가 보내기' 혹은 '집안일 거들기' 항목과 연관된 롤플레이 질문입니다. 친구의 집에 놀러간다고 가정하고 음식 준비에 관해 질문하라는 것은, 결국 집들이(파티)에 관한 전반적인 것을 질문해도 된다는 것입니다. 친구가 선호하는 음식의 종류, 집들이의 규모 및 초대 손님의 연령층 등에 대해 물어볼 수 있습니다. 친한 친구의 집에 놀러간다고 가정하면 보다 편하고 자연스럽게 답안을 만들어갈 수 있을 것입니다.

Model Answer

| Opening |

Hello? Jina? Hi. This is Suji. I called you to ask you a few questions about the party you are throwing this Saturday.

여보세요? 지나야. 안녕, 나 수지야. 이번 주 토요일에 네가 여는 파티에 관해 몇 가지 물어보려고 전화했어.

| What Food to Bring to the Party |

You are having a potluck party, right? Cool. So what kind of dish do you want me to bring? An appetizer? A main dish? A dessert? Oh, okay. You want me to bring a dessert? Sure. What do you prefer? Chocolate, coffee, cake, or pie? Oh, you want a little bit of everything? No problem.

각자 음식을 조금씩 준비해오는 파티라고 했지? 좋아. 그럼, 내가 어떤 음식을 가져 갔으면 좋겠어? 전채 요리? 주 요리? 디저트? 아, 알았어. 디저트 가져오라고? 그렇게 할게. 초콜릿, 커피, 케이크, 파이 중에서는 뭐가 좋아? 아, 조금씩 다 가져왔으면 좋겠어? 문제 없어.

| Party Time and Location |

How do I get to your place from the nearest station? It's only two blocks away from the station? Great! Then I can even stop by at a nearby ice cream shop. I'll see you at your place at 7 p.m. on Saturday.

가장 가까운 지하철역에서 너희 집까지는 어떻게 가야 돼? 역에서 두 블록밖에 안 된다고? 최고야! 그럼 가까운 아이스크림 집에 들러도 되겠다. 그럼 토요일 저녁 7시에 너희 집으로 갈게.

| Closing |

I can't wait for the party. See you soon. Bye.

파티가 정말 기다려진다. 곧 만나. 안녕.

More Questions

〈요리하기〉에 관련하여 더 나올 수 있는 OPIc 질문들을 정리한 코너입니다. 질문에 대한 brainstorming을 해보세요.

1. Tell me about the first time you cooked. What did you cook? Who did you cook for? How did you like the food?
2. What is the most unique dish you've ever had? When did you have it? Who were you with?
3. Do you often eat out? Where do you go to dine? What do you order?

On Your Own

앞에서 주어진 Model Answer을 바탕으로, 아래의 빈칸에 들어갈 수 있는 다양한 대체 가능한 어휘 및 표현들을 참고하여 학습자 본인만의 모범 답안을 직접 만들어보세요.

I Opening I

Hello? Jina? Hi. This is Suji. I called you to ask you a few questions about the party you are throwing this Saturday.

I What Food to Bring to the Party I

You are having a potluck party, right? Cool. So what kind of dish do you want me to bring? An appetizer? A main dish? A dessert? Oh, okay. You want me to bring a
ⓐ_____? Sure. What do you prefer? ⓑ_____?
Oh, you want ⓒ_____? No problem.

I Party Time and Location I

How do I get to your place from the nearest station? It's only two blocks away from the station? Great! I'll see you at your place at 7 p.m. on Saturday.

I Closing I

I can't wait for the party. See you soon. Bye.

I Opening I
Hello? Jina? Hi. This is Suji. I called to ask you a few questions about the party you are throwing this Saturday.

I What Food to Bring to the Party I You are having a potluck party, right? Cool. So what kind of dish do you want me to bring? An appetizer? A main dish? A dessert? Oh, okay. You want me to bring a ⓐ **main dish**? Sure. What do you prefer? ⓑ **Pasta, *jabche*, California rolls, or fried rice noodles**? Oh, you want ⓒ *jabche*? No problem.

I Party Time and Location I How do I get to your place from the nearest station? It's only two blocks away from the station? Great! I'll see you at your place at 7 p.m. on Saturday.

I Closing I I can't wait for the party. See you soon. Bye.

본인이 만든 답안에 아래의 요소들이 포함되었는지 점검해 봅시다.

	Checklist
☐	전화 걸 때 인사말
☐	신분 밝히기
☐	전화 건 목적(파티 문의) 말하기
☐	어떤 음식 준비할지 문의
☐	파티 장소 및 시간 확인
☐	마무리 인사

Unit 34 Cooking 2

요리하기 2

Warm Up

A Guess the Question & Answer
사진을 보면서 예상 질문과 답변을 먼저 추측해 봅시다.

B Listen & Talk
친구 집에 음식을 갖고 가는 도중에 생긴 돌발상황에 관한 대화를 연습해 봅시다. 🎧 05-15

A Shoot. Are you all right?

B That was really close. I'm fine. How about you?

A I'm okay. But I think I got a scratch on my car.

B Oh, no. The food... It's all ruined. What should we do? The party begins in 15 minutes.

A Call Suji and tell her that we will be late. We can drop by at a nearby restaurant for food, but I think I should call the insurance company first.

B Go ahead. I'll talk to Suji about the accident. She'll understand. I'm sure the guests will be patient as well. Don't worry.

A 이런. 너 괜찮아?

B 정말 큰 일 날 뻔 했다. 난 괜찮아. 넌?

A 나도 괜찮아. 그런데 차가 좀 긁힌 것 같아.

B 이런, 안 돼. 음식 좀 봐… 다 망가졌네. 우리 어떡하지? 15분 뒤면 파티가 시작하잖아.

A 수지한테 전화해서 늦을 거라고 얘기해. 근처 식당에 들르면 음식이야 사갈 수 있지만, 난 우선 보험사에 전화해야 할 것 같아.

B 그래. 난 수지에게 사고가 났다고 얘기할게. 이해할 거야. 손님들도 분명 기다려 줄 거야. 염려 마.

Vocabulary

shoot 영어로 '제길'을 완화시켜서 한 말 | **close** (위험한 상황이) 가까스로 모면한 | **get a scratch on ~** ~에 스크래치가 나다 | **ruined** 망가진 | **drop by at ~** ~에 잠시 들르다 | **insurance company** 보험 회사 | **be patient** 인내하다, 참다

Key Expressions

아래 제시된 각 expression의 구조를 이해하고, 자기만의 표현들을 생각해 봅시다.

Expression 1   a minor car accident: 경미한 자동차 사고

저는 방금 경미한 자동차 사고가 났습니다. → I was just in **a minor car accident**.

제 렌터카는 경미한 교통사고로 인해 스크래치가 났습니다.
→ My rental car got a scratch in **a minor car accident**.

저는 고속도로에서 일어난 경미한 자동차 사고 때문에 교통 체증에 걸렸습니다.
→ I was stuck in traffic due to **a minor car accident** on the highway.

Expression 2   on one's way to ~: ~에 가는 길에

저는 당신의 집에 후식을 갖고 가는 길이었습니다.
→ I was **on my way to** your place with the dessert.

나의 사촌은 교회 가는 길에 저를 태워다 줬습니다. → My cousin gave me a ride **on his way to** church.

민호는 호텔에 가는 길에 휴대폰을 잃어버렸습니다.
→ Minho lost his cellular phone **on his way to** the hotel.

Expression 3   bump into ~: ~에 부딪히다, 우연히~를 만나다

내 차를 주차하다가, 나는 다른 차와 부딪혔다. → Parking my car, I **bumped into** another car.

내 동생은 유리 문에 부딪혀서 이마를 다쳤습니다.
→ My brother **bumped into** the glass door and hurt his forehead.

동호는 길을 가다 그의 고등학교때 친구를 우연히 만났습니다.
→ Dongho **bumped into** his high school friend on the street.

Expression 4   be a relief: 마음이 놓이다, 부담에서 벗어나다

와, 그것 참 마음이 놓이는 일이네요. → Well, that **is a relief**.

그가 회복되었다는 소식을 듣게 되어 마음이 놓였습니다.
→ It **was** truly **a relief** to hear about his recovery.

은행 대출을 다 갚을 수 있어서 정말 다행입니다
→ **It's a** huge **relief** that we were able to pay back the bank loans.

Expression 5   be patient: 인내하다, 기다리다

손님들에게 기다려달라고 전해주세요. → Ask your guests to **be patient**.

잠시 기다려주세요. 거의 다 도착했습니다. → Please **be patient**. We are almost there.

마음 가운데 풀리지 않은 질문들에 대하여 인내하십시오.
→ **Be patient** about all the unanswered questions in your heart.

Topic Question & Model Answer

🎧 05-16

Topic Question

Here's a problem you have to resolve. The food you prepared for the party got damaged on the way to the party venue. Call your friend and explain the situation. 여기 당신이 해결해야 할 문제가 있습니다. 당신이 파티에 가져가려고 준비했던 음식이 파티 장소에 가던 중에 손상되었습니다. 친구에게 전화해서 상황을 설명해보세요.

> **TIP FOR THE OPIc**
>
> 앞서 나온 '집에서 휴가 보내기' 혹은 '집안일 거들기' 항목과 연관된 롤플레이 심화 질문입니다. 친구의 집에 가던 길에 예상치 못한 상황으로 인해 음식물이 손상되었다면 당황스럽겠지요. 먼저 친구에게 상황 설명을 하고, 사과를 한 후에 있을 법한 대안을 제시해준다면 출제자의 의도에 맞는 답안이 될 것입니다. 롤플레이에서는 답안의 내용도 중요하지만, 상황에 맞는 목소리를 연출하는 것도 필수입니다. 약간의 role-playing을 통해 한 등급 올려보시기 바랍니다!

Model Answer

| Opening |

Hello, Jina? Hi. How are you? Cool. Are there a lot of people coming tonight? There are already 15 people at your place?

여보세요, 지나야? 안녕, 잘 지내? 그렇구나. 오늘 저녁에 손님 많이 와? 벌써 15명이나 왔다고?

| Why I'm Late for the Party |

Jina, I'm terribly sorry to tell you this, but I was just in a minor car accident. I was on my way to your place with the desserts, but I bumped into the car in front of me. Nope. Nobody is hurt. But the food is ruined. The desserts don't look good. I should get some new ones.

지나야, 이 얘기하기 정말 미안한데, 나 방금 가벼운 차 사고가 났어. 디저트 가지고 네 집으로 가던 길이었는데, 앞서 가던 차를 박았어. 아냐. 아무도 안 다쳤어. 그런데 음식이 엉망이 됐어. 디저트가 보기 딱해. 새 것을 사야겠어.

| Suggestions |

So people are having the appetizers now? Oh, that's a relief. I'll go to a nearby bakery and get the best desserts it has. But I'm going to be a little late because the traffic is pretty bad right now. Ask your guests to be patient because the desserts are coming.

응, 사람들이 이제 전채 요리를 먹는 중이야? 와, 정말 다행이다. 근처 빵집에 있는 최고의 디저트를 준비해갈게. 그런데 지금 교통 체증이 너무 심해서 내가 좀 늦을 것 같아. 손님들에게 조금만 참고 디저트를 기다려달라고 부탁해줘.

| Closing |

Okay, I'll get to your place as soon as possible. See you. Bye.

그래, 최대한 빨리 너희 집으로 갈게. 곧 만나! 안녕.

More Questions

〈요리하기〉에 관련하여 더 나올 수 있는 OPIc 질문들을 정리한 코너입니다. 질문에 대한 brainstorming을 해보세요.

1. What kind of dish do you cook the most often? Do you have a special recipe? Give me the details of your cooking process.

2. Did you learn how to cook from anyone? For example, did your mother teach you how to cook? Tell me how you first got interested in cooking.

On Your Own

앞에서 주어진 Model Answer을 바탕으로, 아래의 빈칸에 들어갈 수 있는 다양한 대체 가능한 어휘 및 표현들을 참고하여 학습자 본인만의 모범 답안을 직접 만들어보세요.

I Opening I

Hello, Jina? Hi. How are you? Cool. Are there a lot of people coming tonight? There are already many people at your place?

I Why I'm Late for the Party I

Jina, I'm terribly sorry to tell you this, but I just ⓐ_____.
ⓑ_____. I was on my way to your place with ⓒ_____,
but I ⓓ_____. Nope. ⓔ_____. But the food is
ruined. The food doesn't look good. I should get some new food.

I Suggestions I

So people are having the appetizers now? Well, that's a relief. I'll go to a nearby
ⓕ_____. But I'm going to be a little late because I feel a
little pain on my knee. I think I should stop by at a nearby pharmacy. Ask your guests
to be patient because the desserts are coming.

I Closing I

Okay, I'll get to your place as soon as possible. See you.

I Opening I Hello, Jina? Hi. How are you? Cool. Are there a lot of people coming tonight? There are already many people at your place?

I Why I'm Late for the Party I Jina, I'm terribly sorry to tell you this, but I just ⓐ **dropped the food I was taking.** ⓑ **I tripped on a rock.** I was on my way to your place with ⓒ *jabche* and Korean pancakes, but I ⓓ **didn't see a big rock on the street.** Nope. ⓔ **I'm not hurt.** But the food is ruined. The food doesn't look good. I should get some new food.

I Suggestions I So people are having the appetizers now? Well, that's a relief. I'll go to a nearby ⓕ **Korean restaurant and get some new dishes.** But I'm going to be a little late because I feel a little pain on my knee. I think I should stop by at a nearby pharmacy. Ask your guests to be patient because the desserts are coming.

I Closing I Okay, I'll get to your place as soon as possible. See you.

본인이 만든 답안에 아래의 요소들이 포함되었는지 점검해 봅시다.

	Checklist
☐	전화 걸 때 인사말
☐	신분 밝히기
☐	파티에 늦는 이유 설명하기
☐	사과하기
☐	음식물 훼손된 사실 말하기
☐	대안 제시
☐	마무리 인사

Unit 35 Reading 1

독서하기 1 (E-reading)

Warm Up

A Guess the Question & Answer
사진을 보면서 예상 질문과 답변을 먼저 추측해 봅시다.

B Listen & Talk
전자책과 종이책의 차이에 관한 대화를 연습해 봅시다. 🎧 05-17

A Joshua, have you ever read electronic books?	A 죠슈아, 혹시 전자책 읽어본 적 있니?
B Yes, I have. In fact, I read e-books more often than paper books. Why do you ask?	B 응, 있지. 사실 난 종이책보다는 전자책을 더 자주 읽어. 근데 왜 묻는 거야?
A As technology is changing our lives, I thought it might have affected people's reading styles as well.	A 기술 발달로 인해 우리 삶이 달라지는데 어쩌면 사람들의 독서 문화도 영향을 받고 있지 않을까 생각했거든.
B I see. What about you? Do you read e-books?	B 그렇구나. 넌 어때? 전자책을 읽니?
A I tried once, but my eyes got tired very soon. I get a headache when I look at a computer screen for a long time.	A 한 번 읽어본 적이 있는데 눈이 금방 피로해졌어. 난 오랫동안 컴퓨터 화면을 보면 머리가 아프더라고.
B I don't have such a problem. I like e-books because it is easier to purchase them. Also, I don't need any space to keep the books because they are saved on the computer.	B 난 그런 문제는 없어. 내가 전자책을 좋아하는 이유는 구입하기가 더 쉬워서야. 그리고 책이 컴퓨터 안에 저장되어 있으니 책을 보관할 공간이 필요 없잖아.
A That's true.	A 맞아.
B But I like reading paper books, too. It's fun to flip through the pages!	B 하지만 난 종이책을 읽는 것도 좋아해. 종이를 넘기면서 읽는 것이 재미있어!
A Not only that, but I also love to smell old books. They smell like grass and vanilla.	A 그뿐만 아니라 나는 낡은 책 향기를 맡는 것도 좋아해. 마치 풀 내음과 바닐라 향을 섞어 놓은듯 해.
B I like them, too. In addition, seeing the book covers is a lot of fun. Many of them are so inspiring!	B 나도 좋아해. 게다가 책 표지를 보는 것도 상당히 재미있어. 책 표지 가운데 영감을 주는 것들도 많잖아!

Vocabulary
affect 영향을 미치다 | **flip through** (책장 등을) 넘기다, (기사를) 훑어보다 | **inspiring** 영감을 주는

Key Expressions

아래 제시된 각 expression의 구조를 이해하고, 자기만의 표현들을 생각해 봅시다.

Expression 1   the most common method of: 가장 흔한 ~의 방법

사람들이 가장 흔히 독서하는 방법은 종이로 된 책을 읽는 것입니다.
→ **The most common method of** reading these days is reading physical books.

이러닝은 영어를 학습하는 가장 일반적인 방법입니다.
→ E-learning is **the most common method of** picking up English.

요즘 사람들이 가장 흔히 사용하는 결제 수단이 무엇인가요?
→ What is **the most common method of** paying one's bill these days?

Expression 2   a significant rise in + 명사: 눈에 띄는 ~의 증가

전자책을 읽는 비중이 상당히 높아지고 있습니다. → There has been **a significant rise in** e-reading.

지진 발생률이 상당히 높아지고 있습니다.
→ There has been **a significant rise in** the number of earthquakes.

홈스쿨링 학생의 수가 급증하고 있습니다.
→ There is **a significant rise in** the number of homeschooling students.

Expression 3   명사-friendly: ~에 친화적인, ~에 우호적인

그곳은 책을 읽기에 최적의 환경이 갖추어져 있습니다. → They have a very **reader-friendly** environment.

저희 이웃은 지나칠 정도로 애완동물에게 친절합니다. → Our neighbors are extremely **pet-friendly**.

저는 환경친화적일 수만 있다면 무엇이든 합니다. → I do everything I can do to be **ecofriendly**.

Expression 4   search for + 목적어 + online: 온라인으로 ~를 검색하다

그는 온라인으로 원하는 것을 검색하는 것이 더 쉽습니다. → It is easier to **search for** what he wants **online**.

온라인으로 예전 기사를 찾는 것은 꽤 편리합니다. → It's so convenient to **search for** old articles **online**.

온라인에서 원하는 것을 검색할 경우 키워드를 입력하면 됩니다.
→ Type in the key words to **search for** what you want **online**.

Expression 5   e-books and e-journals: 전자책과 전자잡지

그는 전자책이나 전자잡지를 읽는 것을 좋아합니다. → He enjoys reading **e-books and e-journals**.

기회가 주어진다면 저는 전자책과 전자잡지를 발행하고 싶습니다.
→ I want to publish **e-books and e-journals** when I get a chance.

전자책과 전자잡지를 읽을 때면 눈이 쉽게 피로해집니다.
→ My eyes get easily tired when I read **e-books and e-journals**.

Topic Question & Model Answer

🎧 05-18

Topic Question

What's the most common method of reading? Many people read e-books nowadays. What about you? How do you access reading in general? Tell me everything about it. 가장 흔한 독서 방법은 무엇인가요? 요즘 많은 사람들이 전자책을 읽습니다. 당신의 경우는 어떠한가요? 당신은 보통 어떤 방법으로 책을 읽나요? 그에 관해 전부 이야기해보세요.

TIP FOR THE OPIc
독서 관련 질문은 본인이 좋아하는 책의 주인공, 사고의 전환을 가져다 준 책, 주로 독서하는 장소 등에 대해 물어볼 수 있습니다. 난이도 5 이상부터는 전자책에 관한 질문이 자주 등장하기 때문에 전자책을 읽지 않더라도 그에 대한 특징을 서술할 수 있어야 합니다.

Model Answer

| Opening |

I think the most common method of reading these days is still reading physical books. Although there has been a significant rise in e-reading, statistics show that the number of paper book readers far exceeds the number of people who read e-books.

오늘날 가장 흔한 독서 방식은 여전히 종이로 된 책을 읽는 것이라고 생각합니다. 전자책을 읽는 수치가 상당히 높아졌음에도 불구하고, 통계에 따르면 전자책을 읽는 사람보다 훨씬 많은 수의 사람들이 종이책을 읽는다고 합니다.

| Favorite Reading Spot |

I also enjoy reading paper books. I access them by going to used bookstores, bookstores, and libraries. I especially enjoy visiting the ABC Bookstore. It has a very reader-friendly environment. I love to sit at the wooden tables, where I can spend plenty of time with books before purchasing them.

저 역시 종이책을 즐겨 읽습니다. 저는 주로 중고서점이나 서점 혹은 도서관에 가서 책을 봅니다. 저는 특히 ABC 문고에 가는 것을 좋아합니다. 그곳에는 책을 읽기에 최적의 환경이 갖추어져 있습니다. 저는 그곳에 있는 나무 탁자에 앉아서 책을 구입하기 전에 책을 찬찬히 훑어볼 수 있습니다.

| Benefits of E-reading |

Unlike me, my husband enjoys reading e-books and e-journals. He is a tech person who spends hours using the computer. He says he prefers to read e-books to paper books because it is easier to search for what he wants online.

저와 달리 제 남편은 전자책이나 전자잡지를 읽는 것을 좋아합니다. 그는 기계를 잘 만지는 사람으로 몇 시간씩 컴퓨터를 사용합니다. 남편은 온라인으로 읽고 싶은 책을 검색하기가 더 쉽기 때문에 전자책을 선호한다고 합니다.

| Closing |

In summary, people read both physical books and e-books, but the old-style of reading is still more popular even in the 21st century.

요컨대 사람들은 전자책과 종이로 된 책을 모두 읽는데, 21세기에도 여전히 전통적인 독서 방식이 더 선호되고 있습니다.

More Questions

〈독서하기〉에 관련하여 더 나올 수 있는 OPIc 질문들을 정리한 코너입니다. 질문에 대한 brainstorming을 해보세요.

1. You said you like to read books. What is the most inspiring book you have ever read? How did it change your life?
2. Tell me about your favorite author. What do you like about his or her books? Is there any character you like in his or her books?

On Your Own

앞에서 주어진 Model Answer을 바탕으로, 아래의 빈칸에 들어갈 수 있는 다양한 대체 가능한 어휘 및 표현들을 참고하여 학습자 본인만의 모범 답안을 직접 만들어보세요.

I Opening I

I think the most common method of reading these days is still reading physical books. Although there has been a significant rise in e-reading, ⓐ_____.

I Favorite Reading Spot I

ⓑ_____. I access ⓒ_____ by going to bookstores and libraries. I especially enjoy visiting the ABC Bookstore. I love to sit at its wooden tables, where I can spend plenty of time with books before purchasing them.

I Benefits of E-reading I

ⓓ_____, I read e-books and e-journals by ⓔ_____. I prefer to read e-books to paper books ⓕ_____ because it is easier to search for what ⓖ_____ online.

I Closing I

In summary, people read both physical books and e-books, but ⓗ_____ the old style of reading is still more popular ⓘ_____.

I Opening I I think the most common method of reading these days is still reading physical books. Although there has been a significant rise in e-reading, ⓐ **the people around me read more paper books than e-books**.

I Favorite Reading Spot I ⓑ **I enjoy reading both paper books and e-books**. I access ⓒ **paper books** by going to bookstores and libraries. I especially enjoy visiting the ABC Bookstore. I love to sit at its wooden tables, where I can spend plenty of time with books before purchasing them.

I Benefits of E-reading I ⓓ **On the other hand**, I read e-books and e-journals by ⓔ **using my laptop**. I prefer to read e-books to paper books ⓕ **sometimes** because it is easier to search for what ⓖ **I want** online.

I Closing I In summary, people read both physical books and e-books, but ⓗ **it seems like** the old style of reading is still more popular ⓘ **in general**.

본인이 만든 답안에 아래의 요소들이 포함되었는지 점검해 봅시다.

	Checklist
☐	독서 방식의 종류
☐	내가 선호하는 독서 방식
☐	그러한 방식을 선호하는 이유
☐	종이책과 전자책의 특징
☐	종이책과 전자책에 대한 내 의견

Unit 36 Reading 2

독서하기 2 (E-Reading)

Warm Up

A Guess the Question & Answer
사진을 보면서 예상 질문과 답변을 먼저 추측해 봅시다.

B Listen & Talk
온라인 서점 및 일반 서점을 통한 책 구매에 관한 대화를 연습해 봅시다.

🎧 05-19

A Do you purchase books online?	**A** 혹시 온라인으로 책을 구매하니?
B I do. I mostly purchase books online.	**B** 응. 대개 온라인으로 책을 구매하지.
A Which websites do you use?	**A** 어떤 웹사이트를 이용하는데?
B I get books through either Junglezone or G-buy.	**B** 나는 정글존이나 지바이를 통해서 책을 주문해.
A Wow, G-buy sells books?	**A** 와, 지바이에서도 책을 팔아?
B Yes, G-buy sells all kinds of things. Why? Are you trying to buy books online?	**B** 응, 지바이는 온갖 상품을 다 팔아. 왜? 온라인으로 책을 사려고?
A No, I was just wondering if you would like to go to a bookstore with me tomorrow.	**A** 아니, 나랑 내일 같이 서점에 갈 생각이 있는지 궁금했거든.
B Of course! I don't always have to get books online. I like the old ways, too.	**B** 물론이지! 늘 온라인으로만 책을 사야 하는 것은 아니야. 난 오래 된 방식도 좋아해.
A Then what about meeting up at Bamboo & Goonies at 11 a.m. tomorrow?	**A** 그럼 내일 오전 11시에 밤부앤구니스에서 만나는 것이 어때?
B Sure. We can also go to the movies and grab a bite afterward.	**B** 좋아. 그리고 나서 영화도 보고 식사도 할 수 있을 거야.
A Sounds good!	**A** 좋은데!

Vocabulary
purchase online 온라인으로 구매하다 | **old way(s)** 옛날 방식 | **meet up** 만나다 | **grab a bite** 식사를 하다

Key Expressions

🔑 아래 제시된 각 expression의 구조를 이해하고, 자기만의 표현들을 생각해 봅시다.

Expression 1 apply to + 명사: ~에 적용되다

이는 제가 도서를 구입할 때도 마찬가지입니다. → This also **applies to** the way I purchase books.

새로운 관세 관련 무역법은 모든 국가에 적용됩니다.
→ The new tariff-related trade law **applies to** all countries.

이 의료 혜택은 비염 환자들에게 적용됩니다.
→ This medical care **applies to** patients who suffer from nasal allergies.

Expression 2 revolutionary: 획기적인, 혁명적인

세계 최대 온라인 서점인 정글존은 획기적이었습니다.
→ Junglezon, the biggest online bookstore on the planet, has been **revolutionary**.

데님은 의류 시장에 혁명을 일으켰습니다. → Denim has been **revolutionary** in the clothing market.

아담의 발명품은 상당히 획기적입니다! → Adam's invention is very **revolutionary**!

Expression 3 lose business: 사업이 망하다, 가게 문을 닫다

정글존이 생긴 이후 수많은 서점들이 문을 닫았습니다.
→ Numerous bookstores **lost business** after Junglezon appeared.

그들의 사업은 곧 망하게 생겼습니다. → They are about to **lose** their **business**.

거대 상가의 독점으로 인해 수많은 구멍가게들이 문을 닫았습니다.
→ Millions of mom-and-pop stores **lost business** due to the big store's monopoly.

Expression 4 fast delivery: 신속한 배달

그곳의 최대 성공 요인은 신속한 배송과 도서 가격 할인입니다.
→ The key factors to its success are **fast delivery** and discounted books.

시장에서 경쟁력을 갖추기 위해서는 빠른 배송이 필수입니다.
→ **Fast delivery** is essential to be competitive on the market.

빠른 배송이 제품의 품질을 보장해주는 것은 아닙니다.
→ **Fast delivery** does not guarantee the quality of the product.

Expression 5 old-school: 전통적인 방식을 고수하는, 예전 방식의

그럼에도 불구하고 저에게는 예전 방식이 더 잘 맞습니다. → Nonetheless, I am more of an **old-school** type.

그는 주로 예전에 유행하던 음악을 듣습니다. → He usually listens to the **old-school** music.

저희 할아버지께서는 전통적인 방식을 좋아하십니다. → My grandfather likes the **old-school** method.

Topic Question & Model Answer

🎧 05-20

Topic Question

People purchase books through various distribution channels these days. How do you like to purchase books? Do you purchase them online? Why?

요즘 사람들은 다양한 경로를 통해 도서를 구매합니다. 당신의 경우는 어떠한가요? 온라인상으로 구매하나요? 왜 그렇게 하나요?

TIP FOR THE OPIc

보통 독서, 음악 감상, 영화 관람에 대해 이야기해보라고 하면 어떤 책/음악/영화를 좋아하는지에 대해서만 답변하는 경우가 많습니다. 하지만 보다 심화된 질문은 해당 활동을 주로 어디에서, 어떠한 형태로 하는지에 대해 물어보기도 합니다. 나의 취미 및 여가 활동에 대해 포괄적으로 설명할 수 있어야 합니다.

Model Answer

| Opening |

I live in a digital world but I am not a huge fan of technology. I use the computer and my smartphone almost every day, but I try to use them as little as possible.

저는 디지털 시대를 살아가지만 테크놀로지를 크게 좋아하지는 않습니다. 거의 매일같이 컴퓨터와 스마트폰을 사용하지만 저는 언제나 그 사용을 최소화하려고 노력합니다.

| How I Purchase Books |

Naturally, I purchase all the items I need at physical stores. This also applies to the way I purchase books. I usually go to used bookstores and bookstores to get new books. It is so much more fun that way. I like reading physical books, touching the book covers, flipping the pages, and smelling the paper.

그러다 보니 저는 모든 물품을 실제 매장에서 구입합니다. 이는 제가 도서를 구입할 때도 마찬가지입니다. 저는 주로 중고 서점이나 일반 서점에 가서 책을 삽니다. 그 방식이 더욱 재미있습니다. 저는 종이로 된 책을 읽으면서 책의 표지를 만져보고 책장을 넘기면서 그 냄새를 맡는 것을 좋아합니다.

| Closing |

However, I have friends who mainly purchase books online for convenience and for saving time. Junglezon, the biggest online bookstore on the planet, has been revolutionary in the book distribution business. Numerous bookstores lost business after Junglezon appeared. The key factors to its success are fast delivery and discounted books. Nonetheless, I am more of an old-school type. I think I will always buy books at physical bookstores.

하지만 제 주변에는 편의성 및 시간 절약을 위해 온라인으로 도서를 구매하는 친구들이 있습니다. 세계 최대 온라인 서점인 정글존은 도서 유통 시장의 혁명을 일으켰습니다. 정글존이 생긴 이후 수많은 서점들이 문을 닫았습니다. 정글존의 중요한 성공 요인은 신속한 배송과 도서 할인입니다. 그럼에도 불구하고 저에게는 예전 방식이 더 잘 맞습니다. 저는 계속해서 일반 서점에서 책을 살 것 같습니다.

More Questions

〈독서하기〉에 관련하여 더 나올 수 있는 OPIc 질문들을 정리한 코너입니다. 질문에 대한 brainstorming을 해보세요.

1. Where do you like to read books? Do you go to a library or a bookstore? Tell me about the place where you like to read books.

2. What are the benefits of reading books? Do you like to watch movies that are based on books? Why?

On Your Own

앞에서 주어진 Model Answer을 바탕으로, 아래의 빈칸에 들어갈 수 있는 다양한 대체 가능한 어휘 및 표현들을 참고하여 학습자 본인만의 모범 답안을 직접 만들어보세요.

I Opening I

I live in a digital world but ⓐ_____. I use the computer and my smartphone almost every day, but I try to use them as little as possible.

I How I Purchase Books I

ⓑ_____. I usually go to used bookstores and bookstores to get new books. It is so much more fun that way. ⓒ_____.

I Closing I

ⓓ_____, I have friends who mainly purchase books online for convenience and for saving time. Junglezon, the biggest online bookstore on the planet, has been revolutionary in the book distribution business. Numerous bookstores lost business after Junglezon appeared. The key factors to its success are the fast delivery and discounted books. Nonetheless, ⓔ_____.
ⓕ_____.

I Opening I I live in a digital world but ⓐ **technology is not my favorite thing**. I use the computer and my smartphone almost every day, but I try to use them as little as possible.

I How I Purchase Books I ⓑ **However, I use both physical and online stores to purchase books**. I usually go to used bookstores and bookstores to get new books. It is so much more fun that way. ⓒ **But when I am in a hurry to purchase books, then I use an online bookstore**.

I Closing I ⓓ **Unlike me**, I have friends who mainly purchase books online for convenience and for saving time. Junglezon, the biggest online bookstore on the planet, has been revolutionary in the book distribution business. Numerous bookstores lost business after Junglezon appeared. The key factors to its success are fast delivery and discounted books. Nonetheless, ⓔ **I love the atmosphere in physical bookstores**. ⓕ **I hope that we always have some physical bookstores around so that we can spend time in them reading books**.

본인이 만든 답안에 아래의 요소들이 포함되었는지 점검해 봅시다.

	Checklist
☐	도서 구입 방식의 종류
☐	온라인 도서 구입의 특징
☐	서점을 통한 도서 구입의 특징
☐	온라인 도서 구입으로 인한 영향
☐	내가 선호하는 도서 구입 방식
☐	내가 그 방식을 선호하는 이유

The Music of Speech

강세를 두어야 하는 어휘의 특징을 익히고 그에 따라 답안을 말하는 연습을 해봅시다.

강세를 두는 어휘의 특징

1) 감탄사이다 2) 최상급이다 3) 형용사/부사이다
4) 문장 안에서 key word 역할을 하는 명사나 동사인 경우가 많다

Model Answer 27   🎧 05-21

There have been a lot of changes in the ways we use gadgets to listen to music. I remember that the CD player was a very popular device to listen to music in the 90s. Also, a small cassette player called the Walkman was loved by people of all ages. These days, gadgets have become much smaller and much more functional. Many people carry their smartphones to listen to music. Most of the smartphones are only the size of your palm, so they are very light. With a smartphone, you can also access the Internet, watch movies, chat for free on Kakao-Talk, and do much more. Advanced technology has even simplified the composing process. A close friend of mine is a composer, and he uses his iPad to make music. He says that it has become a lot easier to write music because the device has all kinds of different instrumental sounds. Overall, I think current technology has brought many changes in the way people play and listen to music.

Model Answer 28   🎧 05-22

I like to listen to all kinds of music. My taste in music changes depending on what I do and how I am feeling. Generally, I listen to a variety of genres from jazz to rock music. Back in my early 20s, my favorite music genre was hip-hop. However, when I was in my mid-20s, I fell in love with classical music. I often listened to classical music when I was working on papers in my room. It was easier to concentrate on my school assignments with classical music on because it doesn't have lyrics. These days, I listen to CCM songs the most. I like CCM songs because the melodies are touching, and the lyrics are therapeutic. I usually play CCM songs when I do the dishes or cook. When I listen to music, I either play my favorite list on my cell phone or tune into the radio. That way, I can enjoy music almost anytime. Music is something that is precious to me. It is something we should be grateful to have in our lives.

Model Answer 29   🎧 05-23

Hello? Is this the Doremi Music School? Hi. My name is Suji, and I'm interested in your vocal training class. I guess I am a beginner. I've never had vocal training before. I'd like to know the difference in the cost of the one-to-one class and the group class. It's nearly five times more expensive! In that case, I will take the group lesson. I don't think I can afford the one-to-one lesson. Do you have an afternoon class? Cool. Is there anything I should prepare for the class? Just eat well and drink enough water? That's easy. Do you offer any kind of discount if I invite a friend to take the class as well? 10% off? Nice! My last question: Who's going to be my teacher? It's Yuri from J.O.P. Entertainment? Great! I'll visit your institute within a week. Thank you. Bye.

Model Answer 30 🎧 05-24

Hello. Is this Yuri? Hi. This is Suji. I signed up for your vocal training class this Monday. I'm terribly sorry, Yuri, but I had some issues come up at the last minute. I have to go out of town for an urgent business trip next week. My boss just called me this morning to make the arrangements. I'll be out of town the entire week next week, so I will miss the next two classes. I wonder if I might make up the classes I miss another time. That's great. I didn't know you had such a system in place. When is the makeup class scheduled? You have it every Saturday? Sure, I can be there. Also, is it possible for my friend to delay the start of her class, too? She's very shy and doesn't want to attend class without me. Thank you. That's so nice of you. Thank you again. I'll get back to you when I return from my trip. Bye.

Model Answer 31 🎧 05-25

I think I've been interested in dancing since I was young. I remember the first time I danced in front of people. I was 6. There was a family gathering, and good music was on TV. I naturally started dancing and have enjoyed it ever since. I guess I have a natural talent for dancing. As long as there's good music, I just dance along to the song no matter when it is or where I am. I feel free when I'm dancing, and I think it's one of the best ways to express myself. It's also a good way to relieve my stress.

Model Answer 32 🎧 05-26

Hi. Are you the secretary of this dance school? Okay. Hi, Mijoo. My name is Jiyoung and I want to take the jazz dance class. I talked to one of your staff members the other day and asked the person to put my name on the list for the open class. I just came to join the class, but I can't find my name on the list! I'm not sure what happened. Would you please check what went wrong? Can I still take the open class? Yes, I brought my ID card. Here you go. Well, thank you for your help. I guess the other staff member made a mistake. Oh, so he misspelled my name. Jaehyung? No, no. My name is J-I-Y-O-U-N-G. Not Jaehyung. It's all right. Thank you for your help. Bye.

Model Answer 33　　🎧 05-27

Hello? Jina? Hi. This is Suji. I called you to ask you a few questions about the party you are throwing this Saturday. You are having a potluck party, right? Cool. So what kind of dish do you want me to bring? An appetizer? A main dish? A dessert? Oh, okay. You want me to bring a dessert? Sure. What do you prefer? Chocolate, coffee, cake, or pie? Oh, you want a little bit of everything? No problem. How do I get to your place from the nearest station? It's only two blocks away from the station? Great! Then I can even stop by at a nearby ice cream shop. I'll see you at your place at 7 p.m. on Saturday. I can't wait for the party. See you soon. Bye.

Model Answer 34　　🎧 05-28

Hello, Jina? Hi. How are you? Cool. Are there a lot of people coming tonight? There are already 15 people at your place? Jina, I'm terribly sorry to tell you this, but I was just in a minor car accident. I was on my way to your place with the desserts, but I bumped into the car in front of me. Nope. Nobody is hurt. But the food is ruined. The desserts don't look good. I should get some new ones. So people are having the appetizers now? Oh, that's a relief. I'll go to a nearby bakery and get the best desserts it has. But I'm going to be a little late because the traffic is pretty bad right now. Ask your guests to be patient because the desserts are coming. Okay, I'll get to your place as soon as possible. See you. Bye.

Model Answer 35　　🎧 05-29

I think the most common method of reading these days is still reading physical books. Although there has been a significant rise in e-reading, statistics show that the number of paper book readers far exceeds the number of people who read e-books. I also enjoy reading paper books. I access them by going to used bookstores, bookstores, and libraries. I especially enjoy visiting the ABC Bookstore. It has a very reader-friendly environment. I love to sit at the wooden tables, where I can spend plenty of time with books before purchasing them. Unlike me, my husband enjoys reading e-books and e-journals. He is a tech person who spends hours using the computer. He says he prefers to read e-books to paper books because it is easier to search for what he wants online. In summary, people read both physical books and e-books, but the old-style of reading is still more popular even in the 21st century.

Model Answer 36 🎧 05-30

I live in a digital world but I am not a huge fan of technology. I use the computer and my smartphone almost every day, but I try to use them as little as possible. Naturally, I purchase all the items I need at physical stores. This also applies to the way I purchase books. I usually go to used bookstores and bookstores to get new books. It is so much more fun that way. I like reading physical books, touching the book covers, flipping the pages, and smelling the paper. However, I have friends who mainly purchase books online for convenience and for saving time. Junglezon, the biggest online bookstore on the planet, has been revolutionary in the book distribution business. Numerous bookstores lost business after Junglezon appeared. The key factors to its success are fast delivery and discounted books. Nonetheless, I am more of an old-school type. I think I will always buy books at physical bookstores.

More Expressions & Vocabulary ▶ Hobbies

Music Genres
- classical music 클래식 음악
- ballad 발라드
- jazz 재즈
- dance music 댄스 음악
- hip-hop 힙합
- soundtrack 사운드트랙
- gospel 가스펠
- electronic music 전자 음악

Musicians
- composer 작곡가
- girl group 여자 그룹
- boy band 남자 밴드
- lead singer (그룹의) 리드 보컬
- solo artist 솔로 가수
- singer-songwriter 싱어송라이터

Descriptive Words for Music
- soft 부드러운
- relaxing 편한
- warm 따뜻한
- calm 고요한
- gentle 온화한
- healing 치유하는
- melodious 선율이 예쁜, 듣기 좋은
- soothing 달래는, 위로하는
- upbeat 경쾌한
- funky 비트가 강한

Why I Listen to Music
I feel relaxed. 저는 긴장이 풀립니다.
I can relieve my stress.
저는 스트레스를 해소할 수 있습니다.
I feel less bored on the bus/subway.
저는 버스/지하철에서 덜 지루합니다.
It's easier to concentrate on my work/studying.
업무/공부에 집중하기가 더 쉽습니다.

Dancing/Club Description
- stage 무대
- dance floor 춤추는 공간
- entrance 입구
- lighting 조명
- bar 바
- cover charge 입장료
- dark 어두운
- smoky 연기가 많은
- pounding 쿵쾅거리는
- crazy 열기가 넘치는
- crowded 사람들이 붐비는
- excited 신난, 흥분한
- dress up 옷을 차려 입다
- dress code 복장 규정

Korean Food
- Korean barbecue 갈비
- kimchi stew 김치찌개
- bean paste stew 된장찌개
- seaweed soup 미역국
- rice cakes in hot sauce 떡볶이
- pork belly 삼겹살
- side dish 반찬

Tastes & Flavors
- mild 담백한
- salty 짠
- greasy 느끼한
- juicy (고기나 과일이) 즙이 풍부한
- spicy 매콤한
- hot 매운

Book Genres
- science fiction 공상 과학 서적
- satire 풍자 문학
- drama 드라마
- mystery 미스터리
- action and adventure 액션 및 모험
- romance 로맨스
- self help 자기 개발 서적
- health 건강 서적
- biography 전기
- autobiography 자서전
- guide 가이드북
- travel 여행
- children's 아동 서적
- religion, spirituality 신앙, 영성 서적
- science 과학
- history 역사
- poetry 시
- encyclopedia 백과 사전
- dictionary 사전
- comic book 만화책
- art 예술 서적
- cookbook 요리책
- journal 일기

CHAPTER 6 운동

Sports

Unit 37	**Jogging (Walking) 1** 조깅(걷기) 1
Unit 38	**Jogging (Walking) 2** 조깅(걷기) 2
Unit 39	**Hiking** 하이킹
Unit 40	**Fitness Club 1** 헬스클럽 1
Unit 41	**Fitness Club 2** 헬스클럽 2

Chapter 6은 스포츠에 대해 다룹니다. 그 중에서도 일상에서 쉽게 할 수 있는 조깅, 걷기, 하이킹 및 헬스클럽에서 운동하기에 대해 다룹니다. 가까운 공원에서 조깅하기(걷기), 근처 산에서 하이킹 하기, 헬스클럽 다니기, 헬스클럽 등록하기를 선택하면 장소와 운동 방법을 묘사하는 것에 대한 부담이 적습니다. 또한 이들은 구기 종목처럼 규정이 복잡하지 않고 요가나 수영처럼 상황 묘사가 애매하거나 관련 어휘가 어렵지 않기 때문에 영어로 답안을 기술하기에 용이한 편입니다.

✚ Brainstorming Point

When?	when I usually jog/walk/hike/go to the gym (언제 주로 운동하는지) the last time I went jogging/walking/hiking/worked out (마지막 운동한 시기)
Where?	where I go to jog/walk/hike/work out (어디서 운동하는지) my favorite mountain (내가 좋아하는 산) where I recommend going to jog/walk/hike/work out (추천 운동 장소)
What?	what I like about jogging/walking/hiking/working out (운동의 장점) what to prepare when jogging/walking/hiking/working out (준비 사항) what to do to avoid injuries while jogging/walking/hiking/working out (부상을 피하기 위한 안전 수칙) the most memorable event while jogging/walking/hiking/working out (기억에 남는 일)
Who?	who I jog/walk/hike/work out with (함께 운동하는 사람) who inspired me to start jogging/walking/hiking/working out (동기 부여한 사람)
Why?	why jogging/walking/hiking/working out is good for your health (몸에 좋은 이유) why jogging/walking/hiking/working out is better than other sports (다른 운동보다 좋은 이유)
How?	how I started jogging/walking/hiking/working out (운동 시작한 계기) how many times I jog/walk/hike/work out a week (일주일에 몇 번 운동하는지)

Unit 37 Jogging (Walking) 1

조깅(걷기) 1

Warm Up

A Guess the Question & Answer
사진을 보면서 예상 질문과 답변을 먼저 추측해 봅시다.

B Listen & Talk
조깅(걷기)의 장점 및 준비 사항에 관한 대화를 먼저 연습해 봅시다.

🎧 06-01

A You look like you are in such good shape these days. What's your secret?	**A** 너 요즘 정말 몸이 좋아진 것 같아! 대체 비밀이 뭐야?
B Thanks. I just started jogging a month ago.	**B** 고마워. 한 달 전부터 조깅을 하고 있어.
A Jogging? But you are more the yoga type.	**A** 조깅? 너 원래 요가 좋아하잖아.
B I know, but the weather is too good to stay inside these days. I thought it would be better to enjoy the outdoors while exercising.	**B** 알아. 그런데 요즘 날씨가 워낙 좋아서 실내에 있기가 아깝잖아. 야외에서 운동하면서 자연을 느끼고 싶었어.
A That's why you started running. How do you like it so far?	**A** 그래서 조깅을 시작한 거구나. 그래서 해보니까 어때?
B Great. I don't need to pay for it, and I can jog anytime I'm free. I can also take in the beauty of spring.	**B** 아주 좋아. 돈 낼 필요도 없고 내가 시간 될 때 아무 때나 할 수 있고. 봄의 아름다움도 만끽하고.
A It sounds like jogging is a perfect form of exercise for you.	**A** 듣고 보니 너한테는 조깅이 아주 딱 맞는구나.
B It is! The air is fresh outside, and I feel lighter whenever I jog. Of course, I apply sunscreen on my face to avoid getting a sunburn.	**B** 그렇다니깐! 바깥 공기가 신선하고 조깅할 때마다 더 가벼워지는 기분이야. 물론, 얼굴 타는 게 싫어서 자외선 차단제를 꼭 바르지.
A I should jog with you sometime soon.	**A** 너랑 조만간 같이 조깅해야겠다!
B Anytime. Don't forget to bring your MP3 player. It's always better with music.	**B** 언제든지. MP3 플레이어 챙기는 거 잊지 말고. 음악이 있는 게 언제나 더 나으니까.

Vocabulary
be in good shape 몸매를 유지하다 | **enjoy the outdoors** 바깥 전경을 즐기다 | **so far** 이제까지 | **take in** ~을 소화하다, (문맥상) ~을 감상하다 | **feel light** 몸이 가볍다고 느끼다 | **apply** 화장품을 바르다 | **sunscreen** 자외선 차단제 | **avoid getting a sunburn** 살이 타는 걸 방지하다

Key Expressions

🔑 아래 제시된 각 expression의 구조를 이해하고, 자기만의 표현들을 생각해 봅시다.

Expression 1 — **be limited to ~:** ~에 한정되다, 구애받다

특정 장소나 시간에 구애받지 않습니다. → It's not **limited to** certain places or time.

유감스럽지만 그 사업에 대한 저의 지식은 한정적입니다.
→ Regrettably, my knowledge of the business **is limited**.

오늘의 손님은 초대장을 받은 분들로 한정됩니다.
→ Today's guests **are limited to** those who received invitation cards.

Expression 2 — **work out:** 운동하다

저는 어릴 적에 헬스클럽에서 운동을 하고는 했습니다.
→ I used to **work out** at a gym when I was younger.

건강을 유지하려면 규칙적으로 운동을 하십시오. → **Work out** on a regular basis to stay healthy.

저와 제 남자친구는 지난주부터 함께 운동을 하기 시작했습니다.
→ My boyfriend and I started **working out** together last week.

Expression 3 — **hard to imagine / can't imagine ~:** ~의 모습을 상상할 수 없는 / 상상하기 힘들다

저는 다시는 러닝 기구 위를 달리는 제 모습을 상상할 수가 없습니다.
→ I **can't imagine** myself running on a treadmill again.

꿈이 없는 인생은 상상하기 어렵다. → It's **hard to imagine** a life without dreams.

나는 그가 집안일을 하는 것을 상상할 수가 없다.
→ I **can't imagine** him doing all the household chores.

Expression 4 — **keep up with ~:** ~을 유지하다, ~을 따라잡다

저는 건강을 유지하고자 하는 분들에게 조깅을 권합니다.
→ I recommend jogging to those who want to **keep up with** their health.

네 속도 따라가려니까 힘들어. → It is stressful to try to **keep up with** you.

빠르게 변화하는 환경을 따라가는 것은 쉽지 않습니다.
→ It's not easy to **keep up with** the rapidly changing environment.

Expression 5 — **stay fit / stay in shape:** 체력 관리하다, 몸매를 유지하다

조깅은 체력 관리에 좋은 운동입니다. → It's good to jog to **stay fit**.

저는 몸매 관리를 위해 칼로리를 계산합니다. → I calculate calories to **stay fit**.

창현은 건강관리를 위해 채식주의자가 되었습니다. 그는 그 방법이 통했다고 하네요!
→ Changhyun became a vegetarian to **stay in shape**. He says it worked.

Topic Question & Model Answer

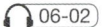 06-02

Topic Question

What are the benefits of jogging (walking)? How is jogging (walking) different from other sports?

조깅(걷기)의 장점에는 뭐가 있나요? 조깅(걷기)는 타 운동 종목과 비교했을 때 어떻게 다른가요?

TIP FOR THE OPIc

조깅(걷기)은 스포츠 항목 중 가장 무난한 종목입니다. 소재가 비교적 친숙하여 질문이 다양하게 변형된다 할지라도 당황하지 않고 풀 수 있습니다. 조깅(걷기)의 장점은 다른 운동에 비해 장소나 시간의 제약이 거의 없다는 점, 별도의 비용이 들지 않는다는 점, 특별한 운동 방법이나 도구가 필요하지 않다는 점 등일 것입니다. 여러 명과 함께 할 수 있지만 혼자서도 얼마든지 할 수 있다는 점도 장점이 될 수 있습니다.

Model Answer

| Opening |

There are many benefits to jogging.

조깅은 많은 장점이 있습니다.

| Merits of Jogging |

First of all, it doesn't cost much. As long as you have a pair of sneakers, you are free to jog. In addition, it's not limited to certain places or time. You are able to jog in any public area anytime. Well, of course for females, it would be safe to run with someone when it gets dark. Another reason I like jogging is that I can enjoy the fresh air and beautiful scenery when I jog at the park. I used to work out at a gym when I was younger, but, since I now jog at the park, I can't imagine myself running on a treadmill again.

무엇보다도, 돈이 많이 안 듭니다. 운동화 한 켤레만 있으면 조깅을 얼마든지 할 수 있습니다. 또한 특정한 시간과 장소의 구애를 받지 않습니다. 공공장소라면 언제든지 조깅을 할 수가 있습니다. 뭐, 여자라면 당연히, 밤이 되면 다른 사람과 함께 뛰어야 안전할 것입니다. 제가 조깅을 좋아하는 또 하나의 이유는 공원에서 맑은 공기와 아름다운 경치를 즐길 수 있기 때문입니다. 저는 어릴 적 헬스클럽에서 운동을 하고는 했었는데, 이젠 공원에서 조깅을 하다 보니, 다시는 트레드밀에서 뛸 수가 없을 것 같습니다.

| Closing |

I highly recommend jogging to those who want to be healthy and to stay fit. I guess these are some of the benefits of jogging.

저는 건강을 지키고 몸매를 관리하고 싶은 분들에게 조깅을 하라고 적극 추천합니다. 이러한 점들이 바로 조깅의 장점이라고 생각합니다.

More Questions

〈조깅(걷기)〉에 관련하여 더 나올 수 있는 OPIc 질문들을 정리한 코너입니다. 질문에 대한 brainstorming을 해보세요.

1. What do you prepare before you go jogging? In addition, are there any special tips you can share for when you go jogging?

2. You indicated that you jog. Tell me about the place you like to go jogging. Is it a park? What do you like about it?

3. Many people enjoy jogging and swimming. Talk about the differences between jogging and swimming. Which one do you prefer? Why?

On Your Own

앞에서 주어진 Model Answer을 바탕으로, 아래의 빈칸에 들어갈 수 있는 다양한 대체 가능한 어휘 및 표현들을 참고하여 학습자 본인만의 모범 답안을 직접 만들어보세요.

I Opening I

There are many benefits to jogging.

I Merits of Jogging I

First of all, ⓐ_____. As long as you have a pair of sneakers, you are free to jog. In addition, it's not limited to certain places or time. You are able to jog in any public area anytime. Well, of course for females, it would be safer to run with someone ⓑ_____. Another reason I like jogging is that ⓒ_____. I used to ⓓ_____ when I was younger, but, since I now jog at the park, I can't imagine myself ⓔ_____.

I Closing I

I highly recommend jogging to those who want to be healthy and to stay fit. I guess these are some of the benefits of jogging.

I Opening I There are many benefits to jogging.

I Merits of Jogging I First of all, ⓐ **it doesn't require any special equipment**. As long as you have a pair of sneakers, you are free to jog. In addition, it's not limited to certain places or times. You are able to jog in any public area anytime. Well, of course for females, it would be safer to run with someone ⓑ **on an isolated road**. Another reason I like jogging is that ⓒ **there's a nice walking track at the park**. I used to ⓓ **play tennis** when I was younger, but, since I now jog at the park, I can't imagine myself ⓔ **hitting balls in such a limited space**.

I Closing I I highly recommend jogging to those who want to be healthy and to stay fit. I guess these are some of the benefits of jogging.

본인이 만든 답안에 아래의 요소들이 포함되었는지 점검해 봅시다.

	Checklist
☐	혼자서도 할 수 있다
☐	장소 및 시간의 제한이 거의 없다
☐	규칙이 복잡하지 않다
☐	운동 기구가 없어도 된다
☐	자연을 만끽할 수 있다
☐	수강료를 지불할 필요가 없다

Unit 38 Jogging (Walking) 2

조깅(걷기) 2

Warm Up

A Guess the Question & Answer
사진을 보면서 예상 질문과 답변을 먼저 추측해 봅시다.

B Listen & Talk
조깅(걷기)의 유의 사항에 관한 대화를 먼저 연습해 봅시다.

🎧 06-03

> **A** Is there anything I should keep in mind before jogging? Do you have any tips or things I should watch out for?
>
> **B** Yes, there are a few things. I would say first, do enough warmup exercises before jogging. Stretch your muscles and relax your body. Drink enough water.
>
> **A** Sure. Very basic things can make a huge difference. Is there anything else I should know?
>
> **B** Keep your own pace when you jog. Don't try to be fast. Remember that you're not in a race. Just enjoy it.
>
> **A** That's a good point. Thanks. I'll focus on keeping my own pace.
>
> **B** I also recommend that you take a bottle of water and a towel. You might sweat a lot when the temperature is high.
>
> **A** Okay. I want to start jogging right away. I feel lighter already.
>
> **B** How about going to the Han River Park this evening? We can chill out at a nearby cafeteria afterward.
>
> **A** Awesome! Let's do that.

> **A** 조깅하기 전에 내가 유념해야 할 부분이 있어? 조심할 부분이나 팁이 될 만한 것 있어?
>
> **B** 응, 몇 가지 있어. 먼저 조깅하기 전에 준비운동을 하라고 말해주고 싶어. 근육을 늘려주고 몸의 긴장을 풀어줘. 물도 충분히 마시도록 해.
>
> **A** 그래. 아주 기본적인 사항들이 커다란 차이를 만드니까. 내가 알아야 할 또 다른 것이 있니?
>
> **B** 조깅할 때 너만의 페이스를 유지해. 빨리 가려고 하지 말고. 달리기 경주가 아니라는 것을 명심하고 그냥 즐겨.
>
> **A** 좋은 지적이야. 고마워. 내 속도를 유지할게.
>
> **B** 또한 물 한 병과 수건 하나를 챙겨가면 좋아. 기온이 높아지면 땀을 많이 흘릴 수 있거든.
>
> **A** 응. 당장 조깅을 시작하고 싶어! 벌써부터 몸이 가벼워지는 것 같아.
>
> **B** 오늘 저녁 한강 공원에 가는 건 어때? 조깅하고 나서 근처 카페테리아에서 머리도 식히고.
>
> **A** 좋아! 그렇게 하자.

Vocabulary
keep in mind 유념하다 | **watch out for** ~를 조심하다 | **warmup exercise** 준비 운동 | **stretch one's muscles** 근육을 이완시키다 | **relax one's body** 몸의 긴장을 풀어주다 | **make a difference** 변화를 만들다 | **keep one's own pace** 자기만의 속도를 유지하다 | **be in a race** 경주에 참여하다 | **focus on** ~에 집중하다 | **right away** 곧바로 | **chill out** (머리를) 식히다, 긴장을 풀다

Key Expressions

> 아래 제시된 각 expression의 구조를 이해하고, 자기만의 표현들을 생각해 봅시다.

Expression 1　　**keep in mind:** 유념하다, 주의하다, 기억하다

가장 중요한 점은 알맞은 신발을 고르는 것에 유념해야 한다는 것입니다.
→ The most important thing you should **keep in mind** is to select the right shoes.

내가 당신에게 회의에 관하여 알려준 모든 상세 정보를 기억하세요.
→ **Keep in mind** all the details I told you about the meeting.

내일까지 청구액을 납입해야 하는 것을 기억하세요.
→ Please **keep in mind** that you have to pay the bill by tomorrow.

Expression 2　　**be more [less] prone to ~:** 더[덜] ~하기 쉽다, 더[덜] ~ 하는 경향이 있다

만일 편한 신발을 신지 않는다면, 발목을 삐는 등 부상을 당하기 더 쉽습니다. → If you don't wear the right shoes, you **are more prone to** get an injury like a sprained ankle.

아이들은 어른들보다 단 것을 더 잘 먹습니다. → Kids **are more prone to** eat sweets than adults.

여름에는 동물들이 전염병에 걸리기 더 쉽습니다. → In summer, animals **are more prone to** diseases.

Expression 3　　**muscle pain:** 근육통

그렇지 않으면, 온 몸에 근육통을 느낄 것입니다.
→ Otherwise, you will have **muscle pain** all over your body.

세호는 복싱을 하고 난 이후 온 몸에 근육통을 느꼈습니다.
→ Seho had **muscle pain** all over his body after boxing.

나의 삼촌은 심각한 근육통으로 인해 약을 먹고 있습니다.
→ My uncle is taking pills due to his severe **muscle pain**.

Expression 4　　**relax one's muscles:** ~의 근육을 이완시키다

이렇게 하면, 근육을 이완시키고 몸 상태가 조깅할 준비가 됩니다.
→ This way, you can **relax your muscles** and prepare your body to jog.

사우나는 근육을 이완시키는 데에 도움이 됩니다. → The sauna helps you **relax your muscles**.

마사지를 받고 나니 근육이 풀렸습니다. → My **muscles are relaxed** after getting a massage.

Expression 5　　**prevent:** ~를 방지하다

그렇게 하면 햇볕에 그을리거나 기미가 생기는 것을 방지할 수 있습니다.
→ You will be able to **prevent** getting a sunburn and avoid getting freckles.

사고를 방지하기 위해 교통 신호를 지키세요. → Traffic signals are necessary to **prevent** accidents.

Topic Question & Model Answer

🎧 06-04

Topic Question

Tell me about a few things you should do to prevent injuries while jogging.

조깅할 때 부상을 방지하기 위해 해야 할 일 몇 가지를 얘기해 보세요.

TIP FOR THE OPIc

조깅(걷기)은 비교적 쉬운 운동이긴 하지만, 역시나 유념해야 할 부분들이 있습니다. 여름철엔 일사병에 걸리지 않도록 기온이 가장 높은 오후 시간에는 가급적 운동을 피하고, 평소에도 물병을 들고 다니거나 자외선 차단제를 듬뿍 바르고 모자를 쓰도록 합니다. 조깅 중 큰 소리로 음악듣는 것은 위험하므로 가급적 자제하는 것이 좋겠고요. 해가 질 무렵에는 안전을 위해 다른 사람과 함께 운동을 하는 것이 좋겠습니다.

Model Answer

| Opening |

I think the most important thing you should keep in mind is to choose the right shoes. If you don't wear the right shoes, you are more prone to injuries like sprained ankles. You will also have sore feet.

저는 조깅할 때 유의할 가장 중요한 점은 바로 적절한 신발을 고르는 것이라고 생각합니다. 편한 신발을 신지 않으면, 발목을 삐기가 쉽고 발에 통증이 생기기도 쉽습니다.

| Jogging Safety Rules |

In addition, it's always important to do enough warmup exercises before jogging. Otherwise, you will feel muscle pain all over your body. I always stretch for about 10 to 15 minutes before I jog. This way, you can relax your muscles and prepare your body to jog. I also take a bottle of water when I jog. It is important to drink enough water while you exercise. This is especially important on sunny days since you might sweat a lot, so it's good to bring something to drink.

또한, 조깅 전에 준비 운동을 충분히 하는 것은 언제나 중요합니다. 그렇지 않으면, 온 몸에 근육통이 생길 것입니다. 저는 조깅을 하기 전에 언제나 10분에서 15분 정도 스트레칭을 합니다. 이런 식으로 하면, 몸이 유연해지고 조깅을 할 준비가 될 것입니다. 저는 또한 조깅을 할 때 물 한 병을 들고 다닙니다. 운동하는 동안 충분한 물을 마시는 것은 중요합니다. 특히 햇볕이 강한 날이면, 땀이 많이 나기 때문에, 마실 것을 준비하는 것이 좋습니다.

| Closing |

Finally, if you are sensitive to sunlight, I recommend that you apply enough sunscreen products on your face and wear either sunglasses or a cap. That way, you will be able to avoid getting a sunburn and developing freckles.

마지막으로 만일 자외선에 민감하다면, 얼굴에 자외선 차단제를 충분히 바르고 선글라스나 모자를 착용할 것을 추천합니다. 그렇게 하면, 피부 그을림이나 기미 발생을 방지할 수 있을 것입니다.

More Questions

〈조깅(걷기)〉에 관련하여 더 나올 수 있는 OPIc 질문들을 정리한 코너입니다. 질문에 대한 brainstorming을 해보세요.

1. Why do you jog? Are there any benefits to jogging?
2. Do you have a memorable event from when you were jogging? When was it? What happened?
3. How did you get interested in jogging? Were you on a diet? Or did you have any health issues?

On Your Own

앞에서 주어진 Model Answer을 바탕으로, 아래의 빈칸에 들어갈 수 있는 다양한 대체 가능한 어휘 및 표현들을 참고하여 학습자 본인만의 모범 답안을 직접 만들어보세요.

| Opening |

I think the most important thing you should keep in mind is

ⓐ_____. If you don't wear **ⓑ**_____,

ⓒ_____.

| Jogging Safety Rules |

In addition, it's always important to do enough warmup exercises before jogging. Otherwise, you will feel muscle pain all over your body. I always stretch for about 10 to 15 minutes before I jog. This way, you can relax your muscles and prepare your body to start jogging. I also take a **ⓓ**_____ when I jog. This is especially important on sunny days since you might sweat a lot, so it's good to bring something to

ⓔ_____.

| Closing |

Finally, if you are sensitive to sunlight, I recommend that you apply enough sunscreen products on your face and wear either sunglasses or a cap. That way, you will be able to avoid getting a sunburn and developing freckles.

| Opening | I think the most important thing you should keep in mind is **ⓐ to wear comfortable clothes when jogging**. If you don't wear **ⓑ comfortable clothes**, **ⓒ you won't be able to jog properly**.

| Jogging Safety Rules | In addition, it's always important to do enough warmup exercise before jogging. Otherwise, you will feel muscle pain all over your body. I always stretch for about 10 to 15 minutes before I jog. This way, you can relax your muscles and prepare your body to start jogging. I also take a **ⓓ towel** when I jog. This is especially important on sunny days since you might sweat a lot, so it's good to bring something to **ⓔ wipe off your sweat**.

| Closing | Finally, if you are sensitive to sunlight, I recommend that you apply enough sunscreen products to your face and wear either sunglasses or a cap. That way, you will be able to avoid getting a sunburn and developing freckles.

본인이 만든 답안에 아래의 요소들이 포함되었는지 점검해 봅시다.

Checklist
☐ 조깅할 때 유의할 점
☐ 편한 신발 신기
☐ 양말 신기
☐ 준비 운동 하기
☐ 물통 챙기기
☐ 자외선 차단제 바르기
☐ 모자(선글라스, 수건) 챙기기

Unit 39 Hiking

하이킹

Warm Up

A Guess the Question & Answer
사진을 보면서 예상 질문과 답변을 먼저 추측해 봅시다.

B Listen & Talk
하이킹을 시작한 계기에 관한 대화를 먼저 연습해 봅시다.

🎧 06-05

A Look at the flowers! Aren't they beautiful?

B They're marvelous. Do you want to go hiking this weekend? It's even more beautiful in the mountains.

A Sure. Do you often go hiking?

B I go once a month. I like to get out of the city sometimes.

A Where do you go hiking? Do you go by yourself?

B I joined an online community for hikers. We go to different places every month.

A That's interesting. How did you start hiking?

B Both my parents love hiking. They love nature and fresh air. I used to think hiking was boring, but, after following them a couple times, I've really come to enjoy it a lot.

A Cool. I'll pack a nice lunch for hiking this weekend.

B Great. I'll bring a frozen water bottle with some snacks.

A 저기 꽃들 좀 봐! 아름답지 않아?

B 신비롭다. 우리 같이 이번 주말에 하이킹 갈래? 산 위에서는 경치가 훨씬 아름답잖아.

A 물론이지. 넌 하이킹 자주 가?

B 한 달에 한 번. 가끔은 도심 생활에서 벗어나고 싶거든.

A 넌 어디로 하이킹 가? 혼자서 가?

B 등산을 좋아하는 사람들을 위한 온라인 커뮤니티에 가입했어. 매달 다른 곳으로 등반을 가.

A 흥미롭다. 하이킹은 어떻게 시작했어?

B 우리 부모님 모두 하이킹을 좋아하셔. 자연을 사랑하시고 맑은 공기를 좋아하시지. 나는 하이킹이 지루한 거라고 생각했었는데, 부모님을 따라 몇 번 가다 보니, 이젠 등산이 아주 재미있어졌어.

A 잘됐다. 이번 주말 등산용 도시락은 내가 싸올게.

B 아주 좋아. 난 얼음물과 간식을 좀 가져올게.

Vocabulary | marvelous 놀라울 정도로 멋진(아름다운), 신기한 | go hiking 등산 가다 | online community 온라인 커뮤니티 | hiker 등산객 | pack a lunch 도시락을 싸다 | frozen water bottle 얼린 물병

Key Expressions

아래 제시된 각 expression의 구조를 이해하고, 자기만의 표현들을 생각해 봅시다.

Expression 1 — 숫자 + nights and + 숫자 + days: ~박 ~일

저는 청계산에 가서 2박 3일간 있었습니다.
→ I went to Chungye Mountain and stayed for **2 nights and 3 days**.

그 커플은 하와이에 5박 7일간 머무를 예정입니다.
→ The couple will stay in Hawaii for **5 nights and 7 days**.

저는 3박 4일 동안 베니스를 여행할 계획입니다.
→ I'm planning to travel to Venice for **3 nights and 4 days**.

Expression 2 — all night: 밤새도록

우리는 산 위에서 고기를 구워 먹고 밤새 게임을 했습니다.
→ At the mountain, we had a barbecue party and played games **all night**.

우리는 밤새도록 문서를 작성했습니다. → We worked on the paper **all night**.

그 과학자는 밤새도록 실험을 했습니다. → The scientist conducted experiments **all night**.

Expression 3 — beyond description: 형용할 수조차 없는

자연 경관은 말로 형용할 수 없을 정도였습니다. → The view of nature was **beyond description**.

그녀의 아름다움은 형용할 수조차 없었습니다. → Her beauty was **beyond description**.

히로시마 원폭으로 인한 파괴는 말로 형용할 수조차 없었습니다.
→ The devastation after the Hiroshima bomb explosion was **beyond description**.

Expression 4 — be covered with ~: ~로 덮이다

산 전체가 분홍색, 흰색, 노란색으로 덮여 있었습니다.
→ The entire mountain **was covered with** pink, white, and yellow.

그 식탁은 빨간 시트로 덮여 있었습니다. → The table **was covered with** the red linen.

그 다음 날 아침, 저는 땅이 흰 눈으로 덮인 것을 보았습니다.
→ The next morning, I saw the ground **covered with** white snow.

Expression 5 — bring back (the) memories: 기억을 되돌리다

그 사진들은 여전히 특별한 기억을 되살려줍니다. → The pictures still **bring back** special **memories**.

그의 노래는 지난날의 기억들을 되살려줍니다.
→ His songs are **bringing back the memories** of the old days.

그 벤치는 우리가 처음 만났던 날의 기억을 되살려줍니다.
→ The bench **brings back the memory** of the day we first met.

Topic Question & Model Answer

Topic Question

When was your most memorable hiking experience? Where did you go? Who did you go with? Why was it so special?

가장 기억에 남는 하이킹은 언제였나요? 어디로 갔나요? 누구와 함께 갔나요? 왜 그렇게 특별한가요?

> **TIP FOR THE OPIc**
> 하이킹은 외국인들에겐 스포츠로 여겨지기 때문에 이 항목에 넣었습니다. 하이킹은 주변 경관 등을 묘사하기가 쉬운 편이라 선택 항목으로 추천합니다. 해당 질문은 기억에 남는 하이킹을 묻고 있지만, 하이킹을 같이 갈 사람과의 약속에 관한 롤플레이나 부상 등에 관한 돌발문제가 나올 수 있습니다.

Model Answer

| Opening |

My most memorable hiking trip was last April. I went to the famous Chungye Mountain with my classmates and stayed at a camping site for 2 nights and 3 days.

제게 가장 기억에 남는 하이킹은 바로 지난 4월에 있었습니다. 저는 학과 친구들과 함께 유명한 청계산에 가서 2박 3일간 묵었습니다.

| Memorable Hiking Trip |

It was my most memorable hiking experience because I went with my close friends. At the mountain, we had a barbecue party and played games all night. We went scavenger hunts and mountain climbing, too. The mountain was very fresh and beautiful. The view of nature was beyond description. Most of all, it was the most scenic time of the year. There were flowers blooming everywhere, and the entire mountain was covered with pink, white, and yellow.

제 친한 친구들과 함께 했기 때문에 가장 기억에 남는 하이킹이었던 것 같습니다. 산 위에서 우리는 고기를 구어 먹고 밤새 게임을 하며 놀았습니다. 보물찾기도 하고 등산도 했습니다. 산 위는 매우 상쾌하고 아름다웠습니다. 자연경관은 말로 형용할 수 없을 정도였습니다. 무엇보다도, 연중 가장 아름다운 계절이었습니다. 여기저기 꽃이 만개했고, 온 산이 분홍색, 흰색 그리고 노란색으로 덮여 있었습니다.

| Closing |

We took a lot of pictures, and they still bring back special memories. I can't wait to go hiking again.

우리는 사진을 많이 찍었는데, 사진들을 보면 당시의 특별한 기억이 떠오릅니다. 하이킹에 또 가고 싶어요.

More Questions

〈하이킹〉에 관련하여 더 나올 수 있는 OPIc 질문들을 정리한 코너입니다. 질문에 대한 brainstorming을 해보세요.

1. Suppose that you were injured while hiking. Call the hospital and explain how you got injured and how serious your condition is. In addition, make an appointment to visit the hospital as soon as possible.

2. Here's a situation I want you to act out. You were supposed to go hiking with your friend this weekend. However, you find out there's a family trip planned. Call your friend and explain the situation. Offer some alternative choices.

On Your Own

앞에서 주어진 Model Answer을 바탕으로, 아래의 빈칸에 들어갈 수 있는 다양한 대체 가능한 어휘 및 표현들을 참고하여 학습자 본인만의 모범 답안을 직접 만들어보세요.

I Opening I

My most memorable hiking trip was last ⓐ_____. I went to the famous ⓑ_____ Mountain with my ⓒ_____ ⓓ_____.

I Memorable Hiking Trip I

It was my most memorable hiking experience because I went with my close friends. At the mountain, ⓔ_____. We went scavenger hunts and mountain climbing, too. The mountain was very fresh and beautiful. The view of nature was beyond description. Most of all, it was the most scenic time of the year. There were ⓕ_____ everywhere, and the entire mountain was covered with ⓖ_____.

I Closing I

We took a lot of pictures, and they still bring back special memories. I can't wait to go hiking again.

I Opening I My most memorable hiking trip was last ⓐ **October**. I went to the famous ⓑ **Bukhan** Mountain with my ⓒ **friends** ⓓ **to hike to the top**.

I Memorable Hiking Trip I It was my most memorable hiking experience because I went with my close friends. At the mountain, ⓔ **we got some water at the mineral spring**. We went scavenger hunts and mountain climbing, too. The mountain was very fresh and beautiful. The view of nature was beyond description. Most of all, it was the most scenic time of the year. There were ⓕ **colorful leaves** everywhere, and the entire mountain was covered with ⓖ **red, yellow, and orange**.

I Closing I We took a lot of pictures, and they still bring back special memories. I can't wait to go hiking again.

본인이 만든 답안에 아래의 요소들이 포함되었는지 점검해 봅시다.

	Checklist
☐	기억에 남는 하이킹이 언제인지
☐	어느 산에 갔는지
☐	누구와 함께 갔었는지
☐	산에서 무엇을 했었는지
☐	산의 풍경은 어땠는지

Unit 40 Fitness Club 1

헬스클럽 1

Warm Up

A Guess the Question & Answer
사진을 보면서 예상 질문과 답변을 먼저 추측해 봅시다.

B Listen & Talk
헬스클럽 등록에 관한 대화를 먼저 연습해 봅시다.

🎧 06-07

A How can I help you?	A 어떻게 도와 드릴까요?
B Hi. I just came to check out your fitness club.	B 안녕하세요. 헬스클럽 좀 둘러보러 왔어요.
A Welcome! Right now, we are holding various promotional events.	A 잘 오셨어요! 지금 다양한 판촉 행사를 진행 중이에요.
B What kinds of events? Are you offering any discounts?	B 아, 어떤 행사요? 할인도 해주나요?
A Yes. We are offering a 10 to 30% discount for a personal training program and a regular membership coupon.	A 그럼요. 개인 강습 프로그램 및 정규회원 멤버쉽 쿠폰을 10~30% 할인 판매하고 있어요.
B How much is the personal training program per hour?	B 개인 강습 프로그램은 한 시간에 얼마인가요?
A The original price is 50,000 won, but it is 35,000 won during the promotion.	A 원래는 5만원인데 행사 기간 동안에는 3만 5천원입니다.
B That sounds good. Do you also have any group exercise programs?	B 좋네요. 그룹 운동 프로그램도 있나요?
A We do. We have spinning, yoga, Pilates, and Tae-bo classes.	A 네. 있어요. 스피닝, 요가, 필라테스, 그리고 태보 수업이 진행되고 있어요.
B Are they included in the membership?	B 회원이면 모두 참여 가능한 건가요?
A No, not all of them. You can take one class for free when you sign up for a membership.	A 아니요, 모두 가능한 건 아니에요. 1개 수업에만 무료 참여가 가능해요.

Vocabulary check out 둘러보다, 확인하다 | fitness club 헬스클럽 | hold an event 행사를 주최하다 | promotional event 판촉용 행사 | offer a discount 할인을 제공하다 | personal training program 개인 강습 프로그램 | regular membership 정규 회원 | original price 정상가 | group exercise program 단체 운동 프로그램 | include 포함시키다

Key Expressions

아래 제시된 각 expression의 구조를 이해하고, 자기만의 표현들을 생각해 봅시다.

Expression 1   acquaintance: 지인, 아는 사람

지인으로부터 특별 할인 행사 기간이라고 들었습니다.
→ I heard from an **acquaintance** that you're offering a special discount.

그 화가는 저와 제 남편이 서로 아는 사람입니다.
→ The painter is a mutual **acquaintance** of my husband and me.

그는 제 언니의 지인입니다. 저는 그를 두어 번 밖에는 만난 적이 없습니다.
→ He's an **acquaintance** of my sister. I've only met him a couple of times.

Expression 2   plenty of: 꽤 많은

그 정도면 기구가 꽤 많네요. → That's **plenty of** equipment.

저는 20대에 꽤 많은 곳에 가봤습니다. → I went to **plenty of** places when I was in my 20s.

우리는 나눠 먹을 수 있는 음식이 많습니다. 언제든지 마음껏 와서 드세요.
→ We have **plenty of** food to share. Feel free to come over and have some anytime.

Expression 3   lose weight: 몸무게를 줄이다

저는 몸무게를 줄여야 합니다. → I need to **lose weight**.

저는 지난 겨울 몸무게가 많이 줄었습니다. → I **lost** a lot of **weight** last winter.

세계 탑모델인 지젤은 뉴욕 패션 주간 동안 무대에 오르기 위해 몸무게를 줄였습니다. → Gisele, the top model in the world, **lost weight** to be on the catwalk during New York Fashion Week.

Expression 4   avoid injury: 부상을 피하다

저는 어떠한 종류의 부상도 피하고 싶습니다. → I want to **avoid** any kind of **injury**.

스케이트를 탈 때는 항상 다른 사람들로부터 적당한 거리를 두어 부상을 피하시오.
→ Always keep a distance from other skaters to **avoid injuries**.

유연성과 균형을 갖는 것은 운동할 때 부상을 피하기 위해 중요한 요소들입니다.
→ It's important to possess flexibility and balance to **avoid injuries** while playing sports.

Expression 5   free counseling: 무료 상담

행사 기간 동안 무료 상담을 진행한다고요?
→ You are offering **free counseling** during the event period?

명수는 채용박람회에서 무료 상담을 받았습니다.
→ Myungsoo got some **free counseling** at the job fair.

Topic Question & Model Answer

🎧 06-08

Topic Question

There is a new fitness club open in town. Call the fitness club and ask 3 to 4 questions about the registration and more.

동네에 새로운 헬스클럽이 개점했습니다. 전화를 걸어 등록 절차 및 기타 사항에 대한 질문을 3~4개 해보세요.

TIP FOR THE OPIc

헬스에 관한 롤플레이 질문입니다. 6번 항목에서 헬스를 선택하지 않을지라도 헬스 관련 질문은 종종 출제되고는 합니다. 미국인의 일상과 밀접한 문화이기 때문에 롤플레이로 변형이 되어 나올 수 있습니다. 위의 질문은 롤플레이의 가장 기본이 되는 정보에 관한 것입니다. 우선, 비용에 대한 질문을 빼놓을 수 없을 것입니다. 또한 헬스클럽의 특징인 운동 프로그램이나 운동 기구 등에 대해 질문할 수 있습니다. 이 밖에도 위치, 운영 시간 등도 물어볼 수 있을 것입니다.

Model Answer

| Opening |

Hello? Is this the Slim Fitness Center? Hi. I'm interested in becoming a member. I heard from an acquaintance that you're offering a special discount during the promotional event period.

여보세요? 거기 슬림 헬스클럽인가요? 안녕하세요, 회원 가입에 관심이 있는데요. 아는 분으로부터 프로모션 행사 기간 동안에 특별 할인을 진행한다고 들었어요.

| Questions about the Fitness Club |

I want to sign up for 6 months. How much would that be? 500,000 won? That's a bargain. Can I rent shirt and pants? Cool. In addition, what kinds of exercise equipment do you have? Oh, that's plenty of equipment. Do you have personal trainers as well? I need to lose weight, but I want to avoid any kind of injury. You are offering free counseling during the event period? Great! My last question: Are there any group exercise programs? Spinning, yoga, Pilates, and Tae-bo classes? There's even a nightclub dance class? I love it!

6개월간 등록을 하고 싶은데요. 그러면 얼마가 되나요? 50만원이요? 그 정도면 상당히 좋은 가격이네요. 셔츠와 바지도 대여 가능한가요? 좋네요. 참, 어떤 운동 기구가 구비되어 있나요? 아, 그 정도면 많이 구비해 놓으셨네요. 개인 트레이너도 있나요? 살을 빼고 싶은데 부상을 입기는 싫거든요. 행사 기간 동안 무료 상담을 진행한다고요? 잘 됐네요! 마지막 질문이에요: 그룹 운동 프로그램은 없나요? 스피닝, 요가, 필라테스 그리고 태보 수업이 있다고요? 나이트클럽 댄스반도 있어요? 정말 좋은데요!

| Closing |

I'd better visit right away. Thanks.

당장 가봐야겠네요. 고맙습니다.

More Questions

〈헬스클럽〉에 관련하여 더 나올 수 있는 OPIc 질문들을 정리한 코너입니다. 질문에 대한 brainstorming을 해보세요.

1. Tell me about the exercise machines you use at the gym. Which one do you use the most often? Why?
2. Since when did you join the fitness club? Do you go there by yourself or with a friend?
3. Do you have a personal trainer at the gym? Who taught you how to use the equipment?

On Your Own

앞에서 주어진 Model Answer을 바탕으로, 아래의 빈칸에 들어갈 수 있는 다양한 대체 가능한 어휘 및 표현들을 참고하여 학습자 본인만의 모범 답안을 직접 만들어보세요.

I Opening I

Hello? Is this Slim Fitness Center? Hi. I'm interested in becoming a member. I heard from ⓐ_____ that you're offering a special discount ⓑ_____.

I Questions about the Fitness Club I

I want to sign up for ⓒ_____. How much would that be? ⓓ_____ won? That's a bargain. Can I rent shirt and pants? Cool. In addition, what kinds of exercise equipment do you have? Oh, that's plenty of equipment. Do you have personal trainers as well? I need to ⓔ_____. You are offering free counseling during the event period? Great! My last question: Are there any group exercise programs? ⓕ_____? There's even a ⓖ_____? I love it!

I Closing I

I'd better visit right away. Thanks.

I Opening I Hello? Is this the Slim Fitness Center? Hi. I'm interested in becoming a member. I heard from ⓐ **a friend** that you're offering a special discount ⓑ **during the vacation season**.

I Questions about the Fitness Club I I want to sign up for ⓒ **3 months**. How much would that be? ⓓ **100,000** won? That's a bargain. Can I rent shirt and pants? Cool. In addition, what kinds of exercise equipment do you have? Oh, that's plenty of equipment. Do you have personal trainers as well? I need to ⓔ **measure my body fat and develop an organized workout plan**. You are offering free counseling during the event period? Great! My last question: Are there any group exercise programs? ⓕ **Body combat, cross fit, and aerobics**? There's even a ⓖ **zumba dance class**? I love it!

I Closing I I'd better visit right away. Thanks.

본인이 만든 답안에 아래의 요소들이 포함되었는지 점검해 봅시다.

	Checklist
☐	전화 걸 때 인사말하기
☐	상대방(헬스클럽) 확인하기
☐	전화 건 목적(회원 등록) 얘기하기
☐	운동복 대여하는지 문의하기
☐	운동 기구 종류 문의하기
☐	개인 트레이너 있는지 문의하기
☐	그룹 운동 프로그램 종류 문의하기
☐	마무리 인사하기

Unit 41 Fitness Club 2

헬스클럽 2

Warm Up

A Guess the Question & Answer
사진을 보면서 예상 질문과 답변을 먼저 추측해 봅시다.

B Listen & Talk
헬스클럽에서 운동하는 것에 관한 대화를 먼저 연습해 봅시다.

🎧 06-09

A Hello, Jaeseok? Hey, how's it going?

B Good. Thanks. How are you?

A I'm doing great. Um, are you still interested in signing up for the gym?

B Sure. I need to do some weight training. My girlfriend is visiting me this summer.

A Your girlfriend who lives in Sydney?

B Yeah. We haven't seen each other for half a year. I want to impress her.

A You'd better start right away then. Vacation season is just around the corner.

B I know. When are you free to sign up?

A How about tonight? I get off at 6.

B Cool. Shall we meet in front of Happy Bank?

A Yeah, that sounds awesome. See you there. Bye.

A 여보세요, 재석? 어떻게 지내?

B 잘 지내. 고마워. 넌?

A 아주 좋아. 음, 너 아직도 헬스클럽 등록에 관심 있어?

B 그럼. 근력 운동 좀 해야 돼. 올 여름에 여자친구가 오거든.

A 와, 시드니에 있다는 여자친구?

B 그럼. 반 년째 못 봤어. 놀라게 해주고 싶어.

A 그럼 바로 시작해야겠네! 곧 휴가철이잖아.

B 알아. 넌 언제 등록할 수 있어?

A 오늘 밤은 어때? 난 6시면 끝나.

B 좋아. 우리 행복 은행 앞에서 만날까?

A 좋지. 거기서 봐. 안녕.

Vocabulary How's it going? 어떻게 지내? | sign up 등록하다 | weight training 근력 운동 | impress somebody ~에게 (좋은) 인상을 주다 | get off at ~ ~시에 마치다, 있던 장소를 떠나다 | be free to ~ ~하기에 가능하다, 자유롭다

Key Expressions

🗝 아래 제시된 각 expression의 구조를 이해하고, 자기만의 표현들을 생각해 봅시다.

Expression 1   **leave a message:** 메시지를 남기다

저는 메시지를 남기고 있습니다. → I'm **leaving a message**.

메시지를 남기시겠습니까? → Would you like to **leave a message**?

나리는 오늘 아침 그녀의 친구에게 메시지를 남겼습니다.
→ Nari **left a message** for her friend this morning.

Expression 2   **pick up the phone:** 전화를 받다

당신은 전화를 받지 않습니다. → You're not **picking up the phone**.

그는 그녀가 바로 전화를 받지 않자 짜증이 났습니다.
→ He got annoyed because she didn't **pick up the phone** right away.

저는 회담 중에 전화를 받을 수가 없었습니다.
→ I was not able to **pick up the phone** during the conference.

Expression 3   **guide** + 사람 + **to ~:** ~를 ~로 인도하다, 안내하다

그녀는 호텔까지 안내해 줄 사람이 필요합니다. → She needs someone to **guide** her **to** the hotel.

부디 저를 그 교회로 안내해주시겠습니까? → Would you please **guide** me **to** the church?

그 소년은 그의 할아버지의 손을 잡고 대저택으로 안내해 드렸습니다.
→ The young boy held his grandfather's hand and **guided** him **to** the mansion.

Expression 4   **no one else but** + 사람: 다른 누구도 아닌 어떤 사람

그녀는 여기에 관광차 왔는데 저 말고는 다른 누구도 아는 사람이 없습니다.
→ She's here to sightsee and knows **no one else but** me.

나는 다른 누구도 아닌 당신과 결혼하고 싶습니다. → I want to marry **no one else but** you.

이 초상화는 다른 누구도 아닌 제 모습입니다. → This portrait could be of **no one else but** me.

Expression 5   **be available:** 가능하다, ~할 수 있다

당신이 가능한지 알려주세요. → Let me know if you **are available**.

당신은 오늘밤 저녁을 함께 할 수 있나요? → **Are** you **available** to join me for dinner tonight?

당신이 그녀를 이번 주말 파티에 에스코트 해줄 수 있나요?
→ Will you **be available** to escort her to the party this weekend?

Topic Question & Model Answer

🎧 06-10

Topic Question

You made an appointment with your friend to sign up for the fitness center tonight. However, an urgent matter came up, and you can't make it. Leave a message with your friend and explain why you can't sign up tonight. In addition, reschedule the appointment.

당신은 오늘 저녁 친구와 함께 헬스클럽에 등록하기로 했습니다. 하지만 갑자기 긴급 상황이 발생하여 약속을 지킬 수가 없습니다. 친구에게 음성 메시지를 남기고 오늘 밤 왜 등록할 수 없는지 설명해보세요. 또한 약속을 다시 잡아보세요.

TIP FOR THE OPIc

앞서 나온 헬스클럽 관련 롤플레이 문제의 콤보입니다. 겉보기에는 헬스 관련 질문 같지만, 사실은 '약속을 취소한 것에 대한 배경 설명 및 rescheduling'을 하는 것이 질문의 핵심입니다. 약속을 지키지 못할 때에는 1) 질병 2) 가족의 질병 3) 비상 업무 발생 4) 교통사고 등을 이유로 설명할 수 있습니다. 먼저 상대방에게 진심 어린 사과를 한 이후에 배경 설명을 하고, 새로 약속을 잡는 것이 순서입니다. 롤플레이 질문에 대한 답안을 만들 때에는 목소리 톤이 답안 내용만큼 중요하다는 사실을 기억하기 바랍니다.

Model Answer

| Opening |

Hi, Dongho. This is Jaeseok. I'm leaving a message since you're not picking up the phone.

동호야 안녕! 나 재석이야. 네가 전화를 안 받기에 음성 메시지를 남겨.

| Appointment Cancellation and Apology |

I know we are supposed to sign up for the Slim Fitness Center tonight. I'm really sorry, Dongho, but can I take a rain check? I have a friend visiting Seoul this week, and she's arriving this evening. She needs someone to pick her up at the airport and guide her to the hotel. She's here to sightsee and knows no one else but me. I thought her arrival time was late at night, but I just found out it is actually 6 p.m. I'm sorry again.

음, 우리 오늘 저녁에 같이 슬림 헬스클럽에 등록하러 가기로 한 걸 알아. 동호야, 정말 미안한데, 우리 약속을 다음으로 미룰 수 있을까? 이번 주에 서울에 오는 친구가 한 명 있는데 오늘 저녁 도착해. 내가 공항에서 친구를 픽업해서 호텔까지 안내해줘야 할 것 같아. 관광차 한국에 왔는데 나 말고는 아는 사람이 아무도 없거든. 오늘 밤 늦게 도착하는 줄 알았는데 방금 보니까 저녁 6시 도착이더라고. 다시 한 번 정말 미안해.

| Rearrangement and Closing |

I will be free on Thursday anytime after work, so please let me know if you are available. Talk to you soon. Bye.

나는 목요일에 업무 마치고 아무 때나 시간이 되니까, 너도 가능한지 알려줘. 곧 연락해! 안녕.

More Questions

〈헬스클럽〉에 관련하여 더 나올 수 있는 OPIc 질문들을 정리한 코너입니다. 질문에 대한 brainstorming을 해보세요.

1. You indicated that you work out at a gym. Is the gym near your house? How do you get there?
2. What do you do before and after working out at the gym?
3. What are some things you should keep in mind to avoid injuries while working out at the gym?

On Your Own

앞에서 주어진 Model Answer을 바탕으로, 아래의 빈칸에 들어갈 수 있는 다양한 대체 가능한 어휘 및 표현들을 참고하여 학습자 본인만의 모범 답안을 직접 만들어보세요.

I Opening I

Hi, Dongho. This is Jaeseok. I'm leaving a message since you're not picking up the phone.

I Appointment Cancellation and Apology I

I know we are supposed to sign up for the Slim Fitness Center tonight. I'm really sorry, Dongho, but can I take a rain check? ⓐ_____.

ⓑ_____.

ⓒ_____.

I'm sorry again.

I Rearrangement and Closing I

I will be free on Thursday anytime after work, so please let me know if you are available. Talk to you soon. Bye.

I Opening I Hi, Dongho! This is Jaeseok. I'm leaving a message since you're not picking up the phone.

I Appointment Cancellation and Apology I I know we are supposed to sign up for the Slim Fitness Center tonight. I'm really sorry, Dongho, but can I take a rain check? ⓐ **I have to work overtime tonight.** ⓑ **We have people visiting from headquarters next week, and my boss wants to impress them.** ⓒ **My team has to finish the current project, and the schedule will be too tight.** I'm sorry again.

I Rearrangement and Closing I I will be free on Thursday anytime after work, so please let me know if you are available. Talk to you soon. Bye.

본인이 만든 답안에 아래의 요소들이 포함되었는지 점검해 봅시다.

	Checklist
☐	전화 걸 때 인사말 하기
☐	상대방 확인하기
☐	자신이 누군지 밝히기
☐	음성 메시지 남기는 이유(약속 변경) 말하기
☐	약속 변경 사과하고 이유 설명하기
☐	언제로 변경할지 물어보기
☐	메시지 확인하면 연락 달라고 하기
☐	마무리 인사하기

The Music of Speech

강세를 두어야 하는 어휘의 특징을 익히고 그에 따라 답안을 말하는 연습을 해봅시다.

강세를 두는 어휘의 특징
1) 감탄사이다 2) 최상급이다 3) 형용사/부사이다
4) 문장 안에서 key word 역할을 하는 명사나 동사인 경우가 많다

Model Answer 37 🎧 06-11

There are many benefits to jogging. First of all, it doesn't cost much. As long as you have a pair of sneakers, you are free to jog. In addition, it's not limited to certain places or time. You are able to jog in any public area anytime. Well, of course for females, it would be safe to run with someone when it gets dark. Another reason I like jogging is that I can enjoy the fresh air and beautiful scenery when I jog at the park. I used to work out at a gym when I was younger, but, since I now jog at the park, I can't imagine myself running on a treadmill again. I highly recommend jogging to those who want to be healthy and to stay fit. I guess these are some of the benefits of jogging.

Model Answer 38 🎧 06-12

I think the most important thing you should keep in mind is to choose the right shoes. If you don't wear the right shoes, you are more prone to injuries like sprained ankles. You will also have sore feet. In addition, it's always important to do enough warmup exercises before jogging. Otherwise, you will feel muscle pain all over your body. I always stretch for about 10 to 15 minutes before I jog. This way, you can relax your muscles and prepare your body to jog. I also take a bottle of water when I jog. It is important to drink enough water while you exercise. This is especially important on sunny days since you might sweat a lot, so it's good to bring something to drink. Finally, if you are sensitive to sunlight, I recommend that you apply enough sunscreen products on your face and wear either sunglasses or a cap. That way, you will be able to avoid getting a sunburn and developing freckles.

Model Answer 39 🎧 06-13

My most memorable hiking trip was last April. I went to the famous Chungye Mountain with my classmates and stayed at a camping site for 2 nights and 3 days. It was my most memorable hiking experience because I went with my close friends. At the mountain, we had a barbecue party and played games all night. We went scavenger hunts and mountain climbing, too. The mountain was very fresh and beautiful. The view of nature was beyond description. Most of all, it was the most scenic time of the year. There were flowers blooming everywhere, and the entire mountain was covered with pink, white, and yellow. We took a lot of pictures, and they still bring back special memories. I can't wait to go hiking again.

Model Answer 40   06-14

Hello? Is this the Slim Fitness Center? Hi. I'm interested in becoming a member. I heard from an acquaintance that you're offering a special discount during the promotional event period. I want to sign up for 6 months. How much would that be? 500,000 won? That's a bargain. Can I rent shirt and pants? Cool. In addition, what kinds of exercise equipment do you have? Oh, that's plenty of equipment. Do you have personal trainers as well? I need to lose weight, but I want to avoid any kind of injury. You are offering free counseling during the event period? Great! My last question: Are there any group exercise programs? Spinning, yoga, Pilates, and Tae-bo classes? There's even a nightclub dance class? I love it! I'd better visit right away. Thanks.

Model Answer 41   06-15

Hi, Dongho. This is Jaesuk. I'm leaving a message since you're not picking up the phone. I know we are supposed to sign up for the Slim Fitness Center tonight. I'm really sorry, Dongho, but can I take a rain check? I have a friend visiting Seoul this week, and she's arriving this evening. She needs someone to pick her up at the airport and guide her to the hotel. She's here to sightsee and knows no one else but me. I thought her arrival time was late at night, but I just found out it is actually 6 p.m. I'm sorry again. I will be free on Thursday anytime after work, so please let me know if you are available. Talk to you soon. Bye.

More Expressions & Vocabulary ≫ **Sports**

It was a close game.
그 경기는 막상막하였습니다.

Our team made it to the finals.
우리 팀은 결승에 진출했습니다.

We cheered for the team.
우리는 그 팀을 응원했습니다.

I jog along the stream.
저는 개울가를 따라 조깅합니다.

I can get some fresh air while jogging.
저는 조깅하면서 맑은 공기를 마십니다.

I listen to music while jogging.
저는 조깅을 하면서 음악 감상을 합니다.

Swimming is a great way to stay in shape.
수영은 몸매 유지를 위한 좋은 방법입니다.

I learned how to do the butterfly last week.
저는 지난주에 접영을 배웠습니다.

I need a kickboard to swim.
저는 킥보드가 있어야 수영할 수 있습니다.

My doctor recommended that I start swimming.
담당 주치의가 수영을 시작하라고 권고했습니다.

I took a break since I had a cramp in my foot.
저는 발에 쥐가 나서 잠시 휴식을 취했습니다.

CHAPTER 7 여행

Traveling

Unit 42	**Domestic Business Trip** 국내출장
Unit 43	**Overseas Business Trip** 해외출장
Unit 44	**Vacation at Home 1** 집에서 보내는 휴가 1
Unit 45	**Vacation at Home 2** 집에서 보내는 휴가 2
Unit 46	**Domestic Travel** 국내여행
Unit 47	**Overseas Travel** 해외여행

Chapter 7은 출장 및 여행, 집에서 보내는 휴가에 관해 다룹니다. 다른 항목에 비해 '장소(where)'와 특히 더 밀접한 관계가 있습니다. 출장 지역, 여행지, 집의 특성에 관해 생각해보고, 해당 장소에 따라 활동(what)이 어떻게 달라지는지 정리해두면 좋습니다. 여행과 관련해서는 질문의 내용이 다양하게 변형되어 나오는 경우가 많지만, 각 unit에 제시된 질문들을 기본으로 하여 생각의 폭을 다각화(branch out)하면 바람직한 답변을 이끌어낼 수 있습니다.

+ Brainstorming Point

When?
- when I last went on a business trip/trip (마지막 출장/여행간 시기)
- when I first traveled overseas (처음 해외여행한 경험)

Where?
- the most memorable city I have been to (기억에 남는 도시)
- where I would recommend to go sightseeing in Korea (한국의 추천 관광지)
- where I would like to visit on my next vacation (다음 휴가지)

What?
- what I do during a business trip (출장 기간에 하는 일)
- what to prepare for a business trip/trip (출장/여행갈 때 준비 사항)
- what kinds of activities I do during the trip (여행가서 하는 일)
- what I need to consider when I travel (여행갈 때 고려할 점)

Who?
- who helped me with the trip (여행갈 때 도움 준 사람)
- who I want to travel with (함께 여행가고 싶은 사람)
- people I met at the travel spot (여행지에서 만난 사람들)

Why?
- why I like to travel overseas/in my country (국내/외 여행을 좋아하는 이유)
- why I have to go on a business trip (출장 가는 이유)

How?
- how I plan an itinerary (여행 일정표를 어떻게 계획하는지)
- how I make a budget for a trip (여행 경비를 어떻게 계획하는지)

Unit 42 Domestic Business Trip

국내출장

Warm Up

A Guess the Question & Answer
사진을 보면서 예상 질문과 답변을 먼저 추측해 봅시다.

B Listen & Talk
국내출장에 관한 대화를 먼저 연습해 봅시다.

🎧 07-01

A Did you attend the conference in Daejeon last week?

B Yes. I made a presentation on behalf of the Seoul office and was even the English MC for the opening ceremony.

A Oh, you had the honor of being the MC for the opening ceremony? Your boss must have liked that.

B I don't know about that, but I did get some nice feedback after the presentation.

A Good for you. What kinds of sessions did you have during the conference?

B We invited the press to introduce our new product line. A few guest speakers also gave lectures on strategic marketing. The rest of the sessions were the same as usual.

A I see. Aren't you a little tired of attending conferences now? There must be a lot to take care of before and after the trip.

B Sure. I feel overwhelmed by the amount of work sometimes. But I don't want to give up on attending conferences since they're a great way to develop my business skills.

A 지난주에 대전에서 열린 회의에 참여했다며?

B 응. 서울 사무소 대표로 프레젠테이션도 하고 개막식때 영어 사회도 봤어.

A 어머, 개막식 사회를 맡았었단 말이야? 네 상사가 흐뭇했겠네!

B 그건 잘 모르겠지만 프레젠테이션 끝나고 나서는 좋은 평을 받았어.

A 잘됐네. 이번 회의에는 어떤 세션들이 있었어?

B 기자단을 초청해서 신제품 라인을 소개했어. 그리고 몇몇 초대 강사들이 전략적 마케팅에 대한 강의를 했어. 나머지 세션들은 평소랑 같았어.

A 그렇구나. 매번 회의 참석하는 게 좀 지겹지는 않아? 출장 다녀오기 전후로 할 일이 많잖아.

B 그럼. 때때로 업무량에 눌리기도 하지. 하지만 내 업무 능력을 쌓는 데에는 회의 참석하는 것 만한 게 없어서 포기하고 싶지 않아.

Vocabulary make a presentation 프레젠테이션을 하다 | on behalf of ~ ~를 대신하여, ~을 대표하여 | opening ceremony 개막식 | have the honor of ~ ~를 하는 영광을 얻다 | get feedback 피드백을 받다 | product line 생산 라인 | give a lecture 강의를 하다 | strategic marketing 전략적 마케팅 | feel overwhelmed 압도당하다 | business skill 비즈니스 능력

Key Expressions

아래 제시된 각 expression의 구조를 이해하고, 자기만의 표현들을 생각해 봅시다.

Expression 1   **every quarter:** 매 분기마다

저는 매 분기마다 국내 출장을 갑니다. → I go on domestic business trips **every quarter**.

우리는 매 분기마다 데이터를 업데이트 합니다. → We update our data **every quarter**.

우리 회사는 매 분기마다 회계 감사를 시행합니다. → My company conducts an audit **every quarter**.

Expression 2   **branch office:** 지점

우리 회사는 16개 도시에 지점이 있습니다. → Our company has **branch offices** in 16 other cities.

우리는 인도네시아에 지점을 여는 것을 계획하고 있습니다.
→ We are planning to set up a **branch office** in Indonesia.

제 아버지는 예전에 보스턴 지점에서 근무하셨습니다.
→ My father used to work for the Boston **branch office**.

Expression 3   **on behalf of ~:** ~를 대신/대표하여

저는 언제나 제 팀을 대표하여 회의에 참석합니다.
→ I always attend the conference **on behalf of** my team.

저는 제 사장님을 대신하여 전화 드리는 겁니다. → I'm calling you **on behalf of** my boss.

우리는 정부를 대신하여 그 사건에 대한 사과를 합니다.
→ We apologize for the incident **on behalf of** the government.

Expression 4   **require:** ~를 필요로 하다

출장을 가는 것은 많은 업무를 필요로 합니다. → Going on a business trip **requires** a lot of work.

이 직업은 상당한 노력을 요할 것입니다. → This job **requires** a great deal of effort.

법은 당신 소득의 3.3%를 지불할 것을 요구합니다.
→ The law **requires** you to pay 3.3% of your income as taxes.

Expression 5   **come up with ~:** ~를 떠올리다, 제시하다, 내놓다

저는 시장에 대해 많은 것을 배우고 새로운 아이디어를 떠올리게 됩니다.
→ I learn a lot about the market, and I am able to **come up with** fresh ideas.

정부는 총기 밀수입을 단속하기 위한 해결책을 내놓았습니다.
→ The government **came up with** a solution to cut down on gun trafficking.

처벌을 면하기 위해서는 합리적인 이유를 제시해야 할 것입니다.
→ You'd better **come up with** a good reason to avoid any punishment.

Topic Question & Model Answer

Topic Question

How often do you go on domestic business trips? What's your role? In addition, what are the difficulties of going on business trips?

당신은 얼마나 자주 국내출장을 가나요? 당신의 역할은 무엇인가요? 또한, 출장의 어려움은 무엇인가요?

TIP FOR THE OPIc

국내출장 편은 직장인 분들이 자주 선택하는 항목입니다. 질문 중에는 국내/해외여행과도 연계되어 나올 수 있는 유형이 있으므로, 학생들도 참고하는 게 좋습니다. 출장은 직장생활의 일부입니다. 평소의 업무가 출장과 어떠한 관련이 있는지, 출장 가서 하는 주요 업무, 출장을 통해 기대하는 성과에 대해 질문할 수 있습니다. 그 밖에도 출장 준비 과정, 기억에 남는 출장 등, 여행 편과 유사한 패턴의 질문도 나올 수 있으므로 다각도로 브레인스토밍 해두면 좋을 것입니다.

Model Answer

| Opening |

I go on domestic business trips every quarter. My company has branch offices in 16 other cities, and the regular conference is held in different regions each quarter. I always attend the conference on behalf of my team.

저는 매 분기마다 국내 출장을 갑니다. 우리 회사는 전국 16개 도시에 지점 사무실이 있는데, 매 분기마다 다른 지역에서 정기 총회가 개최됩니다. 저는 항상 제 부서를 대표하여 회의에 참석합니다.

| My Role and Difficulties |

I make presentations on the outcome of our marketing strategies and sales record. Going on a business trip requires a lot of work in addition to my office work, so it's tiring. I often stay at the office all night to finish my work when I have an upcoming business trip.

그곳에서 저는 우리 부서의 마케팅 전략의 결과 및 영업 실적에 대한 프레젠테이션을 합니다. 출장을 가는 것은 사무실 업무 외의 많은 것을 요구하기 때문에 매우 피곤합니다. 그래서 출장을 앞둔 기간에는 줄곧 밤샘 작업을 하고는 합니다.

| Benefits of Business Trips |

However, attending the conference is a great way to develop my business skills. I learn a lot about the market and come up with fresh ideas. Whenever the trip is over, I always realize that there's no gain without pain.

하지만 회의에 참석하는 것은 저의 비즈니스 능력을 개발시키는 데에 큰 도움을 줍니다. 시장에 대한 많은 정보를 얻게 되고 새로운 아이디어를 떠올리게 됩니다. 출장을 마치면, 저는 늘 노력없이는 얻는 것도 없다는 것을 깨닫게 됩니다.

More Questions

〈국내출장〉에 관련하여 더 나올 수 있는 OPIc 질문들을 정리한 코너입니다. 질문에 대한 brainstorming을 해보세요.

1. Do you often go on business trips? What kinds of work do you do to prepare for business trips?
2. When was your last business trip? Where did you go? Did you have a successful trip?
3. Have you ever faced an embarrassing moment during a business trip? Tell me everything that happened.

앞에서 주어진 Model Answer을 바탕으로, 아래의 빈칸에 들어갈 수 있는 다양한 대체 가능한 어휘 및 표현들을 참고하여 학습자 본인만의 모범 답안을 직접 만들어보세요.

I Opening I

I go on domestic business trips ⓐ_____. My company has

ⓑ_____ on behalf of my team.

I My Role and Difficulties I

I make ⓒ_____. Going on a business trip requires a lot of work in addition to my office work, so it's tiring. I often stay at the office all night to finish my work when I have an upcoming business trip.

I Benefits of Business Trips I

However, ⓓ_____ is a great way to develop my business skills.

I learn ⓔ_____. Whenever the trip is over, I always realize that there's no gain without pain.

I Opening I I go on domestic business trips ⓐ **twice a year**. My company has ⓑ **factories in different cities, and I visit the factory for meetings and inspections** on behalf of my team.

I My Role and Difficulties I I make ⓒ **reports about the factory's facilities and the management system**. Going on a business trip requires a lot of work in addition to my office work, so it's tiring. I often stay at the office all night to finish my work when I have an upcoming business trip.

I Benefits of Business Trips I However, ⓓ **visiting the factories** is a great way to develop my business skills. I learn ⓔ **a lot by observing the manufacturing process**. Whenever the trip is over, I always realize that there's no gain without pain.

본인이 만든 답안에 아래의 요소들이 포함되었는지 점검해 봅시다.

	Checklist
☐	얼마나 자주 국내 출장을 가는지
☐	어디로 출장을 가는지
☐	출장의 목적
☐	출장 가서 하는 일
☐	출장의 어려움
☐	출장을 통해 얻는 점

Unit 43 Overseas Business Trip

해외출장

Warm Up

A Guess the Question & Answer
사진을 보면서 예상 질문과 답변을 먼저 추측해 봅시다.

B Listen & Talk
해외출장에 관한 대화를 먼저 연습해 봅시다.

🎧 07-03

A How was your business trip?

B It was very successful. We had a lot of visitors during the exhibition.

A Did you secure any contracts?

B We did. Around 20 companies ordered our new products and signed contracts.

A Your team must be very excited with the results.

B We are. You know how hard we've been working for this exhibition.

A Sure. By the way, how was Las Vegas? Were you able to do any sightseeing or watch a show?

B No way. I was tied up with work the entire week. I was only able to look down at the city from my hotel room. Of course, the night view was crazy as usual.

A When is your next trip?

B It's in 2 months in Geneva. I don't want to think about it now. I need some rest.

A 출장 어땠어?

B 매우 성공적이었어. 전시회 내내 방문객이 아주 많았어.

A 계약도 좀 성사됐어?

B 그럼. 20개 정도의 회사들이 우리 신제품을 주문하고 계약을 맺었어.

A 너희 부서에서 정말 좋아했겠네.

B 응. 우리가 이번 전시회를 위해서 얼마나 열심히 준비했는지 알잖아.

A 그럼. 그나저나, 라스 베가스는 어땠어? 관광을 하거나 쇼 본 거는 없어?

B 전혀. 일주일 내내 일만 하다 왔어. 호텔방에서 감상한 게 전부야. 물론 야경은 언제나처럼 끝내줬지.

A 다음 출장은 언제야?

B 2달 뒤에 제네바로 가. 지금은 생각도 하기 싫어. 좀 쉬어야겠어.

Vocabulary

business trip 출장 | exhibition 전시회 | order 주문하다 | sign a contract 계약을 맺다 | sightseeing 관광 | be tied up with ~ ~에 (시간이) 묶여있다

Key Expressions

아래 제시된 각 expression의 구조를 이해하고, 자기만의 표현들을 생각해 봅시다.

Expression 1   industry: 업계, 산업

그것은 전자업계에서 가장 큰 전시회 중의 하나였습니다.
→ It was one of the biggest exhibitions in the electronic **industry**.

그는 건설업계에 종사합니다. → He works for the construction **industry**.

관광산업에 대한 투자가 증가하고 있습니다. → There's a growing investment in the tourism **industry**.

Expression 2   promote: ~을 판촉하다, 홍보하다, 장려하다

저는 회사의 제품을 판촉하기 위해서 전시회에 참가했습니다.
→ I attended the exhibition to **promote** my company's products.

그들은 그들의 브랜드 이미지를 홍보하기 위해 많은 돈을 투자했습니다.
→ They invested a lot of money to **promote** their brand's image.

한국 정부는 출산율을 장려하기 위해 노력하고 있습니다.
→ The Korean government is trying to **promote** ways to increase the birth rate.

Expression 3   display: ~를 전시하다, 선보이다

우리 부스는 최신 휴대폰과 LED TV를 선보였습니다.
→ Our booth **displayed** mobile phones and LED TVs on.

화면에 에러 메시지가 나타났습니다. → There was an error message **displayed** on the screen.

그 가게는 가장 최신의 시계 디자인을 선보였습니다. → The store **displayed** the watches' latest designs.

Expression 4   draw attention: 관심을 끌다, 주목을 받다

우리는 기자단과 방문객의 큰 관심을 얻었습니다.
→ We **drew** a huge amount of **attention** from the press and visitors.

그 NGO는 대중의 주목을 끌기 위해 힘쓰고 있습니다.
→ The NGO is aiming to **draw attention** to the public.

그 재즈 페스티벌은 미디어의 큰 관심을 얻었습니다.
→ The jazz festival **drew** a huge amount of **attention** from the media.

Expression 5   reach a goal: 목표를 달성하다

우리는 매출 목표를 달성할 수 있었습니다. → We were able to **reach** our sales **goal**.

저는 제 목표를 달성하기 위해 취미 생활을 포기했습니다. → I gave up my hobbies to **reach** my **goal**.

우리는 특정한 목표를 달성하기 위해서는 동기 부여가 필요합니다.
→ We need motivation to **reach** certain **goals**.

Topic Question & Model Answer

🎧 07-04

Topic Question

When was your last overseas business trip? Where did you go? What was the purpose of the trip?

당신이 마지막으로 해외출장 갔던 것은 언제입니까? 어디로 갔나요? 출장의 목적은 무엇이었나요?

> **TIP FOR THE OPIc**
>
> 해외출장은 부서 및 업계에 따라 다르기는 하겠지만, 비교적 해당되는 분들이 적은 항목입니다. 또한 국내출장에 비해 횟수가 적은 것이 일반적입니다. 따라서 관련 질문에 대해 답을 준비할 때에는 '선택과 집중' 전략을 세우는 것이 좋습니다. 한 두가지 기억에 남는 해외출장 경험 가운데 특별히 목적지(국가, 도시)가 인상적이었던 곳을 선택하여, 해당 지역의 특징, 뜻밖에 일어난 사건, 업무 수행 과정 및 결과 등에 대해 브레인스토밍 해두면 좋습니다.

Model Answer

| Opening |

My last business trip was in February of this year. I went to Las Vegas to attend one of the biggest exhibitions in the electronic industry.

제 마지막 출장은 올 2월에 있었습니다. 저는 전자 산업계에서 가장 규모가 큰 전시회 중의 하나에 참여하기 위해 라스베가스에 다녀왔습니다.

| Purpose of the Business Trip |

Since I'm the manager of the Overseas Sales Department, I attended the exhibition to promote my company's products. It was a 5-day exhibition, and many global companies came to show off their cutting-edge products and technology. Our booth displayed the newest mobile phones and LED TVs. We drew a huge amount of attention from the press and visitors. In addition, we were able to reach our sales goal.

저는 해외영업 부서의 과장으로 있기 때문에, 회사의 제품을 홍보하기 위해 전시회에 참여했습니다. 5일 간 진행된 전시회에는 세계적인 기업들이 다수 참가하여 그들의 최신 제품 및 신기술을 선보였습니다. 우리 회사 부스에서는 최근에 출시된 휴대 전화 및 LED TV를 전시했었습니다. 우리 부스는 언론과 방문객의 큰 관심을 얻었습니다. 뿐만 아니라, 우리는 매출 목표도 달성할 수 있었습니다.

| Closing |

Overall, the trip was very satisfying and rewarding.

아무쪼록 매우 만족스럽고 보람된 출장이었습니다.

More Questions

〈해외출장〉에 관련하여 더 나올 수 있는 OPIc 질문들을 정리한 코너입니다. 질문에 대한 brainstorming을 해보세요.

1. Tell to me about the entire procedure regarding your overseas business trips. What do you prepare in the office, and what do you do when you arrive at your destination?

2. What was your most memorable overseas business trip? When did you go, and to which city did you go? Why was it so memorable?

3. What's the difference between a domestic business trip and an overseas business trip? Which one is more demanding? Why do you think that is so?

On Your Own

앞에서 주어진 Model Answer을 바탕으로, 아래의 빈칸에 들어갈 수 있는 다양한 대체 가능한 어휘 및 표현들을 참고하여 학습자 본인만의 모범 답안을 직접 만들어보세요.

❙ Opening ❙

My last business trip was in ⓐ_____. I went to
ⓑ_____.

❙ Purpose of the Business Trip ❙

Since I'm the manager of the Overseas Sales Department, I
ⓒ_____. It was a ⓓ_____ trip, and I
ⓔ_____.
ⓕ_____.
They were happy with the price we suggested and said that the product would be competitive in their market.

❙ Closing ❙

Overall, the trip was very satisfying and rewarding.

❙ Opening ❙ My last business trip was in ⓐ **April this year**. I went to ⓑ **the Netherlands to meet one of our major clients**.

❙ Purpose of the Business Trip ❙ Since I'm the manager of the Overseas Sales Department, I ⓒ **went on the business trip to introduce our new products**. It was a ⓓ **3-day** trip, and I ⓔ **had meetings with the person in charge of the Distribution Department**. ⓕ **Our client company was very interested in our new products and asked for samples**. They were happy with the price we suggested and said that the product would be competitive in their market.

❙ Closing ❙ Overall, the trip was very satisfying and rewarding.

본인이 만든 답안에 아래의 요소들이 포함되었는지 점검해 봅시다.

	Checklist
☐	마지막으로 해외출장을 갔던 시기
☐	출장 지역
☐	출장의 목적
☐	출장을 통해 이룬 업적
☐	기억에 남는 에피소드
☐	전체적인 출장 소감

Unit 43 Overseas Business Trip

Unit 44 Vacation at Home 1

집에서 보내는 휴가 1

Warm Up

A Guess the Question & Answer
사진을 보면서 예상 질문과 답변을 먼저 추측해 봅시다.

B Listen & Talk
집에서 휴가를 보내는 방법에 관한 대화를 먼저 연습해 봅시다.

🎧 07-05

A How do you spend your free time at home? Have you made changes from the way you used to spend it in the past?	**A** 넌 요새 집에서 어떻게 여가 시간을 보내? 예전이랑 좀 달라진 게 있어?
B Yes, I've made a lot of changes. I was a couch potato when I was young, but I don't even think about watching TV these days.	**B** 응, 달라진 점 많지. 어릴 적에는 소파에 누워서 TV만 봤는데, 요즘에는 TV 켤 생각도 안 해.
A What do you mean? You don't watch TV at all?	**A** 무슨 말이야? TV를 전혀 안 봐?
B No. I never turn on the TV on my own. I spend more time on the Internet or listen to music when I'm free at home.	**B** 응. 내가 TV를 켤 때는 없어. 난 주로 인터넷을 하거나 음악 감상을 하면서 집에서 쉬는 편이야.
A Right. There are so many things to do online these days. Once, I was addicted to online chatting and had a hard time concentrating on my work.	**A** 그렇구나. 하긴 요새는 온라인상에서 할 수 있는 게 정말 많잖아. 난 예전에 온라인 채팅에 중독되어서 업무에 집중하는 게 어려울 정도였어.
B I understand. Well, these days, I'm spending more time on household chores.	**B** 이해해. 음, 나는 요새 집안일을 하는 데에 시간을 더 들이고 있어.
A Really? You don't look like the type to do that. Don't get me wrong. I just can't imagine you wearing rubber gloves and doing household chores.	**A** 진짜? 넌 집안일 안 하게 생겼어. 오해는 말고. 그냥 네가 고무장갑을 끼고 집안일 하는 모습이 상상이 안 돼.

Vocabulary | **make changes** 변화를 일으키다 | **couch potato** 하루 종일 소파에 앉아서 TV만 시청하는 사람 | **turn on the TV** TV를 켜다 | **be addicted to ~** ~에 중독되다 | **rubber gloves** 고무장갑 | **household chore** 집안일

Key Expressions

아래 제시된 각 expression의 구조를 이해하고, 자기만의 표현들을 생각해 봅시다.

Expression 1   be addicted to ~: ~에 중독되다

저는 실제로 TV에 중독되었었습니다. → I **was** practically **addicted to** watching TV.

많은 할리우드 스타들은 약물에 중독되어 있습니다.
→ A huge number of Hollywood stars **are addicted to** drugs.

요즘 많은 아이들은 컴퓨터 게임에 중독되어 있습니다.
→ Lots of children **are addicted to** computer games these days.

Expression 2   get upset about/over ~: ~에 대해 화나다

어머니께서 그 일로 매우 화나셨던 것이 기억납니다.
→ I remember my mother would **get** very **upset about** it.

그는 그 결과로 인해 매우 화가 났습니다. → He **got** very **upset over** the outcome.

여론은 그 주지사의 거짓말에 대해 매우 화가 났습니다.
→ The public **got** very **upset about** the governor's lie.

Expression 3   help out + 사람 + with + (동)명사: ~를 ~함으로써 돕다

저는 어머니의 집안일을 돕기 위해 더 많은 시간을 보내려고 합니다.
→ I try to spend more time **helping out** my mother **with** the household chores.

그는 제가 램프를 고치는 일을 도와줬습니다. → He **helped** me **out with** fixing the lamp.

자원봉사자들은 노숙자들을 위한 도시락 포장을 도와줬습니다.
→ The volunteers **helped** them **out with** packing the lunches for the homeless.

Expression 4   handle: ~를 다루다, 처리하다

어머니께서 연세가 드시는데 혼자 집안일을 다 하시는 것을 보기가 안쓰럽습니다.
→ It's hard to see her **handling** all the chores by herself as she's aging.

저는 그녀가 어떻게 그 모든 일을 혼자 다룰 수 있는지 모르겠습니다.
→ I don't know how she can **handle** all those things by herself.

그 승무원은 터무니없는 승객을 다루느라 고생했습니다.
→ The flight attendant had a hard time **handling** the outrageous passenger.

Expression 5   be free from ~: ~로부터 자유롭다

그래서 저는 일이 없을 때마다 설거지를 합니다. → So, whenever I**'m free from** work, I do the dishes.

나는 네가 모든 짐으로부터 자유로웠으면 좋겠어. → I want you to **be free from** your burdens.

나는 스트레스로부터 자유롭기 위해 여행을 갔습니다. → I went on a trip to **be free from** stress.

Topic Question & Model Answer

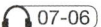

Topic Question

How differently do you spend your free time at home these days compared to the past? What kinds of changes have you made in the way you spend your free time?

당신이 현재 집에서 휴가를 보내는 모습은 과거와 비교했을 때 어떻게 달라졌나요? 당신이 여가 시간을 보내는 방식에는 어떠한 변화들이 있나요?

TIP FOR THE OPIc

'집에서 보내는 휴가'는 여가 시간을 어떻게 보내는지에 관한 질문 항목입니다. 집에서 푹 쉬는 것이 가장 편하고 흔한 광경입니다. 집에서 하는 활동을 생각해보면, TV 시청하기, 인터넷서핑 하기, 음악 감상하기, 밀린 청소하기, 책 읽기 등을 떠올릴 수 있을 것입니다. 과거와 현재의 시간 보내기 패턴을 비교할 때에는 위의 활동 가운데 1~2 가지를 과거와 현재로 나누어 비교, 설명할 수가 있습니다.

Model Answer

| Opening |

When I was young, I used to spend a lot of time watching TV and playing games at home. I was practically addicted to watching TV, and I remember my mother would get very upset about that. She encouraged me to read more books, and I was able to spend more time reading later.

저는 어렸을 때 집에서 TV를 보거나 게임을 하는 데에 많은 시간을 보냈습니다. 제가 사실상 TV 시청에는 중독되다시피 해서 엄마께서 무척 화를 내셨던 것이 기억납니다. 엄마는 제게 독서를 권장하셨고, 나중에 저는 책을 읽는 데에 더 많은 시간을 할애하게 되었습니다.

| Free Time at Home as a Grown Up |

These days, I try to spend more time helping out my mother with the household chores in my free time. It's hard to see her handling all the chores by herself as she's aging. So, whenever I'm free from work, I do the dishes, fold the laundry, vacuum the floor, and so on. Besides, I spend more time on the Internet than watching TV. I think the reason is that I find things online more entertaining.

요즘 저는 집에서 엄마의 집안일을 더 도와 드리고자 노력합니다. 연세가 드시면서 혼자 모든 집안일을 다 해내시는 것을 보기가 안쓰럽습니다. 그래서 저는 일이 없을 때마다 설거지, 세탁된 옷 접기, 청소기 돌리기 등을 합니다. 그 밖에도 저는 TV 시청보다는 인터넷을 하는 데에 더 많은 시간을 들입니다. 요즘에는 온라인상에 흥미로운 것들이 더 많은 것 같습니다.

| Closing |

These are a few of the changes in the way I spend my free time at home.

이러한 점들이 제가 집에서 여가 시간을 보낼 때 달라진 몇 가지입니다.

More Questions

〈집에서 보내는 휴가〉에 관련하여 더 나올 수 있는 OPIc 질문들을 정리한 코너입니다. 질문에 대한 brainstorming을 해보세요.

1. If you could visit someone's house right now, whose house would you visit? Why?

2. Do you prefer to spend your free time at home or outside? What is different about having a vacation at home versus a vacation away?

앞에서 주어진 Model Answer을 바탕으로, 아래의 빈칸에 들어갈 수 있는 다양한 대체 가능한 어휘 및 표현들을 참고하여 학습자 본인만의 모범 답안을 직접 만들어보세요.

I Opening I

When I was young, I used to spend a lot of time watching TV and ⓐ_____ at home. I was practically addicted to watching TV, and I remember my mother would get very upset about that. She encouraged me to ⓑ_____, and I was able to spend more time ⓒ_____ later.

I Free Time at Home as a Grown Up I

These days, I try to spend more time helping out my mother with the household chores in my free time. It's hard to see her handling all the chores by herself as she's aging. So, whenever I'm free from work, I ⓓ_____, and so on. Besides, I spend more time ⓔ_____ than watching TV. I think the reason is that I ⓕ_____.

I Closing I

These are a few of the changes in the way I spend my free time at home.

I Opening I When I was young, I used to spend a lot of time watching TV and ⓐ **listening to music** at home. I was practically addicted to watching TV, and I remember my mother would get very upset about that. She encouraged me to ⓑ **do my school work first**, I was able to spend more time ⓒ **studying** later.

I Free Time at Home as a Grown Up I These days, I try to spend more time helping out my mother with the household chores in my free time. It's hard to see her handling all the chores by herself as she's aging. So, whenever I'm free from work, I ⓓ **cook, set the table, water the plants**, and so on. Besides, I spend more time ⓔ **reading the newspaper** than watching TV. I think the reason is that I ⓕ **find more things to learn through newspapers**.

I Closing I These are a few of the changes in the way I spend my free time at home.

본인이 만든 답안에 아래의 요소들이 포함되었는지 점검해 봅시다.

	Checklist
☐	어릴 적 집에서 휴가를 보낸 모습
☐	TV 시청 및 친인척과의 모임
☐	컴퓨터 게임하기
☐	현재 집에서 휴가를 보내는 모습
☐	집안일 하기 및 요리하기
☐	인터넷 서핑하기
☐	친구 초대하기

Unit 45 Vacation at Home 2

집에서 보내는 휴가 2

Warm Up

A Guess the Question & Answer
사진을 보면서 예상 질문과 답변을 먼저 추측해 봅시다.

B Listen & Talk
집에서 휴가를 보내는 방법에 관한 대화를 먼저 연습해 봅시다.

🎧 07-07

A Have you watched the new episode of *Outing with Daddy* yesterday?

B Sure! I never miss that one. I can't start my weekend without watching the show on Saturday.

A You must really enjoy the show. What do you like about it?

B The kids. They are so lovely. It's funny to see how they react to different situations.

A I know. They are so pure and adorable. In addition, I like that the show depicts the heart-warming relationships between the fathers and the kids.

B True. Unlike many other provocative TV shows, *Outing with Daddy* is full of warm messages.

A Plus, it makes me laugh all the time. I can't help laughing when I see the kids behaving in such unexpected ways.

B No wonder it's so popular.

A 어제 '아빠랑 여행가기' 방송한 거 봤어?

B 그럼! 난 그 프로그램은 절대 놓치지 않아. 토요일에 그걸 안 보면 주말을 시작할 수가 없어.

A 너 그 방송 정말 좋아하는구나. 어떤 점이 좋은데?

B 아이들. 정말 사랑스럽잖아. 다른 상황 속에서 어떻게 반응하는지 보는 게 재미있어.

A 알아. 정말 순수하고 사랑스럽지. 또한 방송에서 그리는 아빠와 아이들 간의 마음 따뜻한 관계가 보기 좋아.

B 맞아. 다른 선정적인 TV 프로그램들과 달리, '아빠랑 여행가기'는 따뜻한 메시지로 가득해.

A 뿐만 아니라, 언제나 웃음을 안겨주잖아. 아이들이 전혀 예상 못한 행동을 할 땐 웃음을 참을 수가 없어.

B 왜 그렇게 인기가 많은지 알겠네.

Vocabulary | **episode** (방송물일 경우) 1회 방송 분량 | **react** 반응하다 | **adorable** 사랑스러운 | **depict** 묘사하다 | **heart-warming** 마음을 따뜻하게 하는 | **unlike** ~와는 달리 | **provocative** 자극적인, 선정적인 | **can't help -ing** ~하는 것을 참지 못하다, ~할 수밖에 없다

Key Expressions

> 아래 제시된 각 expression의 구조를 이해하고, 자기만의 표현들을 생각해 봅시다.

Expression 1   **take a nap:** 낮잠을 자다

저는 TV를 보거나 방에서 낮잠을 잡니다. → I watch TV or **take a nap** in my room.

많은 승객들은 버스에서 낮잠을 잡니다. → Lots of passengers **take naps** on the bus.

저는 어제 하루 종일 낮잠을 잤는데 매우 상쾌합니다.
→ I **took a nap** all day yesterday, so I feel so refreshed.

Expression 2   **productive:** 생산적인

TV 시청은 별로 생산적이지 않습니다. → Watching TV is not very **productive**.

고객사와의 미팅은 꽤 생산적이었습니다.
→ The meeting with our client company was quite **productive**.

많은 사람들이 아침에 생산적인 반면에, 어떤 사람들은 밤에 더 생산적입니다. → While many people are **productive** in the morning, some people are more **productive** at night.

Expression 3   **light-hearted:** 가벼운, 유쾌하고 근심이 없는

저는 가벼운 프로그램을 시청하는 것을 좋아합니다. → I like watching **light-hearted** shows.

그는 마음이 가벼운 상태였습니다. → He was in a **light-hearted** mood.

너무 심각해하지마. 가끔은 좀 가볍게 지내도 좋아.
→ Don't be too serious. It's okay to be **light-hearted** sometimes.

Expression 4   **across the country:** 전국적으로

그들은 전국에 있는 다른 지역으로 캠핑을 갑니다.
→ They go camping in different areas **across the country**.

그 병은 전국적으로 퍼졌습니다. → The disease spread **across the country**.

전국에 많은 비가 내렸습니다. → There was heavy rain **across the country**.

Expression 5   **pure and adorable:** 순수하고 사랑스러운

아이들은 매우 순수하고 사랑스럽습니다. → The kids are so **pure and adorable**.

내 딸은 순수하고 사랑스러운 강아지를 키웁니다.
→ My daughter is raising a **pure and adorable** puppy.

그녀는 그 드레스를 입으니 순수하고 사랑스러워 보였습니다.
→ She looked **pure and adorable** in the dress.

Topic Question & Model Answer

 07-08

Topic Question

You indicated in the survey that you spend your free time at home. What do you do when you stay home? Do you watch TV? If so, what is your favorite show? Why do you think the show is interesting? 당신은 설문조사에서 여가시간을 집에서 보낸다고 했습니다. 집에 있을때 무엇을 하나요? TV 시청을 하나요? 만일 그렇다면, 가장 좋아하는 프로그램은 무엇인가요? 왜 그 프로그램이 재미있나요?

> **TIP FOR THE OPIc**
>
> TV 시청하기는 예전에 background survey 항목으로 있다가 없어진 항목입니다. 하지만 일상에서 쉽게 할 수 있는 활동이기 때문에 종종 다른 항목들과 연계되어 질문이 나옵니다. 좋아하는 TV 프로그램 및 출연진에 관한 질문, 혹은 롤플레이 질문에서 '직접 질문하기' 유형으로 변형이 되어 나올 수도 있습니다.

Model Answer

| Opening |

When I have free time at home, I usually clean my room. Since I work from Monday to Friday, I have no time for household chores on weekdays. So I like to clean on weekends. I simply change the bed cover and arrange the books on my desk. Sometimes I mop the floor and vacuum the carpet.

저는 집에서 쉴 때 주로 방청소를 합니다. 월요일부터 금요일까지 일하기 때문에, 주중에는 집안일을 할 겨를이 없습니다. 그래서 주말에 청소하는 것을 좋아합니다. 저는 단순히 침대 커버를 갈아 끼우거나 책상 위의 책들을 정리합니다. 가끔은 바닥을 닦고 카펫을 청소기로 돌립니다.

| My Favorite TV Show |

When I am done with the household chores, I watch TV or take a nap in my room. I don't spend much time watching TV because that's not very productive. I watch TV around 1 hour a week. I like watching light-hearted shows with funny episodes. One of my favorite shows is *Outing with Daddy* on ABC. It's a reality show starring five male celebrities and their kids. The kids are between 7 and 9 years old. In each episode, the celebrities and their kids go camping in different areas across the country. I love this show because the kids are so pure and adorable. In addition, it's full of humor.

집안일을 마치면, 저는 TV를 보거나 방에서 잠을 잡니다. 저는 TV를 시청하는 게 별로 생산적이지 않기 때문에 많은 시간을 할애하지는 않습니다. 저는 일주일에 1시간 정도 TV를 봅니다. 저는 가벼운 내용의 재미있는 프로그램을 좋아합니다. 좋아하는 프로그램 하나는 ABC에서 하는 '아빠랑 여행가기'입니다. 이 프로그램은 리얼리티 프로그램으로 다섯 명의 남자 연예인과 그들의 자녀가 출연합니다. 아이들은 7살에서 9살 사이입니다. 각 방송마다 출연진들은 전국 곳곳으로 캠핑을 갑니다. 저는 아이들이 정말 순수하고 사랑스러워서 이 프로그램을 좋아합니다. 또한, 재미도 있습니다.

| Closing |

I recommend that you watch the show if you have free time at home. I'm sure you will love it!

집에서 여가 시간이 있으면 이 프로그램을 시청해 보세요. 아마 무척 재미있을 걸요!

More Questions

〈집에서 보내는 휴가〉에 관련하여 더 나올 수 있는 OPIc 질문들을 정리한 코너입니다. 질문에 대한 brainstorming을 해보세요.

1. These days, many people spend their time surfing the Internet. Do you like Internet surfing? Which website do you visit the most often? Give me some details about your favorite website.

2. When was the last time you spent some free time at home with your family? What did you do? Did you do anything interesting?

앞에서 주어진 Model Answer을 바탕으로, 아래의 빈칸에 들어갈 수 있는 다양한 대체 가능한 어휘 및 표현들을 참고하여 학습자 본인만의 모범 답안을 직접 만들어보세요.

I Opening I

When I have free time at home, I usually ⓐ_____.
Since I work from Monday to Friday, I have no time ⓑ_____. So I like to
ⓒ_____ on weekends. I ⓓ_____.

I My Favorite TV Show I

When I ⓔ_____, I watch TV. I ⓕ_____.
I watch TV around ⓖ_____. I like watching light-hearted shows with funny episodes. One of my favorite shows is ⓗ_____. It's a reality show starring
ⓘ_____. In each episode, the celebrities ⓙ_____.
I love this show because ⓚ_____.

I Closing I

I recommend that you watch the show if you have free time at home. I'm sure you will love it!

I Opening I When I have free time at home, I usually ⓐ **listen to music while sitting at my desk**. Since I work from Monday to Friday, I have no time ⓑ **to relax on weekdays**. So I like to ⓒ **rest in my room** on weekends. I ⓓ **read books or rest on the couch for hours**.

I My Favorite TV Show I When I ⓔ **feel bored**, I watch TV. I ⓕ **think it's a great way to relieve my stress**. I watch TV around ⓖ **2 to 3 hours on the weekend**. I like watching light-hearted shows with funny episodes. One of my favorite shows is ⓗ *Never Give Up* on ABC. It's a reality show starring ⓘ **six male celebrities**. In each episode, the celebrities ⓙ **have to complete a mission**. I love this show because ⓚ **the plot is simple and hilarious**.

I Closing I I recommend that you watch the show if you have free time at home. I'm sure you will love it!

본인이 만든 답안에 아래의 요소들이 포함되었는지 점검해 봅시다.

	Checklist
☐	얼마나 자주 TV를 시청하는지
☐	가장 좋아하는 TV 프로그램
☐	언제 방영하는 방송인지
☐	해당 프로그램 출연진
☐	해당 프로그램의 종류
☐	프로그램의 특색 및 장점

Unit 46 Domestic Travel

국내여행

Warm Up

A Guess the Question & Answer
사진을 보면서 예상 질문과 답변을 먼저 추측해 봅시다.

B Listen & Talk
국내여행에 관한 대화를 먼저 연습해 봅시다. 🎧 07-09

A What's your vacation plan this summer?

B I'm flying to Jeju Island to stay at a close friend's house.

A Enjoy the weather there. Have you booked your ticket for the flight yet?

B Yes, I made a reservation last month. It was 20% off the original price.

A Nice. Have you planned your itinerary?

B No. I trust my local friend in Jeju. He is good at planning things.

A Well, have a wonderful trip!

B Thanks.

A If you have time, rent a car and drive from Sinsan-ri to Seongsan Ilchulbong. You will get to see one of the most romantic views on Earth.

B Sure. I'll keep that in mind.

A 이번 여름휴가 계획이 어떻게 돼?

B 제주도에 사는 친한 친구 집에 좀 머물다 오려고.

A 가서 날씨를 만끽하고 오렴. 비행기 표는 이미 예약한 거야?

B 응. 지난달에 예약했어. 원가의 20% 할인가에 구매했어.

A 잘 됐네. 여행 일정표는 짰어?

B 아니. 제주도에 있는 내 친구를 믿어. 일정 하나는 끝내주게 계획하는 친구거든.

A 그럼, 좋은 여행하고 오길 바래!

B 고마워.

A 만일 시간이 되면, 차를 대여해서 신산리에서 성산일출봉을 따라 드라이브 해봐. 지구상에서 가장 낭만적인 광경을 보게 될 거야.

B 그래. 기억해둘게.

Vocabulary
vacation plan 휴가 계획 | stay at ~에서 머물다 | book a ticket 표를 예매하다 | make a reservation 예약하다 | original price 정상가 | plan an itinerary 일정표를 계획하다 | keep in mind 염두에 두다

Key Expressions

> 아래 제시된 각 expression의 구조를 이해하고, 자기만의 표현들을 생각해 봅시다.

Expression 1   **hard to tell [talk about] ~:** ~라고 가늠[말]하기가 어렵다

제가 여행하는 방식이 어떻게 달라졌는지 설명하는 것은 쉽지 않습니다.
→ It's **hard to talk about** how the way I travel has changed.

이 금 반지가 진짜인지 아닌지 가늠하기가 쉽지 않습니다.
→ It's **hard to tell** whether this gold ring is fake or real.

다른 회사의 인수가 회사를 위한 옳은 결정이었는지 가늠하기가 어렵다.
→ It's **hard to tell** if the takeover was a good decision for the company.

Expression 2   **take care of ~:** ~을 책임지다, 소중히 여기다

그들이 모든 과정을 책임졌습니다. → They **took care of** all the procedures.

훌륭한 리더라면 직원들의 권리를 소중히 여겨야 합니다.
→ A good leader has to **take care of** the rights of his or her employees.

우리는 선조로부터 물려받은 문화유산을 돌볼 책임이 있습니다.
→ We are responsible for **taking care of** the cultural heritage from our ancestors.

Expression 3   **plan an itinerary:** 일정표를 계획하다

저는 또한 여행 일정표를 계획하고 제 짐을 챙깁니다.
→ I also **planned** my travel **itinerary** and packed my bag.

일정표 짜는 거 잊지 마세요. → Don't forget to **plan an itinerary**.

제 비서는 방문 대표단의 일정표를 정리하여 줬습니다.
→ My secretary **planned an itinerary** for the delegates.

Expression 4   **ticketing process:** 티켓 발권 과정

티켓 발권 과정이 매우 간단해졌습니다. → The **ticketing process** has become very simple.

티켓 발권 과정을 위해 신분증을 가져오는 것을 잊지 마세요.
→ Don't forget to bring your ID card for the **ticketing process**.

공항에서 티켓 발권 과정 중에 약간의 다툼이 있었습니다.
→ There was a small argument during the **ticketing process** at the airport.

Expression 5   **much easier:** 훨씬 쉬운

저 혼자 여행하는 것은 훨씬 쉽습니다. → It's **much easier** to travel by myself.

당신 혼자 일하는 것보다는 함께 일하는 것이 훨씬 쉽습니다.
→ It's **much easier** to work together than to work by yourself.

Topic Question & Model Answer

Topic Question

You indicated in the survey that you like to travel. Do you travel differently now than you used to? Talk about it.

당신은 설문조사에서 여행하는 것을 좋아한다고 했습니다. 당신은 현재 예전과 다르게 여행하나요? 그것에 대해 말해보세요.

> **TIP FOR THE OPIc**
> 국내여행에서는 여행지에 관한 질문이 나오기도 하지만, 여행의 준비 과정이나 여행 물품 목록에 관한 질문이 출제될 가능성도 높습니다. 과거와 현재의 여행 패턴을 비교, 설명하라는 질문은 주로 Level 5 이상에서 나오는데, 여행지의 선호도 및 함께 여행가는 사람이 과거랑 현재 어떻게 다른지를 설명할 수 있습니다. 질문이 어렵다고 느껴질수록 단순화해서 생각하는 것이 좋습니다.

Model Answer

| Opening |

I like to travel, but it's hard to talk about how the way I travel has changed.

저는 여행하는 것을 좋아하지만, 저의 여행 방식이 어떻게 달라졌는지를 설명하는 것은 쉽지 않습니다.

| Past vs. Present Travel Patterns |

When I was young, I simply followed my parents. They took care of all the procedures, so all I had to do was pack my bag. These days, I travel alone, so I make sure I have my ID card and also see if I have enough cash and my credit cards. I also plan my travel itinerary and pack my bag. On the other hand, I think the biggest change in how I travel these days is probably the e-ticketing system.

제가 어릴 적엔, 단순히 부모님을 따라 여행을 하였습니다. 부모님께서 여행의 전 과정을 책임지셨기에, 저는 그저 짐만 싸면 됐습니다. 요즘 들어서는 주로 혼자 여행하는 편이라, 신분증을 챙겼는지 살피고 또한 신용카드 및 현금이 넉넉히 있는지 확인합니다. 저는 여행 일정표도 짜고 짐 가방도 쌉니다. 다른 한편, 최근 들어 여행할 때의 가장 큰 변화는 아마도 이티켓 시스템일 것입니다.

| Closing |

Thanks to advanced technology, the ticketing process has become very simple. It's way easier to travel by myself.

기술이 발전한 덕분에, 항공권을 구입하는 절차가 매우 간편해졌습니다. 혼자 여행하는 것이 훨씬 쉬워졌어요!

More Questions

〈국내여행〉에 관련하여 더 나올 수 있는 OPIc 질문들을 정리한 코너입니다. 질문에 대한 brainstorming을 해보세요.

1. You are planning to visit your friend's city. Call your friend and ask 3 to 4 questions about the geography of the city.
2. Tell me about a city you've traveled to in your country. How is it different from the city you live in?
3. What are some attractions of domestic traveling? How often do you travel in your country?

앞에서 주어진 Model Answer을 바탕으로, 아래의 빈칸에 들어갈 수 있는 다양한 대체 가능한 어휘 및 표현들을 참고하여 학습자 본인만의 모범 답안을 직접 만들어보세요.

| Opening |

I like to travel, but it's hard to talk about how the way I travel has changed.

| Past vs. Present Travel Patterns |

When I was young, I simply followed my parents. They took care of all the procedures, so all I had to do was ⓐ_____. These days, I travel alone, so I make sure I have my ID card and also see if I have enough cash and my credit cards. I also

ⓑ_____.

On the other hand, I think the biggest change in how I travel these days is probably

ⓒ_____.

| Closing |

Thanks to ⓓ_____, traveling has become more dynamic. It's way easier to travel by myself.

| Opening | I like to travel, but it's hard to talk about how the way I travel has changed.

| Past vs. Present Travel Patterns | When I was young, I simply followed my parents. They took care of all the procedures, so all I had to do was ⓐ **get on the car**. These days, I travel alone, so I make sure I have my ID card and also see if I have enough cash and my credit cards. I also ⓑ **make a reservation for the hotel and search for information on my travel destination**. On the other hand, I think the biggest change in how I travel these days is probably ⓒ **that I use the car rental system at the travel spot**.

| Closing | Thanks to ⓓ **my driver's license**, traveling has become more dynamic. It's way easier to travel by myself.

본인이 만든 답안에 아래의 요소들이 포함되었는지 점검해 봅시다.

	Checklist
☐	어릴적 여행 패턴
☐	부모님과 함께 한 여행
☐	주로 간 여행지
☐	지금의 여행 패턴
☐	혼자 하는/친구들과의 여행
☐	여행지의 다양성
☐	비행기표 발권의 편리함

Unit 46 Domestic Travel

Unit 47 Overseas Travel

해외여행

Warm Up

A Guess the Question & Answer
사진을 보면서 예상 질문과 답변을 먼저 추측해 봅시다.

B Listen & Talk
해외여행에 관한 대화를 먼저 연습해 봅시다. 🎧 07-11

A Hello, Minjung. What's up?	**A** 여보세요. 민정이? 안녕, 무슨 일이야?
B Surprise! I'm back in Seoul.	**B** 짜잔! 나 서울로 돌아왔어.
A Welcome home. How was your trip?	**A** 귀국한 걸 환영해. 여행은 어땠어?
B It was amazing. Rome was the most mysterious city I've ever been to.	**B** 대단했어. 로마는 내가 가본 곳 중에 가장 신비로운 도시였어.
A I told you that you'd love Rome. Did you do anything fun during the trip?	**A** 네가 로마 좋아할 거라고 했잖아. 여행 기간 동안 재미있는 일 없었어?
B You'd better hold your breath. I'm engaged!	**B** 잠깐 숨 좀 골라봐. 나 약혼했어!
A Engaged?	**A** 약혼했다고?
B Yes, to this fantastic Italian man.	**B** 응, 정말 환상적인 이탈리안 남자랑.
A I'm speechless. You always have interesting stories after a trip, but nothing can beat this.	**A** 할 말을 잃었어. 넌 늘 여행을 가면 흥미로운 뉴스를 가져 왔지만, 이번만큼 엄청난 적은 없었어.
B I know. I'm so happy that I've finally met my Mr. Right.	**B** 알아. 드디어 내 짝을 만나서 정말 행복해.
A I can't wait to meet him.	**A** 얼른 그를 만나고 싶어.

Vocabulary What's up? 무슨 일이야? | mysterious 신비한, 비밀스러운 | hold one's breath 잠시 숨을 고르다 | be engaged 약혼하다 | speechless 깜짝 놀라서 할 말을 잃은 | beat ~을 능가하다, ~을 때리다 | Mr. Right 완벽한 남자, 짝

Key Expressions

🔑 아래 제시된 각 expression의 구조를 이해하고, 자기만의 표현들을 생각해 봅시다.

Expression 1	**experience different lifestyles:** 다른 삶의 방식을 경험하다

그들은 다른 삶의 방식과 문화를 경험하고 싶어 합니다.
→ They want to **experience different lifestyles** and cultures.

해외여행은 다른 삶의 방식을 경험하는 기회입니다.
→ Overseas travel is the opportunity to **experience different lifestyles**.

저는 미국에서 공부하면서 또 다른 삶의 방식을 경험할 수 있었습니다.
→ I was able to **experience a different lifestyle** while I studied in the United States.

Expression 2	**in my case:** 제 경우에는

제 경우에는 새로운 문화를 경험하기 위해 다른 나라들을 여행하는 것을 좋아합니다.
→ **In my case**, I love to travel to other countries to experience new cultures.

제 경우에는 10개 이상 통장으로 나누어 저축을 합니다.
→ **In my case**, I spread my money over 10 different bank accounts.

제 경우에는 민감성 피부 때문에 직접 화장품을 만들어 사용합니다.
→ **In my case**, I make my own cosmetics because I have sensitive skin.

Expression 3	**broaden one's horizons:** 시야를(지평을) 넓히다

저는 새로운 사람들을 만남으로써 지평을 넓힐 수가 있습니다.
→ I can **broaden my horizons** by meeting new people.

좋은 교육은 시야를 넓혀줍니다. → A good education **broadens one's horizons**.

저는 생각의 폭을 넓히기 위해 경제지를 구독합니다.
→ I subscribe to a financial magazine to **broaden my horizons**.

Expression 4	**communicate with ~:** ~와 의사소통을 하다

영어는 사람들과 소통을 더 잘할 수 있도록 도와줍니다.
→ English helps me to **communicate** better **with** people.

정직은 사람들과 소통함에 있어서 기본이 되는 요소입니다.
→ Honesty is the basic factor to consider when we **communicate with** people.

다양한 관점을 이해하기 위해서는 다른 사람들과 열린 소통을 하도록 하세요.
→ Try to openly **communicate with** others to understand various perspectives.

Expression 5	**consider:** 고려하다

저는 또한 날씨와 안전을 고려합니다. → I also **consider** the weather and safety.

저는 사업보다 우정이 더 중요하다고 여깁니다. → I **consider** friendship more important than business.

당신이 그 제안을 신중하게 고려해야 한다고 생각합니다. → I think you'd better **consider** the offer carefully.

Topic Question & Model Answer

 07-12

Topic Question

Why do you think people like to travel overseas? What do people consider when they travel to other countries?

당신은 왜 사람들이 해외여행을 좋아한다고 생각하나요? 사람들은 다른 나라를 여행할 때 무엇을 고려하나요?

> **TIP FOR THE OPIc**
> 해외여행에 관한 질문은 출제 범위가 넓습니다. 여행지에서 누군가로부터 도움을 받은 적은 없는지, 친인척 혹은 지인의 거주 여부, 여행지를 선택한 이유 및 특별한 경험은 무엇인지 등에 관해 질문할 수 있습니다. 현지인들의 특색 및 한국과의 문화적 차이에 대해 물어보기도 합니다. 여행지의 숙박 시설이나 날씨, 음식 등에 대해서도 생각해보는 것이 좋습니다.

Model Answer

| Opening |

I think people travel overseas because they want to experience different lifestyles and cultures.

저는 사람들이 해외여행을 하는 이유는 바로 색다른 삶의 모습과 문화를 경험하기 위함이라고 생각합니다.

| Benefits of Traveling Overseas |

In my case, I love to travel to other countries because I can meet new people and broaden my horizons. Whenever I meet nice people while I travel, I exchange email address and keep in touch with them. Also, I love to taste local food and enjoy the exotic view of other cities.

저의 경우, 새로운 사람들을 만나고 생각의 폭을 넓힐 수가 있기 때문에 다른 나라로 여행하는 것을 좋아합니다. 저는 여행을 하면서 좋은 사람들을 만날 때마다, 이메일 주소를 교환하고 그들과 계속 연락하며 지냅니다. 또한, 저는 현지 음식을 맛보고 다른 도시의 이국적인 풍경을 감상하는 것을 좋아합니다.

| What to Consider When I Travel |

I prefer to visit countries that use English since I can then communicate with people. Some of the countries I've visited are the U.S., the UK, and Canada. When I visit other countries, I also consider the weather and safety.

저는 주로 영어권 국가를 방문하는 것을 좋아하는데, 그것은 현지 사람들과의 의사소통이 가능하기 때문입니다. 제가 여행한 몇몇 국가는 바로 미국, 영국, 그리고 캐나다입니다. 저는 다른 나라들을 방문할 때, 현지의 날씨 및 안전도 고려합니다.

| Closing |

I guess these are some of the things people consider when they travel abroad.

아마 이러한 점들이 바로 사람들이 해외여행을 할 때 고려하는 점들일 것입니다.

More Questions

〈해외여행〉에 관련하여 더 나올 수 있는 OPIc 질문들을 정리한 코너입니다. 질문에 대한 brainstorming을 해보세요.

1. When was your first visit overseas? What did you do? Tell me everything about your first trip.
2. Tell me about a memorable event you had during your overseas trip. What happened? Did you get any help from your friend?
3. Which country is the most memorable to you? What were the people like?

On Your Own

앞에서 주어진 Model Answer을 바탕으로, 아래의 빈칸에 들어갈 수 있는 다양한 대체 가능한 어휘 및 표현들을 참고하여 학습자 본인만의 모범 답안을 직접 만들어보세요.

| Opening |

I think people travel overseas because they want to experience different lifestyles and cultures.

| Benefits of Traveling Overseas |

In my case, I love to travel to other countries because I can meet new people and broaden my horizons. ⓐ_____.

| What to Consider When I Travel |

I prefer to visit countries ⓑ_____. Some of the countries I've visited are ⓒ_____. When I visit other countries, I also consider ⓓ_____.

| Closing |

I guess these are some of the things people consider when they travel abroad.

| Opening | I think people travel overseas because they want to experience different lifestyles and cultures.

| Benefits of Traveling Overseas | In my case, I love to travel to other countries because I can meet new people and broaden my horizons. ⓐ **Once I've been to Los Angeles and it was truly a melting pot of a city. It was great to experience the cultural diversity.**

| What to Consider When I Travel | I prefer to visit countries ⓑ **with mild weather because I love to rest under the sun while traveling.** Some of the countries I've visited are ⓒ **Spain, Italy, Singapore, and the Philippines.** When I visit other countries, I also consider ⓓ **the exchange rate and safety.**

| Closing | I guess these are some of the things people consider when they travel abroad.

본인이 만든 답안에 아래의 요소들이 포함되었는지 점검해 봅시다.

Checklist

- [ ] 해외여행의 장점
- [ ] 다양한 문화와 생활을 경험
- [ ] 견문을 넓히는 여행
- [ ] 현지 음식 맛보기
- [ ] 이국적인 풍경 감상하기
- [ ] 선호하는 해외여행지
- [ ] 해외여행할 때 고려할 점

The Music of Speech

강세를 두어야 하는 어휘의 특징을 익히고 그에 따라 답안을 말하는 연습을 해봅시다.

강세를 두는 어휘의 특징
1) 감탄사이다 2) 최상급이다 3) 형용사/부사이다
4) 문장 안에서 key word 역할을 하는 명사나 동사인 경우가 많다

Model Answer 42   07-13

I go on domestic business trips every quarter. My company has branch offices in 16 other cities, and the regular conference is held in different regions each quarter. I always attend the conference on behalf of my team. I make presentations on the outcome of our marketing strategies and sales record. Going on a business trip requires a lot of work in addition to my office work, so it's tiring. I often stay at the office all night to finish my work when I have an upcoming business trip. However, attending the conference is a great way to develop my business skills. I learn a lot about the market and come up with fresh ideas. Whenever the trip is over, I always realize that there's no gain without pain.

Model Answer 43   07-14

My last business trip was in February of this year. I went to Las Vegas to attend one of the biggest exhibitions in the electronic industry. Since I'm the manager of the Overseas Sales Department, I attended the exhibition to promote my company's products. It was a 5-day exhibition, and many global companies came to show off their cutting-edge products and technology. Our booth displayed the newest mobile phones and LED TVs. We drew a huge amount of attention from the press and visitors. In addition, we were able to reach our sales goal. Overall, the trip was very satisfying and rewarding.

Model Answer 44   07-15

When I was young, I used to spend a lot of time watching TV and playing games at home. I was practically addicted to watching TV, and I remember my mother would get very upset about that. She encouraged me to read more books, and I was able to spend more time reading later. These days, I try to spend more time helping out my mother with the household chores in my free time. It's hard to see her handling all the chores by herself as she's aging. So, whenever I'm free from work, I do the dishes, fold the laundry, vacuum the floor, and so on. Besides, I spend more time on the Internet than watching TV. I think the reason is that I find things online more entertaining. These are a few of the changes in the way I spend my free time at home.

Model Answer 45

🎧 07-16

When I have free time at home, I usually clean my room. Since I work from Monday to Friday, I have no time for household chores on weekdays. So I like to clean on weekends. I simply change the bed cover and arrange the books on my desk. Sometimes I mop the floor and vacuum the carpet. When I am done with the household chores, I watch TV or take a nap in my room. I don't spend much time watching TV because that's not very productive. I watch TV around 1 hour a week. I like watching light-hearted shows with funny episodes. One of my favorite shows is *Outing with Daddy* on ABC. It's a reality show starring five male celebrities and their kids. The kids are between 7 and 9 years old. In each episode, the celebrities and their kids go camping in different areas across the country. I love this show because the kids are so pure and adorable. In addition, it's full of humor. I recommend that you watch the show if you have free time at home. I'm sure you will love it!

Model Answer 46

🎧 07-17

I like to travel, but it's hard to talk about how the way I travel has changed. When I was young, I simply followed my parents. They took care of all the procedures, so all I had to do was pack my bag. These days, I travel alone, so I make sure I have my ID card and also see if I have enough cash and my credit cards. I also plan my travel itinerary and pack my bag. On the other hand, I think the biggest change in how I travel these days is probably the e-ticketing system. Thanks to advanced technology, the ticketing process has become very simple. It's way easier to travel by myself.

Model Answer 47

🎧 07-18

I think people travel overseas because they want to experience different lifestyles and cultures. In my case, I love to travel to other countries because I can meet new people and broadenes my horizons. Whenever I meet nice people while I travel, I exchange email address and keep in touch with them. Also, I love to taste local food and enjoy the exotic view of other cities. I prefer to visit countries that use English since I can then communicate with people. Some of the countries I've visited are the U.S., the UK, and Canada. When I visit other countries, I also consider the weather and safety. I guess these are some of the things people consider when they travel abroad.

CHAPTER 8 사회적 이슈

Social Issues

Unit 48	**Public Transportation 1** 대중교통 1
Unit 49	**Public Transportation 2** 대중교통 2
Unit 50	**Technology 1** 테크놀로지 1
Unit 51	**Technology 2** 테크놀로지 2
Unit 52	**Recycling 1** 재활용 1
Unit 53	**Recycling 2** 재활용 2
Unit 54	**Police Officer 1** 경찰 1
Unit 55	**Police Officer 2** 경찰 2
Unit 56	**Hospital 1** 병원 1
Unit 57	**Hospital 2** 병원 2
Unit 58	**Bank 1** 은행 1
Unit 59	**Bank 2** 은행 2
Unit 60	**Opening a Bank Account** 은행 계좌 개설

Chapter 8은 사회적 이슈(돌발 문제)에 관해 다룹니다. 즉, background survey에서 선택하지 않은 소재에 관한 질문을 다룹니다. 사회적 이슈에 관한 질문은 한국의 문화 및 사회 현상과 관련된 질문을 합니다. 이때 우리의 일상에서 지나치기 쉬운 소재에 대해 질문하는 경우가 많아서 응시생이 오히려 당황하기 쉽습니다. 한국의 대중교통, 테크놀로지, 재활용, 경찰, 병원, 은행 등에 대해 질문할 수 있습니다. 더 나아가 한국의 약속 문화, ID 발급 과정 및 교육 제도에 대해서 물어볼 수도 있습니다. 출제 빈도가 높은 소재 위주로 학습하는 것이 바람직해 보입니다.

✛ Brainstorming Point

When?	the last time I went to the hospital/bank (마지막으로 병원/은행 간 때) when I usually take a taxi/the bus/the subway (언제 주로 택시/버스/지하철을 타는지) when I had a problem with technology (테크놀로지 문제가 발생한 적) when the recycling policy was adopted (재활용 정책이 도입된 시기)
Where?	the bank/hospital I usually go to (내가 자주 가는 은행/병원) where the bank/hospital is located (그 은행/병원이 위치한 곳)
What?	my favorite public transportation system/device (가장 좋아하는 대중 교통편/기기) a personal experience with a police officer (경찰관과 있었던 일) the advantages and disadvantages of the public transportation system (대중교통 제도의 장단점) benefits of recycling (재활용 정책의 장점)
Who?	the doctor/nurses/staff at the hospital (병원의 의사/간호사/직원들) bank tellers (은행 직원들) Korean police officers (한국의 경찰관) who taught me how to use technology (테크놀로지 사용법을 가르쳐준 사람)
How?	how Koreans recycle trash (한국인들의 쓰레기 재활용 방법) how to open a bank account (은행 계좌 개설 방법)

Unit 48 Public Transportation 1

대중교통 1

Warm Up

A Guess the Question & Answer
사진을 보면서 예상 질문과 답변을 먼저 추측해 봅시다.

B Listen & Talk
한국의 대중교통 체계에 관한 대화를 연습해 봅시다.

🎧 08-01

A How's the traffic in your city?

B Come on. I live in Seoul. The traffic is crazy, and the drivers are wild. I don't know how I survive on the roads every day.

A Do you drive every day? Do you ever use public transportation?

B Sure, I do. I take both the bus and subway. But I prefer the subway because it's always on time. In addition, it's easy to transfer.

A Do you recommend that I take the subway as well?

B Definitely. It takes you to most of the tourist spots in Seoul. They are easy to find as long as you have a subway map.

A Cool. What about the buses? I like to enjoy the view outside when the weather is good.

B Well, I think that depends on the traffic conditions. I get a headache when I see so many cars on the road.

A 네가 사는 도시의 교통은 어때?

B 이봐. 난 서울에 살잖아. 교통은 복잡하고 운전자들은 거칠어. 내가 매일같이 어떻게 도로 위에서 살아남는지 모르겠어.

A 너는 매일 운전해? 대중교통은 이용 안 해?

B 물론, 이용해. 버스랑 지하철 둘 다 이용해. 그렇지만 지하철이 늘 제시간에 오니까 더 좋아. 환승하기도 쉬워.

A 나도 지하철을 타는 게 더 나을까?

B 물론이지. 지하철을 타면 서울 대부분의 관광지에 갈 수 있어. 또 지하철 지도만 있으면 찾기도 쉬워.

A 잘됐네. 버스는 어때? 난 날씨가 좋으면 바깥 풍경을 보는 걸 좋아하거든.

B 음, 난 교통 상황에 따라 다른 것 같아. 도로 위에 차가 가득한 걸 보면 난 좀 어지럽거든.

Vocabulary survive 살아남다 | public transportation 대중교통 | transfer 환승하다 | take one to ~ ~를 (장소)로 데려가다 | tourist spot 관광지 | as long as ~하는 한 | traffic condition 교통 상황

Key Expressions

🔑 아래 제시된 각 expression의 구조를 이해하고, 자기만의 표현들을 생각해 봅시다.

Expression 1 — well developed: 발달이 잘 된

한국의 대중교통 체계는 잘 발달되어 있습니다.
→ The public transportation system in Korea is **well developed**.

이 학생은 우수한 실력을 갖추고 있습니다. → This student's skills are **well developed**.

우리나라는 IT 산업이 잘 발달되어 있습니다. → The IT industry in my country is **well developed**.

Expression 2 — a hub of ~: ~의 중심지

그곳은 서울의 주요 대중교통 중심지입니다. → It's **an** important **hub of** public transportation in Seoul.

페이스북은 소셜 네트워킹의 중심 공간입니다. → Facebook is **a hub of** social networking.

홍콩은 아시아 금융권의 중심지로 알려져 있습니다. → Hong Kong is known as **a** financial **hub of** Asia.

Expression 3 — multiple: 다수의, 복합적인

저희 집 주변에서 여러 개의 버스 노선이 있습니다. → There are **multiple** bus lines near my house.

제이크의 삶에는 복합적인 문제들이 있습니다. → Jake has **multiple** problems in his life.

그는 그 노래로 인해 수많은 상을 수상했습니다. → He has received **multiple** awards for the song.

Expression 4 — one way: 편도의

편도 가격이 1달러 50센트 정도 밖에 안 됩니다.
→ It costs only about a dollar and a half for a **one-way** trip.

편도 요금이 얼마인가요? → How much is the fare for **one way**?

현수는 두바이행 편도 티켓을 구입했습니다. → Hyunsoo got a **one-way** ticket to Dubai.

Expression 5 — well paved: 길이 잘 포장된

버스 전용 차선은 도로가 잘 포장되어 있습니다. → The bus-only lane is **well paved**.

산 위의 산책로는 잘 닦여 있었습니다. → The walking trail on the mountain was **well paved**.

저는 그 나라의 고속도로가 잘 포장된 점이 인상적이었습니다.
→ I was impressed by the **well-paved** highways in the country.

Topic Question & Model Answer

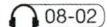 08-02

Topic Question

Tell me about the public transportation system in your country. How is it different from that of other countries?

당신의 나라에 대중교통 체계에 대하여 말해보세요. 다른 나라들의 대중교통 체계와 어떻게 다른가요?

> **TIP FOR THE OPIc**
>
> 한국의 대중교통 체계에 대해 얘기해보라고 하면 당황하기 쉽습니다. 하지만 내가 평소 타는 버스, 지하철, 마을버스 및 택시를 떠올리면 얘깃거리가 생깁니다. 외국에 나가본 경험이 없더라도, 내가 생각하는 한국 대중교통제도의 우수한 점을 언급하면 자연스럽게 다른 나라와 비교가 될 수 있습니다. 특히 한국은 IT강국입니다. 이러한 점은 T-money card 제도, 버스 도착 시간 알림판에서도 발견할 수 있습니다. 지하철은 세계 1,2위를 다툴 정도로 우수한 서비스 및 시설을 갖추고 있습니다. 이러한 점들을 고려하며 브레인스토밍 해봅시다.

Model Answer

| Opening |

There are several kinds of public transportation systems in Korea. These include subways, buses, and taxis. They are very well developed.

한국에는 여러 종류의 대중교통편이 있습니다. 이에는 전철, 버스, 택시가 포함됩니다. 모든 교통편은 잘 발달되었습니다.

| Merits of Korean Public Transportation |

There is an express bus terminal near my house. It's an important hub for public transportation in Seoul. There are multiple bus and subway lines near my house. I use both subways and buses to get to other places. The prices are reasonable, and the systems are convenient. They cost only about one dollar for a one-way trip, and transfers are free. In addition, Korean subways are always on time, and the bus-only lanes are well paved. We also have electronic screens installed at many bus stops to let people know when their buses will arrive.

제 집 근처에는 고속버스 터미널이 있는데, 서울 대중교통의 주요 중심지입니다. 제 집주변에는 수많은 버스 노선 및 지하철 노선이 있습니다. 저는 이동을 할 때 버스와 지하철을 모두 이용합니다. 가격이 합리적이고 교통편이 편리합니다. 편도로 약 1달러정도밖엔 안 되고, 무료 환승입니다. 뿐만 아니라, 한국의 지하철은 늘 제 시간에 도착하며, 버스 전용차선이 잘 포장되어 있습니다. 한국에는 또한 많은 버스 정류장에 전자 스크린이 설치되어 있어서 언제 버스가 도착할지 알려줍니다.

| Closing |

These are some of the merits of the Korean public transportation system.

이러한 점들이 한국 대중교통 체계의 몇 가지 장점입니다.

More Questions

〈대중교통〉에 관련하여 더 나올 수 있는 OPIc 질문들을 정리한 코너입니다. 질문에 대한 brainstorming을 해보세요.

1. Tell me about the public transportation system in your city. What kinds of public transportation do your neighbors use the most?

2. Do you think the public transportation system in your city is well developed? Why do you think that way?

앞에서 주어진 Model Answer을 바탕으로, 아래의 빈칸에 들어갈 수 있는 다양한 대체 가능한 어휘 및 표현들을 참고하여 학습자 본인만의 모범 답안을 직접 만들어보세요.

I Opening I

There are several kinds of public transportation systems in Korea. These include subways, buses, and taxis. They are very well developed.

I Merits of Korean Public Transportation I

ⓐ_____.

I also take both subways and buses to get to other places. The prices are reasonable, and the systems are convenient. They cost only about one dollar for a one-way trip, and transfers are free. In addition, ⓑ_____.

ⓒ_____.

I Closing I

These are some of the merits of the Korean public transportation system.

I Opening I There are several kinds of public transportation systems in Korea. These include subways, buses, and taxis. They are very well developed.

I Merits of Korean Public Transportation I ⓐ **Most people take subways and buses. There are people who take taxis, but I don't think that's very common**. I also take both subways and buses to get to other places. The prices are reasonable, and the systems are convenient. They cost only about one dollar for a one-way trip, and transfers are free. In addition, ⓑ **Korean subways and buses have multiple lines, so you can go almost everywhere in the cities**. ⓒ **The payment system is very convenient, too. People use T-money cards, which are rechargeable smart cards that can be used to pay subway, bus, and taxi fares**.

I Closing I These are some of the merits of the Korean public transportation system.

본인이 만든 답안에 아래의 요소들이 포함되었는지 점검해 봅시다.

	Checklist
☐	한국 대중 교통편의 종류
☐	한국 지하철의 장점
☐	한국 버스의 장점
☐	한국 대중교통제도의 특징
☐	우리나라에만 있는 혜택

Unit 49 Public Transportation 2

대중교통 2

Warm Up

A Guess the Question & Answer
사진을 보면서 예상 질문과 답변을 먼저 추측해 봅시다.

B Listen & Talk
한국 대중교통체계의 장점에 관한 대화를 연습해 봅시다.

🎧 08-03

A I think the taxi driver cheated me. I paid way too much.

B Oh, no. Why didn't you call me for help?

A I was in a hurry. I didn't even realize how much I was paying.

B Next time, take the bus instead. In fact, the bus can be faster than a taxi.

A Yeah? I thought taxis were faster than buses.

B Not always. There are bus-only lanes in Seoul. They are well paved, and the buses run really fast. In addition, check your destination and see if there are any buses that go straight to that place. That way, you'll save a huge amount of time on the road.

A Sounds great. Thanks for the information.

B No problem. Anytime you feel confused with the lifestyle in this city, feel free to contact me.

A 택시 기사가 날 속인 것 같아. 요금을 너무 많이 냈어.

B 저런. 왜 나한테 전화해서 도와달라고 안 했어?

A 서두르느라고. 내가 얼마를 지불하고 있는지도 몰랐어.

B 다음에는 버스를 타. 사실, 버스가 택시보다 빠를 수도 있어.

A 그래? 나는 택시가 버스보다 빠른 줄 알았어.

B 항상 그런 건 아니야. 서울에는 버스 전용 차선이 있거든. 도로가 잘 포장되어 있고 버스들이 정말 빨리 달려. 또한 네 목적지를 확인한 다음 직행 버스가 있는지 알아봐. 그렇게 하면 길 위에서 보내는 시간을 상당히 줄일 수 있어.

A 훌륭하군. 알려줘서 고마워.

B 별 것도 아닌데 뭐. 서울에 머물면서 생활하는 데에 궁금한 점이 있으면 언제든지 연락해.

Vocabulary
be in a hurry 서두르다, 다급하다 | realize 깨닫다, 알아차리다 | bus-only lane 버스 전용차선 | well paved (길이) 잘 포장된 | go straight 직행하다 | feel confused with ~ ~를 혼동하다, 헷갈리다 | feel free to ~ ~하는 것을 마음껏 하다

Key Expressions

> 아래 제시된 각 expression의 구조를 이해하고, 자기만의 표현들을 생각해 봅시다.

Expression 1   a [the] means of ~: ~의 수단, 방법

주요 대중교통 수단은 버스와 지하철입니다.
→ **The** main public **means of** transportation are buses and subways.

제스처는 의사소통의 한 방법입니다. → Gestures are **a means of** communication.

교육은 우리의 능력을 개발하는 방법이 될 수 있습니다. → Education is **a means of** developing our skills.

Expression 2   economical: 경제적인, 실속 있는

둘 다 매우 경제적입니다. → They are both very **economical**.

때로는 신용카드를 사용하는 것이 현금을 사용하는 것보다 경제적입니다.
→ Sometimes using a credit card is more **economical** than using cash.

저는 실속 있는 가격으로 책을 한 묶음 샀습니다.
→ I bought a bunch of books, and the prices were very **economical**.

Expression 3   disadvantage: 불이익, 단점

각자 고유의 장단점이 있습니다. → Each has its own advantages and **disadvantages**.

컴퓨터 게임을 하는 것에는 안 좋은 점이 많습니다.
→ There are many **disadvantages** to playing computer games.

기술 발달로 인한 단점 가운데 하나는 바로 표절이 쉬워졌다는 것입니다.
→ One of the **disadvantages** of advanced technology is easier access to plagiarism.

Expression 4   rush hour: 교통량이 많은 시간 (출퇴근 시간)

출퇴근 시간에는 교통이 정말 안 좋습니다. → During **rush hour**, the traffic is really bad.

출퇴근 시간에 도로는 자동차로 꽉 찹니다. → The road is packed with cars during **rush hour**.

출퇴근 시간에는 교통사고가 많이 납니다. → There are lots of car accidents during **rush hour**.

Expression 5   be on time: 제 시간에 오다, 시간을 지키다

지하철은 언제나 제 시간에 도착합니다. → The subway **is** always **on time**.

어째서 의사들은 제 시간을 지킬 수 없는 걸까? → Why can't doctors **be on time**?

태호는 언제나 시간을 엄수합니다. 그는 약속에 늦는 법이 없습니다.
→ Taeho **is** always **on time**. He is never late for appointments.

Topic Question & Model Answer

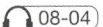

Topic Question

What are the advantages and disadvantages of the public transportation system in your country? What do you like to do when you use public transportation?

당신 나라의 대중교통 체계의 장점과 단점은 무엇입니까? 대중교통을 이용할 때 당신이 좋아하는 것은 무엇입니까?

TIP FOR THE OPIc

한국 대중교통 체계의 장단점을 설명하라는 질문입니다. 평소 대중교통 이용시 편리한 점과 불편한 점을 이야기하면 됩니다. 등·하굣길이나 출퇴근길에 겪었던 일을 구체적으로 제시하면 좋습니다. 도로 상황은 시간대에 따라 달라지므로, 상황에 따라 어떠한 교통편을 선호하는지 설명하면 설득력이 있습니다. 또한 음악을 듣거나 낮잠을 자거나 창밖의 풍경을 감상하는 것 등의 활동을 간략히 언급할 수 있습니다.

Model Answer

| Opening |

The main means of public transportation in Korea are buses, subways, and taxis. I often take buses and subways. They are both very economical and convenient, but each has its own advantages and disadvantages.

한국의 주요 대중교통수단은 버스 지하철 그리고 택시입니다. 저는 자주 버스와 지하철을 탑니다. 모두 경제적이면서도 편리하고, 각각의 장단점이 있습니다.

| Good Points and Bad Points |

I prefer to take buses when the weather is nice. I love to enjoy the view outside and to listen to music. However, on rainy days or during rush hour, the traffic is really bad, and there is no way to arrive at my destination on time. So, when I commute to work, I usually take the subway since it is always on time. If there's one thing I dislike about the subway, there are always some people selling products and making noise. Other than that, I'm happy with the Korean subway system.

저는 날씨가 좋을 때는 버스 타는 것을 선호합니다. 바깥 전경을 보며 음악을 듣는 것을 좋아합니다. 하지만 비가 오거나 출퇴근 시간에는 교통 상황이 안 좋아서 제 때에 목적지에 도착할 방법이 없습니다. 그래서 저는 통근할 때 주로 지하철을 타는데, 언제나 시간을 엄수하기 때문입니다. 지하철 이용을 할 때 싫은 점 하나는 바로 상품 판매를 하며 소란을 피우는 사람들이 늘 있기 때문입니다. 그것 말고는 한국의 지하철 제도가 만족스럽습니다.

| Activities on the Subway |

When I'm on the subway, I always use my smartphone to read online articles or to watch the news. Sometimes I take a nap when I feel really tired.

저는 지하철에 있을 때 언제나 스마트폰으로 온라인 기사를 읽거나 뉴스를 봅니다. 가끔 정말 피곤하면 낮잠을 자기도 합니다.

More Questions

〈대중교통〉에 관련하여 더 나올 수 있는 OPIc 질문들을 정리한 코너입니다. 질문에 대한 brainstorming을 해보세요.

1. Do you often take taxis? On what occasions do you take taxis? Is the service good in your country?
2. What do you think about public transportation in your country? Do you want to make any changes to the system?
3. Which type of public transportation do you use the most? Why?

On Your Own

앞에서 주어진 Model Answer을 바탕으로, 아래의 빈칸에 들어갈 수 있는 다양한 대체 가능한 어휘 및 표현들을 참고하여 학습자 본인만의 모범 답안을 직접 만들어보세요.

I Opening I

The main means of public transportation in Korea are buses, subways, and taxis. I often take buses and subways. They are both very economical and convenient, but each has its own advantages and disadvantages.

I Good Points and Bad Points I

I prefer to take buses when ⓐ_____. However,

ⓑ_____.

ⓒ_____.

ⓓ_____.

I Activities on the Subway I

When I'm on the subway, I always use my smartphone to read online articles or to watch the news. Sometimes I take a nap when I feel really tired.

I Opening I The main means of public transportation in Korea are buses, subways, and taxis. I often take buses and subways. They are both very economical and convenient, but each has its own advantages and disadvantages.

I Good Points and Bad Points I I prefer to take the bus when ⓐ **it goes straight to my destination**. However, ⓑ **when the bus has too many stops on the way, I would rather take the subway.** ⓒ **Korean subway is always on time. It's easy to transfer to other lines, too.** ⓓ **So I often take the subway when the traffic is bad on the roads.**

I Activities on the Subway I When I'm on the subway, I always use my smartphone to read online articles or to watch the news. Sometimes I take a nap when I feel really tired.

본인이 만든 답안에 아래의 요소들이 포함되었는지 점검해 봅시다.

	Checklist
☐	한국 대중교통의 종류
☐	버스의 이용의 장단점
☐	지하철 이용의 장단점
☐	택시 이용의 장단점
☐	개인 사례 및 소감 말하기

Unit 50 Technology 1

테크놀로지 1

Warm Up

A Guess the Question & Answer
사진을 보면서 예상 질문과 답변을 먼저 추측해 봅시다.

B Listen & Talk
첨단 제품이 고장 난 상황에 관한 대화를 연습해 봅시다.

🎧 08-05

A Oh, no. I think my computer is broken.
B What's wrong?
A The screen just went black. It's not working at all!
B Did you save the files you were working on?
A Yes, I saved them on my computer!
B What about on your thumb drive?
A I couldn't find it, so I only saved them on the computer.
B Don't be upset. I'm trying to see if I can do something about it.
A I'm very frustrated. I spent hours on my final papers, and I can't imagine doing them all over again.
B Let me see… I don't think your computer cord was plugged in! Your computer battery might have just run out.
A Really? But I plugged it in!
B Nope. It was almost plugged in. Now let's see if your computer turns on again.
A Oh, it's working! You are my lifesaver. Thank you.
B No worries. I'm happy your files are safe.

A 오, 이런. 내 컴퓨터가 고장 난 것 같아.
B 뭐가 잘못 되었는데?
A 방금 화면이 나갔어. 전혀 작동되지가 않아!
B 작업 중이던 파일은 저장했어?
A 응, 내 컴퓨터에 저장했어!
B 네 USB에는?
A 안 보이길래 컴퓨터에만 저장했지.
B 속상해하지마. 내가 할 수 있는 일이 있나 한 번 볼게.
A 너무 절망스러워. 몇 시간 동안 기말 리포트를 작성했는데, 그것을 어떻게 다시 할 수 있겠어.
B 내가 좀 볼게… 컴퓨터가 전원에 연결되지 않은 거 같아! 단지 컴퓨터 배터리가 다 된 거 같은데.
A 정말? 하지만 내가 전원을 연결했어!
B 그렇지 않아. 연결될 뻔 했겠지. 자 이제 컴퓨터가 다시 켜지는지 보자.
A 오, 다시 작동된다! 넌 내 생명의 은인이야. 고마워.
B 아니야. 네 파일이 모두 무사하다니 기뻐.

Vocabulary
computer is broken 컴퓨터가 고장 나다 | **screen went black** 화면이 나갔다 | **thumb drive** USB (USB가 엄지손가락만 하다고 해서 이렇게 부르기도 함) | **can't imagine -ing** ~할 상상조차 못하다 | **run out of battery power** 배터리가 나가다 | **plug in** (전기 코드)를 꽂다

Key Expressions

아래 제시된 각 expression의 구조를 이해하고, 자기만의 표현들을 생각해 봅시다.

Expression 1　명사 + be동사 + everywhere: ~가 모든 곳에 있다

테크놀로지는 어디에서나 찾아볼 수 있습니다. → Technology **is everywhere**.

도시 곳곳에 고양이가 흩어져 있습니다. → Cats **are everywhere** in the city.

모든 곳이 기쁨으로 가득합니다. → Joy **is everywhere**.

Expression 2　self-taught: 독학해서 배운, 스스로 터득한

사용법은 제 스스로 터득했습니다. → I am **self-taught**.

그녀는 독학으로 사진 찍는 법을 배웠으며 매우 성공하였습니다.
→ She is a **self-taught** photographer and is very successful.

그는 독학으로 소프트웨어 개발자가 된 사람이었습니다. → He was a **self-taught** software developer.

Expression 3　follow the instructions: 설명서를 따라하다, 지시를 따르다

스마트폰은 사용설명서를 이해하면 사용하기가 쉽습니다.
→ Smartphones are easy to use if you **follow the instructions**.

지시 사항 대로 하는 것이 좋을 것입니다. → You'd better **follow the instructions**.

저는 창의적이고 싶기 때문에 항상 배운 대로 하지는 않습니다.
→ I don't always **follow the instructions** because I want to be creative.

Expression 4　have an issue with + 명사: ~에 대한 문제가 있다

제 노트북에 문제가 생기면 늘 제 남동생이 처리해줍니다.
→ Whenever I **have an issue with** my laptop, my brother takes care of it.

집주인과 아무런 문제도 없으신가요? → Do you **have any issue with** your landlord?

저는 계약 내용에 관하여 아무런 이의가 없습니다.
→ I do not **have any issues with** the contents of the contract.

Expression 5　주어 + owe + 사람: ~가 ~에게 빚을 지다

저는 그에게 빚진 것이 많습니다. → I **owe** him a lot.

넌 나한테 점심 살 일이 있어. → You **owe** me lunch.

우리는 그에게 목숨을 빚졌습니다. → We **owe** him our lives.

Topic Question & Model Answer

🎧 08-06

Topic Question

What kind of technology do you use the most often? Did anyone teach you how to use that technology? When was it?

당신은 어떤 종류의 테크놀로지를 가장 많이 사용하나요? 당신에게 테크놀로지를 사용하는 법을 가르쳐준 사람이 있나요? 그것이 언제였나요?

> **TIP FOR THE OPIc**
> 테크놀로지는 21세기 사회의 흐름에 큰 영향을 미치는 요소입니다. 따라서 이 주제는 OPIc이 도입된 후로부터 지금까지 단골 주제로 등장하고 있는데, 특히 테크놀로지 사용법을 누구로부터 배운 경험이 있는지에 관한 질문이 자주 출제됩니다. 이 경우, 전자 기기 사용법을 배운 사례에 대해 구체적으로 이야기하면 됩니다.

Model Answer

| Opening |

Technology is everywhere: smartphones, laptops, and DVD players, just to name a few. Even houses and automobiles have the latest technology nowadays.

테크놀로지는 어디에서나 찾아볼 수 있습니다: 스마트폰, 노트북 컴퓨터, DVD 플레이어 등은 그 일부에 지나지 않습니다. 심지어 요즘에는 주택이나 자동차도 최신 테크놀로지를 갖추고 있습니다.

| Technology in My Life |

Naturally, people living in the modern age use all kinds of technology in their everyday lives. I use my smartphone 7 days a week. I am self-taught. Smartphones are easy to use as long as you follow the instructions in the manuals. I think that smartphones are truly the most revolutionary invention of the 21st century. They have made our lives so convenient.

당연하게도 현대 사회의 사람들은 일상에서 여러 종류의 테크놀로지를 사용합니다. 저 역시 주 7일 스마트폰을 사용합니다. 사용법은 스스로 터득했습니다. 스마트폰 사용은 사용 설명서만 보면 쉽게 터득할 수 있습니다. 저는 21세기의 가장 혁신적인 발명품은 바로 스마트폰이라고 생각합니다. 스마트폰 덕분에 우리 삶은 훨씬 더 편리해졌습니다.

| Closing |

On the other hand, I often use my laptop to work on my papers. Whenever I have an issue with my laptop, my brother takes care of it. He is a computer engineer, and I owe him a lot. It is a blessing that there is someone in the family who knows about technology!

다른 한편 저는 문서 작성을 하기 위해 노트북 컴퓨터를 사용합니다. 제 노트북에 문제가 생기면 늘 제 남동생이 해결해줍니다. 동생은 컴퓨터 엔지니어인데, 제가 빚진 적이 많습니다. 가족 중 테크놀로지를 잘 다루는 사람이 있다는 것은 참으로 감사한 일입니다!

More Questions

〈테크놀로지〉에 관련하여 더 나올 수 있는 OPIc 질문들을 정리한 코너입니다. 질문에 대한 brainstorming을 해보세요.

1. What kinds of technology do you usually use at school/work? Did you learn how to use them? Who taught you?
2. What kinds of technology do you use the most often?

On Your Own

앞에서 주어진 Model Answer을 바탕으로, 아래의 빈칸에 들어갈 수 있는 다양한 대체 가능한 어휘 및 표현들을 참고하여 학습자 본인만의 모범 답안을 직접 만들어보세요.

I Opening I

Technology is everywhere. It is used in ⓐ_____, ⓑ_____, and ⓒ_____, just to name a few. Even houses and automobiles have the latest technology nowadays.

I Technology in My Life I

Naturally, people living in the modern age use all kinds of technology in their everyday lives. I use my ⓓ_____ ⓔ_____. I am self-taught. ⓕ_____ are easy to use as long as you follow the instructions in the manuals. I think that ⓖ_____ is truly the ⓗ_____. It has made my life ⓘ_____.

I Closing I

On the other hand, I use my laptop often to ⓙ_____. Whenever I have an issue with my ⓚ_____, my brother takes care of it. He is a ⓛ_____, and I owe him a lot. It is a blessing that there is someone in the family who knows about technology!

I Opening I Technology is everywhere. It is used in ⓐ **businesses**, ⓑ **transportation systems**, and ⓒ **schools**, just to name a few. Even houses and automobiles have the latest technology nowadays.

I Technology in My Life I Naturally, people living in the modern age use all kinds of technology in their everyday lives. I use my ⓓ **home theater system** ⓔ **almost every day**. I am self-taught. ⓕ **Home theater systems** are easy to use as long as you follow the instructions in the manuals. I think that ⓖ **a home theater system** is truly the ⓗ **best technology to have at home**. It has made my life ⓘ **much more enjoyable**.

I Closing I On the other hand, I use my laptop often to ⓙ **update my website**. Whenever I have an issue with my ⓚ **website**, my brother takes care of it. He is a ⓛ **web designer**, and I owe him a lot. It is a blessing that there is someone in the family who knows about technology!

본인이 만든 답안에 아래의 요소들이 포함되었는지 점검해 봅시다.

	Checklist
☐	자주 사용하는 테크놀로지
☐	테크놀로지 사용을 배운 경험
☐	언제 배웠는지
☐	어떤 것에 관해 배웠는지
☐	누구로부터 배웠는지
☐	어떻게 활용하고 있는지

Unit 51 Technology 2

테크놀로지 2

Warm Up

A Guess the Question & Answer
사진을 보면서 예상 질문과 답변을 먼저 추측해 봅시다.

B Listen & Talk
테크놀로지의 지속적인 발전에 관한 대화를 연습해 봅시다.

🎧 08-07

A It's really hard to catch up with all the latest technology. How did you even major in computer science?

B Then how did you major in biology? We are just good at different things.

A It's not the same thing. You don't have to use biology when you work, but I have to use computers at work every day.

B But isn't your life so much easier because of technology?

A It's the opposite. It's actually making my life more complicated.

B Do you remember the days we used to use floppy disks to save files? Now we can save them in thumb-drives.

A Yes, some things got easier to do thanks to technology. But I believe that technology has advanced enough. Do you think people need to use more advanced technology?

B I don't think it is only a matter of necessity. It is more people's desire. That's also why people like me have jobs.

A All right. But the new technologies are a lot of stress to a person like me.

A 최신 기술을 따라잡는 것은 너무 어려워. 너는 어떻게 컴퓨터를 전공하기까지 했어?

B 그러면 너는 어떻게 생물학을 전공했니? 우리는 그저 잘하는 게 다를 뿐이야.

A 경우가 달라. 너는 공부할 때 생물학을 사용할 일이 없지만, 나는 매일 작업을 할 때 컴퓨터를 사용해야 해.

B 하지만 기술 발달로 인해 삶이 훨씬 편리해지지 않았어?

A 그 반대야. 기술 발달로 인해서 삶이 더욱 복잡해지고 있어.

B 예전에 플로피 디스크에 파일을 저장하던 시절을 기억해? 이젠 USB에 저장할 수 있잖아.

A 그래, 새로운 기술 덕분에 편리해진 점도 있지. 하지만 나는 기술 발달이 충분히 이루어졌다고 믿어. 우리가 더 발달된 기술을 사용해야 한다고 생각하니? 난 더 이상 기술을 발달할 필요가 없다고 생각해.

B 필요성 때문만은 아니라고 생각해. 오히려 사람들의 열망 때문이지. 그것이 바로 나 같은 사람에게 일자리가 있는 이유잖아.

A 알았어. 하지만 나같은 사람한테는 새로운 기술들이 상당한 스트레스야.

Vocabulary | catch up with ~ ~를 따라잡다 | complicated 복잡한 | floppy disk 플로피 디스크 (과거 사용되던 정사각형 모양의 손바닥 만한 크기의 데이터 저장용량 장치) | necessity 필요성 | rely on ~ ~에게 의지하다

Key Expressions

○━ 아래 제시된 각 expression의 구조를 이해하고, 자기만의 표현들을 생각해 봅시다.

Expression 1　go black: (전원, 전기 등이) 꺼지다

갑자기 제 노트북 화면이 나갔습니다. → My laptop suddenly **went black**.

갑자기 방 안의 모든 것이 꺼졌습니다. → Everything in the room suddenly **went black**.

도시 전체가 갑자기 정전되었습니다. → The entire city suddenly **went black**.

Expression 2　reboot the machine: 기계를 재부팅하다

저는 그저 재부팅하면 될 것이라고 생각했습니다. → I thought I should just **reboot the machine**.

때때로 기계를 작동시키기 위해서는 그저 재부팅만 하면 됩니다.
→ Sometimes, we just have to **reboot the machine** to make it work.

기계를 재부팅하기 전에 모든 것을 확실히 저장하도록 하십시오.
→ Make sure you save everything before you **reboot the machine**.

Expression 3　submit an article: 기사를 제출하다

저는 다음 날 오전까지 기사를 제출해야 했습니다. → I had to **submit** my **articles** by the morning.

우리는 편집장님에게 모든 기사를 송부해야 합니다.
→ We have to **submit** all the **articles** to the editor-in-chief.

저는 기사를 제출하고 나면 긴장을 풀기 위해 탁구를 칩니다.
→ After I **submit** my **articles**, I play ping-pong to relax.

Expression 4　extension (on): (~에 대한) 연장

저는 결국 다음 날 제 상사에게 전화를 걸어 마감일을 연기해달라고 요청했습니다.
→ I ended up calling my boss the next day to ask for an **extension on** my deadline.

많은 사람들이 결제일을 연기합니다. → Many people get **extensions on** their bill payments.

저는 오늘 아침에 붙임 머리를 했습니다. → I got hair **extensions** this morning.

Expression 5　retrieve: 복구하다

저는 노트북을 수리 센터로 가지고 가서 모든 것을 복구할 수 있었습니다.
→ I carried my laptop to the repair shop and was able to **retrieve** everything.

저는 예전 핸드폰에 저장되었던 사진을 복구하는 데 실패했습니다.
→ I failed to **retrieve** the photos on my old phone.

그들이 저희들로부터 훔쳐간 모든 재산을 되찾고 싶습니다.
→ I want to **retrieve** all the property they stole from us.

Topic Question & Model Answer

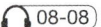 08-08

Topic Question

Tell me about a time you had a technology-related problem. When was it? What happened? How did you resolve it? Tell me the story in detail.

테크놀로지에 관해 문제가 발생했던 경우에 대해 말씀해 주세요. 언제였나요? 무슨 문제였나요? 그것을 어떻게 해결했나요? 자세히 이야기해보세요.

TIP FOR THE OPIc

테크놀로지를 사용하다가 문제가 발생한 경험은 누구에게나 한 번쯤은 있을 것입니다. 휴대폰이 물에 잠겨서 데이터가 다 날아간 경험, 컴퓨터가 다운되어서 작성 중이던 데이터를 잃어버린 경험, 네비게이션 기기만 믿고 갔는데 잘못된 방향으로 길을 든 경험 등을 생각해볼 수 있을 것입니다. 그러한 상황이 언제 일어나서 어떻게 해결했는지를 설명해줍니다.

Model Answer

| Opening |

I was working on my laptop in my room and reviewing my articles when my laptop suddenly went black. It wasn't a battery problem. The laptop was plugged in.

방에서 노트북으로 기사를 검토하고 있었을 때 갑자기 노트북 화면이 나갔습니다. 배터리 문제는 아니었습니다. 전원은 연결된 상태였습니다.

| An Unforgettable Experience |

As bizarre as the situation was, I thought I should just reboot the machine. I tried turning it off and turning it on again, but that didn't fix it. It was too late to call the repair shop, and there was no one at home to help me. I was speechless. I had to submit my articles by the morning, and the only place they were saved was my laptop! I ended up calling my boss the next day to ask for an extension on my deadline. Then, I carried my laptop to the repair shop and was able to retrieve everything I had saved on my hard drive.

좀처럼 없던 일이라 재부팅만 하면 될 것이라고 생각했습니다. 전원을 끄고 다시 켜봤지만 다시 켜지지가 않았습니다. 시간이 너무 늦어서 수리 센터에 갈 수는 없었고 집에서도 도와줄 사람이 없었습니다. 저는 아무 말도 할 수가 없었습니다. 다음 날 오전까지 기사를 제출해야 했는데 작업한 문서가 저장된 곳은 제 노트북뿐이었습니다! 저는 결국 다음 날 상사에게 전화를 걸어 마감일을 연기해달라고 요청했습니다. 그런 후에 노트북을 수리 센터로 가지고 가서 하드드라이브에 저장된 모든 것을 복구할 수 있었습니다.

| Closing |

It wasn't the happiest way to solve my problem. But I learned that I should always save my files on a USB as well as on my computer.

그것은 최상의 해결책은 아니었습니다. 하지만 이 일을 통해 문서 저장은 노트북뿐만 아니라 USB에도 해야 한다는 점을 깨달았습니다.

More Questions

〈테크놀로지〉에 관련하여 더 나올 수 있는 OPIc 질문들을 정리한 코너입니다. 질문에 대한 brainstorming을 해보세요.

1. Technology has both a positive side and a negative side. What do you like and dislike about technology?
2. Technology has transformed our lives in many ways. How does technology affect your life?

On Your Own

앞에서 주어진 Model Answer을 바탕으로, 아래의 빈칸에 들어갈 수 있는 다양한 대체 가능한 어휘 및 표현들을 참고하여 학습자 본인만의 모범 답안을 직접 만들어보세요.

I Opening I

I was working on my laptop in my ⓐ_____ and reviewing my

ⓑ_____ when my laptop suddenly went black. It wasn't a battery problem. The laptop was plugged in.

I An Unforgettable Experience I

ⓒ_____ reboot the machine. I tried turning it off and turning it on again, but that didn't fix it. It was too late to call the repair shop, and there was no one at home to help me. I was speechless. I had to

ⓓ_____, and the only place they were saved was my laptop! I ended up calling my boss ⓔ_____ to ask ⓕ_____.

Then, I carried my laptop to the repair shop and was able to retrieve everything I had saved on my hard drive.

I Closing I

It was ⓖ_____. But I learned that I should always save my files on a USB as well as on my computer.

I Opening I I was working on my laptop in my ⓐ **office** and reviewing my ⓑ **presentation materials** when my laptop suddenly went black. It wasn't a battery problem. The laptop was plugged in.

I An Unforgettable Experience I ⓒ **All I could think of was to** reboot the machine. I tried turning it off and turning it on again, but that didn't fix it. It was too late to call the repair shop, and there was no one at home to help me. I was speechless. I had to ⓓ **give a presentation the next morning**, and the only place they were saved was my laptop! I ended up calling my boss ⓔ **that night** to ask ⓕ **if anyone could replace me**. Then, I carried my laptop to the repair shop and was able to retrieve everything I had saved on my hard drive.

I Closing I It was ⓖ **a nightmare**. But I learned that I should always save my files on a USB as well as on my computer.

본인이 만든 답안에 아래의 요소들이 포함되었는지 점검해 봅시다.

Checklist
☐ 테크놀로지 문제가 발생했던 적
☐ 무엇에 관한 문제였는지
☐ 언제 문제가 발생했는지
☐ 왜 문제가 발생했는지
☐ 문제 해결을 위해 한 일
☐ 문제 해결의 결과

Unit 52 Recycling 1

재활용 1

Warm Up

A Guess the Question & Answer
사진을 보면서 예상 질문과 답변을 먼저 추측해 봅시다.

B Listen & Talk
쓰레기 분리수거 정책에 관한 대화를 연습해 봅시다.

🎧 08-09

A Sweetheart, can you take out the trash later?	**A** 얘야, 있다가 쓰레기 좀 버려줄래?
B Yes, Mom.	**B** 네, 엄마.
A Make sure to separate it correctly.	**A** 분리해서 버리는 것 잊지 말고.
B Of course. I used to do this all the time.	**B** 그럼요. 늘 제가 했던 일이잖아요.
A I know, but you were away for a while. We also have a new food disposal policy.	**A** 그렇지만 한동안 여기 없었잖니. 새로운 음식물 쓰레기 처리 규정이 생겼어.
B What is it?	**B** 그게 뭔데요?
A We have to put the food waste in the yellow cans in front of our apartment building. They have scales on the top.	**A** 우리 아파트 건물 앞에 있는 노란색 통에 음식물 쓰레기를 버려야 해. 통 위에는 저울이 설치되어 있어.
B Why do they have scales on the top?	**B** 왜 저울이 설치되어 있어요?
A They are to weigh the food trash so that each household can pay tax accordingly.	**A** 집집마다 버리는 음식물 쓰레기의 무게를 재서 그에 대한 세금을 내도록 하기 위한 거야.
B We have to pay tax for our own food trash?	**B** 음식물 쓰레기에 대한 세금을 내야 한다고요?
A Yes, honey. The government introduced it last year to reduce and recycle food waste.	**A** 그렇단다. 작년부터 정부가 음식물 쓰레기를 줄이고 또 재활용하기 위해 도입을 했어.
B I guess many things have changed while I was gone.	**B** 저 없는 동안 많은 변화가 있었네요.

Vocabulary

take out 가지고 나가다 | **separate** 분리하다 | **correctly** 올바르게 | **disposal** 폐기, 처리 | **scale** 저울

Key Expressions

아래 제시된 각 expression의 구조를 이해하고, 자기만의 표현들을 생각해 봅시다.

Expression 1 — **distinctive**: 차별화된, 분명한, 독특한

저는 한국의 재활용 정책이 매우 특별하다고 생각합니다. → I think our recycling policy is quite **distinctive**.

그의 직업 정신은 상당히 독특합니다. → His work ethic is quite **distinctive**.

이 작가는 독특한 문체를 가지고 있습니다. → This author has a **distinctive** writing style.

Expression 2 — **charge tax**: 세금을 부과하다

한국 정부는 음식물 쓰레기에도 세금을 부과합니다.
→ The Korean government also **charges tax** on leftover waste trash.

고객이 시장에서 비닐 봉지를 사용할 경우 개당 10센트의 세금이 부과됩니다.
→ Shoppers are **charged a tax** of 10 cents for every plastic bag they use at markets.

알래스카 주는 소득세 및 판매세를 부과하지 않습니다.
→ The state of Alaska **charges** neither income tax nor sales **tax**.

Expression 3 — **growing concern about**: ~에 대한 커지는 근심

음식물 쓰레기에 대한 고민이 커져가고 있었습니다.
→ There has been **growing concern about** food trash.

저는 한국에서 도덕이 붕괴되는 것에 대해 크게 우려하고 있습니다.
→ I have a **growing concern about** the collapse of morality in Korea.

아이들이 폭력적 미디어에 노출되는 것에 대한 염려가 커지고 있습니다.
→ We have a **growing concern about** our kids' exposure to violent media.

Expression 4 — **be estimated (at/to)**: (~으로) 집계되다, 추정되다

지난 몇 년간 처리 비용이 연간 1조원에 이르는 것으로 집계되었습니다.
→ Its disposal **was estimated at** almost 1 trillion won in the past few years.

한국의 자살률은 OECD 국가 중 가장 높은 편인 것으로 추정됩니다.
→ Korea's suicide rate **is estimated to** be the highest among OECD countries.

10대 청소년 중 약 25%는 학교에서 괴롭힘을 당하는 것으로 추정되고 있습니다.
→ It **is estimated** that about 25% of teenagers are being bullied at school.

Expression 5 — **environmentally**: 환경적으로

그 문제는 환경적인 측면에서 더욱 심각했습니다. → The problem was even worse, **environmentally**.

그들은 환경적으로 안전한 제품을 만듭니다. → They make **environmentally** safe products.

이 샴푸는 환경친화적입니다. → This shampoo is **environmentally** friendly.

Topic Question & Model Answer

Topic Question

Tell me about the recycling policy in your country. How is it different than in other countries?

당신이 사는 나라의 쓰레기 재활용 정책에 대해 말해보세요. 다른 나라들의 정책과 어떻게 다른가요?

> **TIP FOR THE OPIc**
> 재활용 정책에 관한 질문입니다. 난이도 4이상부터는 비교 및 대조에 관한 질문이 자주 출제됩니다. 다른 나라의 재활용 정책에 대해서 모르더라도 한국의 재활용 정책 두 세가지 (쓰레기 분리수거, 음식물 쓰레기 처리 등)에 대해 이야기하면 질문 의도에 맞는 답을 할 수 있습니다.

Model Answer

| Opening |

It is not easy to compare Korea's recycling policy with other countries'. However, I think our recycling policy is quite distinctive.

한국의 재활용 정책을 다른 나라의 정책과 비교하기는 쉽지 않습니다. 하지만 저는 한국의 재활용 정책이 매우 특별하다고 생각합니다.

| Distinctive Policy |

We not only separate papers, cans, plastic bags, and bottles from other garbage, but the Korean government also charges a tax on leftover trash. We put food waste in perishable bags and weigh it before we throw it in the food trash cans. It sounds complicated, but it makes sense since there has been growing concern about food waste. The expense of annual food waste and its disposal has been estimated at almost 1 trillion won in the past few years. Besides, the problem is even worse, environmentally.

종이, 캔, 비닐 봉지 및 빈 병을 분리수거를 하는 것은 물론, 한국 정부에서 음식물 쓰레기에도 세금을 부과합니다. 음식물 쓰레기를 자연 분해용 봉지에 버리고 그것의 무게를 잰 다음 정해진 쓰레기통에 버립니다. 복잡한 정책 같지만, 이는 음식물 쓰레기 문제에 대한 고민이 커져가는 가운데 나타난 적절한 해결 방안입니다. 지난 몇 년간 음식물 쓰레기 및 음식물 쓰레기 처리 비용이 연간 1조원에 이르는 것으로 집계되었습니다. 게다가 환경적으로는 더욱 심각한 문제입니다.

| Closing |

Although there is extra work due to the new recycling policy, I see that even my family has reduced food waste most of the time. We believe that our participation is keeping the Earth greener.

새로운 정책으로 인해 할 일이 더 늘어나기는 했지만, 저희 가족만 하더라도 그 후 음식물 쓰레기가 줄어든 것을 경험했습니다. 저희의 참여로 지구가 더 깨끗이 보존된다고 생각합니다.

More Questions

〈재활용〉에 관련하여 더 나올 수 있는 OPIc 질문들을 정리한 코너입니다. 질문에 대한 brainstorming을 해보세요.

1. How do you recycle? Since when have you been recycling? How do you encourage others to recycle?

2. When was the last time you recycled trash? Did you have any trouble while you were recycling? What happened?

On Your Own

앞에서 주어진 Model Answer을 바탕으로, 아래의 빈칸에 들어갈 수 있는 다양한 대체 가능한 어휘 및 표현들을 참고하여 학습자 본인만의 모범 답안을 직접 만들어보세요.

I Opening I

It is not easy to compare Korea's recycling policy to other countries'. However, I think
ⓐ_____.

I Distinctive Policy I

We not only separate ⓑ_____, but the Korean government also charges a tax on leftover food waste. We put food waste in perishable bags and weigh it before we throw it in the food trash cans. It ⓒ_____, but it makes sense since ⓓ_____. The expense of annual food waste and its disposal has been ⓔ_____ 1 trillion won in the past few years. Besides, the problem is even worse, environmentally.

I Closing I

Although there is extra work due to the new recycling policy, ⓕ_____. We believe that our participation is keeping the Earth greener.

I Opening I It is not easy to compare Korea's recycling policy to other countries'. However, I think ⓐ **we have a well-established recycling policy**.

I Distinctive Policy I We not only separate ⓑ **landfill trash from recyclables**, but the Korean government also charges a tax on leftover food waste. We put food waste in perishable bags and weigh it before we throw it in the food trash cans. It ⓒ **is a lot of work**, but it makes sense since ⓓ **land pollution has been getting worse**. The expense of annual food waste and its disposal has been ⓔ **almost** 1 trillion won in the past few years. Besides, the problem is even worse, environmentally.

I Closing I Although there is extra work due to the new recycling policy, ⓕ **it is worth doing because it has been reducing the amount of food waste**. We believe that our participation is keeping the Earth greener.

본인이 만든 답안에 아래의 요소들이 포함되었는지 점검해 봅시다.

	Checklist
☐	한국의 분리수거 문화
☐	가정에서 하는 분리수거
☐	음식물 쓰레기 처리법
☐	밖에서 하는 분리수거
☐	재활용의 환경적 효과
☐	재활용의 경제적 효과

Unit 53 Recycling 2

재활용 2

Warm Up

A Guess the Question & Answer
사진을 보면서 예상 질문과 답변을 먼저 추측해 봅시다.

B Listen & Talk
쓰레기로 인한 환경오염에 관한 대화를 연습해 봅시다. 🎧 08-11

A Do you know that there's an island where nobody lives but is filled with trash?

B Is the island used as a landfill?

A No. It's just covered with trash that was floating on the ocean. Take a look at this video.

B That's pretty shocking! I don't know how people can be so careless about nature. The Earth is seriously polluted!

A That's true. A lot of people worry about purchasing new houses and getting nice cars, but few people truly care about the planet's ecology.

B Scientists say that the Earth is on brink of a mass extinction due to deforestation. They also say that bees are hindered by radiation when they are trying to produce honey.

A How terrible. I had goosebumps the other day when I watched a video about ice melting near Antarctica. The ice was melting so fast.

B I heard about that, too. The water level is constantly rising but people seem to be so indifferent.

A 혹시 쓰레기로 가득 찬 무인도가 있다는 사실 알고 있니?

B 쓰레기 매립지로 사용되는 섬이야?

A 아니. 바다에 떠다니던 쓰레기가 가득 차서 그렇게 된 거야. 이 동영상 한 번 봐.

B 매우 충격적이네! 난 사람들이 어쩜 그렇게 자연을 소홀히 여기는지 모르겠어. 지구가 심각하게 오염되었잖아!

A 맞아. 많은 사람들이 새로 집을 사고 좋은 차를 사는 것은 신경 쓰지만 정작 생태계를 걱정하는 사람은 거의 없어.

B 과학자들에 의하면 지구는 삼림 벌채로 인해서 다수의 생물 멸종 위기를 코앞에 두고 있대. 뿐만 아니라 전자파 때문에 꿀벌이 꿀을 만드는 것도 방해를 받는다고 하더라고.

A 정말 끔찍하군. 며칠 전 남극 대륙의 얼음에 관한 동영상을 봤는데 소름이 끼치더라고. 얼음이 빠르게 녹고 있었어.

B 나도 그에 대해 들은 적 있어. 해수면이 계속해서 상승하고 있는데 사람들은 무관심해 보여.

Vocabulary
landfill 쓰레기 매립지 | **ecology** 생태계 | **on the brink of ~** ~의 직전에 있는 | **mass extinction** 대량 멸종 | **deforestation** 삼림 벌채 | **hinder** 방해하다 | **radiation** 방사선, 전자파 | **goosebumps** 소름

Key Expressions

아래 제시된 각 expression의 구조를 이해하고, 자기만의 표현들을 생각해 봅시다.

Expression 1 — **separate the garbage:** 쓰레기를 분류하다

먼저 쓰레기를 종이, 캔, 유리, 재활용이 가능한 병으로 분류합니다.
→ We first **separate the garbage** into papers, cans, glasses, and recyclable bottles.

우리는 쓰레기를 매립용과 재활용으로 분류할 의무가 있습니다.
→ We are obligated to **separate the garbage** into trash and recyclables.

우리는 20년 이상 쓰레기를 분리해왔습니다.
→ We have been **separating the garbage** for over two decades.

Expression 2 — **belong in:** ~에 속하다

그리고 나서 쓰레기를 해당 분리수거함에 버립니다.
→ Then we throw the garbage in the section it **belongs in**.

그는 마치 이 세상 사람이 아닌 것처럼 행동합니다. → He acts as if he doesn't **belong in** this world.

양말과 속옷은 맨 위 서랍에 넣습니다. → Socks and underwear **belong in** the top drawer.

Expression 3 — **landfill trash:** 매립용 쓰레기

매립용 쓰레기만 따로 모아두는 곳도 있습니다. → We also have a section for **landfill trash** only.

절대로 매립용 쓰레기를 재활용 쓰레기통에 버려서는 안 됩니다.
→ We should never toss **landfill trash** into the recycling bins.

매립용 쓰레기가 수거된 후에 어디로 가는지 궁금합니다.
→ I wonder where all the **landfill trash** goes once it is collected.

Expression 4 — 명사 + **seems to be just too much:** ~이 지나쳐 보이다

처음에는 새로운 정책이 너무 지나쳐 보였습니다. → At first, this new policy **seemed to be just too much**.

그 판결은 너무 지나친 것 같았습니다. → The sentence **seemed to be just too much**.

그녀의 화장은 너무나도 과해 보였습니다. → Her makeup **seemed to be just too much**.

Expression 5 — **establish a** + 명사 + **culture:** ~ 문화를 세우다

저는 한국이 재활용 문화를 성공적으로 정착시켰다고 봅니다.
→ I think Korea has **established a** successful recycling **culture**.

저희의 우선 순위는 긍정적인 가족 문화를 형성하는 것이었습니다.
→ Our priority was to **establish a** positive family **culture**.

우리는 더 나은 인터넷 문화를 만들 수 있습니다. → We can **establish a** better Internet **culture**.

Topic Question & Model Answer

Topic Question

How do people recycle in your country? When do you usually recycle? Describe each step of recycling from the beginning to the end.

당신 나라에서는 어떻게 재활용을 하나요? 당신은 언제 주로 분리수거를 하나요? 쓰레기 분리수거를 하는 과정을 전부 말해보세요.

TIP FOR THE OPIc

환경 문제는 21세기 최대의 사회적 이슈 중 하나입니다. 따라서 OPIc에서 재활용 정책에 관한 질문이 등장하는 것은 자연스러운 일입니다. 실제로 재활용 정책이 어떻게 이루어지고 있는지, 그로 인한 환경적 효과는 어떠한지 등에 대해 이야기하면 됩니다.

Model Answer

| Opening |

We did our recycling this morning. We do it once a week in our neighborhood. I often forget which day we recycle on, but my parents remind me all the time.

저희는 오늘 아침 분리수거를 했습니다. 저희 동네에서는 주 1회 분리수거를 합니다. 저는 분리수거 요일을 자주 잊지만 부모님께서 늘 알려주십니다.

| Recycling Process |

We first separate the garbage into papers, cans, glasses, recyclable bottles, and plastic bags at home. Then, we take them out to the front of the apartment building and throw them in the section in which they belong. We also have a section for landfill trash only. Later, the garbage pickup company comes and collects everything.

저희는 먼저 집에서 쓰레기를 종이, 캔, 유리, 재활용이 가능한 병 그리고 비닐봉지로 분류합니다. 그리고 나서 아파트 단지 앞에 있는 분리수거함에 분류하여 버립니다. 저희 동네에는 매립용 쓰레기만 따로 모아두는 곳도 있습니다. 그러면 나중에 쓰레기를 수거해가는 회사에서 와서 가져갑니다.

| Closing |

On the other hand, the Korean government started to charge a tax on food leftovers. At first, this new policy seemed to be just too much. However, according to statistics, it is actually reducing a large amount of food leftovers. I think Korea has established a successful recycling culture. I hope that our efforts make the world greener.

한편, 한국 정부는 최근 음식물 쓰레기에 세금을 부과하기 시작했습니다. 처음에는 이 새로운 정책이 너무 지나치다 싶었습니다. 하지만 통계에 따르면, 상당량의 음식물 쓰레기가 줄었다고 합니다. 저는 우리나라가 재활용 문화를 성공적으로 정착시켰다고 봅니다. 이러한 노력이 세상을 더 푸르게 만드는데 일조하기를 바랍니다.

More Questions

〈재활용〉에 관련하여 더 나올 수 있는 OPIc 질문들을 정리한 코너입니다. 질문에 대한 brainstorming을 해보세요.

1. Tell me about the recycling process in your neighborhood. Please describe the entire process in as much detail as possible.
2. Tell me how your family and neighbors recycle. Do they participate well?

On Your Own

앞에서 주어진 Model Answer을 바탕으로, 아래의 빈칸에 들어갈 수 있는 다양한 대체 가능한 어휘 및 표현들을 참고하여 학습자 본인만의 모범 답안을 직접 만들어보세요.

| Opening |

We did our garbage recycling this morning. We do it once a week in our neighborhood. ⓐ_____.

| Recycling Process |

ⓑ_____ separate the garbage into papers, cans, glasses, recyclable bottles, and plastic bags at home. Then, we take them out to the front of the apartment building and throw them in the section in which they belong. We also have a section for landfill trash only. ⓒ_____.

| Closing |

On the other hand, the Korean government started to charge a tax over food leftovers. At first, this new policy ⓓ_____. However, ⓔ_____. I think Korea has established a ⓕ_____ recycling culture. I hope that our efforts ⓖ_____.

| Opening | We did our garbage recycling this morning. We do it once a week in our neighborhood. **ⓐ We usually do it every Tuesday**.

| Recycling Process | ⓑ We have to separate the garbage into papers, cans, glasses, recyclable bottles, and plastic bags at home. Then, we take them out to the front of the apartment building and throw them in the section in which they belong. We also have a section for landfill trash only. **ⓒ All of our neighbors recycle really well**.

| Closing | On the other hand, the Korean government started to charge a tax on food leftovers. At first, this new policy **ⓓ sounded crazy**. However, **ⓔ more and more people say that the world may come to an end due to environmental pollution**. I think Korea has established a **ⓕ brilliant** recycling culture. I hope that our efforts **ⓖ help the Earth last longer**.

본인이 만든 답안에 아래의 요소들이 포함되었는지 점검해 봅시다.

	Checklist
☐	우리나라 재활용 정책의 종류
☐	우리나라 재활용 정책의 특징
☐	쓰레기 분리수거 방법
☐	쓰레기 분리수거 참여 현황
☐	재활용 정책의 효과

Unit 53 Recycling 2

Unit 54 Police Officer 1

경찰 1

Warm Up

A Guess the Question & Answer
사진을 보면서 예상 질문과 답변을 먼저 추측해 봅시다.

B Listen & Talk
경찰관의 역할에 관한 대화를 먼저 연습해 봅시다.

🎧 08-13

A My brother says he wants to be a police officer.

B A police officer? I thought he always wanted to be a pilot.

A I know. He just changed his mind after watching the movie *Two Cops*.

B He must have enjoyed the movie very much. But it's actually dangerous to be a police officer.

A That's what I told him. They have to chase criminals, stand in the middle of the road to control traffic, and even fight rioters. That's just to name a few of the things they do.

B True. But let your brother do what he wants. Being a pilot doesn't sound that safe to me either.

A You're right. I guess I should just encourage him to follow his heart.

B Sure. He will be able to discover what he truly wants to do.

A 내 남동생이 경찰관이 되고 싶대.

B 경찰관? 난 비행기 조종사가 되고 싶다고 한 줄 알았는데.

A 그러니까 말이야. '투캅스'라는 영화를 보고 생각이 바뀌었나봐.

B 아. 영화를 너무 재미있게 봤나보네. 하지만 경찰관으로 살아가는 건 사실 위험한 일이잖아.

A 그렇게 얘기해줬어. 경찰관들은 범죄자들을 추격하고, 도로 한복판에서 교통 관리를 하고, 시위가 일어나면 맞서 싸우기까지 하잖아. 그 밖에도 하는 일이 훨씬 많지.

B 맞아. 하지만 네 남동생이 원하는 걸 하게 해. 내 생각에는 비행기 조종사도 똑같이 위험한 직업이야.

A 네 말이 맞아. 마음 가는 대로 하라고 격려해줘야겠어.

B 그럼. 본인이 진정 무엇을 하고 싶은지 발견하게 될 거야.

Vocabulary
change one's mind ~의 생각을 바꾸다 | **chase** 명사 ~의 뒤를 쫓다, 추격하다 | **control traffic** 교통을 통제하다 | **fight rioters** 시위에 맞서 싸우다 | **just to name a few** (많은 것 중에) 몇 가지를 언급하다 | **follow one's heart** ~의 마음을 따르다 | **discover** 발견하다

Key Expressions

🔑 아래 제시된 각 expression의 구조를 이해하고, 자기만의 표현들을 생각해 봅시다.

Expression 1   control: 통제하다, 단속하다, 자제시키다; 통제, 제어

그들은 교통질서를 관리합니다. → They **control** traffic.

우리의 감정을 제어하는 것은 어려운 일입니다. → It's hard to **control** our feelings.

한국은행은 물가상승을 제어하기 위하여 새로운 정책을 도입했습니다.
→ The Bank of Korea adopted a new policy to keep inflation under **control**.

Expression 2   keep + 사물/사람 + safe: ~를 안전하게 보호하다, 유지하다

경찰들은 동네 사람들의 안전을 보호해줍니다. → Police officers **keep** people **safe** in every town.

저는 엄마에게 그 편지들을 서랍에 안전하게 보관해달라고 부탁했습니다.
→ I asked my mom to **keep** the letters **safe** in her drawer.

그 선생님은 학생들을 낯선 이로부터 보호하기 위해 문을 걸어 잠갔습니다.
→ The teacher locked the door to **keep** the students **safe** from the stranger.

Expression 3   head (to + 장소): ~를 향하다, ~로 가다

가끔 저는 늦게 퇴근합니다. → Sometimes I **head** home late because of my job.

그 관광객은 바로 호텔로 향했습니다. → The tourist **headed to** the hotel right away.

우리는 회의를 마치고 커피숍으로 향했습니다. → We **headed to** the coffee shop after the meeting.

Expression 4   be held in/at/on + 장소: ~에서 (행사가) 일어나다

공공장소에서는 데모가 일어납니다. → Demonstrations **are held in** public areas.

그 행사는 학교 캠퍼스에서 열릴 것입니다. → The event will **be held on** the school campus.

그녀의 결혼식은 박물관 옆의 정원에서 진행되었습니다.
→ Her wedding **was held in** the garden next to the museum.

Expression 5   chase: ~를 추격하다

경찰관들은 범죄자를 추격합니다. → Police officers **chase** criminals.

돈을 쫓아가는 삶을 살지 마세요. → Don't live your life **chasing** money.

그 개는 고양이를 잡기 위해 빨리 달렸습니다. → The dog ran fast to **chase** the cat.

Topic Question & Model Answer

 08-14

Topic Question

Tell me about the police officers in your country. What kinds of roles do they have? Give me some examples.

당신 나라의 경찰관들에 대해 말해보세요. 그들은 어떤 역할을 하고 있나요? 몇 가지 예를 들어 말해보세요.

TIP FOR THE OPIc

한국의 경찰관에 관한 질문입니다. 우리나라 경찰관의 역할에 제한하지 말고, 누구나 일반적으로 떠올릴 수 있는 경찰관의 역할에 대해 말하면 됩니다. 교통위반을 단속하는 것, 범죄자를 추격하는 것, 치안유지, 사이버 수사, 등 말할 수 있습니다. 이러한 역할을 영어로 어떻게 표현하는지 다음 답안을 참고하여 연습해 봅시다.

Model Answer

| Opening |

Korean police officers are in charge of various things.

한국의 경찰관들은 여러 가지 역할을 담당하고 있습니다.

| Responsibilities of Police Officers |

First, they control traffic, especially when it's late at night. I see many police officers standing on the road to catch drunk drivers and speeders. Second, police officers keep people safe in every town. Sometimes when I head home late after work, I see police cars moving slowly around my neighborhood. I feel very safe when I see them. Next, Korean police officers often watch demonstrations that are held in public areas. When there are riots or strikes, we always see police officers standing nearby.

첫째, 그들은 교통을 단속하며, 특히 밤늦은 시간에 교통 관리를 합니다. 저는 많은 경찰관들이 도로 위에서 음주운전자나 과속 운전자들을 단속하는 것을 봅니다. 둘째, 경찰관들은 동네마다 주민들을 안전하게 지킵니다. 늦은 퇴근길에 저는 가끔 경찰차들이 동네를 천천히 돌고 있는 것을 발견합니다. 저는 그들을 볼 때 무척 안심을 하게 됩니다. 다음으로는, 한국의 경찰관들은 공공장소에서 시위를 감시합니다. 시위나 파업이 있을 때, 인근에 배치된 경찰관들을 목격합니다.

| Closing |

Police officers must have many other responsibilities, including chasing criminals. I guess these are just a few of the ones that I can think of.

이 밖에도 경찰관들은 범죄자를 쫓는 일을 포함해서, 다른 수많은 책임을 지닙니다. 제 생각에는 이 정도가 한국 경찰관들의 역할인 것 같습니다.

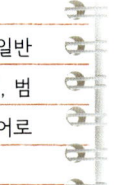

More Questions

<경찰관>에 관련하여 더 나올 수 있는 OPIc 질문들을 정리한 코너입니다. 질문에 대한 brainstorming을 해보세요.

1. Describe the police officers in your country. What do their uniforms look like? What colors are police cars?
2. Have you ever made a report to the police in your life? When did you do that? What happened?
3. Suppose you hear a thief break into your house. It's late at night, and you are in your bedroom. Call the police and ask a few things to get some help.

On Your Own

앞에서 주어진 Model Answer을 바탕으로, 아래의 빈칸에 들어갈 수 있는 다양한 대체 가능한 어휘 및 표현들을 참고하여 학습자 본인만의 모범 답안을 직접 만들어보세요.

I Opening I

Korean police officers are in charge of various things.

I Responsibilities of Police Officers I

First, they control traffic, especially when ⓐ_____.

ⓑ_____.

Second, police officers keep people safe in every town. Sometimes when I head home late after work, I see police cars moving slowly around my neighborhood. I feel very safe when I see them. Next, Korean police officers often look into

ⓒ_____.

I Closing I

Police officers must have many other responsibilities, including chasing criminals. I guess these are just a few of the ones that I can think of.

I Opening I Korean police officers are in charge of various things.

I Responsibilities of Police Officers I First, they control traffic, especially when ⓐ **it is heavy**. ⓑ **When there's a car accident, police officers are always the first to arrive at the spot**.
Second, police officers keep people safe in every town. Sometimes when I head home late after work, I see police cars moving slowly around my neighborhood. I feel very safe when I see them. Next, Korean police officers often look into ⓒ **domestic violence and violence at school**.

I Closing I Police officers must have many other responsibilities, including chasing criminals. I guess these are just a few of the ones that I can think of.

본인이 만든 답안에 아래의 요소들이 포함되었는지 점검해 봅시다.

	Checklist
☐	한국 경찰관들의 역할
☐	교통질서 유지
☐	음주(과속)운전자 단속
☐	시위 및 파업 제재
☐	시민 안전 관리
☐	범죄자 추격

Unit 55 Police Officer 2

경찰 2

Warm Up

A Guess the Question & Answer
사진을 보면서 예상 질문과 답변을 먼저 추측해 봅시다.

B Listen & Talk
경찰관과 있었던 개인적인 경험에 관한 대화를 먼저 연습해 봅시다.

🎧 08-15

A Have you ever had a personal experience with a police officer?

B Yeah, a couple of times. Once, I saw a big fight at the subway station. So I called 112.

A That was brave of you. Did the police come right away?

B I hope so. I left the spot right away after I made the call.

A Good. You did your duty anyway. What's the other experience you had with the police?

B Last week, there was a rock festival in my town. It was okay to hear people singing and playing the music aloud during the daytime. However, the festival went on till late at night, and I got upset about that.

A Sure. You don't want to be bothered after your bedtime. So did you call the police again?

B Yes, I did. Thankfully, they came to the area right away and made them stop the music. I think I did the right thing as a citizen.

A 경찰관과 개인적으로 겪은 일 있어?

B 응, 두 번. 한 번은 지하철역에서 큰 싸움을 목격했어. 그래서 112에 전화했지.

A 굉장히 용기 있었네. 경찰들이 곧바로 왔어?

B 그랬었길 바래. 난 신고한 다음에 바로 그 자리를 떠났거든.

A 잘했어. 어쨌거나 네 할 일을 했는데. 경찰관과 있었던 또 다른 경험은 뭐야?

B 지난주에 우리 동네에 록 페스티벌이 있었어. 낮에는 사람들이 노래하고 음악을 크게 틀어놓는 건 괜찮은데, 페스티벌을 밤늦게까지 하니까 뚜껑이 확 열리더라고.

A 당연하지. 자려고 하는데 방해 받으면 싫지. 그래서 또 경찰에 전화한 거야?

B 응, 그랬어. 감사하게도, 경찰관들이 바로 현장에 왔고 음악 소리도 조용해졌어. 나는 내가 시민으로서의 도리를 했다고 생각해.

Vocabulary | a personal experience 개인적인 경험 | a big fight 큰 싸움 | leave the spot 자리를 떠나다 | make the call 전화를 걸다 | be bothered 방해 받다 | do the right thing 올바른 일을 하다 | citizen 시민

Key Expressions

아래 제시된 각 expression의 구조를 이해하고, 자기만의 표현들을 생각해 봅시다.

Expression 1 — **a report on ~**: ~에 관한 보도

저는 TV에서 범죄에 대한 보도가 있을 때마다 경찰관들을 보게 됩니다.
→ I see police officers on TV when there's **a report on** crime.

그들은 그 피난민에 대한 보도를 했습니다. → They made **a report on** the refugees.

준하는 지구 온난화에 대한 보고서를 작성했습니다. → Junha made **a report on** global warming.

Expression 2 — **arrest**: 체포하다

경찰관들은 범죄자들을 체포합니다. → Police officers **arrest** criminals.

그는 기물을 파손하여 체포되었습니다. → He was **arrested** for damaging the facility.

그 사장은 뇌물수수죄로 붙잡혔습니다. → The CEO was **arrested** for bribery.

Expression 3 — **investigate**: 조사하다

저는 어떻게 그들이 범죄자들을 조사하는지 궁금합니다. → I wonder how they **investigate** criminals.

그 연구는 우리 신체에 미치는 마늘의 효과를 조사하고 있습니다.
→ The study **investigates** the effects of garlic on our bodies.

본사에서는 사람을 보내서 우리 사무실을 조사하게 했습니다.
→ The head office sent some people to **investigate** our office.

Expression 4 — **be penalized**: 벌금을 부과받다

어떤 사람들은 과속을 해서 벌금을 부과 받습니다. → Some people **are penalized** due to speeding.

그 운전자는 빨간 신호등을 위반하여 벌금을 부과받았습니다.
→ The driver **was penalized** for running the red light.

그 남자는 홈페이지에 헛소문을 작성하여 벌금을 부과받았습니다.
→ The man **was penalized** for posting rumors on the website.

Expression 5 — **be ticketed for ~**: ~로 인해 딱지를 떼다

많은 운전자들은 불법주차로 단속 딱지를 떼입니다.
→ Many other drivers **are ticketed for** parking in the wrong places.

세나는 고속도로에서 너무 천천히 운전했기 때문에 딱지를 부과 받았습니다.
→ Sena **was ticketed for** driving too slow on the highway.

그 운전자는 운전 중에 휴대 전화를 사용했다는 이유로 딱지를 떼였습니다.
→ The driver **was ticketed for** using his cell-phone while driving.

Topic Question & Model Answer

🎧 08-16

Topic Question

Tell me about an experience you had with a police officer. When was it? What happened?

당신이 경찰관과 겪었던 경험에 대해 말해보세요. 언제였나요? 무슨 일이 있었나요?

TIP FOR THE OPIc

경찰관과 있었던 개인적인 경험을 얘기해보라는 질문입니다. 많은 분들이 당황하기 쉽습니다. 살면서 경찰에게 붙잡히거나, 경찰서에 가거나, 경찰의 단속을 받는 경우는 흔치 않을 수 있기 때문입니다. 이럴 경우엔 평소 주변에서 볼 수 있는 경찰관의 모습에 대해 얘기하는 것으로 답안을 대체할 수 있습니다. 여러분이 이러한 난이도 있는 질문에 대해 얼마나 차분하고 순발력 있게 답변할 수 있는지를 보고자 하는 것이 질문의 출제 의도입니다. 아래의 모범 답안을 참고해 보세요.

Model Answer

| Opening |

I don't actually have any particular experiences with a police officer.

저는 사실 경찰관과 있었던 특별한 경험은 없습니다.

| Personal Experience with Police Officers |

The only chance I get to see police officers is on the road. When traffic is bad, I often see police officers controlling traffic. I also often see police officers on the news on TV when there's a report on crimes. Whenever the police arrest criminals, I wonder how they investigate and catch them. I've also seen people caught for speeding by the police. Many other drivers are ticketed for parking in the wrong places.

제가 경찰관들을 볼 수 있는 기회는 도로 위에서 뿐입니다. 교통 상황이 안 좋으면, 저는 종종 교통을 통제하는 경찰관들을 보게 됩니다. 저는 또한 TV에서 범죄에 대한 뉴스 보도가 있을 때 경찰관들을 자주 봅니다. 경찰이 범죄자들을 체포할 때마다, 저는 그들이 어떻게 조사에 착수하고 범인들을 붙잡게 되는지 궁금합니다. 저는 또한 과속으로 인해 경찰관으로부터 잡히는 사람들을 봤습니다. 다른 많은 운전자들은 불법 주차로 딱지를 떼입니다.

| Closing |

These are some of the cases regarding the police that I have experienced first hand.

이러한 점들이 제가 경찰관들에 관련하여 직접적으로 경험한 몇 가지 사항들입니다.

More Questions

〈경찰관〉에 관련하여 더 나올 수 있는 OPIc 질문들을 정리한 코너입니다. 질문에 대한 brainstorming을 해보세요.

1. Do you often see police officers? When do you see them? What are their roles?
2. Have you ever been caught by the police for breaking the law? When was it? Which law did you break?
3. What are the responsibilities of the police in your country? What do you think their most important duty is? Why?

앞에서 주어진 Model Answer을 바탕으로, 아래의 빈칸에 들어갈 수 있는 다양한 대체 가능한 어휘 및 표현들을 참고하여 학습자 본인만의 모범 답안을 직접 만들어보세요.

| Opening |

ⓐ_____.

| Personal Experience with Police Officers |

ⓑ_____.

Then, I saw a police station nearby, so I went in. I saw a few police officers sitting at their desks. ⓒ_____.

He kindly explained where the building was located and even drew a rough map for me.

ⓓ_____.

| Closing |

This is the only case regarding the police that I have experienced first hand.

| Opening | ⓐ **I remember that I once went to the police station to ask for directions to a building. It was my first visit to the city.**

| Personal Experience with Police Officers | ⓑ **I was supposed to interview with a company that day, but I got lost.** Then, I saw a police station nearby, so I went in. I saw a few police officers sitting at their desks. ⓒ **I went to one of them and asked if he knew the building I was looking for.** He kindly explained where the building was located and even drew a rough map for me. ⓓ **Thanks to his help, I was able to find the building and safely arrived at the interview venue in time.**

| Closing | This is the only case regarding the police that I have experienced first hand.

	Checklist
☐	경찰관에 얽힌 에피소드
☐	범죄를 신고한 경험
☐	무단횡단하다 단속된 경험
☐	운전하다가 벌금 부과당한 경험
☐	TV에서 본 경찰관 역할

본인이 만든 답안에 아래의 요소들이 포함되었는지 점검해 봅시다.

Unit 56 Hospital 1

병원 1

Warm Up

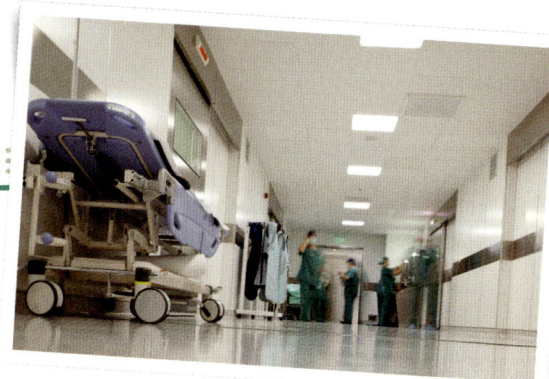

A Guess the Question & Answer
사진을 보면서 예상 질문과 답변을 먼저 추측해 봅시다.

B Listen & Talk
병원 진료에 관한 대화를 연습해 봅시다.

🎧 08-17

A Do you know any oriental clinic that is good with acupuncture?

B Yeah, I know one next to my office. Why? Do you need to get acupuncture?

A I do. I sprained my ankle this morning while I was jogging.

B That must hurt. You'd better visit the doctor. I'll give you her number.

A Thanks. Is the doctor reliable?

B She has a good reputation in this field. Many of my co-workers have been treated by her, and they have all been satisfied.

A Great. I'll make a reservation right away.

B I hope you get better soon.

A Thanks.

A 침 잘 놓는 한의원 혹시 알아?

B 응, 우리 사무실 옆에 하나 있어. 왜? 침 맞아야 돼?

A 응. 오늘 아침 조깅하다가 발목을 삐었거든.

B 아프겠구나. 병원에 가봐야겠다. 선생님 번호 알려줄게.

A 고마워. 선생님은 신뢰할 만한 분이야?

B 이 분야에서는 명성이 자자하셔. 회사 동료들이 많이 가서 치료를 받았는데 다들 만족해 해.

A 잘됐다. 당장 예약해야겠어.

B 쾌차하길 바래.

A 고마워.

Vocabulary | oriental clinic 한의원 | acupuncture 침 | sprain one's ankle 발목을 삐다 | visit the doctor 병원에 가다 | reliable 신뢰할 만한 | have a good reputation 명성이 높다 | field 분야 | treatment 치료 | make a reservation 예약하다

Key Expressions

🔑 아래 제시된 각 expression의 구조를 이해하고, 자기만의 표현들을 생각해 봅시다.

Expression 1　**for many years: 다년간, 여러 해 동안**

저는 그 병원에 다년간 다녔습니다. → I have been going to the clinic **for many years**.

저는 수년간 피아노 치는 것을 연습했습니다. → I've been practicing the piano **for many years**.

그 여인은 여러 해 동안 잃어버린 아들을 찾았습니다.
→ The woman searched for her lost son **for many years**.

Expression 2　**a regular checkup: 정기 검진**

저는 정기 검진을 받으러 갑니다. → I go for **a regular checkup**.

1년에 한 번은 정기 검진을 받으세요. → Get **a regular checkup** once a year.

정기 검진을 받는 것은 중요합니다. → It is crucial to have **regular checkups**.

Expression 3　**waiting room: 대기실**

그곳엔 잘 갖춰진 대기실이 있습니다. → They have a nice **waiting room**.

대기실은 매우 아늑하게 느껴졌습니다. → The **waiting room** felt very cozy.

많은 사람들은 대기실에서 줄을 섰습니다. → Many people were lined up in the **waiting room**.

Expression 4　**pick up: 들다, 줍다**

저는 항상 패션 잡지 하나를 골라 봅니다. → I always **pick up** one of the fashion magazines.

저는 상자에 있는 초콜릿 한 조각을 골랐습니다. → I **picked up** a piece of chocolate from the box.

그 선생님은 바닥에 있는 분필을 주웠습니다. → The teacher **picked up** the chalk on the floor.

Expression 5　**wait for one's turn: ~의 순서를 기다리다**

저는 제 순서를 기다리는 동안 책을 봅니다. → I read books while I **wait for my turn**.

인내하고 네 차례를 기다려라. → Be patient and **wait for your turn**.

저는 물을 마시기 위해 제 차례를 기다려야 했습니다. → I had to **wait for my turn** to drink water.

Topic Question & Model Answer

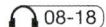

Topic Question

Which dental clinic do you visit? How often do you go there? Why do you go to that clinic? Give me a good description of the dental clinic that you go to.

당신은 어느 치과에 가나요? 얼마나 자주 가나요? 왜 그 치과에 가나요? 당신이 가는 치과에 대해 자세히 묘사해보세요.

TIP FOR THE OPIc

치과에 관한 질문입니다. 사실 치과에 정기적으로 가는 분들은 많지 않습니다. 하지만 누구나 한 번 쯤은 치과에서 치료 받은 경험이 있을 것입니다. 충치 치료, 신경 치료, 사랑니 발치, 스케일링, 교정 등 다양한 이유로 진료를 받을 수 있습니다. 또한 치과 내부 설명은 곧 병원 내부를 떠올리면 됩니다. 일반적인 병원 내부 시설 및 직원, 분위기 등을 생각하며 묘사하면 어렵지 않게 답안을 만들어볼 수 있습니다.

Model Answer

| Opening |

I go to the ABC Dental Clinic in my city. It takes only 10 minutes to walk there from my apartment. My family and I have been going to this dental clinic for many years.

저는 동네에 있는 ABC 치과에 갑니다. 제가 거주하는 아파트에서 도보로 10분밖에 안 걸립니다. 제 가족과 저는 여러 해 동안 이 병원을 다녔습니다.

| Description of the Dental Clinic |

We visit this clinic because it's close to our place and the service is good. In addition, the dentist and the nurses are friendly. I go to the clinic once a year. I go for a regular checkup to see if my teeth are healthy. Many people say it's scary to go to the dentist. However, I feel comfortable whenever I visit the clinic. The clinic has a nice waiting room with various magazines and beverages.

우리는 이 치과가 집에서 가깝고 친절해서 갑니다. 또한 치과 의사 선생님과 간호사들도 친절합니다. 저는 매해 한 번씩 그 치과에 갑니다. 제 치아가 건강한지 보기 위해 정기 검진을 받습니다. 많은 사람들은 치과에 가는 것이 무섭다고 합니다. 하지만 저는 병원에 갈 때마다 편한 느낌입니다. 병원에는 잘 갖춰진 대기실이 있는데, 다양한 잡지와 음료가 비치되어 있습니다.

| Atmosphere of the Clinic and Closing |

I always pick up one of the fashion magazines there while I wait my turn. I like that soft classical music plays there all the time.

저는 항상 패션 잡지 하나를 골라 들고 순서를 기다리며 봅니다. 저는 그들이 잔잔한 클래식 음악을 늘 틀어놓는 것이 좋습니다.

More Questions

〈병원〉에 관련하여 더 나올 수 있는 OPIc 질문들을 정리한 코너입니다. 질문에 대한 brainstorming을 해보세요.

1. There's a situation I want you to act out. One of your family members got sick all of a sudden. Call your doctor, explain your family member's symptoms, and ask 3 to 4 questions to get some help.

2. How often do you go to the hospital? What's the purpose of your visit?

3. Tell me about an episode you had at the hospital. When was it? What happened? I want to know all about it.

On Your Own

앞에서 주어진 Model Answer을 바탕으로, 아래의 빈칸에 들어갈 수 있는 다양한 대체 가능한 어휘 및 표현들을 참고하여 학습자 본인만의 모범 답안을 직접 만들어보세요.

| Opening |

I go to the ABC Dental Clinic ⓐ_____. It takes only 10 minutes to walk there from my school. I have been going to this dental clinic for a couple years.

| Description of the Dental Clinic |

I visit this clinic because ⓑ_____ and the service is good. In addition, the dentist and the nurses are friendly. I go to the clinic ⓒ_____. I go to ⓓ_____. Many people say it's scary to go to the dentist. However, I feel comfortable whenever I visit the clinic. The clinic has a nice waiting room with various magazines and beverages.

| Atmosphere of the Clinic and Closing |

I always pick up one of the fashion magazines there while I wait my turn. I like that soft classical music plays there all the time.

| Opening | I go to the ABC Dental Clinic ⓐ **nearby my school campus**. It takes only 10 minutes to walk there from my school. I have been going to this dental clinic for a couple years.

| Description of the Dental Clinic | I visit this clinic because ⓑ **it's close to my school** and the service is good. In addition, the dentist and the nurses are friendly. I go to the clinic ⓒ **every month**. I go to ⓓ **get my braces checked**. Many people say it's scary to go to the dentist. However, I feel comfortable whenever I visit the clinic. The clinic has a nice waiting room with various magazines and beverages.

| Atmosphere of the Clinic and Closing | I always pick up one of the fashion magazines there while I wait my turn. I like that soft classical music plays there all the time.

본인이 만든 답안에 아래의 요소들이 포함되었는지 점검해 봅시다.

	Checklist
☐	내가 다니는 병원 이름
☐	어디에 위치하는지
☐	언제부터 다녔는지
☐	왜 그곳에 가는지
☐	병원 의사 및 직원 묘사
☐	실내 분위기 묘사

Unit 57 Hospital 2

병원 2

Warm Up

A Guess the Question & Answer
사진을 보면서 예상 질문과 답변을 먼저 추측해 봅시다.

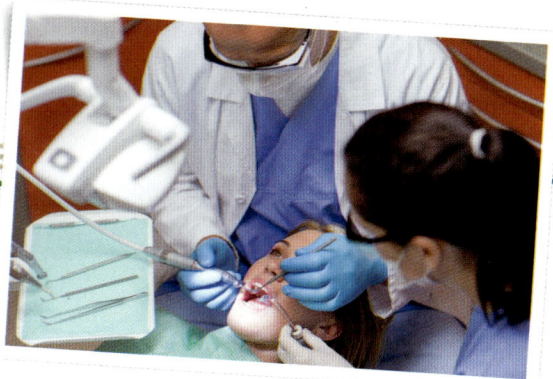

B Listen & Talk
치과 치료에 관한 대화를 연습해 봅시다. 🎧 08-19

A When was the last time you went to the dentist?
B Last month. I went for a regular checkup.
A Was there anything wrong with your teeth?
B No, they were all fine. But the dentist said that one of my wisdom teeth is coming in.
A Is that a problem?
B It could be if the tooth invades other one's space.
A Then will you have to get your tooth pulled?
B In case it affects other tooth, I shall have to get it pulled.
A Ouch. I hate having teeth pulled.
B So do I. I always take a deep breath before I get my teeth pulled.

A 마지막으로 치과에 간 게 언제야?
B 지난 달. 정기 검진 받으러 다녀왔어.
A 치아에 문제는 없었어?
B 아니, 다 괜찮았어. 그런데 선생님이 나보고 사랑니가 하나 자라고 있대.
A 그게 문제야?
B 다른 치아의 공간을 침범하면 그럴 수 있지.
A 그러면 치아를 뽑아야 되는 거야?
B 다른 치아를 아프게 하면, 아마 뽑아야 할 거야.
A 아이쿠. 난 이 뽑는 게 정말 싫어.
B 나도 마찬가지야. 난 언제나 이를 뽑기 전엔 심호흡을 크게 한 번 해.

Vocabulary
go to the dentist 치과에 가다 | a regular checkup 정기 검진 | wisdom tooth 사랑니 | invade 침범하다 | space 공간 | get one's tooth [teeth] pulled ~의 치아를 뽑아내다 | take a deep breath 심호흡을 크게 하다

Key Expressions

아래 제시된 각 expression의 구조를 이해하고, 자기만의 표현들을 생각해 봅시다.

Expression 1   have teeth pulled [cleaned]: 이를 뽑다[스케일링을 하다]

저는 사랑니 중 하나를 뽑기 위해 마취를 해야 했습니다.
→ I had to go under anesthesia to **have** one of **my wisdom teeth pulled**.

저는 스케일링을 하고 나서 상쾌해졌습니다. → I felt fresh after **having my teeth cleaned**.

저는 이를 뽑으러 치과에 가는 것이 항상 두렵습니다.
→ I always dread going to the dentist to **have a tooth pulled**.

Expression 2   family ritual: 가족 의식(의례)

그것은 해마다 우리 가족이 하는 가족의식입니다. → It's a **family ritual** that we do every year.

우리는 하나의 가족 의식처럼 크리스마스에 카드를 주고 받습니다.
→ We exchange cards on Christmas as a **family ritual**.

금요일마다 멕시칸 음식을 먹는 것은 제 가족의 의식처럼 되었습니다.
→ Having Mexican food on every Friday became our **family ritual**.

Expression 3   very skillful: 매우 능숙한, 숙련된

그는 친절하고 매우 숙련되었습니다. → He is friendly and **very skillful**.

래빈이는 웹 디자인을 매우 능숙하게 합니다. → Raebin is **very skillful** at web-designing.

세라가모씨는 구두를 만드는 솜씨가 뛰어납니다. → Mr. Seragamo is **very skillful** at making shoes.

Expression 4   recover quickly: 쾌차하다, 빨리 회복하다

뿐만 아니라, 저는 매우 빨리 회복했습니다. → In addition, I **recovered** very **quickly**.

주희는 치료를 받은 후에 빨리 회복되었습니다. → Juhee **recovered quickly** after the treatment.

제 할아버지께서는 그 약을 드신 후에 빠르게 회복되셨습니다.
→ My grandfather **recovered quickly** after taking the medicine.

Expression 5   give a shot: 주사를 놓다

저는 그가 주사를 놓았을 때 별로 아프지 않았습니다. → I felt little pain when he **gave** me **a shot**.

그 의사는 그 환자에게 주사를 놨습니다. → The doctor **gave a shot** to the patient.

그 간호사는 갓 태어난 아기에게 주사를 놓았습니다. → The nurse **gave a shot** to the newborn baby.

Topic Question & Model Answer

Topic Question

When was the last time you went to the dental clinic? What did you do there? Was the doctor friendly? Tell me everything about your last visit to the dental clinic.

당신이 언제 가장 최근 치과에 간 적은 언제였나요? 그곳에서 무슨 일이 있었죠? 의사 선생님은 친절했나요? 치과에 마지막으로 간 것에 대해 모든 것을 말해보세요.

TIP FOR THE OPIc

마지막으로 치과에 갔던 경험에 대해 얘기하라는 질문입니다. 지난달(last month)이나 지난주(last week)에 갔었고 방문 목적은 치아 스케일링 혹은 정기 검진이었다고 얘기하면 됩니다. 물론, 실제 치과에 최근 다녀온 경험이 있는 분은 경험을 바탕으로 말을 하면 될 것입니다. 의사 선생님이나 직원들이 치료를 잘해주거나 친절하게 대해준다고 말하는 것이 일반적입니다.

Model Answer

| Opening |

I went to the dental clinic last month. I went there with my family. It was for a regular checkup. I had my teeth cleaned after the checkup. It's a family ritual that we do every year.

저는 지난달 치과에 갔었습니다. 가족과 함께 갔었습니다. 정기 검진을 위한 것이었습니다. 저는 검진 후 스케일링을 했습니다. 매년 저희 가족이 하는 의례적인 일입니다.

| Description of the Dentist |

The dental clinic we went to is located in our city. We've been going there ever since we moved to our current house, so we are familiar with the dentist. The dentist is in his early 60s. He is friendly and very skillful. Once, I had to go under anesthesia to have one of my wisdom teeth pulled, but I felt little pain when he gave me a shot in my gums. In addition, I recovered very quickly.

저희 가족이 다녀온 치과는 동네에 있는 것입니다. 우리는 지금 살고 있는 집에 이사 온 이후로 계속 그 치과만 다녔기 때문에 치과 의사와도 친숙합니다. 선생님은 60대 초반이십니다. 그 분은 친절하시며 매우 능숙하게 치료하십니다. 한번은 제가 사랑니를 뽑기 위해서 마취를 해야 했는데, 잇몸에 주사를 놓으실 때 통증을 거의 못 느꼈습니다. 또한 회복도 매우 빨랐습니다.

| Closing |

The nurses and staff members are kind, too. They have become like old friends. I don't think our family will visit any other dental clinic.

간호사와 직원들도 친절합니다. 그들은 마치 오래된 친구들 같습니다. 제 가족이 다른 치과를 가는 일은 없을 것 같아요.

More Questions

〈병원〉에 관련하여 더 나올 수 있는 OPIc 질문들을 정리한 코너입니다. 질문에 대한 brainstorming을 해보세요.

1. When was the last time you went to the hospital? What was the purpose of your visit? Did you get any treatment?
2. Tell me about a hospital in your neighborhood. What does it look like? How many doctors and nurses are there? Give me a good description of the hospital.

On Your Own

앞에서 주어진 Model Answer을 바탕으로, 아래의 빈칸에 들어갈 수 있는 다양한 대체 가능한 어휘 및 표현들을 참고하여 학습자 본인만의 모범 답안을 직접 만들어보세요.

| Opening |

I went to the dental clinic ⓐ_____ It was for a regular checkup.

ⓑ_____.

| Description of the Dentist |

The dental clinic we went to is located in ⓒ_____. I've been going there ever since ⓓ_____, so I'm familiar with the dentist. The dentist is in ⓔ_____. She is friendly and very skillful. Once, I had to go under anesthesia to get a ⓕ_____ pulled, but I felt little pain when she gave me a shot in my gums. In addition, my recovery was fast.

| Closing |

The nurses and staff are kind, too. They have become like old friends. I don't think I will visit any other dental clinic.

| Opening | I went to the dental clinic ⓐ **last week**. It was for a regular checkup. ⓑ **I go to the dentist once a year unless there's a problem with my teeth**.

| Description of the Dentist | The dental clinic I went to is located in ⓒ **the same building as my office**. I've been going there ever since ⓓ **I started working at my current office**, so I'm familiar with the dentist. The dentist is in ⓔ **her mid-40s**. She is friendly and very skillful. Once, I had to go under anesthesia to get a ⓕ **decayed tooth** pulled, but I felt little pain when she gave me a shot in my gums. In addition, my recovery was fast.

| Closing | The nurses and staff are kind, too. They have become like old friends. I don't think I will visit any other dental clinic.

본인이 만든 답안에 아래의 요소들이 포함되었는지 점검해 봅시다.

	Checklist
☐	언제 마지막 치과에 갔는지
☐	방문 목적이 무엇이었는지
☐	어디에 있는 병원인지
☐	치료 받을 때 아프진 않았는지
☐	의사 및 직원들은 어떤지

Unit 58 Bank 1

은행 1

Warm Up

A Guess the Question & Answer
사진을 보면서 예상 질문과 답변을 먼저 추측해 봅시다.

B Listen & Talk
내가 이용하는 은행에 관한 대화를 연습해 봅시다.

🎧 08-21

A Do you often go to the bank?	A 넌 은행에 자주 가?
B Not really. Maybe once a year?	B 아니 안 그래. 1년에 한 번 정도?
A That's a surprise. I thought you would be very strict with your budget.	A 놀라운걸. 난 네가 생활비 예산에 있어 굉장히 엄격할 줄 알았어.
B I am. It's only that I use the Internet banking system instead of visiting the bank myself.	B 맞아. 다만 은행에 직접 가지 않고 인터넷 뱅킹 제도를 이용할 뿐이야.
A The Internet banking system?	A 인터넷 뱅킹 제도?
B Yes. I can check my bank account, wire money, and even pay my bills for the national insurance service plan.	B 응. 계좌 확인도 하고, 송금도 하고 국가보험료도 납부할 수 있어.
A It sounds so complicated to me. I still check my bankbook at the bank.	A 나한테는 너무 복잡할 것 같아. 나는 여전히 은행에 가서 통장을 확인하는데.
B That's fine. We just have different preferences for managing our finances. You can also get free consulting on your saving plans at the bank.	B 좋은데 뭘. 각자 다른 재정 관리법을 선호하는 것뿐이지. 또 은행에 가면 무료로 저축 관련 상담도 받을 수 있잖아.
A Sure. It's good to get advice from experts.	A 물론이지. 전문가의 조언을 받는 건 좋은 거야.

Vocabulary
be strict with ~ ~에 대해 엄격하다 | Internet banking system 인터넷 뱅킹 시스템 | check one's bank account ~의 계좌를 확인하다 | wire money 송금하다 | pay one's bills 금액을 지불하다 | national insurance service plan 국민보험제도 | complicated 복잡한 | free consulting 무료 상담 | saving plans 저축 계획 | get advice from ~ ~로부터 조언을 받다 | expert 전문가

Key Expressions

아래 제시된 각 expression의 구조를 이해하고, 자기만의 표현들을 생각해 봅시다.

Expression 1   **mainly use + 명사:** ~를 주로 이용하다

저는 한국의 KBC 은행을 주로 이용합니다. → I **mainly use** KBC Bank in Korea.

지은이는 그녀의 그림에 주로 보라색을 사용했습니다. → Jieun **mainly used** purple in her painting.

저는 계산할 때 주로 신용카드를 사용합니다. → I **mainly use** my credit card when I pay the bills.

Expression 2   **nationwide:** 전국적으로, 전국의

그 은행은 전국에서 가장 많은 지점을 보유하고 있습니다.
→ The bank has the most branches **nationwide**.

그 상점은 전국에 200개가 넘는 지점이 있습니다.
→ The store has more than 200 branches **nationwide**.

그 케이블 방송국은 그 쇼를 전국적으로 방영했습니다.
→ The cable TV station broadcasted the show **nationwide**.

Expression 3   **check one's bankbook:** ~의 통장을 확인하다

저는 통장을 확인하기 위해 은행에 갑니다. → I visit the bank to **check my bankbook**.

엄마는 내 통장을 확인하여 내가 진실을 말하는지 확인했습니다.
→ My mom **checked my bankbook** to see if I was telling the truth.

통장을 확인해서 그들이 정확한 금액을 보냈는지 보아라.
→ **Check your bankbook** and see if you were sent correct amount of money.

Expression 4   **pay one's bills/rent/loans (for) ~:** ~(에 대한) 청구액/집세/대출금을 납부하다

저는 국민 보험제도의 청구액을 납부합니다. → I **pay my bills for** the national insurance service plan.

당신은 집세를 지불했습니까? → Have you **paid your rent**?

저는 대출금을 갚는데 3년이 걸렸습니다. → It took 3 years for me to **pay off my loans**.

Expression 5   **talk to (an expert):** (전문가와) 얘기하다

언제나 전문가와 얘기하는 편이 낫습니다. → It's always better to **talk to an expert**.

우리는 집을 구매하는 것에 관해 전문가와 얘기했습니다.
→ We **talked to an expert** about purchasing a house.

무슨 문제가 있으면, 미스터 신에게 말하십시오. 그는 직업 상담 전문가입니다.
→ If there are any problems, **talk to** Mr. Shin. He's an expert job consultant.

Topic Question & Model Answer

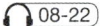

Topic Question

Tell me about the banks in your country. Which one do you use the most often? What does it look like? What do you do when you visit the bank?

당신 나라의 은행에 대해 말해보세요. 가장 자주 이용하는 은행은 어디인가요? 그 은행의 모습은 어떤가요? 은행에 갈 때 당신은 무엇을 하나요?

TIP FOR THE OPIc

한국의 은행에 관한 질문입니다. 내가 자주 가는 은행 혹은 일반적인 은행의 모습을 기준으로 브레인스토밍하면 됩니다. 자주 가는 은행 이름은 내게 가장 친숙한 은행 이름을 언급하는 것이 말하기에도 편할 것입니다. 또한 은행 내부 시설에 관해서는 ATM(현금자동입출금기), 은행 창구, 대기실 등에 대해 얘기할 수 있습니다. 점심시간 혹은 월말에는 붐빈다는 점, 은행 대기 좌석에 비치된 잡지와 음료수, 친절한 직원 등을 설명할 수 있습니다. 은행가는 목적은 저축, 계좌 개설, 통장 확인, 예적금 가입 등을 말하면 됩니다.

Model Answer

| Opening |

I mainly use KBC Bank in Korea. It is one of the top three major banks and has the largest branches nationwide.

저는 보통 한국의 KBC 은행을 이용합니다. 3대 은행 중의 하나이며, 전국적으로 가장 많은 지점을 보유하고 있습니다.

| My Favorite Bank |

The KBC Bank in my neighborhood is neat and clean. When I arrive at the bank, the first thing I see is the security guard welcoming visitors. Then, I see the bank tellers sitting at their desks. Their uniforms are white and navy blue. The bank tellers are friendly and fast.

우리 이웃에 있는 KBC 은행은 깨끗하고 잘 갖춰져 있습니다. 은행에 가면, 가장 먼저 보게 되는 것은 고객들을 환영해주는 경비원입니다. 그리고는 책상 앞에 앉아 있는 은행 직원들을 보게 됩니다. 그들의 유니폼은 흰색과 남색으로 이루어져 있습니다. 은행 직원들은 친절하며 신속하게 일합니다.

| Purpose of the Visit |

I visit the bank about once a week to check my bankbook or to pay my bills for the national insurance service plan. Sometimes I ask the bank teller for advice on strategic saving plans. It's always better to talk to an expert.

저는 일주일에 한 번 정도 은행에 가서 통장을 확인하여 국민 보험료를 납부합니다. 가끔은 은행 직원에게 전략적인 저축 계획에 관해 물어보고는 합니다. 전문가에게 얘기하는 것이 낫다고 언제나 생각합니다.

| Closing |

Overall, I'm pretty satisfied with the service and system at KBC Bank.

아무쪼록 저는 KBC 은행의 서비스 및 제도에 꽤 만족합니다.

More Questions

〈은행〉에 관련하여 더 나올 수 있는 OPIc 질문들을 정리한 코너입니다. 질문에 대한 brainstorming을 해보세요.

1. Do you often go to the bank? Which bank do you go to? What do you do there?
2. Are you good at saving money? How many bank accounts do you have?
3. Tell me about the bank you go to. How's the service? Are the bank tellers friendly? How are they dressed?

On Your Own

앞에서 주어진 Model Answer을 바탕으로, 아래의 빈칸에 들어갈 수 있는 다양한 대체 가능한 어휘 및 표현들을 참고하여 학습자 본인만의 모범 답안을 직접 만들어보세요.

| Opening |

I mainly use KBC Bank in Korea. It is one of the ⓐ_____.

| My Favorite Bank |

The KBC Bank ⓑ_____. When I arrive at the bank, the first thing I see is the security guard welcoming visitors. Then, I see the bank tellers sitting at their desks. ⓒ_____.

| Purpose of the Visit |

I visit the bank about ⓓ_____ to check my bankbook or to ⓔ_____. Sometimes I ask the bank teller for advice on strategic saving plans. It's always better to talk to an expert.

| Closing |

Overall, I'm pretty satisfied with the service and system at KBC Bank.

| Opening | I mainly use KBC Bank in Korea. It is one of the **ⓐ biggest banks in the nation**.

| My Favorite Bank | The KBC Bank **ⓑ next to my office is neat and clean**. When I arrive at the bank, the first thing I see is the security guard welcoming visitors. Then, I see the bank tellers sitting at their desks. **ⓒ I can also see the ATM in the corner and the loan counselors sitting on the other side of the bank**.

| Purpose of the Visit | I visit the bank about **ⓓ once a month** to check my bankbook or to **ⓔ withdraw some cash**. Sometimes I ask the bank teller for advice on strategic saving plans. It's always better to talk to an expert.

| Closing | Overall, I'm pretty satisfied with the service and system at KBC Bank.

본인이 만든 답안에 아래의 요소들이 포함되었는지 점검해 봅시다.

Checklist
내가 자주 가는 은행 이름
은행의 특징 및 시설
은행 내부 직원 묘사
은행 시설물 묘사
방문 목적 설명
은행에 대한 소감

Unit 59 Bank 2

은행 2

Warm Up

A Guess the Question & Answer
사진을 보면서 예상 질문과 답변을 먼저 추측해 봅시다.

B Listen & Talk
은행의 내부를 묘사하는 대화를 연습해 봅시다.

🎧 08-23

A Which bank do you use the most often?

B I mainly use Happy Bank.

A Why do you go to Happy Bank? Is the service good?

B Sure. The service is satisfying. It also has branches in almost every city, so it's convenient to use.

A What about the facilities? What do you see when you go there?

B The facilities? I just see some ATMs and a small machine that provides numbers so that you can wait for your turn. There is also a big TV screen on the ceiling. Oh, and there's a small screen on the wall that displays the currency rate.

A I see. It sounds very typical.

B What else did you expect? Banks all look the same. It's only that Happy Bank has the most branches nationwide.

A 넌 어떤 은행을 가장 자주 이용해?

B 난 주로 행복은행에 가.

A 왜 행복은행에 가는데? 서비스가 좋아?

B 그럼. 서비스가 만족스러워. 그리고 거의 모든 동네마다 지점이 있어서 이용하기도 편리해.

A 시설은 어떤데? 은행에 가면 뭐가 있어?

B 시설? 그냥 ATM이랑 번호표 기계가 보이지. 그리고 천장에 달린 커다란 TV도 있고. 아, 또 벽에 걸린 환율 동향 표시 기계도 있지.

A 그렇구나. 되게 평범하네.

B 뭘 기대했는데? 은행이 다 똑같이 생겼지 뭐. 그 은행은 다만 전국에 가장 많은 지점이 개설되었을 뿐이야.

Vocabulary

satisfying 만족스러운 | facilities 시설물 | ATM 현금 자동 입출금기 (Automated Teller Machine) | display 전시하다, 나타내다 | currency rate 환율 | typical 전형적인 | have the most branches 가장 많은 지점을 보유하다 | nationwide 전국적으로

Key Expressions

아래 제시된 각 expression의 구조를 이해하고, 자기만의 표현들을 생각해 봅시다.

Expression 1 changes have occurred: 변화들이 생겼다

달라진 점이 분명히 있을 것입니다. → There must be some **changes** that **have occurred**.

그 도시에는 놀라울 만한 변화들이 생겨났습니다. → Remarkable **changes have occurred** in the city.

그들이 새 정책을 도입한 이후에 많은 변화들이 생겼습니다.
→ Many **changes have occurred** after the new policy was adopted.

Expression 2 the hours of service: 업무(운영) 시간

그 중 하나는 바로 업무 시간이 달라진 것입니다. → One of the changes is **the hours of service**.

우리는 영국문화원에 전화하여 업무 시간을 물어봤습니다.
→ I called the British Council to ask **the hours of service**.

우체국 업무시간은 오전 9시부터 오후 6시까지입니다.
→ **The hours of service** at the post office are from 9 to 6.

Expression 3 bring many changes to ~: ~에 많은 변화를 가져오다

기술 발달은 은행 시스템에 많은 변화를 가져왔습니다.
→ Advanced technology has **brought many changes to** the banking system.

세계화는 우리 문화에 많은 변화를 가져왔습니다.
→ Globalization has **brought many changes to** our culture.

경기 침체는 시장에 많은 변화를 일으켰습니다.
→ The economic downturn has **brought many changes to** the market.

Expression 4 be performed by ~: ~에 의해 ~가 수행되다, 음악이 연주되다

은행 직원들은 많은 일을 담당했었습니다. → Lots of work used to **be performed by** bank tellers.

그 청년은 많은 기적을 일으켰습니다. → Miracles **were performed by** the young man.

그 음악은 스페인 음악가에 의해 연주되었습니다. → The music **was performed by** a Spanish artist.

Expression 5 be replaced by ~: ~로 대체되다

그 노동자들이 기계들에 의해 대체되어 왔습니다. → The workers **have been replaced by** machines.

그의 역할은 다른 사람에 의해 대체되었습니다. → He **was replaced by** another person.

존 대신 수가 회의에 참석하였습니다. → John **was replaced by** Sue at the meeting.

Topic Question & Model Answer

🎧 08-24

Topic Question

Did you go to the bank with your parents when you were younger? How was it different from the banks you visit these days?

당신이 어릴 때 부모님과 은행에 갔었나요? 요즘 당신이 가는 은행과 어떻게 다른가요?

> **TIP FOR THE OPIc**
>
> 한국의 은행이 과거와 현재 달라진 점을 얘기하라는 질문입니다. 어릴 적 은행에 갔던 기억은 잘 안 날 것입니다. 하지만 최근 몇 년간 달라진 점들을 1~2가지 언급하더라도 과거와 현재의 차이를 말할 수 있습니다. 예를 들어 업무 시간 변경, 신용 카드 발급, 인터넷 뱅킹이나 모바일 뱅킹의 도입, 기계를 사용한 청구액 납부 등이 은행의 달라진 모습이라고 할 수 있습니다.

Model Answer

| Opening |

I can't really remember the banks I visited during my childhood. I don't think I went to a bank until I became high school student. Of course, I realize that there must be some changes that have occurred at banks since then.

저는 어릴 적에 갔던 은행에 대해서는 잘 기억이 나지 않습니다. 고등학생이 되기 전까지는 은행에 가지 않았던 것 같습니다. 물론, 과거와 현재 은행이 달라진 점은 분명히 있을 것이라고 생각합니다.

| Changes in Korean Banks |

One of the changes is the hours of service. Korean banks used to be open from 9 a.m. to 4:30 p.m. However, these days, they are open until 4 p.m. Advanced technology has also brought many changes to the bank system. In the past, there weren't any Internet banking or mobile banking services, but these days, all Korean banks use both systems. In addition, work that used to be performed by bank tellers is now done by machines. It has become more convenient to pay bills and to check one's account.

그 중 하나는 바로 업무 시간의 변화입니다. 예전에 한국의 은행들은 오전 9시에 개점해서 오후 4시 30분까지 영업했습니다. 하지만 요새는 오후 4시까지만 합니다. 또한 기술의 발달은 은행 제도에도 많은 변화를 가져왔습니다. 과거에는 인터넷 뱅킹이나 모바일 뱅킹이 안 됐는데, 요새는 모든 한국의 은행들이 시행하고 있습니다. 또한, 은행 직원들이 담당하던 업무들은 이제 기계가 많이 대체하고 있습니다. 덕분에 청구액 납부 및 통장 정리가 훨씬 쉬워졌습니다.

| Closing |

These are some of the changes that have occurred at Korean banks.

이러한 점들이 한국의 은행에 나타난 몇 가지 변화입니다.

More Questions

〈은행〉에 관련하여 더 나올 수 있는 OPIc 질문들을 정리한 코너입니다. 질문에 대한 brainstorming을 해보세요.

1. Have you ever had an embarrassing moment at the bank? For example, were you ever unable to get a service since you didn't bring your ID card? Or have you ever left your check card at the ATM?

2. Do you think the banking system in your country is convenient? Why do you think so?

On Your Own

앞에서 주어진 Model Answer을 바탕으로, 아래의 빈칸에 들어갈 수 있는 다양한 대체 가능한 어휘 및 표현들을 참고하여 학습자 본인만의 모범 답안을 직접 만들어보세요.

| Opening |

I can't really remember the banks I visited during my childhood. I don't think I went to a bank until I became ⓐ_____. Of course, I realize that there must be some changes that have occurred at banks since then.

| Changes in Korean Banks |

One of the changes is the hours of service. Korean banks used to be open from 9 a.m. to 4:30 p.m. However, these days, they are open until 4 p.m. Advanced technology has also brought many changes to the bank system. In the past, there weren't any Internet banking or mobile banking services, but these days, all Korean banks use both systems. In addition, ⓑ_____.

| Closing |

These are some of the changes that have occurred at Korean banks.

| Opening | I can't really remember the banks I visited during my childhood. I don't think I went to a bank until I became ⓐ **a college student**. Of course, I realize that there must be some changes that have occurred at banks since then.

| Changes in Korean Banks | One of the changes is the hours of service. Korean banks used to be open from 9 a.m. to 4:30 p.m. However, these days, they are open until 4 p.m. Advanced technology has also brought many changes to the bank system. In the past, there weren't any Internet banking or mobile banking services, but these days, all Korean banks use both systems. In addition, ⓑ **they issue credit cards**.

| Closing | These are some of the changes that have occurred at Korean banks.

본인이 만든 답안에 아래의 요소들이 포함되었는지 점검해 봅시다.

Checklist
☐ 한국의 은행의 과거와 현재
☐ 어릴 적 봤던 은행의 모습
☐ 현재 아는 은행의 모습
☐ 과거 은행이 담당한 업무
☐ 달라진 현재 은행의 업무
☐ 은행의 변화로 인한 혜택

Unit 60 Opening a Bank Account

은행 계좌 개설

Warm Up

A Guess the Question & Answer
사진을 보면서 예상 질문과 답변을 먼저 추측해 봅시다.

B Listen & Talk
은행의 계좌 개설 방법에 관한 대화를 연습해 봅시다.

🎧 08-25

A Hi. I would like to open a bank account.
B Do you have a form of photo ID?
A Here's my passport.
B Give me one moment. I need to do a quick background check and copy your ID… What type of bank account do you want to open?
A I need to open one for savings and withdrawal.
B I see. You can open a regular savings account. You can simply keep some cash in it and withdraw money according to your needs.
A I'll get that then. Can I also get a debit card for the account?
B Of course. Do you want the public transportation card function installed on it?
A Yes, I do.
B Here are your photo ID, the passbook for your new bank account, and your debit card with the public transportation card function.
A Thank you.

A 안녕하세요. 저는 계좌를 개설하려고 해요.
B 신분증 있으세요?
A 여기 제 여권이요.
B 잠시만 기다려주세요. 신원조회를 해야 하고 신분증 복사도 해야 해서… 어떤 종류의 계좌를 개설하고 싶으신가요?
A 입출금용 계좌를 개설하려고 해요.
B 그렇군요. 보통 예금 계좌를 개설해드릴 수 있어요. 예금을 하시고 필요하실 때마다 돈을 찾아 쓸 수 있는 통장이죠.
A 그걸로 할게요. 체크 카드도 만들어주실 수 있나요?
B 그럼요. 교통 카드 기능도 추가해 드릴까요?
A 네.
B 여기 고객님 신분증과 개설하신 예금 통장 그리고 교통 카드 기능이 추가된 체크 카드를 드릴게요.
A 감사합니다.

Vocabulary open a bank account 계좌를 만들다 | background check 개인정보 조회 | withdraw 인출하다, 철거하다, 후퇴하다 | savings account 보통 예금 계좌 | debit card (한국의) 체크 카드 | installed 설치된 | passbook 통장

Key Expressions

아래 제시된 각 expression의 구조를 이해하고, 자기만의 표현들을 생각해 봅시다.

Expression 1 — line up: 줄을 서다

은행 직원과 상담하기 위해서는 대기를 해야 합니다. → You should **line up** to talk to the bank teller.

런던에서는 박싱데이 때마다 수백 명의 사람들이 상점 앞에 줄을 섭니다.
→ Hundreds of people **line up** in front of stores on Boxing Day in London.

그의 모든 책은 선반에 가지런히 진열되어 있습니다. → All of his books are **lined up** on the shelves.

Expression 2 — on the spot: 그 자리에서 바로, 즉석에서

그러면 그 자리에서 새로운 계좌를 만들어줄 것입니다. → Then they will help you open one **on the spot**.

그는 그 자리에서 계약서에 날인하였습니다. → He signed the contract **on the spot**.

사장은 즉시 그녀의 임금을 50% 인상해줬습니다. → The CEO gave her a 50% raise **on the spot**.

Expression 3 — keep track of: ~의 현재 상황을 확인하다

입출금 내역 및 잔고를 확인할 수 있습니다.
→ You can **keep track of** your transactions and current balance.

제가 모든 주간 매출을 파악할 수는 없습니다. → I cannot **keep track of** the weekly sales volume.

저는 항상 이메일 현황을 파악합니다. → I always **keep track of** my e-mails.

Expression 4 — physical record: 물리적 기록

통장을 만듦으로써 종이로 된 기록물을 보관하는 것도 좋다고 생각합니다.
→ It is good to have **physical records** in a passbook.

저는 언제나 물리적 기록을 남기기 위해 종이 영수증을 달라고 합니다.
→ I always ask for printed receipts to keep **physical records**.

그 소년의 출생에 관한 물리적 기록이 전혀 없나요?
→ Do you have any **physical records** regarding the boy's birth?

Expression 5 — to sum up: 요컨대, 요약하자면

요컨대 이상은 한국에서 계좌를 여는 과정에 대한 설명이었습니다.
→ **To sum up**, this is the process for opening a bank account in Korea.

요컨대, 저희는 다른 어떤 종류의 음료보다도 물을 더 많이 마셔야겠습니다.
→ **To sum up**, we should drink more water than any other type of beverage.

정리하자면, 자존심을 내려놓는 것이 관계 지속의 핵심 요소입니다.
→ **To sum up**, let going of our egos is the key factor to sustaining relationships.

Topic Question & Model Answer

Topic Question

How do you open a bank account in your country? What is the first thing and the last thing you do when you open a bank account? Tell me about the steps in detail.

당신이 사는 나라에서는 어떤 식으로 계좌를 만드나요? 계좌를 만들 때 제일 먼저 하는 일과 가장 나중에 하는 일이 무엇인가요? 모든 과정을 자세히 말해보세요.

> **TIP FOR THE OPIc**
>
> 은행 계좌 개설 과정에 관한 질문입니다. OPIc에서는 종종 특정한 활동의 과정에 대해 설명하라는 질문이 출제됩니다. 예를 들어 신분증 발급, 통장 개설, 영화 관람 전후에 하는 일, 운동 전에 하는 일, 여행 일정을 세우는 과정 등에 대해 물어볼 수 있습니다.

Model Answer

| Opening |

It is quite simple to open a bank account in Korea. We first need an ID card. It can be your passport, driver's license, or Korean social security card. With an ID card, you can open an account right away.

한국에서 계좌를 만드는 것은 비교적 간단합니다. 우선 신분증이 필요합니다. 여권이나 운전면허증 또는 주민등록증을 가져가면 됩니다. 신분증만 있으면 바로 그 자리에서 계좌를 만들 수 있습니다.

| How to Open a Bank Account |

When you arrive at the bank, you should line up to talk to a bank teller. When it is your turn, show your ID card and ask for a new bank account. Then, the person will help you open one on the spot. In Korea, you automatically receive a passbook when you open a bank account. You can keep track of your transactions and current balance with your passbook. The bank offers the same services as your online account, but it is good to have physical records with a passbook. For your reference, there are several types of passbooks with different functions. Basically, there are passbooks just for savings, for both savings and withdrawals, and for strategic savings.

은행에 도착하면 은행 직원과 상담하기 전에 대기를 해야 합니다. 자신의 차례가 되면 직원에게 신분증을 보여주고 계좌를 만들어달라고 요청합니다. 그러면 담당자가 즉시 새로운 계좌를 만들어줄 것입니다. 한국에서는 계좌를 개설하면 통장도 자동으로 발급됩니다. 통장이 있으면 입출금 내역 및 잔고를 확인할 수 있습니다. 온라인상으로도 동일한 서비스가 제공되지만, 통장을 만듦으로써 종이로 된 기록물을 보관하는 것도 좋다고 생각합니다. 참고로 통장은 그 목적에 따라 여러 가지로 분류됩니다. 기본적으로 보통 저축용, 입출금용, 그리고 적금용 통장이 있습니다.

| Closing |

Next, you can request a debit card along with your bank account and passbook. You can add credit card or transportation card functions to it if you want. To sum up, this is the process of opening a bank account in Korea.

그 다음으로는 계좌와 통장과 함께, 체크 카드를 만들 수 있습니다. 원하면 신용카드 및 교통카드 기능도 추가할 수 있습니다. 요컨대, 이상은 한국에서 계좌를 개설하는 과정에 대한 설명이었습니다.

More Questions

〈은행 계좌 개설〉에 관련하여 더 나올 수 있는 OPIc 질문들을 정리한 코너입니다. 질문에 대한 brainstorming을 해보세요.

1. Which bank do you use the most often? Why do you use its services the most often? How is it different from other banks?

2. Did you ever have an embarrassing experience at a bank? What happened? Did you ask somebody for help? Tell me everything about it.

On Your Own

앞에서 주어진 Model Answer을 바탕으로, 아래의 빈칸에 들어갈 수 있는 다양한 대체 가능한 어휘 및 표현들을 참고하여 학습자 본인만의 모범 답안을 직접 만들어보세요.

I Opening I

It is ⓐ_____ to open a bank account in Korea. We first need an ID card. It can be your passport, driver's license, or Korean social security card. With an ID card, you can ⓑ_____.

I How to Open a Bank Account I

When you arrive at the bank, you should line up to talk to a banker teller. When it is your turn, show your ID card and ask for a new bank account. Then, ⓒ_____. In Korea, you automatically receive a passbook when you open a bank account. The bank offers the same services as your online account, but it is good to have physical records with a passbook. For your reference, there are several types of passbooks with different functions. Basically, there are passbooks ⓓ_____.

I Closing I

Next, you can request a debit card along with your bank account and passbook. You can add credit card or transportation card functions to it if you want. ⓔ_____ a bank account in Korea.

I Opening I It is ⓐ **easy** to open a bank account in Korea. We first need an ID card. It can be your passport, driver's license, or Korean social security card. With an ID card, you can ⓑ **go to a bank to open a new bank account**.

I How to Open a Bank Account I When you arrive at the bank, you should line up to talk to a bank teller. When it is your turn, show your ID card and ask for a new bank account. Then, ⓒ **you will get one after your identification is approved**. In Korea, you automatically receive a passbook when you open a bank account. The bank offers the same services as your online account, but it is good to have physical records with a passbook. For your reference, there are several types of passbooks with different functions. Basically, there are passbooks ⓓ **just for savings, for both savings and withdrawals, and for strategic savings**.

I Closing I Next, you can request a debit card along with your bank account and passbook. You can add credit card or transportation card functions to it if you want. ⓔ **Well, this is how you open** a bank account in Korea.

본인이 만든 답안에 아래의 요소들이 포함되었는지 점검해 봅시다.

	Checklist
☐	계좌를 개설할 때 준비해야 할 것
☐	은행 가서 처음 할 일
☐	계좌 개설 과정
☐	계좌 개설에 관한 참고 사항
☐	한국에서의 계좌 개설의 특징

The Music of Speech

강세를 두어야 하는 어휘의 특징을 익히고 그에 따라 답안을 말하는 연습을 해봅시다.

강세를 두는 어휘의 특징
1) 감탄사이다 2) 최상급이다 3) 형용사/부사이다
4) 문장 안에서 key word 역할을 하는 명사나 동사인 경우가 많다

Model Answer 48 　🎧 08-27

There are several kinds of public transportation systems in Korea. These include subways, buses, and taxis. They are very well developed. There is an express bus terminal near my house. It's an important hub for public transportation in Seoul. There are multiple bus and subway lines near my house. I use both subways and buses to get to other places. The prices are reasonable, and the systems are convenient. They cost only about one dollar for a one-way trip, and transfers are free. In addition, Korean subways are always on time, and the bus-only lanes are well paved. We also have electronic screens installed at many bus stops to let people know when their buses will arrive. These are some of the merits of the Korean public transportation system.

Model Answer 49 　🎧 08-28

The main means of public transportation in Korea are buses, subways, and taxis. I often take buses and subways. They are both very economical and convenient, but each has its own advantages and disadvantages. I prefer to take buses when the weather is nice. I love to enjoy the view outside and to listen to music. However, on rainy days or during rush hour, the traffic is really bad, and there is no way to arrive at my destination on time. So, when I commute to work, I usually take the subway since it is always on time. If there's one thing I dislike about the subway, there are always some people selling products and making noise. Other than that, I'm happy with the Korean subway system. When I'm on the subway, I always use my smartphone to read online articles or to watch the news. Sometimes I take a nap when I feel really tired.

Model Answer 50 　🎧 08-29

Technology is everywhere: smartphones, laptops, and DVD players, just to name a few. Even houses and automobiles have the latest technology nowadays. Naturally, people living in the modern age use all kinds of technology in their everyday lives. I use my smartphone 7 days a week. I am self-taught. Smartphones are easy to use as long as you follow the instructions in the manuals. I think that smartphones are truly the most revolutionary invention of the 21st century. They have made our lives so convenient. On the other hand, I often use my laptop to work on my papers. Whenever I have an issue with my laptop, my brother takes care of it. He is a computer engineer, and I owe him a lot. It is a blessing that there is someone in the family who knows about technology!

Model Answer 51

I was working on my laptop in my room and reviewing my articles when my laptop suddenly went black. It wasn't a battery problem. The laptop was plugged in. As bizarre as the situation was, I thought I should just reboot the machine. I tried turning it off and turning it on again, but that didn't fix it. It was too late to call the repair shop, and there was no one at home to help me. I was speechless. I had to submit my articles by the morning, and the only place they were saved was my laptop! I ended up calling my boss the next day to ask for an extension on my deadline. Then, I carried my laptop to the repair shop and was able to retrieve everything I had saved on my hard drive. It wasn't the happiest way to solve my problem. But I learned that I should always save my files on a USB as well as on my computer.

Model Answer 52

It is not easy to compare Korea's recycling policy with other countries'. However, I think our recycling policy is quite distinctive. We not only separate papers, cans, plastic bags, and bottles from other garbage, but the Korean government also charges a tax on leftover trash. We put food waste in perishable bags and weigh it before we throw it in the food trash cans. It sounds complicated, but it makes sense since there has been growing concern about food waste. The expense of annual food waste and its disposal has been estimated at almost 1 trillion won in the past few years. Besides, the problem is even worse, environmentally. Although there is extra work due to the new recycling policy, I see that even my family has reduced food waste most of the time. We believe that our participation is keeping the Earth greener.

Model Answer 53

🎧 08-32

We did our recycling this morning. We do it once a week in our neighborhood. I often forget which day we recycle on, but my parents remind me all the time. We first separate the garbage into papers, cans, glasses, recyclable bottles, and plastic bags at home. Then, we take them out to the front of the apartment building and throw them in the section in which they belong. We also have a section for landfill trash only. Later, the garbage pickup company comes and collects everything. On the other hand, the Korean government started to charge a tax on food leftovers. At first, this new policy seemed to be just too much. However, according to statistics, it is actually reducing a large amount of food leftovers. I think Korea has established a successful recycling culture. I hope that our efforts make the world greener.

Model Answer 54

🎧 08-33

Korean police officers are in charge of various things. First, they control traffic, especially when it's late at night. I see many police officers standing on the road to catch drunk drivers and speeders. Second, police officers keep people safe in every town. Sometimes when I head home late after work, I see police cars moving slowly around my neighborhood. I feel very safe when I see them. Next, Korean police officers often watch demonstrations that are held in public areas. When there are riots or strikes, we always see police officers standing nearby. Police officers must have many other responsibilities, including chasing criminals. I guess these are just a few of the ones that I can think of.

Model Answer 55

🎧 08-34

I don't actually have any particular experiences with a police officer. The only chance I get to see police officers is on the road. When traffic is bad, I often see police officers controlling traffic. I also often see police officers on the news on TV when there's a report on crimes. Whenever the police arrest criminals, I wonder how they investigate and catch them. I've also seen people caught for speeding by the police. Many other drivers are ticketed for parking in the wrong places. These are some of the cases regarding the police that I have experienced first hand.

Model Answer 56

I go to the ABC Dental Clinic in my city. It takes only 10 minutes to walk there from my apartment. My family and I have been going to this dental clinic for many years. We visit this clinic because it's close to our place and the service is good. In addition, the dentist and the nurses are friendly. I go to the clinic once a year. I go for a regular checkup to see if my teeth are healthy. Many people say it's scary to go to the dentist. However, I feel comfortable whenever I visit the clinic. The clinic has a nice waiting room with various magazines and beverages. I always pick up one of the fashion magazines there while I wait my turn. I like that soft classical music plays there all the time.

Model Answer 57

I went to the dental clinic last month. I went there with my family. It was for a regular checkup. I had my teeth cleaned after the checkup. It's a family ritual that we do every year. The dental clinic we went to is located in our city. We've been going there ever since we moved to our current house, so we are familiar with the dentist. The dentist is in his early 60s. He is friendly and very skillful. Once, I had to go under anesthesia to have one of my wisdom teeth pulled, but I felt little pain when he gave me a shot in my gums. In addition, I recovered very quickly. The nurses and staff members are kind, too. They have become like old friends. I don't think our family will visit any other dental clinic.

Model Answer 58

I mainly use KBC Bank in Korea. It is one of the top three major banks and has the largest branches nationwide. The KBC Bank in my neighborhood is neat and clean. When I arrive at the bank, the first thing I see is the security guard welcoming visitors. Then, I see the bank tellers sitting at their desks. Their uniforms are white and navy blue. The bank tellers are friendly and fast. I visit the bank about once a week to check my bankbook or to pay my bills for the national insurance service plan. Sometimes I ask the bank teller for advice on strategic saving plans. It's always better to talk to an expert. Overall, I'm pretty satisfied with the service and system at KBC Bank.

Model Answer 59

🎧 08-38

I can't really remember the banks I visited during my childhood. I don't think I went to a bank until I became a high school student. Of course, I realize that there must be some changes that have occurred at banks since then. One of the changes is the hours of service. Korean banks used to be open from 9 a.m. to 4:30 p.m. However, these days, they are open until 4 p.m. Advanced technology has also brought many changes to the bank system. In the past, there weren't any Internet banking or mobile banking services, but these days, all Korean banks use both systems. In addition, work that used to be performed by bank tellers is now done by machines. It has become more convenient to pay bills and to check one's account. These are some of the changes that have occurred at Korean banks.

Model Answer 60

🎧 08-39

It is quite simple to open a bank account in Korea. We first need an ID card. It can be your passport, driver's license, or Korean social security card. With an ID card, you can open an account right away. When you arrive at the bank, you should line up to talk to a bank teller. When it is your turn, show your ID card and ask for a new bank account. Then, the person will help you open one on the spot. In Korea, you automatically receive a passbook when you open a bank account. You can keep track of your transactions and current balance with your passbook. The bank offers the same services as your online account, but it is good to have physical records with a passbook. For your reference, there are several types of passbooks with different functions. Basically, there are passbooks just for savings, for both savings and withdrawals, and for strategic savings. Next, you can request a debit card along with your bank account and passbook. You can add credit card or transportation card functions to it if you want. To sum up, this is the process of opening a bank account in Korea.

More Expressions & Vocabulary > Social Issues

Public Transportation
bus line 버스 노선
transportation fare 대중교통 요금
round trip 왕복 여행
transfer from A to B A에서 B로 환승하다
traffic jam 교통체증
get a discount 할인받다
get stuck in traffic 길이 막히다
transfer discount 환승 할인
taxi fare 택시 요금

Bank
open a new account 신규 계좌를 개설하다
loan payment 대출금 납부
get a loan 대출을 받다
deposit 예금
make a withdrawal 인출하다

cash withdrawal 현금 인출
put my debit card into the ATM 직불카드를 현금인출기에 넣다
enter one's PIN 비밀번호를 입력하다
take money out of an ATM 현금인출기에서 돈을 꺼내다
take out a card 카드를 꺼내다
take out a receipt 명세표를 뽑다

Recycling
climate change 기후 변화
contamination 오염
gas emissions 가스 배출
global warming 지구 온난화
greenhouse effect 온실효과
reuse 재사용
food waste shredder 음식물쓰레기 분해기
conserve water 물을 아끼다

OPIc Punch
Actual Test

IH&AL 공략 실전모의고사

OPIc Punch Actual Test에 나오는 질문 및 답안은 실제 기출 문제를 변형하거나 IH 및 AL 레벨 답안 수준으로 맞춘 것입니다. 각 질문마다 어떤 주제에 관한 것인지 명시하였기 때문에, Background Survey 항목 및 돌발 문제(Random Questions), 롤플레이 문제(Role-Playing Questions)에서 어떠한 유형으로 질문이 나오는지 파악할 수 있습니다. 특히 각 주제별 콤보 문제(Combo Questions)의 출제 경향을 파악하여, 비슷한 주제로 여러 개의 질문이 연속으로 나올 때 어떤 식으로 대처할 수 있는지를 살펴볼 수 있습니다. 다음의 Actual Test Set을 참고하여 실전에 대비해 보세요.

Actual Test

> **Topic**   **Self-Introduction**   🎧 09-01

Q1 Let's start the interview now. Tell me a little about yourself.

A Hello. My name is Jiyeon. I'm in my late 20s, and I teach English at SW University. I have a TESOL certificate, so I'm a certified teacher. I love to interact with my students. I am a good counselor. I want to help my students organize their lives better. I try to encourage them in the various circumstances they face in life. For example, the job market is very tough these days, and I see many students giving up on their dreams. My advice to them is to follow their heart instead of money. It could be challenging, but it will be more rewarding in the end. After class, I often take a walk around the campus. I'm also taking online courses to get my master's degree, and I spend a lot of time in my office because of paperwork. I trust this work will lead to more opportunities in my life. Overall, I'm happy with my life and career.

> **Topic**   **Business Trip**   🎧 09-02

Q2 You indicated in the survey that you take business trips to other countries. Can you tell me about your last business trip? Where did you go? What kind of business did you take care of there? What were the results?

A I went on a business trip to Microba's BI Conference in Chicago last month. It was my second visit to the town, and I really enjoyed the event, which was actually a part of the larger TechEd conference. In general, it was well organized and offered pretty good food and excellent WiFi. While there, I had some great discussions with Microba folks, customers, partners, and fellow analysts. I guess there were about 10,000 attendees at TechEd who were allowed to attend the BI sessions. The BI keynote speech was held in a very large auditorium and was probably attended by 1,000 people. My presentation was on performance-directed culture. It was so crowded that it filled the main room. It was quite a surprise to me. I think everything went pretty well during the trip, and I look forward to attending the next conference. I hope it also goes well!

| Topic | **Random Combo_ ID Card 1** | 🎧 09-03 |

Q3 Tell me about the entire process of how an ID card is issued in your country.

A There are a few steps to take to get an ID card issued. First, you need a photo of yourself for the ID card. Next, you need to fill out some paperwork that is provided at the district office. They ask you to write down personal information such as your telephone number and home address. You also need to pay a fee for the ID card to be processed, so it's always important to have some cash with you. Finally, you need to wait for a week or two to receive your ID card. This is the general process for obtaining an ID card in Korea.

| Topic | **Random Combo_ Clothing 1** |  09-04 |

Q4 What kind of clothes do people wear in your country? Is there a special dress code for work?

A I think the dress code for Korean employees depends on their workplaces. If you work for big companies like Samsung or Hyundai, people mostly wear suits. The public sector is also quite conservative, so you don't have many choices. But if you work for the entertainment industry or in the fashion field, your dress code can be a lot more liberal. I think you can wear almost anything you want in these fields. In my case, I work on the planning management team at a foreign company and dress semi-casually. I usually wear jeans and a shirt or a skirt and a cardigan. I try to dress properly for my position. Overall, I think the way Koreans dress depends on their job.

Actual Test

Topic   **Random Combo_ Clothing 2**   🎧 09-05

Q5   How has fashion changed in your country? What did people wear when you were young, and how was that different from the clothes people wear today?

A   I think many things have changed in terms of clothes in Korea. When I was in junior high school, baggy pants were very popular with teens and 20-somethings because hip-hop was really trendy then. My sister and I also used to wear loose jeans, and my mom often asked us not to mess up the floor with our dirty jeans. Of course, we don't dress that way anymore. These days, leggings, skinny jeans, and mini-skirts are trendy with young Koreans. I also enjoy wearing them. I guess Koreans dress differently now than they did in the past.

Topic   **Watching Sports**   🎧 09-06

Q6   Can you tell me about your favorite athlete? What is his or her personality like? Why do you like that athlete?

(for female students)

A   My favorite athlete is South Korean figure skater Yuna Kim. She is one of the most highly recognized athletes in Korea. I like Yuna Kim because she is an excellent skater. She is the current record holder for ladies in the short program, the free skating and the combined total. In addition, Kim's passion for skating never seems to end despite the fact that she already puts on nearly perfect performances. Kim also takes part in various social activities. In 2010, she was appointed a goodwill ambassador for UNICEF. Moreover, she participated as a presenter at an International Olympic Committee briefing on candidate cities for the 2018 Winter Olympics in Durban, South Africa. Her fluent English and appealing gestures during the presentation contributed to the bid. It's no wonder that Koreans call her a national treasure.

(for male students)

A   If I had to choose just one athlete from all fields, I would definitely choose Jisung Park. Park is an extraordinary soccer player. He is the only Korean player to have won the UEFA Champions League and the first Asian to have played in the final of the tournament. His success story has given hope to a lot of Korean youths. When I was studying in London in 2008, I felt so proud to be Korean when I saw my classmates from various nations shout Park's name during games. Park is noted for his exceptional fitness level, discipline, work ethic, and movement. People call him "a man with three lungs" because he constantly runs around in every game. When I remember that he has flat feet, I practically get goosebumps. The fact that he overcame his weakness has challenged a lot of people. People think that if he can do it, then so can they. I hope to write my own success story as well by adopting his spirit.

Topic: Random Combo_ Vacation at Home 1

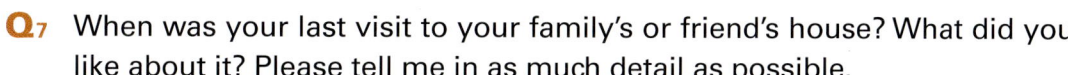

Q7 When was your last visit to your family's or friend's house? What did you like about it? Please tell me in as much detail as possible.

A   I went to my best friend's housewarming party last Saturday. She used to be my roommate but moved out after getting married a couple months ago. I was so glad and a bit excited to visit her new place. I wondered how she decorated her house. As I stepped into her place, I found everything to be so well organized. From the doormat to the LCD TV, it was such a perfect display. I felt like I was in a model home. My favorite item was the modern coffee table in the living room. It was light pink and had a sophisticated design and glossy finish. It was gorgeous. I had a pretty good time there with her other close friends. Next year, I hope I can throw a housewarming party as well. I can't wait.

Actual Test

Topic | **Random Combo_ Vacation at Home 2**　　　　🎧 09-08

Q8 Whose house would you like to visit the most at this moment? Why?

A If I could visit anyone's house at this moment, I would visit Miranda Kerr's house. She is a world-famous top model and is also known as Hollywood actor Orlando Bloom's wife. She recently visited Korea and appeared in several TV shows and magazines. I was very impressed by her down-to-earth attitude and great sense of fashion. I want to visit her place and get some fashion tips. I don't know how she dresses so chic and sexily all the time. She never overdresses or reveals too much, as many other celebrities do. Miranda is also praised for her marriage. As the mother of a son, she said in an interview that she wants to be a good mother before being a good model. I know it sounds silly, but, if I could visit anyone's house at the moment, I would definitely go to Miranda Kerr's.

Topic | **Role-playing_ Vacation at Home 3**　　　　🎧 09-09

Q9 Here's a situation I want you to act out. Suppose that you are organizing a party. Call your friend and leave a message by asking him/her to help you.

A Hi, Eric. Long time, no talk. How have you been? You know, I'm organizing a party for the first Saturday of August. I rented a venue for 50 people at the W Hotel. I was wondering if you could bring some of your hot friends. Trust me. It's going to be the coolest party ever. Oh, and do you know anyone who can take photos at the party? We have a great photo zone and will also choose the most photogenic person of the day. I'd really appreciate if you could recommend someone. I can't wait to hear back from you. There's so much to talk about. Please call me back whenever you get this. Bye.

| Topic | **Role-playing Combo_ Cooking** |

 09-10

Q10 I'd like to give you a situation and ask you to act it out. You are going to throw a party at your house this Saturday. Call your family and friends and invite them to your party. Be sure to give them information about the party.

A Hi Gina. How have you been? Did you remember that it's my parents' 25th wedding anniversary this Saturday? I want to throw a surprise party for them, and I hope you can come celebrate with us. Do you think you can make it? Awesome. It's going to take place at my house. My parents will be downtown to watch the musical *Les Miserables* and will be back home by around 8 p.m. I'm planning to set up the party before they arrive. Would you be able to come a little early and help me decorate the dining room? I owe you so much. Then I will see you at 5 p.m. on Saturday. Almost 30 people will be coming. Thanks and sleep tight.

| Topic | **Role-playing Combo_ Household Chores** |

 09-11

Q11 There is a problem you need to resolve. Your ceiling is leaking on the day of a party. Call the repairman and ask for help. Explain why it should be fixed quickly.

A Hello? Is this the ABC Repair Center? Hi. This is Nari Lee from room 303 in building 105 on Yeoksam Street. Hi. I have a big problem with my ceiling. I don't know what's going on, but the ceiling started leaking all of a sudden. Can you please come over as soon as possible? Oh no. You have to visit 12 other houses first? Please. This is an urgent situation. I'm throwing a party for my parents, and more than 30 guests will be coming in an hour. Please. This is supposed to be a surprise party, and I don't want to spoil it. Wait a minute. What if I pay you double? Is that a deal? What? Three times more? Well, okay. Just come in 10 minutes then. Bye.

Actual Test

Topic **Random_ Health**

Q.12 How do you stay healthy? Why do you think your method is efficient?

A A majority of people think going to the gym or working out intensely for a short period of time is good for their health. But according to research, walking is better for you than exercising at a gym. There are many ways to walk more in our daily lives. For example, you can go up or down the stairs instead of taking the elevator. In addition, you can get off the subway one stop early and walk the rest of the way to your destination. There is an old saying that walking more than 10,000 steps a day helps you become very healthy. Mao Zedong, a former communist revolutionary in China, walked 10,000 steps every day. He was known as a man who did not have to visit the hospital. His walking habits influenced a lot of people. Many Chinese and Koreans follow his exercise philosophy. I am one of them. I try to walk more and ride less. That will improve my health and keep me in shape.

Topic **Random Combo_ Shopping**

Q.13 When did you last go shopping? What did you get? Why?

A I went shopping for a spring jacket a couple days ago. I love shopping, even window shopping. So I look around quite often. This time, I went to a nearby shop and got a tweed jacket on sale. There was a 30% discount on spring products, and I think the price was pretty reasonable. I had always wanted an ivory tweed jacket, and I liked the color, design, and fabric. I liked everything about it. I'm so happy with my choice and think it'll be really useful.

Topic   **Random Combo_ ID Card 2**

Q14 When did you get your first ID card? How did you feel when you received your ID card? On which occasions do you use your ID card?

A I was a high school student when I got my first ID card. It was a national ID card, which proved that I was a grownup. Having a national ID card means that you can watch any kind of movie at the theater, including movies that require you to be at least 18 years of age. But it takes a couple more years to be able to drink alcohol or to go clubbing. When I got my first ID card, I felt weird. I didn't feel like I was a grownup yet. In contrast, I remember some of my friends were very excited and threw parties to celebrate. These days, I always carry at least one form of ID. I usually carry my driver's license. Personally, I like the moment when I take out my passport at the airport. I feel like I'm an important person whenever I get on an airplane.

Topic   **Random_ Holiday**

Q15 What is the most memorable holiday from your childhood? Why is it so memorable for you?

A When I was a child, I loved celebrating Christmas at my grandfather's home in Busan. It had great ocean views and a beautiful garden in front. There was also a small fireplace in the living room. I loved everything about the house. It always gave me special memories of Christmas. The best part of the holiday was having Christmas dinner. Our house was always filled with people. My grandfather used to invite his friends and neighbors, and the meal was usually a potluck party. I love thinking about it. After dinner, we would gather around the Christmas tree and exchange gifts. Sometimes we played *Secret Santa*, and it was so fun. My grandfather died a few years ago, and his home was sold, so now we drive by the place every few years to relive those good memories. I'll never forget those Christmas days with my grandad, and I hope I can make good Christmas memories with my kids as well.

Actual Test 해설

주제: 자기 소개

질문 1 인터뷰를 시작하겠습니다. 자기소개를 해보세요.

답안 안녕하세요, 제 이름은 지연입니다. 저는 20대 후반이며 SW 대학교에서 영어를 가르칩니다. 저는 TESOL 자격증이 있는 영어 강사입니다. 저는 학생들과 교류하는 것을 정말 좋아합니다. 저는 상담을 잘 해줍니다. 제 학생들이 보다 건강한 삶을 살 수 있도록 도와주고 싶습니다. 저는 학생들이 살면서 마주하는 다양한 환경 속에서 힘을 낼 수 있도록 돕고자 합니다. 예를 들어 요즘 취업 시장이 매우 어렵기 때문에 많은 학생들이 꿈을 포기하는 것을 보게 됩니다. 저는 그들에게 돈보다는 마음을 따르라고 조언합니다. 쉽지 않은 결정일 수 있지만, 결국에는 그렇게 하는 것이 훨씬 보람될 것입니다. 수업을 마치면 저는 종종 캠퍼스 주변을 산책합니다. 뿐만 아니라 온라인 석사 과정을 밟고 있어서 사무실에서 과제를 하는 데에 많은 시간을 할애합니다. 저는 지금의 과정이 앞으로 삶을 살아가는 데 있어서 더 많은 기회들을 제공하게 될 것이라고 믿습니다. 아무쪼록 저는 제 삶과 일로 인해 행복합니다.

<Vocabulary & Expressions>
certificate 자격증 a certified teacher 자격증을 소지한 선생님 interact 상호 작용하다 circumstance 환경 job market 취업 시장 give up on ~ ~를 포기하다 challenging 어려운, 난제의 rewarding 보람된 paperwork 문서 작업, 과제 opportunity 기회

주제: 회사 출장

질문 2 당신은 설문조사에서 해외출장을 간다고 했습니다. 마지막으로 다녀온 출장은 언제였나요? 어디로 갔나요? 어떤 임무를 마치고 왔나요? 결과는 어땠나요?

답안 지난달 시카고에서 열린 마이크로바사의 'BI(Business Intelligence) 컨퍼런스'에 다녀왔습니다. 시카고에는 두 번째 방문이었는데, 이번 컨퍼런스는 Tech-Ed 컨퍼런스 산하에 있는 것으로 그 행사를 즐겼습니다. 전반적으로 매우 체계적으로 진행된 회의였습니다. 음식도 깔끔하고 Wifi서비스는 최고였지요. 그 곳에 있으면서 마이크로바사의 임직원, 고객사, 협력사 및 동료 애널리스트들과 성과 있는 토론을 하였습니다. Tech-Ed 컨퍼런스에는 1만여 명 정도의 참석자가 있었는데, 그들은 BI 컨퍼런스에도 참여가 가능했습니다. 하지만 BI 컨퍼런스 참가자가 Tech-Ed 컨퍼런스에 참석할 수는 없었습니다. BI 컨퍼런스의 기조연설은 대강당에서 진행되었는데, 약 1천명의 사람들이 참석하였습니다. 저는 '업무 중심의 문화'라는 주제로 발표를 했는데, 본회의장에 사람들이 넘쳐났습니다. 예상치 못했던 일이라 적잖게 놀랐습니다. 출장동안 전체적으로 잘 진행이 되었던 것 같고, 이제는 다음 컨퍼런스에 참여하는 것을 기대하고 있습니다. 다음 번 출장도 기대가 되네요!

<Vocabulary & Expressions>
B.I. (Business Intelligence) Conference 비즈니스 지능 컨퍼런스 TechEd (Technology Education) conference 테크놀로지 교육 컨퍼런스 well-organized 짜임새 있게 진행된, 체계적으로 기획된 attendee 참석자 keynote speech 기조연설

주제: 돌발문제 콤보_신분증 1

질문 3 당신 나라의 신분증 발급 절차 전체에 대해 말해보세요.

답안 신분증을 발급 받는 데에는 몇 가지 절차가 따릅니다. 첫째, 신분증에 사용될 본인 사진이 있어야 합니다. 다음, 구청에서 주는 종이의 빈칸을 채워야 합니다. 종이에는 전화번호나 집 주소와 같은 개인 정보를 기재해야 합니다. 또한 신분증 발급 수수료를 지불해야 하므로 현금을 소지하는 것이 중요합니다. 마지막으로, 1주일에서 2주일 정도 기다리면 신분증을 발급 받게 됩니다. 이것이 한국에서 신분증을 발급 받기 위한 일반적인 과정입니다.

<Vocabulary & Expressions>
issue 발급하다 ID card (identification card) 신분증 fill out 채우다 paperwork 서류 정리 provide 제공하다 district 지역 process 과정, 처리하다 obtain 습득하다

주제: 돌발문제 콤보_옷차림 1

질문 4 당신이 사는 나라의 사람들은 어떤 옷차림입니까? 직장에서의 특별한 옷차림이 있나요?

답안 저는 한국 직장인들의 옷차림은 그들의 직장에 따라 다르다고 생각합니다. 삼성이나 현대와 같은 대기업에서 근무한다면, 대부분의 직원들은 양복을 입을 것입니다. 공공 부문 역시 꽤 보수적이어서, 선택의 여지가 별로 없습니다. 그러나 만일 연예 산업이나 패션 분야에서 일을 한다면, 훨씬 자유로운 복장을 갖출 수 있습니다. 이와 같은 분야에서는 거의 뭐든지 입어도 되는 것 같습니다. 저의 경우, 외국계 기업의 기획 관리팀에서 일하기 때문에 세미 캐주얼 복장을 갖추어 입습니다. 저는 주로 청바지에 셔츠나 치마에 카디건을 입습니다. 저는 제 직분에 맞는 옷차림을 하려고 노력합니다. 아무쪼록, 저는 한국 사람들의 옷차림은 각자의 직업에 따라 달라진다고 생각합니다.

<Vocabulary & Expressions>
dress code 옷차림 depend on ~에 달려있다 public sector 공공부문 conservative 보수적인 entertainment industry 연예계 fashion field 패션 분야 liberal 자유로운 private institute 사설 학원 semi-casual 세미 캐주얼 dress properly 적절히 차려 입다

주제: 돌발문제 콤보_옷차림 2

질문 5 당신의 나라의 패션 변천사는 어떻습니까? 당신이 어릴 적에 사람들은 무엇을 입었고, 오늘날과 어떻게 달랐습니까?

답안 저는 한국의 옷차림이 많은 면에서 달라졌다고 생각합니다. 제가 중학교를 다닐 때는, 10대와 20대 사이에서 헐렁한 바지가 매우 인기 있었습니다. 당시 힙합이 큰 유행이었기 때문입니다. 제 여동생과 저 역시 느슨한 바지를 곧잘 입었는데, 엄마께서는 저희에게 '바지로

바닥을 쓸지 말라'고 말씀하시고는 했습니다. 물론, 저희는 더 이상 그렇게 입고 다니지는 않습니다. 요즘에는 레깅스, 스키니진, 그리고 미니스커트가 젊은 한국인들 사이에서 인기입니다. 저 역시 그렇게 입는 것을 좋아합니다. 제 생각에 한국인들은 과거와 현재 옷을 좀 다르게 입는 것 같습니다.

<Vocabulary & Expressions>

in terms of ~의 면에서 baggy pants 힙합 바지 trendy 유행하는 loose jeans 느슨한 청바지 mess up 더럽히다, 어질러 놓다 leggings 레깅스(바지)

주제: 스포츠 관람

질문 6 제일 좋아하는 운동선수에 대해 얘기해줄 수 있나요? 그/그녀의 성격은 어떤가요? 왜 그 선수를 좋아하나요?

(여학생용 답안)

답안 제가 가장 좋아하는 한국인 운동선수는 피겨 스케이터 김연아입니다. 그녀는 한국에서 가장 인기 있는 운동 선수 중 하나입니다. 김연아 선수가 좋은 이유는 그녀의 뛰어난 스케이트 실력 때문입니다. 그녀는 현재 쇼트 프로그램과 프리 스케이팅 종목 합계 세계 여자 선수들 가운데 가장 높은 점수를 보유하고 있습니다. 또한 이미 정상에 서 있으면서도 그녀의 스케이트에 대한 열정은 멈추지 않는 것 같습니다. 김연아 선수는 다양한 사회 활동에도 참여하고 있습니다. 2010년에 그녀는 유니세프 친선대사로 임명되었습니다. 뿐만 아니라 남아프리카공화국 더반에서 열린, IOC 위원회의 2018년 동계 올림픽 개최지를 위한 후보 도시를 소개하는데, 한국측 발표자로 참여하였습니다. 그녀의 유창한 영어 실력과 호소력 있는 제스쳐 덕분에 이번 경쟁에서 이길 수 있었습니다. 한국인들이 김연아를 "한국의 보물"이라고 부르는 것은 당연합니다.

<Vocabulary & Expressions>

athlete 운동선수 highly recognized 매우 잘 알려진 combined 통합해서 despite ~에도 불구하고 stand out 눈에 띄는 social activities 사회 활동 be appointed ~로 임명되다 a goodwill ambassador 친선대사 presenter 프레젠테이션을 하는 사람 candidate 후보(자) appealing 호소력 있는 contribute 공헌하다 bid 경매, 경쟁

(남학생용 답안)

답안 만일 제가 모든 종목 중에서 좋아하는 단 한 명의 선수를 꼽아야 한다면, 저는 주저하지 않고 박지성 선수를 꼽을 것입니다. 박지성은 탁월한 축구선수입니다. 그는 UEFA 챔피언 리그에서 우승했던 유일한 한국선수이고 결승전에 출전한 최초의 아시아 선수입니다. 그의 성공담은 한국의 많은 청년들에게 희망이 되었습니다. 제가 2008년에 런던에 공부를 하러 갔을 때, 경기 중 박지성 선수의 이름을 외치는 수많은 외국인 친구들을 목격하면서 한국인으로서의 상당한 자부심을 느꼈습니다. 박지성 선수는 남다른 연습량과 훈련, 직업윤리, 움직임으로 잘 알려져 있습니다. 사람들은 그가 "폐가 3개 달린 사나이"라고 합니다. 그만큼 매 경기마다 쉬지 않고 달리기 때문입니다. 그러나 그가 평발이라는 불리한 신체 조건을 타고 난 것을 안다면, 소름이 납니다. 약점을 뛰어 넘은 사실은, 많은 사람들에게 도전이 되었습니다. '박지성도 했는데, 우리라고 왜 못하겠어?' 라는 마음이겠지요. 저 역시 그의 정신을 닮아서 저만의 성공 스토리를 쓰고 싶습니다.

<Vocabulary & Expressions>

field 분야 definitely 분명히 extraordinary 비범한 final tournament 결승전 exceptional 예외적인, 남다른 discipline 훈련 work ethic 직업의식 flat feet 평발 goosebumps 소름 overcome 극복하다 challenge 도전하다 adopt one's spirit ~의 정신을 받아들이다

주제: 돌발문제 콤보_ 집에서 여가 보내기 1

질문 7 당신 가족 혹은 친구 집에 마지막으로 방문한 것이 언제입니까? 방문했을 때 어떤 점이 좋았나요? 최대한 자세하게 얘기해 보세요.

답안 저는 지난주에 가까운 친구의 집들이에 초대되었습니다. 그 친구는 제 룸메이트였는데, 두 달 전 결혼을 하면서 집을 옮겼습니다. 그녀의 신혼집에 초대받고 정말 기뻤고, 한편 신났습니다. 집을 어떻게 꾸몄을까 매우 궁금했습니다. 집안에 들어서자 모든 게 매우 잘 정돈되어 있었습니다! 현관 깔개에서부터 LCD TV까지 정말 완벽하게 전시되어 있어서 마치 모델하우스에 온 느낌이었습니다. 가장 마음에 드는 것은 거실에 있는 모던한 느낌의 커피 탁자였습니다. 연분홍색의, 세련되게 디자인된, 광택나는 탁자였습니다. 정말 예쁜 탁자였습니다. 친구의 집에서 다른 친한 친구들과 좋은 시간을 보내고 왔습니다. 내년에는 저도 집들이를 했으면 좋겠습니다. 빨리 좀 그렇게 되었으면 좋겠어요!

<Vocabulary & Expressions>

housewarming party 집들이 move out 이사가다 decorate 장식하다 step into~ ~에 발을 들이다 well organized 잘 정돈된 doormat 문 앞에 깔린 작은 카페트 display 전시 sophisticated 세련된 glossy 광택 나는 throw a party 파티를 열다

주제: 돌발문제 콤보_ 집에서 여가 보내기 2

질문 8 당신은 지금 이 순간 누구의 집을 가장 방문하고 싶은가요? 왜 그런가요?

답안 지금 제가 누군가의 집을 맘대로 찾아가도 된다면, 저는 미란다 커의 집에 가고 싶어요. 미란다 커는 세계적인 모델이며, 할리우드 스타 올랜도 블룸의 아내이기도 합니다. 그녀는 최근 한국을 방문하여 국내의 TV 프로그램 및 잡지 인터뷰에 출연하였는데요, 솔직한 성격과 타고난 패션 감각이 매우 인상적이었습니다. 그녀의 집에 놀러 가서 패션 정보 좀 얻고 싶어요! 어쩌면 그렇게 시크하고 섹시하게 옷을 입는지 모르겠어요. 미란다가 오버해서 옷을 입거나 다른 많은 연예인들처럼 과다 노출한 것을 한 번도 못 봤어요. 뿐만 아니라 미란다의 결혼 생활에 대한 칭찬이 자자합니다. 아들을 둔 엄마로써, 그녀는 한 매체와의 인터뷰에서 '좋은 모델이기 전에 좋은 엄마이고

Actual Test 해설

싶다'라는 말을 했습니다. 제 말이 좀 어처구니없이 들릴 수도 있지만, 지금 누군가의 집에 맘대로 놀러 갈 수 있다면, 전 망설임 없이 미란다 커의 집에 갈 거예요!

<Vocabulary & Expressions>
world-famous 세계적으로 유명한   appear in TV / magazine TV 및 잡지에 출연하다   be impressed by ~ ~에 깊은 인상을 받다   down-to-earth 진실한, 현실적인   sense of fashion 패션 감각   overdress 과하게 입다   reveal 드러내다

주제 롤플레잉_집에서 여가 보내기 3

질문 9 여기 상황극이 있습니다. 당신이 파티를 하나 계획한다고 가정해 보세요. 친구에게 연락해서 그/그녀에게 당신을 도와달라고 메시지를 남겨 보세요.

답안 안녕 에릭! 오랜만이야! 어떻게 지냈어? 있잖아, 나 8월 첫째 주 토요일에 파티 하나 주최하거든. W호텔에 50명 규모 파티장 하나 빌렸어. 너랑 네 멋진 친구들 좀 같이 올 수 있나 궁금해서. 날 믿어봐. 최고의 파티가 될 거야. 아, 그리고 혹시 파티에서 사진 찍을만한 사람 있을까? 이번에 사진 찍는 공간을 아주 예쁘게 꾸몄는데, 파티 날에 사진에 가장 멋지게 찍힌 사람을 뽑을 예정이야. 누구 사진 잘 찍는 사람 좀 추천해주면 정말 고맙겠어. 너랑 얼른 통화했으면 좋겠네! 할 얘기가 너무도 많아! 이 메시지 들으면 바로 연락해줘. 안녕.

<Vocabulary & Expressions>
organize a party 파티를 열다   venue 장소   photo zone 포토존 (사진 촬영용 장소)   photogenic 포토제닉 (사진 찍을 때 포즈가 좋은)   appreciate 감사히 여기다   recommend 추천하다   hear back from ~ ~로부터 연락을 받다

주제 롤플레잉 콤보_요리하기

질문 10 여기 상황극이 있습니다. 당신은 이번 토요일에 집에서 파티를 열고자 합니다. 가족 및 친구들에게 전화해서 파티에 초대하고, 파티 관련 정보를 알려주세요.

답안 안녕 지나! 어떻게 지냈어? 너 혹시 이번 주 토요일이 우리 부모님 결혼 25주년인 것 기억해? 내가 부모님을 위해 깜짝 파티를 열려고 하는데 너도 와서 같이 축하해줬으면 좋겠어. 올 수 있을 것 같아? 최고야. 파티 장소는 우리 집이야. 부모님은 그날 시내에서 뮤지컬 "레미제라블" 보시고 집에 저녁 8시에나 도착하실 예정이야. 오시기 전에 파티 준비를 해 놓으려고 해. 너도 좀 일찍 와서 장소 꾸미는 것 좀 도와줄래? 와, 정말 고마워! 그럼 토요일 오후 5시에 봐. 30명 정도 모일 거야. 고맙고 잘 자!

<Vocabulary & Expressions>
wedding anniversary 결혼기념일   a surprise party 깜짝 파티   celebrate 기념하다   downtown 시내   set up 준비하다, 차리다   I owe you 너한테 빚졌어 (보통 "너한테 신세진 마음이 들 정도로 고마워"라는 뜻의 표현으로 사용)   sleep tight 푹 자다

주제 롤플레잉 콤보_집안일

질문 11 당신이 해결해야 할 문제가 있습니다. 파티를 열기로 한 날에 당신 집의 천장에서 물이 샙니다. 수리하는 사람에게 전화에서 도움을 요청하세요. 왜 수리가 급한지 설명하세요.

답안 여보세요? 거기 ABC 수리 센터인가요? 안녕하세요, 역삼로에 위치한 105동303호에 사는 이 나리라고 해요. 다름 아니라 저희 집 천장에 큰 문제가 일어났어요. 무슨 일인지 모르지만 갑자기 천장에서 물이 새기 시작했어요. 지금 당장 와주시겠어요? 저런, 다른 12개의 집부터 방문하셔야 한다고요? 제발 부탁이에요, 지금 아주 긴급 상황이라고요. 제가 부모님을 위해 오늘 파티를 여는데, 서른 명이 넘는 손님들이 1시간 안으로 모일 거란 말이에요. 제발 부탁이에요. 깜짝 파티인데 망치면 안 된다고요. 잠시만요, 제가 만일 2배 더 계산해 드리면 어때요? 그 정도면 됐나요? 네? 3배를 달라고요? 음, 그래요. 10분 안으로만 와주세요. 안녕히 계세요.

<Vocabulary & Expressions>
repair center 수리 센터   ceiling 천장   leaking 물이 새는   urgent 긴급한   supposed to be ~ ~해야 하는   spoil 망치다   a deal 거래가 성사된

주제 돌발_건강

질문 12 당신은 어떻게 건강을 관리하나요? 당신은 왜 그 방법이 효율적이라고 생각하나요?

답안 많은 사람들은 체육관에 가거나 짧은 시간 동안 강도 높게 운동하는 것이 건강에 좋다고 생각합니다. 하지만 한 연구조사에 따르면, 오히려 체육관에서 운동하는 것보다는 걷는 것이 건강에 더 좋다고 합니다. 사실 일상 생활을 하면서 걷는 방법은 많습니다. 예를 들어, 엘리베이터를 타는 대신에 계단을 오르내리는 것이 한 방법일 수 있습니다. 또는 지하철을 한 정거장 빨리 내려서 남은 목적지까지 걸어가는 방법도 있습니다. 옛말에 '하루에 만보를 걸으면 장수한다'고 합니다. 중국의 공산주의 혁명가였던 마오쩌둥은 매일 만보씩 걸었다고 합니다. 그는 생전에 병원에 갈 일이 없었다고 합니다. 마오쩌둥의 걷기 방식은 많은 이들에게 영향력을 미쳤습니다. 많은 중국인과 한국인들이 그의 운동철학을 따릅니다. 저도 그 중 한 명입니다. 더 많이 걷고 차를 덜 타려고 합니다. 그렇게 함으로써 건강을 향상시키고 또 몸매를 유지할 수 있을 것입니다.

<Vocabulary & Expressions>
a majority of people 대다수의 사람들   work out intensely 강도 높게 운동하다   communist revolutionary 공산주의 혁명가   exercise philosophy 운동 철학   keep somebody in shape ~의 몸매를 유지시키다

주제 | 돌발문제 콤보_쇼핑

질문 13 당신이 마지막으로 쇼핑을 간 것은 언제입니까? 무엇을 구매했으며, 왜 그것을 구입했습니까?

답안 저는 며칠 전 봄 재킷을 구입하기 위해서 쇼핑을 갔습니다. 저는 쇼핑을 매우 좋아해서, 심지어는 윈도우 쇼핑만 해도 좋습니다. 때문에 종종 둘러봅니다. 이번에는 가까운 가게에 가서 세일 중인 트위드 재킷을 구입했습니다. 봄 상품이 30% 할인 판매되고 있었는데, 제 생각에는 가격이 매우 합리적이었습니다. 저는 늘 아이보리 색상의 트위드 재킷을 사고 싶었고, 색상, 디자인, 재질도 모두 좋았습니다. 저는 제 선택에 매우 만족하며, 재킷을 아주 유용하게 활용할 것 같습니다.

<Vocabulary & Expressions>
go shopping 쇼핑하러 가다 **window shopping** 윈도우쇼핑 **look around** 둘러보다 **on sale** 세일 중의, 할인이 적용되는 **reasonable** 합리적인 **fabric** 직물, 천

주제 | 돌발문제 콤보_신분증 2

질문 14 당신은 언제 처음 신분증을 받았습니까? 당신의 신분증을 받았을 때 기분이 어땠나요? 어떤 경우에 신분증을 사용하고 있습니까?

답안 제가 처음으로 신분증을 받은 것은 고등학생 때였습니다. 어른이 되었음을 증명해주는 주민등록증이었습니다. 주민등록증은 최소 18세 이상 관람을 요구하는 영화를 영화관에서 볼 수 있다는 의미이기도 합니다. 하지만 술을 마시거나 클럽에 가려면 1년에서 2년 정도의 시간이 더 필요합니다. 처음 신분증을 받았을 때 저는 미묘한 기분이 들었습니다. 아직 어른이 되었다는 느낌은 들지 않았기 때문입니다. 반대로, 제 친구들 몇몇은 들떠서 축하 파티를 열었던 기억이 납니다. 요즘 저는 최소 한 개의 신분증을 가지고 다닙니다. 주로 운전면허증을 갖고 다닙니다. 개인적으로 저는 공항에서 여권을 꺼낼 때가 좋습니다. 비행기를 탈 때마다 제가 중요한 사람이 된 기분입니다.

<Vocabulary & Expressions>
national ID card 주민등록증 **grownup** 성인 **go clubbing** 클럽에 가다 **in contrast** 반대로 **throw a party** 파티를 열다 **carry an ID** 신분증을 갖고 다니다 **driver's license** 운전면허증

주제 | 돌발_명절

질문 15 당신의 어릴 적에 가장 기억에 남는 명절은 언제인가요? 왜 그렇게 기억에 남는 명절인가요?

답안 저는 어릴 적, 부산 외할아버지 댁에서 크리스마스를 보내는 것을 좋아했습니다. 집에서 보이는 바다 전경은 끝내줬고, 집 앞에는 아름다운 정원이 있었습니다. 또한 거실에는 작은 벽난로가 있었습니다. 저는 그 집의 모든 것이 좋았습니다. 그곳에 가면 늘 특별한 크리스마스 추억을 만들어줬습니다. 가장 좋은 점은 바로 크리스마스 저녁 식사였습니다. 우리 집은 언제나 사람들로 붐볐습니다. 외할아버지께서는 종종 친구 분들 및 이웃을 초대하셨기 때문에 저녁 식사는 포틀럭 파티가 되고는 했습니다. 저는 그 때를 상기하는 것이 좋습니다. 식사 후에는 크리스마스 트리 주변에 둘러앉아 선물교환을 하고는 했습니다. 가끔 우리는 시크릿 산타를 했는데, 진짜 재미있었어요! 제 외할아버지는 몇 해 전 돌아가셨고 이제 그 집은 팔려서 우리 가족은 가끔 집 주변을 차로 돌며 예전의 기억을 되살리고는 합니다. 저는 외할아버지와의 크리스마스를 보낸 날들을 잊을 수가 없고, 제 아이들과도 좋은 크리스마스 추억을 만들게 되길 바랍니다.

<Vocabulary & Expressions>
ocean views 오션뷰, 바다 풍경 **give special memories** 특별한 추억을 만들어주다 **drive by** 운전하며 지나가다 **relive good memories** 추억을 상기시키다

* **potluck party** 파티에 초대된 사람들이 각자 본인이 준비한 음식을 갖고 와서 파티장에 있는 다른 사람들과 부페식으로 나누어 먹는 형식의 파티. 덕분에 파티를 주최한 사람은 음식 걱정 없이 장소만 대여해주면 된다.

* **Secret Santa** 크리스마스 이브날 선물을 줄 당사자를 뽑아 몰래 선물을 하는 일종의 이벤트.